Deer Creek
Rich Bar
North Fork
Middle Fork
South Fork
Nelson Cr.
Bidwell's Bar
Feather River
Downieville
S I E R R A N E V A D A
Rough and Ready
Deer Creek
Yuba River
Long Bar
Nevada City
Grass Valley
Marysville
Hock Farm
Bear River
North Fork
Middle Fork
Lake Tahoe
Manhattan Bar
Georgetown
Mormon Island
Sutter's Mill
Coloma
American River
Weber Cr.
South Fork
Hangtown (Placerville)
River
Sutter's Fort
Sacramento
Cosumnes River
Mokelumne River
Mokelumne Hill
Calaveras River
Stockton
Angel Cr.
Carson Cr.
Angel's Camp
Mormon Diggings
Murphy's Creek
Murphy's
Sonora
Jamestown
Woods Cr.
Wood's Creek Diggings
Sullivan's Creek
Stanislaus River
Jacksonville
Hawkins Bar
Tuolumne River
San Joaquin River
Merced River
Agua Fria
Mariposa
Mariposa River

Arkansas in the Gold Rush

The map on the endsheets is from *Gold Dust* by Donald Dale Jackson. Copyright by Donald Dale Jackson. Published by Alfred A. Knopf, Inc.

Arkansas in the Gold Rush

Priscilla McArthur

For Peg,
Thanks for sharing your family papers and your knowledge of Arkansas' early history.
Sincerely,
Priscilla McArthur
11-2-86

August House / Little Rock

PUBLISHERS

1986

Published 1986 by August House, Inc., Publishers, Post Office Box 3223,
Little Rock, AR 72203 501-663-7300

Cover design by Byron Taylor
Design direction by Ted Parkhurst
Typography by Arrow Connection

Printed in the United States of America

10 9 8 7 6 5 4 3 2 1

First edition, 1986

Library of Congress Cataloging-in-Publication Data:

McArthur, Priscilla.
Arkansas in the gold rush.

Bibliography: p.
Includes index.
1. Arkansas—History. 2. California—Gold
discoveries. 3. Arkansas—Emigration and immigration—
History—19th century. 4. Overland journeys to the
Pacific. 5. Pioneers—Arkansas—History—19th century.
6. Pioneers—California—History—19th century.
I. Title.
F411.M33 1986 976.7'05 86-70043
ISBN 0-87483-008-7

This book is printed on archival-quality paper that
meets the guidelines for performance and durability
of the Committee on Production Guidelines for Book
Longevity of the Council on Library Resources.

The author would like to acknowledge the generosity of the following for permission to use materials as cited: Washington County Historical Society, publisher of *Flashback;* Fort Smith Historical Society, publisher of the *Journal;* the Arkansas History Commission; University of Arkansas Library—Special Collections; University of Arkansas at Little Rock Library Archives; Fort Smith Public Library; the Arkansas Gazette Company; Arthur H. Clark Co.; Alfred A. Knopf, Inc.; University of Nebraska Press; University of Oklahoma Press; Mrs. Charlie T. Davis; Duval Johnston, Logan Pritchett; George Toney and Mrs. Frank Wait.

For Charles, Mark and David

and

The Arkansas Territorial Restoration

Foreword

Arkansas remained a frontier area almost to the time of the Civil War, when the telegraph and the railroad—two major symbols of civilization—finally arrived on the scene.

Generally a frontier receives immigrants, and Arkansas grew dramatically in early statehood, but Arkansas also served as a jumping-off point to the west. "G.T.T." (Gone To Texas) became a familiar message, but the most dramatic emigration from Arkansas occurred when gold was discovered in California.

The Arkansas Territorial Restoration interprets the frontier period in Arkansas history and is proud of the role it has played in the production of this work documenting the connection of the Arkansas frontier to the new frontier in California. The Sesquicentennial of Arkansas is a grand opportunity to look back at this remarkable American story.

William Booker Worthen
Executive Director
Arkansas Territorial Restoration

Preface

The lure of the California gold fields has been the subject of numerous monographs, articles and literary works. The gold seekers kept marvelous journals and diaries as well as wrote numerous letters home to family, friends, and newspapers. They left us a well-documented record of their travels, their dreams, their successes, and their failures.

The Arkansas gold seekers were no exception. Their story has been told in bits and pieces and as part of the larger story. Three general works which especially mention Arkansas gold seekers are Owen Coy's *The Great Trek* (1931), Ralph Bieber's *Southern Trails to California* (1937), and Grant Foreman's *Marcy and the Gold Seekers* (1939). But the Arkansas story is worth the telling. The written legacy is vastly richer than these sources suggest.

This volume attempts to assemble all the known records of the Arkansas gold seekers. It especially makes use of the contemporary Arkansas newspapers, but it also includes private sources which have not heretofore been a part of the public record. Foreman and Bieber quoted extensively from the letters of the Arkansas forty-niners, but that was almost fifty years ago and primarily in an effort to redress the grievances against historical neglect of the importance of the southern routes to California. Many of those letters will appear in this volume, but the Arkansas-California story extends beyond 1849. This book is submitted as a small part of the one hundred fiftieth birthday celebration of Arkansas' statehood. More especially it is submitted as a part of the Arkansas Territorial Restoration's efforts to reconstruct the history of early Arkansas.

I began this project while working on the research staff for the Restoration. The National Endowment for the Humanities funded a grant to research and index the *Arkansas Gazette* and other primary sources in an effort to reconstruct early Arkansas history. I am indebted in particular to Bill Worthen, Director of the Arkansas Territorial Restoration, who permitted me to complete the project although I had "removed" to Alabama. Other members of the research team who deserve special thanks for helping me "stake my claim" are Swannee Bennett and Jackie Daughtery.

I wish also to express appreciation to Patricia A. Etter of Tucson, Arizona, who prepared a bibliography of the 1849 journals of the Southern route and was most generous in sharing information on the Little Rock "boys" in California. Her book on Robert Brownlee, an early Little Rock settler and a gold seeker, will be published by the University of Arkansas in 1986. Finally, I wish to acknowledge the tremendous labor performed by Lynda Harper, Troy State University at Dothan/Fort Rucker, who prepared the typed manuscript from my longhand draft. Having tediously deciphered many letters and diaries myself, I can appreciate her fine performance.

Contents

Maps

Illustrations

Appendices

CHAPTER I

The Golden News

"Who will sit quietly at home in the State pining in penury when fortunes are to be had merely for the labor of picking them up in California?"

The accidental discovery of gold in California in January 1848 set in motion a massive migration of people westward across the continent in an attempt to find a fortune in the gold fields. Initially the news was taken as idle rumor even in California, but as newspapers and public figures assigned more and more credence to the news, the tendency was to believe the rumor had substance. It was late summer of 1848 before the news spread 2,000 miles back east and to the Mississippi port cities of New Orleans, Memphis, and St. Louis. It was by steamboat from eastern newspapers one to four weeks old that the news reached the Arkansas River towns of Little Rock, Van Buren and Fort Smith in early autumn. The army report authenticating the discovery and sending gold samples to President James K. Polk was probably the single best evidence for the citizens of Fort Smith. This report was filed by Colonel R. B. Mason, then military Governor of California, and Lieutenant Edward F. Beale, both of whom had served at Fort Gibson and Fort Smith and were well known to Fort Smith folk.[1] As early as September 5, 1848, a group of Fort Smith men were making plans to go to California.[2]

Arkansas newspapers began to print columns entitled, "news from California," which further spread the message and stimulated lively conversation and piqued interest. Letters from Reverend Walter Colton, Alcalde of Monterey, which described gold "lying around waiting to be washed," were copied in the Arkansas papers.[3] The *Batesville Eagle* reported "the whole of California is run wild at this time, after a gold mine—if half we see is to be believed, every man, woman, and child there, will be rich as cream a foot thick." This article also reported that the size of the gold field was "150 miles in length and 50 miles in breadth—wages are as high as $20.00 a day."[4] Gold had become the main topic of conversation and Arkansas, like the rest of the nation, was infected with gold fever. Confirmation was deemed completely official when President Polk acknowledged the gold discovery in his annual message to Congress on December 5, 1849.[5] This speech galvanized the nation into action. "Are you for California?" was the most often asked question in the spring of 1849 as expeditions were being formed throughout the country and throughout Arkansas.

The discovery of gold must have seemed like a wonderful panacea for the nation's economic woes. The Panic of 1837, brought on by overspeculation in land sales, overexpansion in canal and railroad building by the states, and Jackson's war on the Bank of the United States, was to grip the nation for almost a decade. It ended flush times in Alabama and Mississippi. Banks failed, unemployment grew, prices fell (especially land, cotton and farm prices), railroad and canal building stopped, several debt-burdened states ceased to pay interests on their bonds, and some states even repudiated their debts. Distressed and dissatisfied Americans turned the Democrats out in the 1840 log cabin campaign and elected the Whigs to national office. In Arkansas the State and Real Estate Banks failed. Currency was depreciated and worth only "forty-five cents on the dollar;" the treasury was empty; business came to a standstill; fifty houses were vacant in Little Rock.[6] Lack of money caused great hardships on all. The citizens were indebted to the merchants, the merchants were indebted to men of other states, and very little money was coming into the state. The only real source of specie lay on the frontier where the government troops and the Indian trade were located. At exactly the right moment for the national economy and particularly for Arkansas, gold was discovered in California, holding out the promise of relief.

In its broader historical perspective, the Gold Rush was also a part of America's manifest destiny to subdue the continent. Since colonial times Americans had pushed ever westward. The Gold Rush merely interrupted the gradual progression and resulted in Americans leap-frogging over the vast plains to California. Independence and Westport, Missouri, Fort Smith and Van Buren, Arkansas, and Eagle Pass, Laredo, and Brazos Santiago, Texas, were "jumping off" places for the land route to California. Jumping off could not only refer to leaving the states behind, but also leaving steamboats and steam locomotives behind. Emigrants may have reached the outfitting places by riverboat or train, but they left those places on mules, oxen and horses to follow faintly marked trails blazed by fur trappers, government explorers, and missionaries to the Indians. Their departure was not mandated by a printed schedule, but rather by when the grass was sufficient for the animals. This was going to be a primitive American adventure which pitted gold seekers against the land, against nature and the elements, and against hostile Indians.

Knowing that this would probably be the one great adventure of their lives, they wrote about their experience. It was as though they were aware of being participants in an epoch-making movement, so they kept journals and diaries for themselves, for their families and for future publication. Others chronicled their trip in letters which were sequel installments of their adventure.

With emigrants coming from all levels of society, there are naturally numerous eccentricities of style, spelling, grammar and punctuation. Some writings exhibit historical awareness and a flair for the dramatic, others are brief and unembellished trail journals. This only adds to the immediacy of the documents and underscores the individual response to events. The Gold Rush accounts along the northern trails are numerous and the literature is extensive; whereas the accounts of gold seekers along the southern routes are fewer in number and less completely catalogued. Arkansans recorded their Gold Rush experiences, however, and they can claim a great share in America's version of the Iliad and Odyssey.[7]

Arkansas, because it was one of the frontier states bordering the Indian territory and the vast plains, was to have a unique role in funneling the flow of humanity to California. The state had received national notice during the recently concluded Mexican War because the newly completed Fort Smith military post (1846) had not only served as the supply depot for the Southwestern frontier, but had also provided all the military supplies and commissary goods for the U.S. Army units passing through Fort Smith on their way to Mexico. Zachary Taylor was stationed in Fort Smith for the four years prior to his taking command of the Army of the Rio Grande. Three infantry companies from the Fort Smith garrison served in the Mexican War, and during their absence citizens of Fort Smith served as border patrols.[8]

Fort Smith might have settled back to its prewar obscurity had not news of the discovery of gold burst upon the nation. Fort Smith was almost in a direct line to Santa Fe over territory unimpeded by mountains. Besides, Fort Smith was a river port on the Arkansas River where steamboats from St. Louis and New Orleans docked regularly. The Cherokees on Fort Smith's western border were considered peaceable and friendly and on good terms with Arkansans which quieted worries about hostile Indians.

Enterprising Fort Smith town leaders were aware of these advantageous factors and determined to put forth Fort Smith as the best possible assembly and departure point for the trip to California. The best known overland routes were the Santa Fe Trail, the Oregon Trail and the Mormon Trail. But why not a Fort Smith Trail? On September 5, 1848, a number of Fort Smith citizens pledged themselves to go to California and, to promote and organize the project, named as a committee John J. Dillard, former captain in the Arkansas Cavalry in the Mexican War, J. R. Kannady, and John F. Wheeler, editor of the *Fort Smith Herald*.[9] A public meeting was held on September 23, 1848, and resolutions were adopted asking the state legislature to petition congress to authorize the survey and establishment of a national road from Fort Smith to California.[10]

Editor Wheeler, in a determined effort to popularize the Arkansas route and to give it official credibility, wrote to General Matthew Arbuckle, commander at Fort Smith, requesting him to comment on the proposed Arkansas route. General Arbuckle had been stationed on the frontier for thirty years, and his knowledge, experience and integrity were known and respected. Wheeler must have been ecstatic with the general's lengthy response and published it in full requesting other papers in the state and elsewhere to follow suit.

Headquarters 7th Mil. Dept.
Ft. Smith, Nov. 20, 1848

Dear Sir:—I have received your note of the 27th ultimo, requesting information as to the best route on this frontier to California. . . .

I am not at all surprised at the deep interest manifested by the citizens of most of the states of the Union, and particularly of this and the adjoining states, as to the best starting point as well as the most practicable route, because the salubrity of the climate, the richness of the soil, and the many inducements held out for the acquisition of wealth, could not fail to attract the attention of the citizens of the United States, acknowledged to be the most energetic and enterprising people on the globe.

I do not entertain a doubt, but that upon an unpartial examination this would be found to be the best point for emigrants going to New Mexico and California, to assemble, and make preparations for their journey, as everything necessary for their transportation and subsistence can be procured as cheap here, and with as great facility as at any other point.—There are many other advantages which it possesses, the most important of which, is that its location may be considered at the head of navigation of the most important river in the state, where steamboats can reach for a considerable period of each year. In connection with these considerations, it is well ascertained that the route from this place is the nearest that can be found from our frontier to New Mexico and California.

All the information I have been able to obtain convinces me, that a road should be laid out from this point to the head branches of Washita river, a distance of about three hundred fifteen miles, and which is nearly the direct route to our newly acquired territories. It is believed this route should pass entirely on the south of the Canadian river, and approach near to it opposite Chouteau's trading house, which is located on the north side of the river, and but a short distance from it . . . This route would be freer from obstructions, by water courses, than any other that can be selected. It will pass through a country that in a few years will probably furnish all supplies necessary for the subsistence and comfort of travelers. From the headwaters of the Washita, the proposed route would run over a prairie country gently undulating, and well suited for good road, intersecting [Josiah] Gregg's course on his return from Santa Fe to the United States, about sixty or eighty miles from Washita, and continuing with it to the table lands on the western border of the plains—in all a distance of about 165 miles. These table lands are reported to be very fertile, and to afford sufficient wood and water, for considerable settlement. Here the direct route to California would leave Gregg's trail and incline slightly to the southwest for a distance of about 70 miles, to the Pacos—[Pecos River] an eastern branch of the Rio Del Norte [Rio Grande River], proceeding on the same course about 80 miles, to La Joya [Socorro], a village situated upon the Del Norte; and which is believed to be the proper point at which to cross that river on the most direct practicable route to California.

I have availed myself of the most reliable maps in computing the distances on the route I have described which makes the distance from this place to La Joya, on the Del Norte, 630 miles, being, at least 250 miles less than the route from Independence, Missouri. It is true I have computed the distances from this point to the Del Norte, by the maps; yet, from the nature of the ground upon which the road would run, its windings would not, it is believed, increase the distance more than 30 or 40 miles, at the farthest:—still making it more than 200 miles shorter than the Missouri route. In addition, to this, the travel would commence on this route at least one month sooner than on that, as it runs through a much warmer latitude, and vegetation is much earlier, consequently. The truth is, the advantages of this route over all others are so numerous, and important, that it would extend this letter—already too long—to attempt to point them out . . .

Yours respectfully, your
ob't serv't.
M. Arbuckle
Brig. Gen. U.S.A.[11]

In addition to mileage errors, Socorro was not the place where emigrants crossed the Rio Grande as the next pages will show. This letter is a good example of newspaper promotion of a favorite route because of a special bias. Too, general misinformation about distances, maps and routes was common. In the same edition as Arbuckle's response, Wheeler also published a letter from Major B. L. E. Bonneville, another well-known army officer whose opinion would carry weight. Bonneville also praised the route as being shorter, more level, having water and good encampments, and being settled one-third of the way. Then he made this interesting observation:

You still want one thing, however, to make this route perfect. It is a post where the Texan boundary crosses the Canadian River. This point cannot be far from the present settlements (for you are aware they stretch out nearly two hundred miles west of Fort Smith) and would be as it were a half way house, where parties might refresh and rest if necessary. . . . This post would be supplied with as much ease and security as Fort Washita has ever been.

The Government I believe contemplates establishing one or more posts from the States to Santa Fe. If you could secure this for our state, you would indeed have accomplished a service worthy of your efforts.

Your friend.
B. L. E. Bonneville[12]

Fort Arbuckle was established in western Oklahoma in 1851 by Captain Marcy.

The *Fort Smith Herald* had numerous responses to its gold rush news. Ascertaining that it was impossible to answer individually all the inquiries, the agents of the Fort Smith company "making up for California" devised a circular which included all the pertinent information for emigrants. Under a caption "HO! FOR CALIFORNIA," a copy of the circular was printed.[13] The circular contained general instructions regarding the route to be followed, length of journey, departure time, equipment, food, wagons, teams and livestock. Every able-bodied man was required to provide himself with a good gun, plenty of ammunition, and a bowie knife. Young men without funds to purchase an outfit were encouraged to hire on as teamsters. There was no objection to slaves accompanying their owners and it was a common practice among the Arkansas groups. "Each person who wishes to attach himself to the company will please forward his name (if a man of family, then the number and the number of wagons) to either of the undersigned agents who have a register for that purpose."

The Arkansas press was to publish extensively the Fort Smith circular.[14] It was mailed to inquirers all over the country and a copy of the circular was sent to the Arkansas Congressional delegation in an effort to secure their support in publicizing the Arkansas route.[15]

At the same time Fort Smith was taking this initiative, other towns in Arkansas were responding to the news from California and keeping their readers informed about the preparatory activities in Fort Smith. One of the most exciting early notices of actual emigrants to California about which the citizens of Little Rock learned was in the *Arkansas Gazette* on December 8, 1848. "Four emigrants from New York with a mule team and all the necessary fixings, passed throuqh Little Rock today en route to California. They intend to go with the Company from Fort Smith."[16] Taking note of "the subject which now divides the attention of the public, the great Epidemic—California," George B. Hayden, editor of the *Gazette,* informed the citizens of a meeting scheduled at the State House. One of the objects of the meeting was "to consider the propriety of memorializing Congress on the subject of making an appropriation and appointing a corps of engineers to survey and mark out a road from Memphis, Tennessee, to the city of San Francisco in California."[17]

Undoubtedly another object of this meeting was to determine if there was interest among Little Rockians in going to California. That the response was positive is indicated by the Articles of Association announced two weeks later.[18] Originally this was to be a pack-mule company organized along military lines. This would have excluded families as wagons were deemed necessary for their traveling. Succinctly outlined, the articles stated:

> We, who have subscribed our names hereto, agree to form ourselves into an emigrating association, to be styled the "Little Rock and California Association," the immediate purpose of which is, as its name imports, for providing, in the outset, the necessities requisite for a tour so long and arduous and for the purpose of subjecting each and every one to certain rules and regulations, which may lead to harmony, good order, safety and comfort, on the route; and to insure the speedy, comfortable, safe, and certain accomplishment of the proposed undertaking, and to command, upon our arrival in California, that respect which may be due to respectable and intelligent citizens of the U.S. in a strange country, do hereby agree each one for himself, to provide the following articles, and appear with them on the 27th day of March next, at Little Rock, in this state; to wit: one saddle horse and pack mule, one hundred pounds of flour, 25 pounds of crackers, 25 lbs. of coffee, 50 lbs. of bacon, 15 lbs. of salt; one rifle or shot gun, one pair of holster pistols and knife; and each man of every mess of six will bear his proportion of the following additional articles, to wit:—one pack mule extra, one tent, one axe, one handsaw, one auger and drawing knife, one coffee pot, tin cups, one copper kettle of two gallons, one spade.
>
> And it is further agreed that we will, on the first Monday of March next, meet at the capitol in the city of Little Rock, and proceed by ballot to choose the following officers; one captain and three lieutenants, who are required to serve without any pecuniary compensation, and each man failing to place himself under, and observing the rules and regulations hereby and hereafter adopted, shall be subject for the first and second offence to be dismissed from the com-

fe distance from any civilized settlement; and, if not, shall be ildest infliction of military discipline; and the force of this dged to sustain those in command in carrying into effect all ɔt tyrannical or harsh. The vote of the whole company shall atter, etc.

ay desire to join this company may address either of the men named as a committee of reference: James McVicar, Henry Keatts, Robert Brownlee.[19]

ɔmpany as finally organized was not restricted to packers association different from those spelled out above. See the .

ville, Johnson and Pope Counties were also astir with the following the Fort Smith preparations. In early January D. rt Smith on behalf of a company forming in Clarksville "to n regarding the route, regulations, etc." McLean said sixty dy enrolled and another meeting that week would "see at ed names of persons (good, substantial) bound for group was "fitting out wagons and tents."[20] The Clarksville any was one of the largest and best organized of the Arkansas groups. Redmond Rogers and A. D. King were co-captains and John May was first lieutenant. All three were early settlers of Clarksville, highly respected citizens, and recognized as men of "considerable means." A. D. King kept a journal of this company's journey which provides much information about this group of Arkansans and their California experience.[21] Please read the footnote regarding this source.

Van Buren, the county seat of Crawford County located only six miles below Fort Smith on the north bank of the river, realized early that it too could be a rendezvous and departure point for the California emigration. Van Buren could offer the gold seekers a route to the West on the north side of the Arkansas River. The first notice of "HO! FOR CALIFORNIA" in Van Buren was January 27, 1849, and interested persons were told to be in Van Buren on or before April 1.[22] Two weeks later a list of thirty-eight names were printed in the paper with this comment:

> The following named citizens of Crawford County have resolved to emigrate to California, and will as soon as their number increases to 100, organize and elect officers. Among those are some of our oldest and most respectable citizens, the Hon. Eli Bell, late Representative from this county, and for many years a popular sheriff, the Hon. D. C. Price, now a member of the legislature, and a leading man in our county.[23]

This company took the name Van Buren California Association.

Interestingly another Van Buren company was simultaneously organizing and planned to leave about the same time as the first company. It took the name California Emigrating Company and listed its rules and regulations committee and its correspondence committee.[24]

Gold fever was also raging in the Fayetteville area. In early February an organizational meeting was held in Fayetteville and reported:

> A company is now being formed at Fayetteville, Arkansas, consisting of vigorous, enterprising and substantial citizens of Washington and adjoining counties with the intention of paying a visit to the gold mines of California and securing a portion of the rich deposits of that region. The company will start from Fayetteville about the first of April and will pursue the most advantageous route. A committee has been appointed to collect all the facts that can be procured in relation to the several routes.... The company would be willing to receive a number of additional members of the right sort.[25]

Interested persons were instructed to contact Doctor W. R. Cunningham who was corresponding secretary of the Fayetteville Gold Mining Company. The Fayetteville company was to be very impressed with the route chosen by another group simultaneously organizing in the northwest—the Cherokee.

Citizens of the Cherokee Nation who were interested in going to the gold fields met at the courthouse in Tahlequah on February 3. They chose the editor of the *Cherokee Advocate* James S. Vann to chair the meeting. A preamble and resolutions were drawn up including the rationale for emigrating:

> "Whereas the intelligence which has reached us of the California mines is corroborated by official reports, which render it certain that there is sufficient for all...
>
> We, a portion of the Cherokee people, designing to avail ourselves of the inducements held out for bettering our condition" wish to go to California.[26]

Vann, in his editorial comments regarding the meeting, gave additional information. The Cherokees would travel the route marked out the past summer by Lieutenant Buford which pushed northwesterly from Fort Smith to Fort Gibson in the Indian Territory, crossed Grand River, proceeded to the Verdigris and then on to the west side of the Arkansas River near the mouth of the Salt Fork and continued to Fort Mann and Fort Bridger where it joined other westward trails.[27] This would come to be known as the "Cherokee Trail." This trail could be intersected at the Grand Saline River near present-day Salina, Oklahoma, by groups following a northwesterly route from Fayetteville. Vann gave cordial invitation to companies or parts of companies forming in Fayetteville and Bentonville to join with the Cherokees.[28]

Two additional bonuses for the Cherokee route were set forth by Vann. The Cherokee company would travel "more expeditiously" to California since it would "not be encumbered by a large party." The "very great advantage," however, was that the Cherokee were "on the most friendly terms with all the Indian tribes of the prairie; consequently there will be no danger of attacks from our red bretheren."[29] With these advantages in mind the Cherokee company tendered invitations to neighboring states, appointed A. D. Wilson of Fort Gibson, W. H. Holt of Flint, and D. M. Gunter of Tahlequah to open enrollment books for the names of those wishing to join the company.

The following week Vann was especially excited by the reports from the gold fields and even more laudatory of the benefits of traveling with the Cherokee.

> Gold lump after gold lump in rapid succession are revealed and found under the wonder working picks of the gold diggers of California. The last accounts received from the gold diggers throw far in the shade the first accounts given of the productiveness of the gold placers. The little 'thirteen pounders' are lost sight of, when two-hundred-pound lumps are picked out by the butcher knives of those who are now gently disturbing the bowels of the auriferous mountains of the modern El Dorado. And shall we Cherokee not take advantage of the times and be found trying to get to this glorious country? It is free to all to take up their beds and walk; and if we mistake not, . . . there will be a goodly number of enterprising spirits leave (here) for California.

The editorial continued with the report of a Cherokee citizen who has just returned from a trading expedition on the prairies.

> He says the Cherokee can pass across the prairies with perfect safety from the molestation of the Indians on the priaries, as they are on most friendly terms with the Cherokee; but (he) says the Comanche harbor the most hostile feelings towards the citizens of the United States. This we feel our duty to tell our neighbors, that they may prepare themselves to encounter difficulties with the Comanche should they fall in with them. Any persons along the line or in the neighboring states who may wish to avoid any difficulty with the Indians by joining the Cherokee company, are invited to do so.[30]

The Fayetteville company at a subsequent meeting definitely chose the Cherokee route, and by April one hundred and thirteen persons and fifty wagons were registered as members of the Fayetteville Gold Mining Company. The company expected to rendezvous with the Cherokee on the Grand Saline April 21.[31] This group came to be called the Lewis Evans' Company as he was chosen captain.[32]

The gold contagion spread to the smaller towns and more sparsely settled nonborder counties as well. Groups much smaller in number were organized in those areas with the intention of joining larger groups leaving Fort Smith. A group of thirteen from Helena went to Fort Smith via the steamboat *Oella*.[33]

Groups of a half dozen or less each from Fulton, Izard, and Marion counties "calculating" to join the Fort Smith company registered their names with the *Fort Smith Herald*.[34] Hempstead County was also represented by a small party of forty-niners.[35] Batesville citizens were seized with the California fever and a company "of its best citizens" was formed and planned to follow the Fort Smith route.

> Having made their calculations as reflecting men should, and having fully counted 'the cost,' we have no fear of their being disappointed or disheartened, unless the gold dust gives out before they get there.
>
> We can say that California may be proud of such an acquisition to her population; but hope to see them again among us, each man bringing back a jack mule loaded down with the gold dust.[36]

This warm send-off could not have been predicted three months earlier when the *Batesville Eagle* was reporting that the so-called gold of California was really "arsenite of copper, containing a little nickel and zinc, and mixed with iron pyrates" or even "mica."[37]

The editor of the *Batesville Eagle* was C. M. F. Noland, formerly of Little Rock. Noland reported that gold fever had seized some of his best friends in Little Rock and printed the articles of the Little Rock and California Association. He went on to say that he had "rather chance James McVicar and Henry Keatts in such an expedition, than any men" he knew.[38] The *Batesville Eagle* also reprinted articles from the *Arkansas Democrat* about the advantages of the Fort Smith route.[39] A group of fourteen gold seekers were recorded in the *Batesville Eagle*.[40] Three members of the Batesville company, Thomas Hughes, Eli Ward, and Joseph Woodward left later than the main body, packing and overtaking the Batesville group at Fort Holmes.[41]

Other groups of Arkansans, smaller in number and even more eager to reach California, were the pack-mule companies. The first of such groups to leave Fort Smith was a company of young farmers from the vicinity of Greenwood, Arkansas. Nothing is known of what became of them.[42] The W. H. Heath Pack Mule Company, composed of men from several states and other countries left Fort Smith on March 12. Five Arkansans joined this group, among them Asa Scarborough of Union County who arrived at Embarkadaro, [Sacramento] California on July 26, 1849.[43] Scarborough's record seventy-day journey was to be matched with financial success. See page 143.

Arrangements for a Fort Smith Pack Mule Company "composed entirely of young men without families" was to assemble in Fort Smith on March 1. J. N. Wedsworth was in charge of arrangements.[44] A Van Buren pack-mule company led by Maxwell, an old hunter and traveler who accompanied Col. Fremont, was to leave about May 1.[45] Johnson County's pack-mule company was to rendezvous at Fort Smith on April 5 and John Harris and William B. Whiteside were contact persons.[46]

A Cherokee pack-mule company from Fort Gibson was to be of much interest to Arkansans in the border towns. Lovely Rogers, a mixed-blooded Cherokee, and J. N. A. Carter were members of this group. They expected to reach California in sixty-five or seventy days but were "exactly four months and twelve days in getting to the diggings." They did not plan to return to Fort Gibson until they made "twenty thousand apiece."[47] Carter returned in February 1850, and led one of the 1850 Arkansas groups to California.[48]

In addition to these land trekkers, there were a few men in Arkansas who chose the Panama route to San Francisco. Thomas Parsel and M. Abagge were among the Little Rock group. They left New Orleans on March 21 and arrived in Panama April 3. There they were detained until May 4 waiting to obtain passage. Writing to his wife, Parsel said, "If I had any idea of the difficulty of getting away from here, I should never have come this route, but it is too late now. Tell—to tell all his friends, for God's sake, not to come this way, for there are more here than will get away by next Christmas."[49] One of the known factors mitigating against crossing the Isthmian route was its expense. Parsel informed his wife that people were paying $500 to $800 for passage to San Francisco. Ending his letter on a note of real despair, he wrote,

> I do not know if you will ever get this letter. Many have been written which never reached their destination. It is said the agents of the steamship company

open all the letters, and if they contain anything against this route, destroy them. Whether this is true or not I do not know, but it is certain that if the truth had been known, there would not have been one in a hundred who have come this way that would have taken this route.[50]

When Parsel left Panama on May 9, it was on board the schooner *Sylph* as he could not secure steamboat passage. He recounted his suffering and hardship in a letter written after he reached San Francisco.

> The passage was 81 days, and the number on board the small vessel was 225. In the midst of constant rain and terrible storms, to which I was exposed, for I had to sleep on the open deck, with mouldy bread to eat and foul water to drink. You may imagine that my situation was anything but pleasant. Many men would have given odds to have been in a warmer place below, of which you have heard. To stand on deck was to be drenched by rain and exposed to the pitiless storm—to go below was to be crowded into a dark, dirty, dismal hole with 150 men.[51]

Also on the *Sylph's* passenger list was Major John S. Houston from Clarksville.[52]

At least one Arkansan went by way of Cape Horn. Alden M. Woodruff, son of *Gazette* editor William E. Woodruff, went overland to California. Writing to his father from California, he noted, "Dr. Tappe [J. W.] arrived today. Our trip by land has been a long one, but we beat the doctor in his route around the Horn."[53]

The decision having been made to go to California, the most pressing question became, "What is the best route to California?" The Fort Smith promoters were prepared to answer that question. Since making their decision in September to form an emigrating company and to ask Congress to establish a national road from Fort Smith to California, Wheeler, Dillard, and Kannady worked untiringly to promote the Arkansas route. They reviewed for the potential emigres information on this route which was already available from reports of hunters and traders who had traversed the route in the preceding decade. One of the earliest of these trader-explorers was Dr. Josiah Gregg who left Van Buren in April of 1839 with a merchant caravan bound for Santa Fe. He mapped a route along the Canadian River which was a more southernly Santa Fe route. In 1844 he had published his finding in two volumes entitled *Commerce of the Prairies*. Because of Gregg's knowledge and his keen observations, he was able to make the western adventure come alive. His eight trips across the plains in nine years made him the authority on the Santa Fe Trail.[54] The *Fort Smith Herald* on December 28 had already determined to "proceed along the trail marked out by Mr. Josiah Gregg."[55]

Jesse Chisholm, a Cherokee Indian trader, conducted a trading outfit from Fort Gibson to California in 1839, and his experience qualified him to make recommendations about the southern route. Six years later two other Arkansans, Captain D. G. W. Leavitt of Napoleon and Hiram Hudson of Fort Smith, led a company of sixty from Van Buren to Santa Fe using Gregg's route and completing the trip in thirty-one days. This information was presented anew to Arkansans.[56]

For information regarding conditions beyond Santa Fe, the prospective emigrants could rely on the published report of Lieutenant Colonel P. St. George Cooke who was under orders from General Philip Watts Kearny to open a wagon road from Santa Fe to San Diego during the Mexican War in 1846. He followed a route along the Rio Grande to Guadalupe Pass, thence to Tuscon, beyond to the Pima Indian villages, and then along the Gila River to the Colorado River and on to San Diego.[57] Additional information on the route beyond Santa Fe was provided by Lt. Col. W. H. Emory who accompanied General Kearny in 1846 blazing a pack mule trail north of Cooke's wagon trail but converging with Cooke's road at the Pima Indian villages. The Kearny-Emory Trail was to supply much data concerning the Gila route.[58]

One further exploration was often mentioned in the Arkansas papers, that of Lt. Abram Buford who in the summer of 1848 traveled with his dragoons from Fort Gibson to Santa Fe. Buford reported a good road, six hundred and fifty miles long, could be constructed from Fort Smith to Santa Fe.[59] This fresh publication of data on the Arkansas route fed the flames of excitement. Gregg's *Commerce of the Prairies* and the reports by Cooke, Emory and Buford became handbooks for the prospective Arkansas emigrants comparable in importance to Joseph Ware's guidebook for the Oregon and California Trail.[60]

By late fall of 1848 there was every indication that many Americans planned to go to California. The Arkansas papers continued to keep their readers advised of the interesting movements for the gold diggings. The alcade of Monterey underscored the movement when he reported "the whole country was now moving on the mines."[61] The Fort Smith committee stepped up its efforts to attract the gold seekers to the Arkansas route. Fearing that the Mormon Trail to the Salt Lake and the Oregon and California Trail to the Northwest were better known, the committee made a concerted effort to point out the benefits of the Fort Smith route over that of Independence or St. Joseph. The other Arkansas papers were wholeheartedly behind the effort. The following lengthy article in the *State Democrat* proclaims the superiority of the "southern" route and charges that the Missouri papers were not telling their readers about the superior southern route because they would lose money for Missouri:

> Emigration to California—The Shortest And Best Route
>
> From the notices by the press of the organization of parties in almost every section of the Union for the purpose of emigrating to California, we are led to believe that the number of persons who will next spring be found wending their way over the prairies to the farthest West will far exceed the estimates . . . The *Louisville Courier* speaks of the organization of emigrating companies in various towns and neighborhoods of Kentucky; and from its knowledge of the movements for similar purposes in other states it declares that there is little doubt that fifty thousand persons will be on their way to California as soon as the grass of the prairies shall show itself next spring.
>
> In view of these indications we desire to say a few words in relation to the superiority of the southern, or Arkansas, route, over that of the Missouri, or northern, route, in hopes that our remarks will attract the attention of all

emigrants and emigrating parties preparing to remove to California; confidently believing, as we do, that if they will examine for themselves the claims of the two routes, they will not be long in coming to a decision that the southern route presents the most direct, the best, and the cheapest avenue to California. We have frequently during the past year, in our editorial columns and by many communications from persons intimately acquainted with the country west of Arkansas, attempted to awaken public attention to the superiority of the southern route—a matter which, while it is of the greatest importance to emigrants, is of no small moment to the people of our state. And we trust to see the Arkansas press, generally, take this subject in hand, that there may be no lack of information in regard to this matter in other sections of the Union. Let us unite in this movement, and we can place this subject in its true aspect before the whole country, in spite of the efforts that are being made by those persons and presses in Missouri interested in diverting the tide of emigration to California from its natural and direct channel by the Arkansas river and Canadian trail to Santa Fe, to the circuitous and perilous route by the Mississippi and Missouri rivers, and the Independence route to the same point. It is well known that our neighbors of Missouri have long striven, and are still striving by all the means in their power, to prevent the dissemination of a knowledge of the superiority of the Arkansas route, for fear of losing the benefits now accruing to them from their state being made the thoroughfare of the California and Oregon emigration and the Santa Fe trade. As an evidence of this, witness with what unanimity the press of Missouri acted in suppressing the testimony of Lieutenant Buford in relation to the superiority of the Arkansas route. The lieutenant, in command of a company of United States dragoons, left Fort Smith not long since and, by the Canadian trail, reached Santa Fe in a short time without the least difficulty, reporting the route which he traveled as the best and shortest route from the States to Santa Fe. This statement was given by the St. Louis *Republican* on the arrival of the dispatches from Santa Fe; but almost every paper in Missouri printed out of the city of St. Louis, in copying the intelligence, merely mentioned the arrival of Lieutenant Buford, suppressing entirely his flattering, but what is well known to be truthful, notice of the southern route! This fact alone should stimulate the papers in Arkansas to renewed efforts in this matter, since they must clearly see by this example that it depends almost entirely upon them to place the public in possession of the facts in relations to the shortest and best route to Santa Fe, California, and Oregon.

This lengthy article continued with a synopsis of the advantages of the Arkansas route according to "the testimony of gentlemen" who spoke on the basis of their personal travels between Fort Smith and Santa Fe.

...The distance from the head of steamboat navigation on the Arkansas to Santa Fe is less by about three hundred miles than from Independence to Santa Fe. From the early opening of the spring in the latitude of the southern route, caravans are enabled to start from a month to six weeks earlier than on the northern route. The route runs mainly between the forks of the Canadian, on the dividing ridge, which is as level as could be desired and abounds with springs the entire distance. Cattle for transportation and subsistence of all kinds can be purchased at the rendezvous on the Arkansas much more readily and on better terms than at Independence; for it is a fact well known to the people on our western border that drovers and others often come from Missouri into the counties bordering on the Arkansas river for the purpose of purchasing cattle and supplies to sell to the emigrants and traders at the rendezvous at Independence. In addition to this, the Indians have extended their settlements westward to such a distance that emigrants can supply themselves with corn, beef, and other supplies for eight or ten days' travel on the route after leaving the point of rendezvous.

In this article readers were informed about the possibility of one further advantage for the Arkansas route:

> ... it is expected that a detachment of United States soldiers will leave at the same time for Santa Fe and perhaps California, a good opportunity is presented for emigrants who rendezvous at that place (Fort Smith) to avail themselves, through a portion of the route if not through the entire distance, of the protection which this armed escort will afford.

The article ended with the request that "our brethren of the press in every section of the Union" give place to this information in their papers so that "all those who intend making an overland trip to California may not be ignorant of the fact that the *shortest and best route* to the farthest West is through Arkansas."[62]

Arkansas had a very supportive group of congressional advocates who favored the opening of a Southwestern highway. Senators Solon B. Borland and W. K. Sebastian and Representative Robert W. Johnson were all aware of the permanent commercial benefits which such a road could bring to Arkansas. Arkansas could become the center of western trade and travel and this would rapidly accelerate the economic development of the state. Senator Borland was an early advocate of a southern railroad route to the Pacific, and he became the most tireless of Arkansas' congressional advocates.[63] Aware of the public meetings in Fort Smith (September 1848) and in Little Rock (early January 1949) which petitioned Congress to survey and establish a national road from Fort Smith to California, these congressmen increased their pressure on their colleagues. In the Senate on January 3, 1849, Sebastian presented the memorial from the Arkansas General Assembly asking for the highway to California; while in the House of Representatives, Johnson made the presentation. Both bodies referred the matter to a committee, and the Senate Committee on Military Affairs, chaired by Jefferson Davis of Mississippi, reported favorably on January 31.[64]

Senator Borland, however, feared Congress could or would not give final approval and provide appropriations for the project before April 1 when emigrants would be ready to leave Fort Smith. He therefore decided to simultaneously pursue another possibility. Borland communicated in early January with the Secretary of War, William L. Marcy, informing him about the road measure pending in Congress but also asking for a military escort for the protection of the California emigrants leaving Fort Smith in April and "for the purpose of exploring the intervening country acquired lately from

Mexico." Borland received prompt, favorable response, and the Arkansas papers gleefully printed his letter and reported a military escort had been provided.[65] General Arbuckle at Fort Smith received instructions based on this decision which the papers also reported.

Not content to rest his case, Borland again called the Senate's attention to the Arkansas-Canadian-Santa Fe-San Diego as the shortest and best route to the Pacific. He urged immediate official sanction for a survey and requested an army topographical engineer accompany the Fort Smith expedition to prove the excellence of the route for a national road. Senator Borland was partially successful. The War Department ordered Captain Randolph B. Marcy to command a military escort of dragoons and infantry for the protection of the emigrants and Lieutenant James H. Simpson of the topographical engineers to accompany Marcy and make a reconnaissance of the route traveled—but only as far as Santa Fe.[66]

Editor Wheeler was laudatory of Senator Borland's efforts and praised his "industry in pursuing" the matter of the Fort Smith route and "bringing this subject before the people of the United States."[67] Nonetheless 147 citizens of Arkansas who planned to take the Arkansas route to California forwarded a petition to the Secretary of War requesting the continuation of the escort all the way to California. This petition was sent in mid-February.

"Hon. Secy. of War.
"Sir—

"We, the undersigned, citizens of the State of Arkansas, who intend leaving Van Buren and Fort Smith on or about the 1st day of April next for San Francisco, California, respectfully represent that they are desirous that the escort of U.S. Soldiers, and the officer of Topographical Engineers recently ordered to accompany this expedition, should continue with them from Santa Fe through their entire journey to the Pacific Coast; and they indulge the hope that it will not be inconsistent with your views of public expediency to grant their request.

"In communicating with a gentleman of your intelligence, the undersigned do not deem themselves called upon to make any argument in favor of their request, believing as they do that it is only necessary to draw your attention to this matter, to convince you of its propriety, and that the public interest will be served as well as the comfort and safety of thousands of our citizens received by such a movement.

Respectfully

A. Wallace, P. M. Phillips, Augustus Q. Ward, John Austin, Leonard O. Southmayd, William A. Watson, C. G. Scott, Benj. W. Herndon, N. A. Tryon, Geo. C. Pickett, John Thurston, Jos. P. Marcan, R. Stevenson, Geo. W. Clark, S. M. Larimer, D. C. Williams, G. W. Bearden, Eli Bell, James Foosman, Jas. Shannon, Willis Newton, Wash Farris, A. B. Gorman, A. Stevenson, C. F. Snyder, I. Renshaw, James Stinnett, H. B. Howell, James Haygood, Geo. S. Dyer, John T. Carver, Moses Keelly, Harry Love, John Mums, P. Perkins, R. M. Crumi, T. R. Simmons, Jackson Lock, A. R. Foster, H. W. Bell, D. C. Price, John Goddard, T. M. Newton, James Black, T. P. Cunard, A. P. Christy, Asa Roman, Wm. Low, John James, M. W. Barnes, James W. Davis, A. A. Talkington,

Nicholas A. Pryer, Joseph Price, John Waitgrass, E. T. Craige, Jesse Morse, John W. Hatty, Sam Miles, Thos. H. Johnson, Geo. Gross, Jesse Turner, E. B. Bishop, John F. Bowyer, Peter Connorey, S. Willhalf, Jno. Bostick, I. L. McGhee, Ben Moon, Ed. Cunningham, John Henry, W. W. Stevenson, James McVicar, James Murphy, W. P. Officer, A. M. Woodruff, I. C. Stevenson, Samuel McMorris, Thos. Parsel, L. J. C. Duncan, W. W. Adams, Geo. Holmes, Jno. C. Peay, John T. Trigg, P. R. Kenny, J. Ash, Jesup McHenry, William B. Wait, John W. Walker, Reuben Nutter, D. F. Shall, Henry Wilcox, Jno. B. Ogden, W. R. Simms, Jno. Austin, W. B. Barnett, L. C. Morrell, Saml. Kimball, J. Dickson, Wm. F. Pope, Wm. H. Hammond, Richd. T. Jennings, C. P. Bertrand, L. B. Lincoln, Geo. B. Ring, I. W. Parker, E. D. Robins, S. Lowrie, C. A. Cunningham, Jim F. Fagan, G. S. Primm, A. E. Thornton, E. H. English, Wm. E. Ashley, Wm. Brown Jr., J. M. Giles, Silas T. Field, John D. Adams, Wm. B. Bowdon, E. W. McCrackin, E. Manous, Joseph I. Borden, Wm. H. Cousin, S. T. Hudson, J. W. Tappe, Tho. Butterworth, John Krause, A. J. Hutt, G. B. Hayden,. I. B. Gracie, Jacob Lindauer, David Lindauer, W. Chinellwan, A. S. Walker, A. Armstrong, Chas. Rapley, R. L. Dady, Fred L. Garritt, J. W. Clark, J. W. Farley, *William* H. Field."[68]

Senator Borland again championed the cause of his constituents. When the new administration took office in Washington in March 1849, he deemed it advisable to verify the War Department's earlier promises and to ask that the escort be extended all the way to California. In a letter on March 13 to the new Secretary of War, George W. Crawford, he wrote:

> As you are aware, a military escort, with an officer of the Topographical Engineers, has been ordered by your predecessor, to accompany a company of emigrants to California, which proposes to set off about the 1st of April, from the neighborhood of Fort Smith, Arkansas. The order for this escort contemplated its accompanying the emigrants only as far as Santa Fe. Subsequent reflection has satisfied my own mind . . .that to accomplish the purposes for which the order was made, in a manner truly useful to the party of emigrants, and particularly to the government and country, the escort should continue with the expedition entirely across the continent . . .

On March 19 Borland received positive response and the letter and success were reported in the *Arkansas State Gazette,* April 8, 1849.

The enthusiasm and interest of Arkansas citizens in conjunction with Senator Borland's Washington pressure proved a winning combination. The escort was certain and the army appropriation bill of March 3, 1849, authorized an expenditure of $50,000 for the topographical surveys and reports from Fort Smith to the Bay of San Francisco.[69] Lieutenant Simpson arrived in Fort Smith on April 7 with confirmation both of his instructions and of the escort all the way to California.[70]

Borland's letters to the Senate, to the War Department, to W. E. Woodruff in Little Rock, and to Col. John C. McLemore of Fort Smith were all published and only served to further promote and support the Arkansas route.[71] Untiringly in this correspondence, he reiterated the Fort Smith-Santa Fe route was the best for a railroad or a highway. He also maintained that from Santa Fe to the Pacific would require no more than 100 days. As for Fort Smith, Borland praised its mild climate and its accessibility, claiming it could be reached in three weeks from any other city in the States![72]

His enthusiasm was infectious, and Arkansas journalists in a supportive promotional campaign underwrote the senator and the Fort Smith route. An editorial in the *Arkansas Banner* was captioned "The Golden Route" and reported "The *Herald* at Fort Smith publishes an extra containing a circular forcibly setting forth the advantages of an overland route to California through that place.... It contains much information useful to those who contemplate the trip.... We are pleased to see the energy and industry which our friends at Fort Smith exhibit pressing upon public attention the manifest superiority of this route to that of Independence."[73] William Woodruff in a long editorial stated "that humanity demands from the press of the whole country a prompt and widely circulated warning of the dangers" of the northern route, especially after May 1.

> By reliable accounts from the East we learn that the rush of emigration to California continues as large as ever. The last Cincinnati papers state that every boat coming down the river is crowded with Californians; and it is calculated by those who are acquainted with the movements in the eastern states that the emigration will continue as large as it now is through the whole of May and perhaps for some portion of June. From the misrepresentations of individuals interested in attracting this emigration throuqh Missouri to the northern route, and from the want of correct information respecting the Arkansas route, almost all these emigrants are embarking at Cincinnati and Louisville for St. Louis.
>
> In view of these facts we call upon the presses of Ohio, Kentucky, and all along the Ohio River, and everywhere else within earshot of those emigrants who at this time are wending their way to the northern route, to sound the alarm, and warn them of the dangers which threaten them and the privations which they may be obliged to endure—the dreadful sufferings they may be subjected to, and the horrid fate which they may meet—by taking, so late in the season, the northern route to California. If there is any proper time for starting to California from the frontier of Missouri, it is about the first of May. Previous to that period there is no grass for the subsistence of teams; and if, by any means, the departure is delayed much beyond that time, the route is so long and traveling upon it so tedious that winter overtakes the emigrants in the mountains, and the awful scenes of starvation and cannibalism which have been so often enacted on that route must again occur. In addition to these considerations it is reported that nearly thirty thousand emigrants, with their teams, are concentrating on the frontier of Missouri to take the northern route to California. This number, forced by the shortness of the season to start almost simultaneously on the same route, will consume every vestige of forage as they move along; and there will be nothing left for those who come after them but a waste miles upon miles in width, presenting as barren a spectacle as a burnt prairie, or the fields of Egypt after they had been smitten by the plague of locusts.
>
> Whoever will consider seriously upon this matter—whoever will remember the shortness of the summer from the high latitude of this northern route, and the suddenness with which the winter closes in upon it from the great altitude of the country over which the trail lies—must acknowledge the force of our fears for those who take this route after such an immense number have

preceded them. And they cannot fail to see that humanity demands from the press of the whole country a widely circulated warning of the dangers which all the emigrants who take this route so late in the season must prepare to confront. Nothing but a general movement in this matter on the part of the press, now while there is yet time for it to be done, will avail much; and therefore we look with confidence to our *confrères* in every section of the Union to act promptly in this matter. Humanity demands that these crowds of emigrants should not be permitted to rush headlong upon the perils of the northern route, so completely blinded by the glittering dust that they are utterly unable to discern the inevitable destruction which awaits them.

Those emigrants who succeed in reaching Independence prepared to leave with the companies starting during the first part of May, will probably succeed in getting through before very cold weather commences in the mountains over which they must pass; but those who are delayed much beyond the time we have mentioned, ought not to flatter themselves with a prospect of the like success. The delays which emigrants will experience on the river if they proceed by steamboat, for if they disembark at St. Louis and proceed by land to Independence, ought, in our opinion, to influence all who do not arrive farther on their way than the mouth of the Ohio by the *first of May,* to adopt some more southern route than the Independence trail by the South pass; near which, but yet south of it, be it remembered, a portion of Colonel Fremont's party lately suffered such a lamentable fate, on account of the intense cold and the deep snows so common in those mountainous regions.

We are at a loss to conceive any good reasons why the emigrants who are now leaving the eastern states should take the northern route to California. If they abandon that trail, they are by no means denied ingress to the land of promise, except by the dangerous, costly, and circuitous route through the pestilential atmosphere of the Isthmus of Panama. Between these two extremes, the Scylla and Charbdis of these modern voyagers, free alike from the blighting influence of the frosts and snows of a northern region, and the withering effects of gentle breezes under whose wings is hidden the deadly malaria of equatorial climes, lies the shortest route to the Pacific, through our state via Santa Fe and the Old Spanish trail, or by the way of the Gila river, is the only route which can be safely taken by emigrants after the first of May; and besides this, it is the shortest route, as the gold region, according to the accounts, lies between the very same parallels of latitude which mark the southern and northern boundaries of Arkansas. In addition to all this, the escort and companies which have already left our frontier will place the road in such fine condition that those who follow them will find little or nothing to do through the entire route, except to follow a well-marked, well-trod, and well-bridged road. In view of the many advantages which the Arkansas route possesses over all others as a route practicable at nearly all seasons of the year, we believe it will soon be the only route traveled. The American people do not usually reach a point in a roundabout way which can be gained by a direct approach.[74]

And so with much enthusiasm the news of gold was received in Arkansas; the superior route determined, prolificly advertised and a military escort provided; and preparations for expeditions were underway in most all of the towns and hamlets of the state. One gold seeker aptly expressed the feelings of many Arkansans when he wrote, "now the supply of ore is known to be inexhaustible, . . . who will sit quietly at home in the state pining in penury when fortunes are to be had merely for the labor of picking them up in California, the fact now being established that there is gold enough for all."[75]

CHAPTER II

Outfitting at Fort Smith and Van Buren

"Everything needed for California can be had here and as cheap as in Cincinnati or St. Louis."

The enthusiastic promotion of the Arkansas route resulted in thousands of emigrants converging upon Fort Smith and Van Buren. The merchants in both these villages were aware of the trade benefits that would come as a consequence of supplying the needs of the forty-niners. A spirited rivalry was to develop as these two villages, only five miles apart, competed as outfitters for the California gold seekers.

In the introductory editorial comment prefacing the printings of the Fort Smith Circular, these interesting comments were made:

> Fort Smith has between 500 and 1,000 inhabitants and is steadily increasing. Buildings are going up constantly. The Military Post at this place, is in no way connected with the town, but lies without its corporate limits, partly in the state and partly in the Choctaw Nation. Place does much in way of trade for one of its population, there are several wholesale mercantile houses and a large number of retail stores. Mechanics of almost every trade can be found here. There are a number of blacksmith and wagon maker shops where work is done well and cheap. Evidence of prosperity is that there are no vacant houses for those who wish to rent. Everything needed for California can be had here and as cheap as in Cincinnati or St. Louis.[1]

Representative Green J. Clark of Crawford County was preparing an "Emigrants Guide to Arkansas" which described all the counties of the State. His description of these two towns in Crawford County convey the enthusiasm that was present.

> Crawford County is about 150 miles north and west of Little Rock. The Arkansas river runs through the county and is navigable about one third of the year as high as Fort Smith. Van Buren and Fort Smith are the two flourishing towns in the county. Van Buren, the county seat is on the north bank of the Arkansas River and it has a population of about 900 persons, and is destined to become the Pittsburgh of the West. . . .
>
> Fort Smith is located on the south bank of the river about six miles above Van Buren and has a population of about 1,000 persons. Fort Smith is immediately at the head of the navigation and will soon be the rendezvous place of all California emigrants.[2]

The 1850 census reported the population of Van Buren as 549 (404 whites and 145 slaves) and of Fort Smith as 880 (803 whites and 77 slaves).

The merchants in both towns began to advertise with special attention given to the California emigrant. The following three ads were in the *Fort Smith Herald.*

> Tin Ware for California
>
> Darby and Bennett are now manufacturing ware expressly adapted to the use of California Emigrants, and intend to make up and have ready by the time of the starting of the train, ALL ARTICLES NEEDED FOR THE TRIP, which they will sell cheap for cash. Their Pans and Kettles will be useful to every emigrant, as they can be used on the road, and will do to wash gold in after arriving in California.
>
> Travelers wishing anything in the "Tinker's" line would do well to call at the
>
> CALIFORNIA TIN SHOP.

> Medicine for Emigrants
>
> The undersigned are fully prepared to furnish Emigrants with suitable medicines, necessary for their uses, and would most respectfully call their attention to our Drug establishment, where they can procure the proper kinds of the best quality, at greatly reduced prices; especially to those who are bound for the gold regions.
>
> W. H. & M Mayers
> Wholesale & Retail Druggists

> Horses and Mules
>
> 100 Spanish mules and 50 horses—Emigrants and others in want of Mules and Horses for California Expedition are respectfully requested to call on us before purchasing, as we will give the best bargains in the above.
>
> W. H. and M. Mayers

Three wagon makers advertised in Van Buren's *Arkansas Intelligencer* on the same day.[4]

> California Depot
> Wagon-making firm Newland & Bearden.

> California Outfits for Sale—Complete
> Joseph Hawkins—Wagon Maker & Wheelwright

Wallace & Wards   Ho! for California
Emigrants to California seeking articles of *Outfit,* will please look into
Wallace & Wards

Not only did the merchants of the two towns rival each other, but there was competition to provide the best camp site for the gathering emigrants. In September 1848, a sulphur spring was discovered about a mile and a half from Fort Smith.[5] It was to be the camping place of one of the largest companies taking the Fort Smith route—the Western Rovers. The captain of this group was from Mississippi, but the ninety-six men in the company represented all the southern states.[6] Col. John Drennen of Van Buren provided an eighty-acre woods pasture one half mile below Van Buren for the use of the emigrants. A prospective emigrant described this as "a fine place well wooded, for shade or shelter, good grass, fallen wood for fires, immediately on the bank of the river, enclosed by a rail fence."[7]

It was with regard to providing food for the prospective gold seekers that the competition between Fort Smith and Van Buren became rather heated. On February 7 the *Fort Smith Herald* advised its readers:

> *Flour and Bacon* will be in demand. We should advise those being at a distance to bring their flour and bacon here as soon as possible, and if they cannot find sale immediately, to leave it with someone to be sold on commission.—Look to it farmers and traders. Be sure to have a supply on hand. We expect there will be a large party here soon who will have to purchase their provisions, at this place, and will pay cash for them.[8]

And in another ad on the same day:

> Corn!   Corn!   Corn!
> Corn is very much needed here and is now worth 50¢ per bushel. It is thought that 10,000 bushels will be wanted to supply the California emigrants.—Will our friends through the country endeavor to bring in all they can. It will command cash in a few days—not less than 50¢ per bushel.[9]

The *Arkansas Intelligencer* chose to interpret this ad as indicating "need" in Fort Smith and as an inflated price to take advantage of the emigrant. Editor Wheeler shot back in reply the next issue:

> "We would inform the editor of the *Intelligencer* that the citizens of Fort Smith are not in a *'destitute condition'*:—All we designed in our notice was to induce our own farmers and others to bring in their provisions in time as there will be a great demand for them in a few days.—We have no intention of inducing people to come to this place from a distance to join our company, and when they arrive here to have them find every article required for an outfit, scarce and very high. We wish to take no advantage of the emigrant to California. If the editor of the *Intelligencer* has corn in so great an abundance, as to be able to sell it for 30 or 35¢ a bushel, we would inform him that he can sell every bushel he can rake and scrape, at this place, for that price. What say you?[10]

The *Arkansas Democrat* reported from "a citizen of Crawford County: that "Corn is worth only 25¢ per bushel in Crawford County" and that flour in any amount could be had for $4.50 a barrel.

> "Plenty of bacon in the back country for many farmers could not sell their pork at $2.00 per hundred last winter and made bacon of it. I would contract to deliver 50,000 pounds at 5¢ per pound. Emigrants may come on with the expectation of finding at Van Buren, corn, flour, and bacon plenty, and on reasonable terms; certainly much less than they can buy and freight to Fort Smith from any part of the United States.—There will be a good supply of mules and horses for sale at Van Buren, at reasonable prices by the first of March.[11]

Again Editor Wheeler of the *Fort Smith Herald* quickly responded to the Van Buren challenge.

> If citizen will show himself and be a responsible man and furnish said articles, we would refer purchasers to him. Many citizens fear that there will not be enough to meet demand and then our citizens will suffer consequences later.[12]

A prospective emigrant had stopped in Little Rock and undoubtedly met William Woodruff, for on March 11 from Fort Smith he wrote to the *Arkansas State Democrat* regarding conditions in Van Buren and Fort Smith. The letter unintentionally drew attention to the rivalry between the two towns. The writer indicated that he stopped in Van Buren "no more than an hour" but was nonetheless willing to report:

> The place (Fort Smith) is crowded, and I would suggest to emigrants coming up, to stop at Van Buren. It is a larger town, and as more business is done there, the goods are cheaper. Those horses, mules, or oxen, clothing or provisions (the latter in particular) we now get here, were laid in at Van Buren.[13]

The writer went on to say that he found the people of Fort Smith "polite, hospitable, and friendly, and willing to give all the information in their possession."

Another expeditioner from Louisiana, while camping in Fort Smith, wrote home his comments on the two towns. Regarding the Fort Smith garrison he said, "The buildings are put up in handsome style and the officers seem to enjoy life very well." The sojourner had toured the quarters occupied by General Zachary Taylor and comparing it with his quarters at Baton Route, "found it difficult to determine which was the more comfortable of the two." His description of Fort Smith was a town of about 1,000 inhabitants whose chief trade was with the Indians. His description of Van Buren was "a much more finely built town of about 1,100 inhabitants" whose trade was primarily "with a large back-country" and whose "stores are well supplied with goods."[14]

This verbal spat did not continue. Probably the number of emigrants and the increased business opportunities more than compensated the merchants in both towns. Too, the feared shortages did not occur. Maybe the leaders of Fort Smith and Van Buren determined that such snipping could hurt the larger Arkansas cause which championed the southern route as opposed to the northern route from Missouri. This excerpt from a reporter at Fort Smith to the *Arkansas Banner* suggests these conclusions:

> The streets are literally crowded with California wagons and teams.... Nothwithstanding the constant influx of emigrants, provisions are plentiful and as cheap as usual. It is the determination of all to supply those who emigrate from this point at moderate prices; those coming need apprehend no fear of extortion. Those who suppose we wish to speculate upon this movement, would do well to come and see before denouncing that about (which) they know nothing. I allude to the course of some papers who oppose this route . . .[15]

For whatever reason, both towns turned their attention to outfitting the emigrants and helping them meet their April 1 target departure.

The Fort Smith Circular with its general instructions regarding supplies, equipment and preparation continued to be periodically reprinted in the Fort Smith and other Arkansas papers. Its content illustrates the preparatory items the emigrants would be assimilating at the rendezvous points. Horses, mules and oxen could be secured in Fort Smith and Van Buren, but travelers were advised to have their wagons built at home and shipped to Fort Smith. Arkansas had too few wagon makers to meet the needs of Arkansas gold seekers and to accommodate emigrant demands. The *1850 Census of Products and Industry* lists industries which grossed $500 per year. There were no wagon makers listed for Crawford County (Fort Smith and Van Buren); there was one each in Pulaski (Little Rock), Johnson (Clarksville), Benton (Centerville), and Jackson (Newport); there were three in Washington County (Fayetteville). Saddlers, blacksmiths, boot and shoemakers were more numerous. Pulaski listed three, Johnson six, Benton zero, Jackson three, Washington eleven, Yell (Danville) three, and Crawford one. See Appendix A. Outfitters could therefore obtain other required items such as axes, shovels, mattocks, saws, hammers, nails, chisels, augers, drawing knives, tents, lead, and powder on the scene. There are some discrepancies in the *Industry's* listing and the local ads in the Arkansas papers. More industries advertise than are listed in the census indicating that they grossed less than $500 per year; that they were no longer in business or that there were inaccuracies in reporting. In Fort Smith in addition to John Gardner, Saddler and Harness appearing in the census, there were Stephen D. McDonald, Saddler and John Stafford, Bootmaker. In Van Buren the principal blacksmith was McCurry, who "planned to join the rush to California when business should let up."[16] Three wagon-making firms advertise in the *Arkansas Intelligencer* in 1849: Newland and Bearden, Wallace & Wards, and Joseph Hawkins. The *Washinqton Telegraph* in 1849 also had ads from businesses not listed in the 1850 census: Fleming and Beasley, Blacksmithing and J. A. and J. W. Barron, Blacksmithing and Wagon Making.[17]

The food needs for each person varied slightly with the different companies, but those listed in the Fort Smith Circular are representative of the requirements. Each person was to provide 100 pounds of bacon, 150 pounds of flour, 20 pounds of coffee, 30 pounds of sugar, lard, 20 pounds salt, pepper, crackers, pilot's bread, meal, rice, molasses, dried peaches, beans, tea, spices, salaratus (baking powder), and vinegar. All of these items had to be packed in a manner to conserve both space and weight as each wagon was to average about 2,000 pounds. The soda crackers and pilot bread or hard tack were two new bakery products whose production was vastly stimulated by the California Gold Rush. They could be used for the noon meal when fires were not built or when fuel was in short supply. These items were stored in half barrels or large tin boxes for easy packing and handling and to protect their freshness. In Fort Smith the firm of Johnson and Grimes advertised both items for sale.[18]

In early 1849 business was lively and the population of Fort Smith and Van Buren was abnormally swollen. The *Intelligencer* reported "Blacksmiths and wagon makers are all busy; the streets and premises around their shops are thronged with horses and mules waiting to be shod, and with wagons to be repaired."[19] The same paper reported that there was not "an ounce of quicksilver to be had in the town; it was all bought up for California."[20] Thousands of emigrants were camped along the five miles of river bank between Fort Smith and Van Buren. Conditions were so crowded and accommodations so overtaxed by January that farm families six miles from Van Buren were taking boarders.[21] Emigrants were swarming through Little Rock by steamboat, stage, and covered wagon on the way to the Arkansas rendezvous points. Each week the Little Rock papers estimated the additional number "passing this point, bound for Fort Smith." The *Arkansas State Democrat* reported "Every steamer from below comes well freighted with emigrants with their wagons, outfit, etc. . . . It is calculated that about 500 emigrants within the past ten days have passed this point on their way to Van Buren or Fort Smith."[22] The next issue reported "the *Armstrong, White, Cashier*, and *Pennywit* have passed up with about 350 on board, consisting of companies and parts of companies from Tennessee and Mississippi. To this number, if we add those who have passed through our city proceeding by land, we may safely estimate that not less than 1,000 have already gone up to the rendezvous."[23] Still they continued to come so that two weeks later the numbers projected had increased tenfold.

> The camps of those who are going up by land are seen in numerous localities in the vicinity of our city; and the *Cotton Plant* and *Duroc* are hourly expected to arrive from New Orleans with companies from Louisiana and Mississippi. At Memphis, we learn, large crowds are awaiting transportation to Van Buren and Fort Smith. We also see by the Cincinnati and Louisville papers that various parties are constantly leaving those ports, on their way to California by the Arkansas route. From present appearances we shall not be surprised if the number of emigrants leaving our frontier during April, May and June should reach *ten thousand*.[24]

The presence of so many emigrants served to heighten the excitement and sense of impending adventure. Indeed it must have seemed "the whole nation was moving on the mines." The New York City Knickerbocker Company was eighty in number when it came through Little Rock on March 7. Sixty of the eighty dined at the Anthony House.[25] This entirely male company was highly complimented by Arkansans and described as very intelligent, good-looking, gentlemen, enterprising, persevering, and men of spirit.[26] They camped at Sulphur Springs and advertised for horses, mules, and harnesses.[27]

One activity in which all the emigrants were involved was procuring, breaking, and fitting (harnessing) mules. Horse traders such as David Tulloch advertised they would be in Fort Smith with 150–200 Mexican mules of first quality, four years old, low for cash.[28] Auctions and private sales took place daily and harness makers had more demands than seemed possible to meet. Mules were preferred by many to oxen because they traveled faster, but their unmanageability was a real disadvantage. To help prospective emigrants learn to gentle their mules, men such as Denton Offut, a recognized horse trader from Kentucky, came to Fort Smith to conduct lectures. One five-dollar lecture was a "full course" on how to select and gentle horses and mules, how to cure their diseases, and how to prevent stampeding. The lectures ran for four nights, and persons could attend all four for the price of five dollars.[29] "His skill as a horse tamer was remarkable. Passing through the crowded streets you would hear a drum and see him tapping it, and an unbridled horse that he had broken, tamely following him as he lectured to the crowd. He was known in Kentucky as the 'Whisperer' from his methods. He would get a vicious horse in a stall and avoiding bites would cautiously stroke the nose and whisper in the ear. The subdued horse would suffer handling and bridling. The whisper was to fake the crowd. The secret was a strong perfume on his hand that has a singular influence on the animal."[30]

A Fort Smith observer of mule-breaking techniques reported on March 16.

> Breaking mules is the constant occupation of many. The streets are literally crowded with California wagons and teams, the latter learning the rudiments of a mule's education, to wit: plenty of work and little forage. It is quite amusing to witness the expedients resorted to in subduing their fiery and kick-inclining spirits. Sometimes you will see one tied by the head to a post, and his hind leg drawn back as far as possible and tied to another (post). After enduring mortal agony and the unpleasant familiarity of the breaker for an hour or two until he is nearly broken, a pack is fastened upon his back, and (he) is driven until exhausted and yields a willing servant of his master.[31]

Recalcitrant mules and outfitting wagons could not fill all the hours of the day for the weeks and months that some emigrants waited before departure. There was also much time for drinking, gambling and quarreling. The liquor business probably picked up as an air of general celebration prevailed and because the prospectors knew there would be no liquor on the trail. The newspapers, however, were complimentary of the behavior of the emigrants as they tarried in the Arkansas towns. The Little Rock paper wrote, "We most willingly bear testimony to the gentlemanly deportment, sobriety, and exemplary conduct of all the emigrants who passed this point.[32] The Fort Smith paper commented, "The peace and harmony that has heretofore characterized our city, while crowded with California emigrants, speaks volumes in favor of those persons that are emigrating to that golden land of the West. Not a single riot or difficulty so far has occurred."[33] When one also considers that the spring of 1849 was unusually wet in Arkansas, causing far less than ideal camping conditions, the absence of serious social misbehavior is remarkable.

The *Fort Smith Herald* certainly did its part in helping organize, inform and advise the waiting emigrants. Every company arriving in Fort Smith was asked to register the number and names of their members by writing the *Herald* in care of the post office.[34] Many did so, leaving us a record of many travelers we might not otherwise have known. Readers were also informed that there was a mail service for the California country; and therefore they should avail themselves of the "opportunity of obtaining cheap paper by subscribing for the *Herald*."[35] Two weeks after this notice, readers were told:

> The subscription list of the *Herald* is increasing fast. Many of the emigrants subscribe to it to send to their friends. We shall be enabled to give news from the emigrants on the route, earlier than any other paper, therefore, our paper will be of great benefit to the friends of emigrants in the states, besides, it is the cheapest paper in the State, only $2 *per annum* in advance.[36]

A column entitled "Advice to Emigrants" included comments regarding health and cleanliness that indicated possible problems in a town swollen more than double its population.

> As our total is now full of emigrants for California from different parts of the U.S., we would remark that too much care cannot be taken in regard to their health, and a good deal depends upon the healthy state of the system when starting a long journey. Therefore, run into no excess, and pay particular attention to the state of your stomach and bowels.—We learn from experienced military officers that it is very unhealthy to remain at one camp more than a week and it would be better to remove every three or four days, if only for a short distance.
>
> While giving a few words of advice to emigrants, we would also caution our own citizens, and say to them too much care cannot be paid to personal cleanliness, and clearing away from about your premises all filth. A word to the wise is sufficient.[37]

The dreaded disease of all the outfitting towns was cholera, known to be carried by rats, fleas and lice and aggravated by contaminated water. This was a clear warning without using the dreaded word. Soldiers prevented steamboats from New Orleans, one of the pestholes for cholera, from landing at Van Buren when cholera was feared to be on board.[38] Cholera did come to Fort Smith in 1849 on board the steamboat *Oella No. 2* which docked the day after the emigrants departed. The disease spread through the town and to Fort Coffee, Fort Gibson and the Choctaw Agency. It raged until the board of health, backed by the town council, ordered property owners to cleanse their premises and disinfect with lime.[39] The town cleansing and the coming of cold weather ended the epidemic. Cholera did not overtake the Fort Smith wagon train. The Van Buren emigrants were told that when their company was organized, each one would bear a proportionate part of the cost of a chest of medicine and that a doctor would accompany the party.[40] This was a common practice of all the groups.

Much in vogue with forty-niners were the daguerreotypists who could catch a likeness of the gold seeker in his goldfield attire for sending back home to the folks. Fort Smith had its own daguerreotypist, G. S. C. Scott, who had set up shop at Clark's Hotel. He did a booming business "making pictures" of the emigrants in their gold-rush raiment. The *Herald* advised that "Friend Scott was ready at any time to take a likeness. Call and have your *phiz* taken down before leaving for California."[41] Emigrants from the East came in every imaginable attire, but the standard costume became a wool shirt, heavy trousers, stout boots, a wide-brim hat, and for a touch of class and color, a bright sash for the waist. The ready-made clothing industry was stimulated by the forty-niners hasty preparations for the gold fields, and enterprising merchants devised the "proper attire" which included the red or blue flannel shirts, baggy trousers, wide-brimmed felt hats, and trucks and rubber bags for their gear.

The Arkansas papers kept their readers' attention keenly focused on reports of big gold finds in California and new inventions which reportedly made gold searching and washing extremely simple. One such instrument was the Goldometer and Guide invented by one Signor Don Jose D'Alvear, "an eminent Spanish geologist, chemist, and natural philosopher." An entire column in the *Arkansas Gazette* was devoted to this creation. Readers were told, "The Goldometer is so simply an instrument, that a child may learn to operate with it in five minutes. Persons going to California cannot make a better investment. Goldometer $3.00. Guide alone $1.00." There was a New York City mailing address.[42] In addition to being completely impractical, these inventions were to prove an additional overload burden and discarded long before reaching California. There was no reference by the Arkansans to having enriched Signor D'Alvear, but companies from the eastern states departing from Van Buren did have gold-washing machinery. (See next chapter.)

The preparations and plans of the various Arkansas groups were also reported. In March these groups turned to the actual organization of their companies. Meetings were held to draft rules and regulations, to designate officers and their duties, and to write articles of association. See Articles of Association in Appendix B. The articles of association were modeled after a military-type organization and many of the leaders (captains) of the companies were either ex-officers who had recently returned from the Mexican War or experienced frontiersmen. John J. Dillard, captain of the Fort Smith company, was lately captain of the Van Buren Avengers, Company F, Arkansas Cavalry. James McVicar, captain of the Little Rock company, was lately Quartermaster Sergeant of Colonel Yell's cavalry regiment. Undoubtedly, great benefit was seen in such an arrangement whereby officers had prescribed authority and duties and whereby members subscribed to specified obligations and discipline.[43] Such planning and organization was a very common sense approach to a venture beset by numerous fears and uncertainties. Besides they were in the company of U.S. Army dragoons and military organization was very evident.

The duties of the officers prescribed in the articles followed the same general pattern. The captain was to command the company, direct the march, select the camping ground, and "exercise such other authority as might be required by his position;" the first, second, and sometimes third lieutenants were to assist in carrying out orders and to assume command, according to rank, in the event of the captain's death or disability. The secretary kept an account of the business proceedings of the company; the treasurer was in charge of the company's finances. Some companies had a commissary rather than a treasurer whose duty was to purchase provisions for the company while on the route, to employ guides, to purchase mules and horses, and to keep company accounts. Companies having a commissary would have a clerk to keep a journal of each day's travels.[44]

The articles created an administrative council made up of the officers and a specified number of elected members or, as in the case of the Van Buren company, made up of all members serving on a rotating basis. Usually the council inspected wagons and teams and approved for membership. On the trail the council would try members for any infringement of the rules and render punishment based on majority vote of the council. The council would also make assessment of the members for such items as a traveling forge, a medicine chest, and a cable which were then company property. Some of the specified offenses which were mentioned as punishable were drunkenness, gambling, and "violence of peace." All members took a solemn oath to abide by the rules of the council. The concluding sentences in the Little Rock articles well convey the serious nature of the commitment.

> It is expected that every person who has determined to go has made up his mind to endure the hardships of camping out and attending to his horses, wagons, etc., but we are well enough acquainted with such a life to be able to say that those who have made the experiment, heretofore, have uniformly become of robust constitutions, and increased much in flesh. We, the undersigned, members of the "Little Rock and California Association," do approve of the above rules and regulations for its government, and do bind ourselves as men, and do pledge our honor as gentlemen, each one for himself, to obey, enforce, and abide by them.[45]

The Fort Smith Articles contained a couple of items not found in the others. Every member of the company was required to change his underclothing once a week and to carry three pounds of soap. A musician was appointed by the captain, to sound the call for arising, harnessing, folding, taking up the line of march, and for accidents. The Little Rock articles specified that any member who became sick or disabled would be "sustained" by the company.[46] This was the accepted practice in all the companies, however.

Nature was the determining factor in planning an overland journey in 1849. There must be adequate grass on the prairies for livestock before departing, and April 1 became the magical date for the Arkansas Route. Arrival in California should be before the first snows in the mountain passes which meant October 1 became the target date for reaching California for those traveling the northern routes. The distance reckoned to San Francisco on the Arkansas route was 2,290 miles.[47] They counted on averaging fifteen to twenty miles a day with wagons, which would have been three and one-half to four and one-half actual travel months; but they determined not to travel on Sundays and knew that additional days for "laying by" would be necessary. Sunday was not a traveling day, but neither was it strictly a day of rest, for washing, cooking, and repairs were to be a part of Sunday's necessary routine. Other days the company would have to lay by for extensive repairs, resting the animals, illness, poor weather, lost animals and various other contingencies which were expected but were to be kept to a minimum in order to meet the time table. So another month to month and one-half allowance for these factors would extend the trip time to six months.

The broad limits of the time table were projected; yet each day's progress and route were dictated by the need for water, wood, and forage. Nurture and care of the animals was basic to the survival of the emigrants, for to be stranded without motive power would have meant eventual death. The 2,000-pound load limit for wagons was also dictated by the necessity of consideration for the animals. Excess poundage slowed the progress and strained the animals, even though it relieved anxiety about "running out" of food supplies. Too little poundage meant faster progress was imperative and created its own bundle of anxieties. To strike a happy medium between the two was the desired goal and necessitated minute planning of every detail. The forty-niners, especially along the northern routes, were to sadly overload. In consequence of their mistakes, however, the 1850 emigrants were to be much better planner.

A factor important to all emigrants was the expected cost of the journey. The overland trip was clearly acknowledged as the least expensive way to reach California. Arkansans were convinced that their southern route to San Francisco was the best of all because it was three hundred miles shorter than the northern route, it was the best watered and had the best grazing, and it could be used the earliest in the spring; therefore, it was also the cheapest.[48] Arkansans as farmers would have had wagons, teams and most of the required provisions on hand, so their estimated cost of the journey was small. No dollar figures were found in the records. Hastings' *Emigrants Guide* estimated the cost of the journey on the northern route to be $100.[49]

All preparations made, the Arkansas companies began moving to their rendezvous places. The Little Rock and California Association under the command of Captain James McVicar began leaving for Van Buren in small parties on March 25. It was estimated that "about one hundred would take up the line of march."[50]

> At the time our paper goes to press almost all the members of the company have left. The wagons, teams, and all the various *et ceteras* of the outfit of this company are of the most superior quality, and we feel assured that no company will take up the line of march better prepared for the trip. Many of those who compose this company are long members of our city and well known to all of us as men of high character and great energy. They will take with them the best wishes of this community for a speedy and safe journey to El Dorado and the realization of their brightest hopes.[51]

Members of the various groups are listed in Appendix F. William Pope recalling the departure of the Little Rock gold seekers forty-five years later commented on the completeness of the outfit. "The bodies of the wagons were made water tight and fashioned at each end like the bow and stern of a flatboat, and were used to ferry swollen streams." There is no reference by contemporary Little Rock gold seekers to those boat-shaped wagons. Wagons were caulked to impede wetness from river crossings. This reference serves as a good example of Pope's sometimes faulty memory. He noted that they drove young cattle for beef.[52]

The Clarksville Californians created quite a stir when they passed through Van Buren on their way to Fort Smith on April 7. This company was under the command of Captain Redmond Rogers, proceeded

> . . . with flying colors and martial music. In the train were about fifty wagons, all heavily laden with those things which are necessary for the body. From the anxious search of a member for a copy of the Declaration of Independence, we presume that the drum and instrumental choir will not be silent on the next Fourth of July.[53]

The best estimate of the total number of emigrants to choose the Arkansas route in 1849 is about three thousand from at least twenty-five states.[54] New York and the southern states provided the largest number. In addition there were some emigrants on the Arkansas route from the District of Columbia, and from Germany, England, Scotland, and Ireland.[55] A prospective gold seeker wrote from Fort Smith March 11 giving his estimates:

> I have no doubt from the signs and from information, at least 1,200 persons with about 250 wagons and about 2,000 mules or horses and 1,000 oxen will leave this place sometime between the first and fifteenth of April, and about the same number will leave Van Buren about the first of the month.[56]

A citizen of Van Buren corresponding with a Little Rock paper on April 18 agreed with Bieber's estimate.

> This has been a busy day in town; many of the California emigrants took up their line of march. . . . Although *three thousand* emigrants have left here, there is yet a surplus of stock and provisions.[57]

Yet another estimate was made by a correspondent of the *Baltimore Sun* who wrote from Fort Smith on April 28. "From the best calculations possible, more than 900 wagons left here with 2,000 emigrants for California."[58] Exact calculations are impossible, but obviously the number of emigrants was considerable.

What effects were felt on Fort Smith and Van Buren as a result of being outfitting posts? A citizen of Van Buren who did not go to California made this assessment:

> The California emigration has been the source of immense profit to the citizens of Arkansas, and should be encouraged by the press, the public men, and every one. They have left at this point alone, about $60,000 for oxen, horses, mules, bacon, flour, etc, etc., and probably as much or more at Fort Smith. Every branch of business flourished. Next year, after the advantages of this route over all others become published to the world, the whole emigration will go through Arkansas; and our merchants, farmers, stock raisers and all should prepare themselves to meet the demands for the outfit.[59]

The economic benefits for Fort Smith were not short term, as an editorial in late September indicated. The population had increased, nothing was available to rent, and rents were high. The merchants were doing well, having sold fifty per cent more than last year. Mechanics were constantly employed and at liberal wages.[60]

The financial gains for Arkansas, the excitement of having "strangers in our midst," and the high hopes of the Arkansas prospectors all converged to make the spring of 1849 one to be remembered. George Hayden of the *Arkansas Gazette* captured the spirit well when he wrote:

> "Gone to California" is likely to become as significant as "gone to Texas," once was. Among the thousands getting off, there appears to be a sprinkling here and there of those who either won't or can't "meet their engagements." Of course, California is the place where they honestly expect to reap the golden harvest.[61]

Arkansans had been very interested in the Texas revolution and the Texas offer of free land to volunteers who would help them in their cause against Mexico. Arkansans left for Texas in such significant numbers after the revolution that G. T. T. after a man's name needed no explanation. Arkansas' Golden Army of 1849 was on the trail, and Hayden was predicting numerous G. T. C.s.

CHAPTER III

Seeing the Elephant Along the Arkansas Route to Santa Fe

"Everyone is liable to mistakes, and everyone has a right to call a road *very bad* until he sees a worse. My mistake was that I said I had seen 'The Elephant' when getting over the first mountain. I had only seen the tail."

"In nine miles we came to another Elephant."

A phrase which came to be synonymous with "going to California" was "seeing the elephant." This term was in the *Dictionary of American English* as early as 1835, but it came into maximum usage during the California Gold Rush. Specifically it meant to face a particularly severe ordeal, to gain experience by undergoing hardship, or to learn the realities of a situation first hand.[1] Having determined to undertake the venture, the emigrants were eager to be off. When April 1 rolled around the sense of excitement in Fort Smith and Van Buren was scarcely to be contained.

Weather conditions in the spring of 1849 were to cause delays, however. Conditions were unseasonably wet due to deep winter snows and unusually heavy spring rains causing flooding. The river bottoms had become quagmires which would not permit the passage of loaded wagons. While the big company waited for the trail to dry, pack-mule companies, military reconnaissance groups, and impatient smaller detachments began to test the Arkansas-Canadian trail. On March 12, the Heath Pack Mule Company of twenty-four men including Asa Scarborough and four other Arkansans were the first to leave Fort Smith.[2] Captain Fred T. Dent left two days later to prepare a road to the Choctaw Agency.[3] The New York Knickerbocker

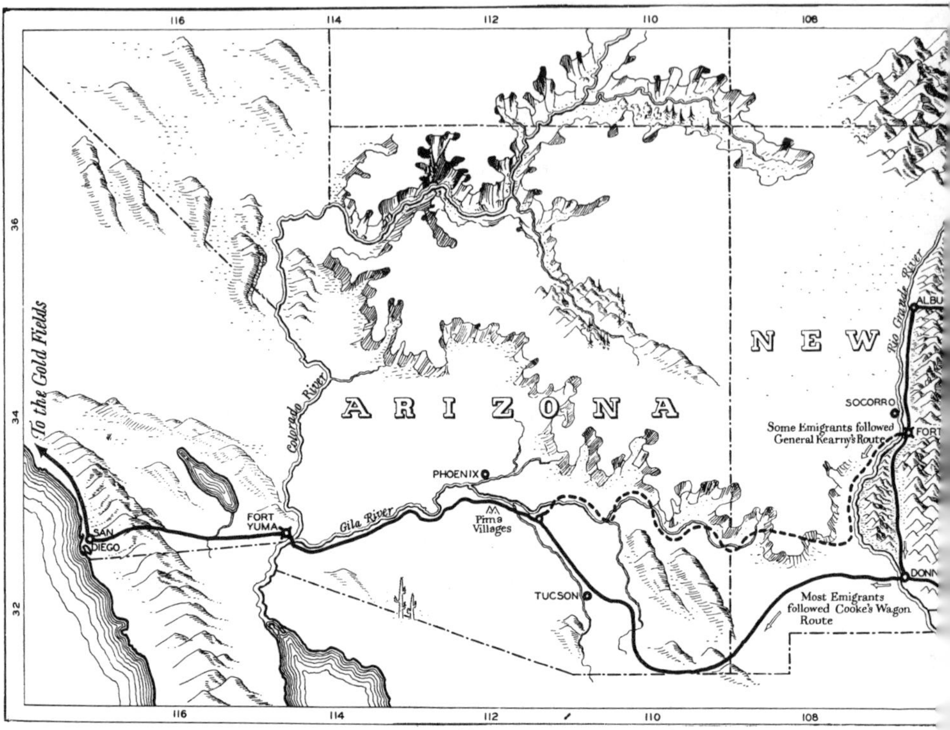

Note: Dona Anna is misspelled on this map.

Exploring Company under the command of Captain John A. N. Ebbetts and numbering eighty men left Fort Smith on March 26. This was a well-equipped, well-organized, and well-off group of emigrants who were much admired by Fort Smith citizens.[4] They started up the south side of the Arkansas River on a route soon to be followed by Captain Marcy and the Fort Smith group. The Helena Company followed the Knickerbockers on March 27.[5]

Then on April 4 the military escort of eighty-five men under the command of Captain Randolph B. Marcy moved out one week in advance of the emigrant caravan to open the road on the south side of the Canadian. Lieutenant J. H. Simpson accompanied the expedition as topographical engineer and Dr. Julian Rogers of Newcastle, Delaware, served as physician.[6]

At long last, Wednesday, April 11, the appointed departure date for the Fort Smith expedition arrived. It was a bright, clear day after a hard rain on Monday night and clouds on Tuesday. A. D. King captured a brief glimpse of the moment in his journal: "Very early this morning the horn was sounded and soon all the wagons were in a line of march for the golden west."[7] "Stretch out!" the long-awaited command of Captain Dillard, who had general charge of the Fort Smith migration in Captain Marcy's absence, set the train in motion. Excitement, tearful farewells, last minute checking, head counting, commands and expletives to teams and mules, and well wishing filled the air. By its very nature it was a noisy, smelly, and impres-

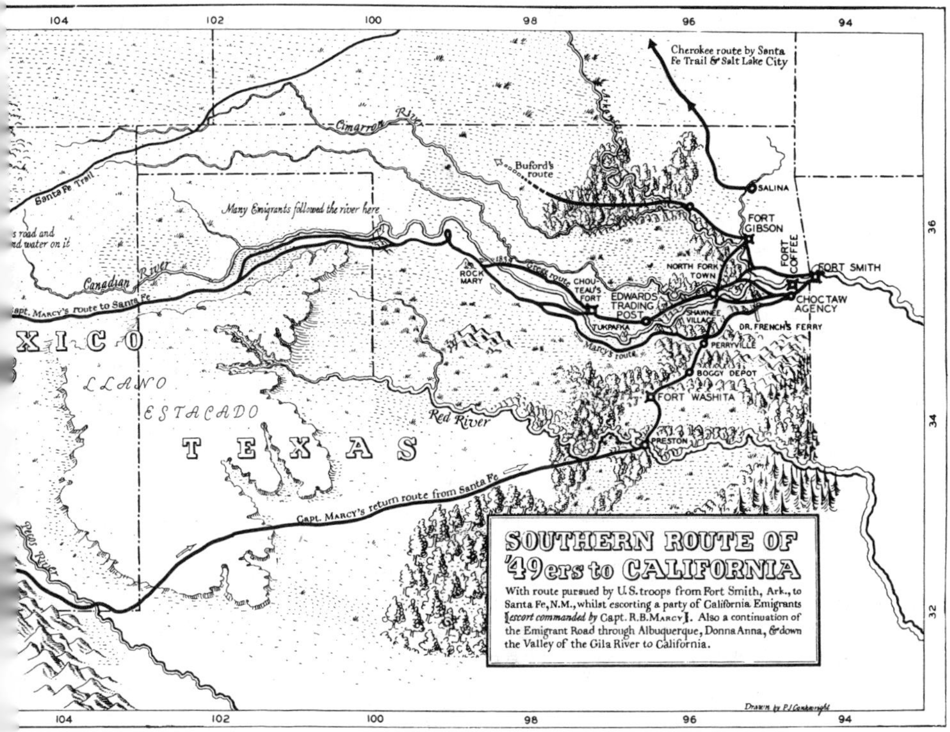

From *Marcy & the Gold Seekers: The Journal of Captain R. B. Marcy, with an Account of the Gold Rush Over the Southern Route,* by Grant Foreman. Copyright 1939 by the University of Oklahoma Press.

sive caravan. Banners streaming from the wagons announced "Ho! for the Diggings." They were off!

The Fort Smith expedition was one of the largest forty-niner groups known to have been under one command. According to Foreman, this first big departure included 479 people, 75 wagons drawn by 500 oxen and as many horses and mules, besides hundreds of saddle and pack horses. The caravan extended its length more than three miles along the road and took one and one-half to two hours to pass a given point.[8] The initial expectation was that the caravan would proceed all the way to California as a unit. Very quickly the experiences on the trail would end that notion and the great company would break up into many smaller units. Realizing that a mass exodus of emigrants would overcrowd the road and overgraze the tender spring grass, Captain Dillard outlined a schedule of systematic departures for companies leaving Fort Smith after April 14.[9]

Groups also departed from Van Buren at staggered times. The Little Rock company left on April 16 and the Van Buren company on April 18. The two were to take the route on the north side of the river and rendezvous at Little River in the Choctaw Nation. "The Van Buren folks, although they only left today, expect to be at Camp Holmes first."[10] Several other groups took up the line of march on April 18. The Empire Mining Company, a group of 35 pack mules and one wagon pulled by four mules, expected to reach Los Angeles in 65 days "with good luck." The observer who witnessed this group's departure was very impressed with its outfit which included "all kinds of machinery and India-rubber fixins including a life boat, capable of carrying 12 men at a time." This group was reportedly composed of young men from "some of the wealthiest families of New York."[11] The Washington City Company, an ox team group, who had in their possession "a gold washing machine which will do the work of 150 men" also left with the Van Buren group. A group from Louisiana and a pack mule company from St. Joseph, Missouri, were mentioned among the emigres for April 18. "Although several hundred left here today, and thinned out the crowd, yet there are small squads that will not leave for three or four days, and some not for a week. . . . Another party is fixing up to leave in May. . . . Many letters have been received here from other States stating that numbers will be here to leave in May."[12]

From Fort Smith and Van Buren the gold seekers journeyed along the Canadian River.

There were two main trails along this route. The "old road" followed along the north bank of the Canadian to Chouteau's trading house and was so described because Gregg's trading party in 1839 and others thereafter had traveled along its course. The "new road" followed along the south bank of the Canadian and was so described because Captain Marcy and Lieutenant Simpson had only begun its survey and construction on April 5. It was sometimes called Marcy's road.[13] The merits and demerits of these two trails were to be hotly debated by the emigrants. One overlander summarized it thus: "The party going from this place (Fort Smith) will strike out a new route south of the Canadian . . . but you know some of our folks do not like to try untried routes—they call it 'experimenting.' In these practical times they prefer a beaten track. Some will go off with the party from Van Buren. I will stick to this company; the U.S. troops will be along and the Indians have more respect for soldiers than emigrants."[14]

The distance from Fort Smith across the Indian Territory was 240 miles. There were four main rendezvous points along this route. At the first three, good camping, water, and supplies could be found. Choctaw Agency, later known as Scullyville, was fifteen miles from Fort Smith. North Fork Town was about thirty-five miles further. Little River, about one hundred twenty-five miles from Fort Smith, had two trading posts, Edward's and Aird's, both popular with the emigrants. This was the last point at which emigrants could purchase supplies before reaching the Mexican settlements. Here Delaware Indians living nearby could sometimes be hired as guides. Chouteau's Trading House or Old Fort Holmes, an abandoned army post, approximately two hundred forty miles from Van Buren was the last vestige of civilization before taking out across the plains where it was believed hostile Indians would attack the emigrants. It was from here that the military escort was deemed necessary for protection; consequently, all the groups waited for or hoped to catch up to Marcy at this point. Chouteau's was sometimes referred to as the "Council Grove" of the Arkansas route.[15] After leaving Chouteau's, the emigrants reached the Cross Timbers or "hilly fringe" of the great prairies, famed for cottonwoods, elm, hackberry, and postoak.[16] They proceeded across the Great Plains, crossed the Pecos River, and reached Anton Chico near Santa Fe, the half way point of the overland trek.

The experiences of the overlanders from Arkansas to Santa Fe along the Canadian can clearly be discerned from their letters. They tell the story with an immediacy that needs little comment. The muddy conditions of the road slowed travel to a mere crawl for the first one hundred fifty miles. Wagons frequently sunk to the axletrees and had to be shoveled and dragged out with ropes. Such conditions naturally prompted the response, "This is the great road you advertised?"——of course, sprinkled with lively profanity! Foreman says that though Captain Marcy does not mention them in his journal, "he had to listen to many grievances and criticisms by the emigrants, of his road, and of the Fort Smith influences which induced them to travel from there."[17] Inexperienced travelers, overloaded wagons, and muddy roads were a poor combination.

W. H. Heath, captain of the first company (pack mule) to leave Fort Smith wrote:

Little River, Indian Territory, March 22, 1849

Dear Sir: Our little company, after passing through many difficulties on account of the roads, has arrived safe at this place. We traveled slow, not being in a hurry and wishing to get our animals inured to the journey. Upon the whole, the price we had to pay for corn is about 50¢. At some places they put on an exorbitant price, knowing that we were obliged to have it; this was done during the first fifty miles of our journey. After we crossed the Canadian, we got corn at from 25¢ to 37½¢ per bushel. When we arrived at this place, we found corn at Edwards's 75¢ a bushel. He, as we are informed, raised 25¢ on the bushel as he saw us crossing the river. At Aird & Vore's we obtained corn at 50¢ a bushel. We shall stay here but a day or two, and then move on about thirty miles farther to an Indian village called Topafico, where, we are informed, we can get feed for our animals very cheap. The grass is not up much here yet; we are told it is much better farther up the Canadian. From the information we get from those who reside in this region, the wagons will have to pursue nearly the same route we have taken. From the best authority we learn that we will have no difficulty with the Comanche. Three of their chiefs have been here lately, and they manifest a very friendly feeling; but, still, we will not be the less on our guard. Our company is now twenty-four strong, and will cross the prairies 'peaceably, if we can—forcibly, if we must.' We intend to be at the Cross Timbers by the first of April. We wish the other pack mule company God speed.

WILLIAM H. HEATH[18]

A. C. Russell of the Helena Company wrote to this hometown paper:

Little River, April 17, 1849

My last letter to S—, dated Canadian river, sixth instant, advised you of the frustration of our original plan of traveling and our reorganization independently of the Cherokee, who failed to make their agreement good. We numbered sixty-eight men, and under the constitution drawn by you, elected officers, etc.—Dorsey, captain; Stephenson, lieutenant. In less than two days after breaking up camp on the Canadian, the Indianans, numbering twenty-two men, and Remington's mess (five) withdrew from the company and determined to pack. After our arrival here, five Tennesseeans who had joined us on the way sold their wagon and are packing from this point.

We have had very bad roads and worse weather all the time. On the thirteenth, after a hard day's travel through drenching rains and deep mud, we encamped three miles east of Little river. On the fourteenth cold rain and north winds prevailed until about four o'clock in the afternoon, when it commenced snowing, and continued to snow during the evening and night, and covered the ground to the depth of three inches. On the fifteenth it cleared away and the snow disappeared. Yesterday we crossed Little river. The crossing was rough and dangerous, but we got over safely. We overtook the New Yorkers here, and found them in confusion and disorder—some packing, some one thing, and some another. A portion of them are still on the east side of the river. The Fort Smith company, numbering thirty men, took up the line of march on or about the tenth. Following the new route surveyed under military orders, they got fifty or sixty miles on the prairie, where they sunk in the quagmire and, at last accounts, were unable to proceed or turn back. What has or will become of them, I know not. The Van Buren and Little Rock company are, I learn, on the road we traveled, which is the only practicable road in this country; and it is wholly impracticable for anything save a train of Indian ponies. I can safely assert that there is not a man who left Fort Smith but regrets, and will always regret, having started on this route. The roads thus far are the worst in the world; and from this point forward there is no road at all, and we have to make our way as best we can, through and over alternate post-oak flats and rugged mountains for one hundred miles. There we strike the prairies and will have tolerable traveling.

Throughout the Indian country we have had to pay from seventy-five cents to a dollar per bushel for corn, and difficult to procure at that. Those who follow us will get none at all at any price. We are going to try the plains without a guide, and expect to reach Santa Fe in five or six weeks from this date. From Santa Fe we will take guides and pack mules ... Stephenson is a man of remarkable energy and sound judgment. He is, by common consent, the leading spirit of our company. Dorsey is a good fellow but inefficient, and has no influence with the men. The boys are about trading their heavy wagons for lighter ones, which, if done, will facilitate our movements materially. The Cherokee are on the road and will, perhaps, join us before we leave here. There are some other parties coming on with a view of uniting with us. We number at present only forty-five men, and would like to have about thirty-five more, which would make our force sufficiently strong. We will, however, move tomorrow with or without recruits. Locke and I surveyed the road fifteen miles yesterday, and found that we will not be able to travel more than seven miles a day through the woods and across ravines. We have, however, passed over too many obstructions to be baffled by any future difficulties. The boys are all in good health and spirits; the mules and horses in as good, and some better, condition than when we started ... If anybody else thinks of going to California, tell them to take any route but this. Stephenson has exchanged our wagon for a light one; Moore has sold his and bought another. We will now reduce our loading and roll onward. If I have an opportunity I will write again, but you will probably hear no more of us till we reach the Pacific, unless we meet a train inward bound from Santa Fe. We will all look anxiously for advices from home when we reach our destination.

A. C. RUSSELL[19]

A member of the Little Rock company with the initials E. W. H., not one of the few names recorded in the Little Rock company, described the more hostile appearance of the Indians, the rapid consumption of food due to hearty appetites, his preference for pack mules, and camp life. The "H. C." mail carrier was Henry Crease.

Near the Cross Timbers, May 4, 1848

. . . We have for some days been encamped in a prairie on a mound which commands a very beautiful and extensive view. We have stopped here for the purpose of preparing to launch out upon the grand prairies, which we are now approaching. The Van Buren company is behind, water-bound, at Little river, and Captain McVicar has gone to meet them for the purpose of expediting their movements. The grass is very fine, and our animals are fast improving. Our progress has been rather slow from Fort Smith, on account of so much wet weather and the road having been so badly cut up by the numerous wagons which have preceded us. But as we will soon have drier weather, and now have more experience, and as we are approaching higher ground, we may expect to make good progress without much difficulty or delay to Santa Fe. We are now approaching the Comanche and are near the country where they range; so that we now keep out a strong guard every night. My initiation as guard was anything but pleasant. The rain poured down in torrents, accompanied with the most terrific thunder and lightning. This wet spell continued for three days.

The Indians now begin to assume a very savage appearance. Those about here all paint and wear scalp locks. We met two the other day almost entirely naked, having only a blanket thrown over their shoulders, and a small piece of cloth about the loins. They were armed with bows and arrows, rode without saddles, and in lieu of a bridle, had a piece of rope tied about the lower jaw of the horse. They were Wichita. About two miles from Little river we met the celebrated Seminole Chief, Wild Cat, with twelve warriors, all painted and in full war costume. They had a plenty of whiskey, which sold at twenty cents per pint. They were all considerably stewed. Old Wild Cat is a fine-looking Indian, and has a countenance that would become a chief of Old Nick's dominions. On his neck, wrists, arms, and waist were silver bands given him at Washington city. The current report here is that he is in league with the Comanche, and appearances seem to corroborate this rumor.

We have not yet reached the buffalo grounds, but trust we shall soon, for we are making rapid progress in the subsistence we took along. You have no idea what an appetite the clear air and excitement of the prairies give us. Each of us swig a quart of strong coffee at a meal, and solids disappear in the same proportion! Thus far on the route the ox teams have done the best, getting along faster than mules and with less labor. I think from what experience I have had that pack mules are the best. The road is very severe on the wagons, and unless they are of the strongest kind they ought not to be taken. H. C., as mail carrier for the company, will take this and all other letters back to Little river. He will have to ride over sixty miles. Our captain arrived last night. We shall not wait any longer for the Van Buren company. Orders have been given for an early start tomorrow morning. I will write you again from Santa Fe.

You must excuse this hasty scrawl, as I write in the midst of much noise and confusion. One is singing, "The Girl I left behind me;" one is playing on the French horn, with a cymbal accompaniment of a handsaw and tent pin; another is telling a tall story, which brings down the tent with thunders of applause; while all around on the outside are various noisy groups at work repairing wagons, making fires, cooking, etc.

E. W. H.[20]

Another member of the Little Rock company wrote from this camp.

"Camp of Little Rock co., May 3, 1849. We are now 26 miles from Little River, and about 25 miles from the Cross Timbers. We encamped here yesterday for the purpose of resting and grazing, and to wait for the Van Buren Company. Tomorrow we leave for Santa Fe.

"We left Fort Smith on the 16th of April, crossed the Canadian on the 24th, the North Fork on the 25th, and Little River on the 1st May. We passed through some of the finest country, richest land, and most beautiful prairie I have ever seen. We have met with some delays on account of the road being so wet; and had considerable work to do in the way of ferrying the rivers, pushing our wagons up the hills, &c., &c. Robbins broke the front hounds of his wagon yesterday, but soon got it repaired. They upset it the day we crossed the Canadian. Capt. McVicar came near being obliged to abandon one of his wagons. One of the wheels gave out, but he was fortunate enough to obtain another that fitted exactly, and therefore there was no detention. We are now in the Kickapoo and Muscogee country, and very near the Camamches [sic]. We keep a guard every night."[21]

Because of three days of continuous rain, they moved camp to find dry ground. Alden Woodruff, son of the *Arkansas Gazette* editor William Woodruff, and another member of the group wrote about these wet conditions.

Camp of Little Rock Company, May 6, 1849

". . . . Moved camp two miles to find a dry place; and it is the only comfortable place I have seen for four days. The ground we occupied from the 2nd to the 5th, was a perfect mud-hole. During the last three or four days it has rained incessantly, and such thunder and lightning! It was terrible. The sun came out today, and every foot of ground, and every bush and shrub in this vicinity is covered with wet blankets, boots, saddles, &c., &c.

We start tomorrow for Santa Fe. The Van Buren company are about five miles this side of Little River, water bound. We shall not wait for them. . . .

—A. M. W."[22]

On May 8 still in "Camp Near Little River," a member wrote "We are now encamped on a high mound in a small island of timber in a prairie, with a very extensive view. The bones of buffaloes are very plenty about camp, wolves are prowling about in countless numbers. The Indians tell us we are within forty miles of the Buffalo range. . . . . We start on our way again to-morrow morning, if it does not commence raining. . . . We have had some hard service. Standing guard on stormy nights is not very pleasant. It gives the wayfarer an opportunity of contemplating the comforts of home. The wolves are seen prowling about, but you are not allowed to shoot at them for fear of alarming the camp."[23]

Thus far on their journey, letters had been written from the major trading posts or returned by a designated mail carrier to those posts. The people at home waited with anxiety and sharp interest for news from the journey. Recipients were generous to share their news with the press, and "news from the West" was a regular feature of the papers. There was usually one month delay between the writing date and the publishing date of the letter. The reassurances in these letters were comforting to families and friends at home, and at the same time many letters became a part of the public record which otherwise would have been lost. The *Fort Smith Herald* on June 6 informed its eager readers that the emigrants had reached "the Plains!" Merchant Aird from Chouteau's fort had accompanied the gold seekers with his loaded merchant wagons into the Cross Timbers. When he had sold all his goods to the travelers, he left them on May 15 and returned to Fort Smith for more supplies. He brought with him many letters dated May 14 and 15 for the gold seekers would not have another opportunity to mail letters until they reached Santa Fe, some four hundred miles distant.

> Our friend Mr. Thomas Aird, of Little river, arrived here on Thursday last. He went on with the Fort Smith company several miles beyond Chouteau's trading house, into the plains, where he said he had a full view of the Wichita mountains and could see far away towards Santa Fe, with nothing to obstruct the view—a vast plain. He left the emigrants on the fifteenth of May, all well, and their hearts cheered with the beautiful prospect before them, besides having a fine prairie to travel over with no obstructions. It has been raining ever since the emigrants left, and the consequence was that they had a very hard time traveling through mud and water all the while, being themselves constantly wet. Yet, notwithstanding all this, they enjoy good health. Mr. Aird informs us that several of the companies waited at Chouteau's a short time and then went on without the troops. The Fort Smith company were (partly) along with the troops on the south side of the Canadian, and a portion still behind, when he left them, but (they) expected to overtake the escort in a day or two. The Van Buren company were still behind all, except the sutler to the troops. Lieutenant Buford had gone back with wagons to assist him along. The Van Buren company will go on with the Fort Smith company and the escort.
>
> Mr. Aird brought in several letters from members of the company to their friends, which we are permitted to make extracts from.[24]

John B. Hockert of Fort Smith wrote Captain J. R. Kannady, one of the promoters of the Fort Smith company who did not go to California.

> Grand Camp, East of Chouteau's
>
> "We are all well and are now camped on a high prairie, which is about twenty miles in breadth; the soil red. This day's travel has been one of more satisfaction than the whole of the journey since we left, for we have not had a wagon bogged this day, which is a thing very uncommon. We have along with us fifty

wagons, and I have seen them all stall ten times each, at least, in a day. It frequently happens that the train is scattered for miles. I expect that you have already learned that we took the old road at the South Fork, which we found but little better than the new one. The troops are at the plains waiting for us. You have doubtless heard many complaints against this route to California, but nothing, according to my judgment, can be alleged against it except wet weather. As much of the new road as I have seen is as good a route as can be found anywhere, for the ground upon which the road runs is comparatively level. You will perceive that those who complain have never had a trial on a journey with a wagon and cannot endure the hardships without complaining. I have traveled in every direction from Fort Smith—north, south, east, and west—and I consider the western route the best that can be found. The ground is wet and the road is new; therefore no one can expect a good road under such circumstances. . . .[25]

T. M. S. Gookin, treasurer of the Fort Smith company, in a long letter which the *Herald* said was "a kind of journal from which we extract the last date," wrote on May 15:

Chouteau's is about four miles east of our camp. We passed the ruins this morning. At last we have got out of the mud, and I can assure you there was rejoicing among us. Even the mules appear to tread with more elasticity since we arrived at the prairies. The Canadian, where we crossed this morning, is as wide (as) the Arkansas at Fort Smith; very rapid but shallow. The banks are not more than two feet above the water, and a rise of that much would overflow the prairies that lie between the river and the hills. Just after crossing, we came to a high red bluff, which commands as beautiful a view as I ever beheld. The river can be seen for miles wending its way along the high prairies, the course of which can be traced by a very slight growth of very small timber. About one o'clock we came to a very fine spring and regretted much that we could not encamp there for the night, but there was not a sufficiency of water for our stock. The troops are twelve miles ahead of us, and if they do not travel tomorrow, we will overtake them.[26]

Mr. J. W. Seaman wrote to Mitchell Sparks, a merchant in Fort Smith and one paragraph was extracted:

I am here as sound as a Spanish dollar. All of my friends are well and have not met with any accident. But there have been at least one hundred breakdowns since (we) left Fort Smith; and it has rained almost every day, and the ground is so rotten that it has been impossible to travel. We are within fifteen miles of the troops; and if it doesn't rain tonight, we will be up with them day after tomorrow, as Captain Marcy is moving very slow so that we may overtake him. The Little Rock company is ten miles ahead; the Tennessee company, about six miles; the Clarksville company passed here ten days ago.[27]

H. J. Share wrote to Editor Wheeler on May 14:

We have made such poor headway that you probably have heard from us from time to time. This much I can say: we have had nothing but bad roads since we left Fort Smith. We crossed the Canadian on the third, and have been ever since traveling about seventy miles, but have recrossed today and have moved out about four miles into the Grand Prairie, and will leave in the morning to join the troops. The members of our company are in good health and spirits, which is something strange, for we have been wet for the last two weeks with but one or two days fair weather. Judging from the rain that has fallen here, the river must be very high at Fort Smith. The Canadian was rising this morning when we crossed. Our company have not all got together yet; the balance are with the troops ahead.[28]

Captain Dillard wrote a letter to his mother which Aird also delivered. It did not, however, appear in the *Herald* until a week after all the other letters. He too commented on the miserable roads and wet bedding, but he was reassuring about the spirit, harmony, and health of the party.

Camp, May 15, 1849

Dear Mother: We arrived at Chouteau's today and camped about four miles across on the south side of the Canadian, crossing it again to the same side Captain Marcy is on. We have regretted leaving his route much. There was much complaint about the roads before we arrived at the Canadian, and all were in favor of crossing over to the old road. We have done so and have been very sorry for it, as we have been compelled to take ropes and pull our wagons out of the mud every day, not making more than from four to five miles per day. You have no idea of the miserable roads we have had to contend with since we left home. It has rained on us every other day for the last week, and we have been compelled to sleep on wet bedding all the time. We are now on the Grand Prairie and have a fair prospect for good roads. I have frequently been awakened from my sleep by the water coming over my bedding, sometimes two or three inches. Notwithstanding all of our troubles and difficulties, there is no company gets along with more harmony than this does. I find them all willing to obey any order given them and to see them enforced. I have tried them in every way, having had as many as one hundred men at work at a time, in mud and water all the while. Sometimes the mud would be over their knees, and I can say that I have not heard one complain. We will fall in with Captain Marcy in two days from this time. The families have had to put up with many inconveniences on account of wet weather. I am truly glad to say that I have never seen so many thrown together and enjoy such good health. We have heard of many dying on the trip, but we have not been detained one day on account of sickness. There has not been a call for a doctor since we crossed the South Fork of the Canadian. I must close, as it is time for me to go and see the guard; it is now eleven o'clock, and I have charge of it.

JOHN J. DILLARD

In the same edition of the *Herald*, Captain Marcy's "official" report of progress was printed, relieving family and friends at home.

"Having an opportunity to send a letter to Edward's Trading House, by an Indian who leaves here in a few minutes, I have the honor to state that we have reached this point (a little above Chouteau's) in safety. We have continued entirely upon the South side of the Canadian from Fort Smith, and have found a road which is much better than that upon the North side, particularly that portion of it from the south of Little River to this place. The emigrants including the Fort Smith Company, were induced to believe that there could not be a road found upon this side of the Canadian, by citizens of Little River, who were interested in having them pass upon the other side; but they were woefully deceived, for we have passed over a most excellent road, while they have been wallowing in the mud and making causeways, for the last two weeks, between Edwards' and this place.

It was Captain Dillard's wish to follow us upon this side of the river, but the majority of the company overruled him, and he acquiesced but I believe they are determined to be controled by him in future. We are now opposite the Cross Timbers, and I have found a good road past them; nearly all the distance through is prairie; so that the practicability of making a road from *Fort Smith to Santa Fe on the south side of the Canadian is settled.* I expect the Fort Smith Company to join us tomorrow, when we shall take up the line of march again, and as we have a good road from here, I trust we shall make more rapid progress than we have been making. Our animals are in better condition than when we left Fort Smith, and our wagons are in fine repair."[29]

Many of the letters are stacatto and give very little information about camp life, chores, and interpersonal relationships among the travelers. It is here that the journals and diaries, which were published at later dates, can give us many more details. The King journal is especially illuminating about the camp life of the Arkansas forty-niners. The following entry for May 9 found them within twenty miles of Chouteau's Trading House. Two daily occurrences for the overlanders, making a corral and setting up and breaking camp, are described.

At our camp this evening we can see the valleys of both the Washita and the Canadian, and we are now upon the ridge dividing the waters of these two rivers. As we are now coming into the vicinity of the Comanche "range," we will arrange our wagons in a corral and post guards. I will give you a bird's-eye view of our encampment and its formation. The ground has been selected by our leader, John Dillard of the Fort Smith Company. The corral, or enclosure to secure the mules, horses and cattle, is first made as follows: the first wagon is driven up to its place and halted; the second is then driven up to the left of the first—the tongues being so near to each other that, after the teams are disengaged, they may be made to cross each other. The third wagon is now driven to the right of the first, and so halted that the left fore wheel of this third wagon will graze or be very near the right hind wheel of the first wagon; the fourth wagon is then driven to the left of the second wagon. Then comes in succession, to take their places in like manner, the fifth, sixth, seventh, eighth, etc., until the whole train is disposed of—they all, in the meantime, having been so arranged that when the enclosure is completed, it will be in the form of an ellipse, or circle. The corral made, the animals are turned out to graze, and a guard detailed to watch them.

Now comes the busy scene of pitching tents, collecting wood, preparing food, etc. The sound of the ax, the metallic sound of the blacksmith's hammer, the merry voice of children, the lowing of cattle, the braying of mules is heard. Some children are playing near the water . . . The older ladies are attending to

> their domestic concerns, in the preparation of a good meal for their families, or a comfortable sojourn until the morrow.
>
> At sunset the signal will be sounded by the blowing of a horn—for the driving up of the animals; the animals will be secured in the corral; the camp watch established for the night; the sweet sound of the flute, perchance will come floating on the ear, or the well accorded voices of a band of happy vocalists, or the merry notes of the violin, accompanied with the tripping sound of feet; all these may be the accompanying circumstances—as they not unfrequently are—of the evening.
>
> The gray of the morning beginning to appear, the animals are again let out to pasture; breakfast then made ready and over, about sunrise; the signal horn is again sounded for bringing up the animals; the tents are struck; the baggage restored to the wagons; the teams hitched up, and the command given, "Forward!" Such is the daily formation, some of the characteristic scenes and the breaking up of an emigrant's camp.[30]

Despite the corral and the guard, escaping livestock delayed departure many times, sometimes for days, as evidenced in numerous journals. One of many examples found in the King journal occurred on May 17: "One of Jim Logan's steers escaped from the corral last night and was found two miles back on the road. Jim says that steer wants to go back to Johnson County, Arkansas!"[31]

Fires at night were built for each "mess" which would number four to six men and their wagon. Messmates were usually friends who associated themselves for the convenience of travel, for protection, to forestall loneliness, or other reasons. These associations were intended to endure until they returned from California. One large tent served the entire mess. In addition to the standard supplies mentioned elsewhere, it was recommended that a mess have a ten-gallon water keg, a keg of vinegar, a keg of molasses, plenty of rope, a bucket of tar, and blankets.[32] The messes practiced all degrees of refinement, but a poor appetite was not the complaint of any. Turkey, deer, antelope, praire dogs, prairie hens, various birds, and buffalo added variety to the usual diet.

The wagon trains adopted travel schedules which would conserve the strength of the animals. It was hoped that twenty miles a day could be achieved and this in seven or eight hours. Some had long noon time breaks to avoid traveling in the heat of the day, but the Clarksville Company traveling with Captain Marcy followed a different routine.

> We generally commence the day's travel about 3 o'clock in the morning, and never later than 4 o'clock, and are ready to encamp by 11 o'clock; this gives ample time for animals to graze before night, when they are driven into camp. The horses and mules are picketed within the enclosure, while the oxen are tied up to the wagons; sentinels are posted ...
>
> Many have supposed that cattle in a journey upon the plains would perform better and keep in better condition by allowing them to graze in the morning before starting upon the day's march, which would involve the necessity of traveling during the heat of the day. These persons are of the opinion that animals will only feed at particular hours of the day, and that the remainder of the day must be allotted them for rest and sleep, and unless these rules are

adhered to they will not thrive. This opinion, however, is, I think, erroneous, and I also think that cattle will adapt themselves to any circumstances, so far as regards their working hours and their hours of rest. If they have been accustomed to labor at particular hours of the day, and the order of things is at once reversed, the working hours being changed into hours of rest, they may not do so well for a few days, but they soon become accustomed to the change, and eat and rest as well as before.

By starting at an early hour in the morning during the summer months, the day's march is over before it becomes very warm; hereas—as I have observed—of the animals are allowed to graze before starting the march must continue during the middle of the day, when the animals—particularly oxen—will suffer much from the heat of the sun, and, so far as my experience goes, will not keep in as good condition, as when the other plan is pursued.

We have adopted this course soon after the commencement of our journey, and our oxen have continued to improve upon it. Another and important advantage to be derived from this course is found in the fact the animals, being tied up during the night, are not liable to be lost or stolen.[33]

This schedule makes even more sense when it is remembered that they were journeying West with the afternoon sun beaming in their faces. It was best for man and beast.

"Nooning," the non-hot meal at midday or mid-morning, was also a time to stretch tired muscles and move about free of a wagon or horse. It was a time to tend the sick, grease axles, check wagons, release the oxen from their yokes, and have some pilot bread or soda crackers and maybe something left from last night's evening meal.

"Laying by" was a term applied to not traveling. There were numerous reasons for laying by—severe sickness of a member of the group, inclement weather, waiting on laggards, lost animals, extensive repairs, or general rest and recuperation after a taxing ordeal. At times of laying by, which was always where water was available, clothes would be washed and spread on bushes and lines to dry; blankets and bedding aired; bodies and hair washed; extensive repairing made; pots of ham and rice or beans (which took too long to cook at regular stops) cooked; bread baked in Dutch ovens; fresh game killed to add variety to the diet; grievances and complaints dealt with, letters and journals updated; and a touch of "civilization" prevailed. The duration of the laying by could be one to four days depending on circumstances, but all were eager to reach the gold fields.

Many of the companies had determined ahead of time not to travel on Sunday so that man and beast could rest. Rev. Robert Lattimer traveled with the Clarksville company and he began his preaching on the very first Sunday while they were still in Fort Smith waiting to begin their expedition. The diary entry for April 8 noted that Rev. Lattimer was a brother-in-law of James and David Logan and that he was leaving his family with his mother-in-law, Mrs. Sarah Logan. A few of the Sunday entries follow:

Sunday, April 15. We had preaching today and dried out our tents.

Sunday, April 22. We had preaching this day by Rev. Robert Lattimer, a Methodist minister.

Sunday, May 13. We are having a general drying out. However, we had preaching services as usual.

Sunday, May 27. Today, in accordance with a rule we have adopted, we "lay by" to give ourselves and animals a chance to rest, and for the animals to graze and recruit. As usual we had a fine sermon delivered today. We are three hundred seventy-four miles from Fort Smith.

Ware's guidebook, one of the most popular handbooks for the overlanders cautioned, "*Never travel on the Sabbath;* we will guarantee that if you lay by on the Sabbath and rest your teams, that you will get to California 20 days sooner than those who travel seven days a week."[34]

The emigrants found time to include merriment in their tedious regimen. The King journal in an earlier quoted passage referred to camp music and dancing. Foreman recounts: "Tailboards of a score of wagons that last night made a dancing floor, are returned to their places."[35] There were a number of women in the Arkansas contingent who will be discussed later. Music pushed back the limitless horizons, soothed lonely hearts, quickened lively spirits, and was psychologically an important release for the emigrants—besides, it was fun and a touch of home. The Gold Rush was to produce a great body of songs. "Oh Susanna" was the tune for the theme song. It may have had several variations. Here is one version.

"Like Argos of the ancient times,
I'll leave this modern Greece;
I'm bound to California mines,
To find the golden fleece.
For those who would work from morn to night
And live on hog and corn,
When one can pick up there at sight
Enough to buy a farm.

Chorus.

"O California! that's the land for me,
I'm going to California the gold dust for to see.

"There from the snowy mountain side,
Comes down the golden sand,
And spreads a carpet far and wide
O'er all the shining land;
The rivers run on golden beds,
O'er rocks of golden ore,
The valleys six feet deep are said
To hold a plenty more.

"O California, etc.

"I'll take my wash bowl in my hand,
And thither wind my way,

To wash the gold from out the sand,
  In California.
And when I get my pocket full,
  In that bright land of gold
I'll have a rich and happy time;
  Live merry till I'm old.

"O California, etc."

The Knickerbocker Company had its own song which they sang on the steamer to Fort Smith, along the route, and around their campfires. They undoubtedly performed it several times while in Fort Smith for the *Herald* featured it in a newspaper article noting that James H. Cooley, a painter in the company, composed the song. Its words convey the sense of adventure, excitement, and downplaying of danger which many gold seekers must have felt.

The New York boys and Yankees too
With some of the real old Jersey Blues
Have thought it would be a very good plan,
To make a draw on Uncle Sam
So draw while you can, the gold is free and plenty
Tis very fine oh! how it shines—(hurrah for California!)

Chorus: Hy, ho! Away we go, o'er the Rocky
Mountains, O!
Hy, ho! Away we go, o'er the Mountains
cap'd with snow.

Our little ones we leave behind,
Our better halves we keep in mind;
And all the good we could impart,
We kindly did before we started.
Hail Yankees, hail, we're now already parted;
So we must try, and not to cry, but cheer the broken
  hearted.

Chorus:

And when we cross the prairie lands,
We'll keep in mind those precious sands,
And if we hear the wild Wah hoo,
We'll cry out, "Injun, is that you?"
So hail, Yankees, hail—'twill be a pleasant journey;
We'll cross the hills at Santa Fe, in trail of General
  Kearney.

Chorus:

Then having found the wealthy prize,
And satisfied our longing eyes,
We'll think of coming home again,
And there contented to remain.
So good-bye to all our friends and relations;
And if we fail to get the gold, we'll see most all creation.

Chorus:[36]

The old stand bys were not forgotten by the Arkansans either. King records: "Everyone seems to be enjoying themselves as there are several fiddles in the company and we are being entertained by some of them with the 'Arkansas Traveler,' 'Billy in the Low Ground,' 'Sally Goodin,' etc."[37] Nor was music confined to times of "laying by." On June 13 the Fort Smith expedition made a record twenty-eight miles across the prairie, and that evening King wrote: "Our company seem to be enjoying themselves much this evening; they have managed to raise some music and are dancing round their camp fire most merrily. It certainly looks as if they were determined to keep up their spirits as we go along."[38] As for the rapid progress, King was especially ajulatory of the good road which they had had since Edward's Trading Post. "Now it has become very fine; and so it continues. Indeed so superior is it that I often wish that I had a fleet horse and a light buggy, that I might skip over it to my satisfaction."[39]

Many of the Arkansans were accomplished frontiersmen and accustomed to killing deer, bear and turkey. But other animals and game along the way always drew their comments. The horned frog or lizard was "a queer stumpy little fellow with spikes all over the top of his head and back, and given to move in the most leisurely manner."[40] Gregg in *Commerce of the Priaires* reported the horned frog "a harmless creature, notwithstanding its uncouth appearance."[41] The prairie dog and his "dog towns" occasioned many comments. Their burrows were raised two or three feet above the ground; and when an intruder approached, they yelped like small toy dogs and scampered to their burrows. Rattlesnakes lived in communion with the prairie dogs using their burrows for shelter and their pups for food. Owls fed on the lizards and chameleons which were plentiful. A dog town could cover an area several square miles.[42] Another animal which drew much comment was the antelope, "a queer-looking rather than a beautiful animal, with curious pronged horns, great bulging eyes. . . . and a morbid curiosity."[43] The antelope provided a wonderful variation in their diet. The Clarksville Company had engaged an Indian interpreter at the Choctaw Agency who had been educated at Dartmouth College and who they called Rover. Rover was to accompany them to Santa Fe. King acknowledged that Rover gave him much of the information about the animals found in his journal. About Rover, King also stated: "He seems to be a splendid gentleman, a finished scholar, a critic on English and Roman literature, a politician, a trapper, and an Indian!"[44] When Rover left the company at Santa Fe, King noted how much he hated to see Rover leave. He acknowledged that Rover was a good and fast penman and that he "has written much of the material contained in my journal and there is much therein which otherwise would have been left out if it had not been for Rover. . . . Rover writes an elegant hand and the language he used is much better than mine."[45]

Of course the buffalo was one of the animals they expected to see when they reached the plains and many letters say "no buffalo yet" or acknowledge a "buffalo wallow" had been sighted. Undoubtedly earlier traders and trappers had talked of buffalo meat as a delicacy and many emigrants were eager to sample the meat. This experience as related by a member of the Van Buren company was less than satisfactory.

> Plenty of buffalo signs, and all eager for the chase. On the 19th of May we had the satisfaction of seeing buffaloes. One was killed and distributed. Now for the delicacy of a prairie supper. It was soon prepared and brought forth—something fresh that we had coveted a mouthful of. And O cracky! in vain were our grinders brought to bear upon it. Its toughness was a quality that absorbed all others; it was abandoned. And I would say for the benefit of the emigrants that as they value hams, dried beef, cheese, dried fruit, rice, etc. at home, so will they be valued in the prairies.[46]

Dick Hudson, a man of much strength in the Clarksville company and known affectionately as "Uncle Dick," had a penchant for being involved in lively animal adventures and loved to relate those adventures to the group in great detail. King records many of Uncle Dick's reports of these encounters which are in the best tradition of Arkansas frontier lore. Although Uncle Dick obviously loved a good story, witnesses sustained these adventures. Some notable and very abbreviated examples were his crawling into a hollow log after a possum which turned out to be a litter of wild pigs and then being charged from the rear by the sow while still in the log. A bear rescued him by killing the sow. He retrieved his gun and killed the bear! Another time he was stalked by a panther into a cave where he was forced to spend the night. When he had no more wood to put on the fire to keep the panther at bay, he waited until the precise moment of the charge and fired his rifle as the animal struck him to the ground "by a powerful blow to the shoulder." Several well-sustained blows with his hunting knife finished the job. Uncle Dick received a painful shoulder wound, the skin stripped to the bone for about three inches. When friends rescued him at dawn, they found an old male panther dead in the cave.[47]

The emigrants along the Arkansas route were blessedly free from cholera which plagued those along the Missouri route. Births, deaths, and illnesses were, however, a part of their journey. One week out of Fort Smith, but only thirty-eight miles from the town, the Chandlers in the Fort Smith company became parents of a baby girl whom they named "California." Dr. Mitchell of the Clarksville company ministered at the birth, and King noted his opinion of the situation:

> Of course, the only thing for the father to do is to remain in camp here til his wife is able to return to their home near Fort Smith as it is out of the question for them to continue on this long and hazardous journey. . . . The Chandlers are quartered in a good tent which is very fortunate as there came up a heavy rain and thunderstorm about the time of the birth of little "California," but they were kept dry from the rain.[48]

King noted the following day that he "understood" the Chandlers would be returning to Fort Smith.

The birth of twins to an unknown couple in the Fort Smith expedition on June 7 occasioned much enthusiasm on the part of both Captain Marcy and Captain Dillard. The two "promising" boys were named "Marcy" and "Dillard" in honor of the military and civilian leaders of the expedition. Captain Marcy's response to the compliment was recorded by King: "If I never see the gold regions myself, I shall have the satisfaction of knowing that my name is represented there. I wish the young gentleman a safe journey to California and much happiness and gold after he gets there and I hope for a speedy recovery for the mother."[49] The mother had suffered much discomfort the week prior to the birth. The King journal on May 31 refers to the "sickness" of one of the emigrant women:

> The wife of one of the emigrants has been sick for several days, and reported tonight as very low. The fatigue and inconveniences to which she is necessarily exposed in a journey over the prairies, has no doubt had a tendency to aggravate her disease. Being a lady of delicate constitution, and never having been subjected to the privations and hardships of a camp life, she is poorly fitted to endure in sickness a march of this kind.
>
> Friday, June 1, 1849. On account of the critical condition of the wife of the emigrant, who is unable to be moved, we are remaining here hoping that her condition will improve sufficient for her to stand travel.

On Saturday they remained encamped and Captain Marcy and his party went on a buffalo hunt. Sunday was to be a travel day as they had been encamped two days and "the sick lady became able to travel." Sunday they made ten miles, Monday seventeen miles, and Tuesday a long, hot march of twenty-two and one-half miles—the longest day's travel of the journey. They "encamped upon a very beautiful, clear stream of spring water" under the shade of huge cottonwood trees with plenty of good grass. "It is one of the best camping places on the road so far and as some of our wagon tires require resetting, we shall "lie over" tomorrow for that purpose." As planned Wednesday June 6 was spent making repairs and the stock enjoying the grass and shade. On Thursday the caravan did not proceed "on account of the illness of the wife of one of the emigrants." King noted that "no one seems in a hurry to leave." Then Friday's entry reveals the nature of the "illness" and notes that eleven and one-half miles were covered. "The reason for our detention (yesterday) has been the addition to the company of two promising boys—twins." A belated salute to "the wife of one of the emigrants!"

Death too was a part of the journey to the halfway point of Santa Fe. A. M. Woodruff of the Little Rock company wrote in his letter to his father concerning a Mr. Roberts of Hempstead County who was very sick and whose recovery was not expected.[50] Another member of the company indicated in his letter, "We are all well except a Mr. Green Roberts, who it is expected will die."[51] A member of the Fort Smith company writing from near Chouteau's notes the death and burial of J. G. Roberts who was traveling with the Little Rock company.

I attended, today, the burial of a young man of the Little Rock company, whose name was J. G. Roberts. He died after an illness of ten or fifteen days. He was as decently interred as the case would admit of. It is true, he had no coffin, but he was neatly wrapped and placed in a vault. His friends appeared deeply affected in paying the last tribute to his earthly remains."[52]

The overland journey was to have a salubrious effect on the health of one Little Rock man. Pope in his recollection of *Early Days in Arkansas* recalled that Elijah Robbins was "in the last stages of consumption when he undertook the trip and no one supposed he would live a month." Robbins' health improved and he arrived in San Francisco "well and strong."[53]

One very plausible explanation for sickness among the overlanders was the quality of the water along the way. After reaching the Cross Timbers the emigrants "passed large quantities of gypsum or plaster of Paris" which made the water taste like epsom salt.[54] The King Journal elaborates on the gypsum formations, the "unpalatable nauseous" water, and the effect on the animals.

> At our encampment tonight we have water but it is bitter and unpalatable, but will answer for cooking when none other can be obtained. Our animals do not know what to make of this gyp water. They put their noses down to it and then they sniff and turn away. Tom Hackney has a fine mule. This animal is the fattest in the camp, as young Tom (17) feeds her on scraps from the leftovers of the mess. He has been trying every way to coax and persuade "Margaret", as he calls her, to drink some of the water, but so far he has been unable to do so. (The next day) after several trials, Tom succeeded in getting Margaret to take a few swallows of water.[55]

Alkali water of this type caused scours, a farm term for diarrhea in animals. Humans undoubtedly did not escape the side effects of the water. For a week this water condition persisted along with a shortage of wood which necessitated the use of buffalo chips for cooking purposes. At last they came to a camp with good water and wood on May 31. It is at this encampment that King noted the critical condition of the sick woman who seven days later produced the twins at the encampment with good spring water which all the emigrants were reluctant to leave.[56]

There were several families among the Arkansas gold seekers. The newspaper listings of men's names only do not reflect this, but journals, diaries and letters often refer to women and children. King's journal reveals that John W. Patrick had with him his wife (unnamed), a seven-year-old daughter, Mary Lee, a son, G. L., and an older daughter, Hanna (18 or 20) who was married to Tom King, and they too were in the Clarksville group. Mark Lee and his wife Nancy Hickey, their son James (12) and a small daugher Martha were also part of the Clarksville contingent. Mark Lee died in California and Nancy married Archibald Naylor and remained in California.[57] "Miss Mary Barton, a very fine young lady," was also along, but no explanation was given of her presence or connections. Captain Redmond Rogers took with him his slave Jane, "a very fine cook." King made his assessment of the female travelers: "It is a hazardous journey for hardened men to attempt, much less taking women and children along, but it is well known that nothing in the past has been too hazardous for a woman to do to follow her loved ones wherever they go."[58] W. W. Stevenson of the Little Rock company maintained, "Females bear the toil of the way much better than the males. I saw but one female grave, but many of the other sex."[59]

Another family group traveling with the Fort Smith company and one which was the subject of much comment was the Dr. John R. Conway family from Little Rock. The Conway family was associated with the earliest days of Arkansas history when five of seven Conway brothers moved to the state. From these five came two governors, one Congressional delegate; an associate justice of the Supreme Court, and emigrant John. John Conway received his medical training in Bardstown, Kentucky, and married Mary Elizabeth Thurston of Kentucky. He was commissioned as a surgeon in the U.S. Army in Illinois during the thirties and removed to Little Rock in 1836. He was also a surveyor, and President John Tyler sent him to survey the Texas-Mexico boundary in 1842. By the time the news of California gold came to Arkansas in 1848, the Conways were the parents of ten children, six boys and four girls, the oldest was Mary, age seventeen. The Conways determined to go to California where, if there were not gold, there would at least be plenty of surveying work. Accordingly, country home, servants, and other interests were sold. Dr. Conway purchased a big army ambulance which was to be pulled by mules, and in this conveyance he installed his family of twelve plus one Negro maid to serve them on their westward journey. To relieve the crowding and to give Mary more freedom, her father provided her a black horse on which she made the seven-and-one-half month journey to California. The beauty of this raven-haired girl upon her black mount would occasion numerous comments from emigrants in many groups.[60]

The King Journal describes Miss Mary at an early date in the journey, and he too recorded the romance of Mary and Lt. M. P. Harrison. This early description is another of the passages which Lt. J. H. Simpson, topographical engineer, filed in his report and King also included in his journal.

> Under a large shady cottonwood tree on the bank of the stream, I see a young lady who has just alighted from her black palfrey, enjoying the luxury of a camp seat, after a fatiguing day's ride. Habited in her riding dress, and with bonnet on, a veil thrown carelessly aside, she is listlessly twirling a switch, and giving heed to the conversation of a young emigrant who is sitting contentedly at her feet.[61]

Lt. Simpson was himself quite smitten by the lovely lady and named a "poundcake" shaped sandstone rock formation rising sixty feet in height in her honor.[62] However, it was two young lieutenants in Marcy's command who fell in love with her and competed for her promise of marriage. She gave her promise to Lt. Harrison, and at the parents' insistence, they were to be married in California. The King journal poignantly recounted what were to be the last few times the young couple ever saw each other.

> Tomorrow we will part from our friends, Captain Marcy, Lieutenants Harrison and Simpson and other fine soldier boys. They will go to Santa Fe, while we go to Albuquerque and cross the Rio Grande. I know that Miss Mary will be sad at the parting from Lt. Harrison, as they have been together every chance in the last few days and tonight they are seen in earnest conversation and I am sure

> that they think a great deal of each other. Everyone in the company loves them both and we are sad that they have to part.[63]

The next day they only traveled ten miles and reached the juncture where the Albuquerque and the Santa Fe roads divided. They were about twenty-five miles west of Anton Chico. King noted that it was still early in the day and the soldiers could have made it on to Santa Fe, but "decided to spend one more night in camp with us." Marcy's entry for June 26 mentions resting two hours at the juncture and then continuing on twenty-two miles to Galisteo. A contingent of the troops could have remained for one last night as King's account noted:

> Our parting was indeed sad this morning when the soldiers marched away over the road northwestward towards Santa Fe. There were tears in the eyes of Lt. Harrison when he bid me a good-bye—whether it was from parting with me I can't say, but I suspect it was from thinking about Miss Mary—and I can't say that my own eyes were any to [sic] dry. I noticed Miss Mary as we were breaking camp this morning and her eyes were red from weeping. I hope that they will meet again.[64]

This was not to be. Lt. Harrison was murdered and scalped by the Indians on October 7 in western Texas on the return march to Fort Smith of Marcy's escort. Marcy and his men were very saddened by the loss of young Harrison. A coffin was fashioned from a wagon bed and lined with charcoal and Harrison was returned to Fort Smith for burial in what became the United States National Cemetery. Lt. Harrison was the older brother of future president Benjamin Harrison.[65] When Mary learned of the event is not known. She did not know at the crossing of the Colorado River on October 27 when Lt. Cave Couts recorded his pleasure in her company for four days and his farewell to her: "May you wed your true love."[66] The ending for this story is conveyed in a letter written May 26, 1850, by D. F. Shall of Little Rock to Elias Conway. The letter relates that the Conways arrived in San Diego after much suffering and loss of possessions. They then moved to Los Angeles and then to the southernmost mines on the San Joaquin River. Then the statement: "Mary is married."[67] Foreman cites correspondence from a niece and a granddaughter of Mary's which confirms her marriage to a sea captain and their having six children.[68]

The Fort Smith expedition was not eager to have Marcy and the escort leave them at Santa Fe. They had come to respect and have genuine affection for the troops. King speaks of the many services performed by the troops to make conditions better for the emigrants. While coming through the quagmire, "they worked the banks down, so that we have no trouble in crossing . . . these creeks."[69] When crossing the plains where timber was not available, "Captain Marcy sent word . . . that we had better procure an extra supply of poles, axles and hounds for our wagons."[70] The emigrants carried these in the "possum bellies" and learned "to throw in a few sticks for cooking" when they thought they might not find wood.[71] The main purpose of the escort was to protect them from the Indians. The only Indians encountered were Comanche and Kiowa with whom Marcy "talked" and from whom he extracted a promise of safe passage for the emigrants. King referred to Marcy, Harrison and Simpson as "gentlemanly fellows" to whon they had become "attached."[72] Nonetheless, having accomplished the safe delivery of the Fort Smith group to the vicinity of Santa Fe, Marcy left them. He reported the distance to Santa Fe, as measured with the claim, 819½ miles.[73]

C H A P T E R IV

Santa Fe and the Elephants Beyond

> After crossing the Colorado River and ascending a hill, "we saw what we have always termed 'the elephant,' which was the brightest, shining sand heaps, I have ever seen."

Santa Fe was the specified point at which Marcy and the military escort were to turn back; it was the half-way mark of the trip to the West; it was the place for rest, recruitment of teams, and outfitting for the last and more difficult portion of the trip to California; it was a decision point as to route, wagons, or pack mules; it was the point where dissension became open and "breaking offs" numerous; it was the place where some turned back. The emigrants now had to make their way over or around the Rocky Mountains. They had been assured of the excellent trails for this leg of the journey and fully expected to reach California in a short time. Little did they realize the dangers and trauma they were yet to face. There were two basic routes from which to choose: one to the northwest via Salt Lake City along the Old Spanish Trail, initially a mule trail to Los Angeles, and one to the southwest along Cooke's Wagon Road and along the Gila River to San Diego. There were, of course, variations of these routes.[1]

Most of the emigrants Arkansas passed the vicinity of Santa Fe between May and September. Many of the from emigrants encamped at other settlements in New Mexico such as Galisteo, Anton Chico, San Miguel or Albuquerque hoping to avoid the exorbitant prices charged in Santa Fe for their needed purchases. The pull of Santa Fe was strong, and interested emigrants from encampments twelve to twenty miles away visited the town. Santa Fe was a part of the United States in 1849, but still a lawless Mexican frontier town. The Arkansas emigrants penned many descriptions of the drinking, gambling, dancing, sporting and killing which went on in Santa Fe. N. L. Birge of the Fort Smith Company said he spent a week in Santa Fe, and "I think it was a little of the hardest place I was ever in. Men shoot one another for past time. Not a day without the enactment of a bloody tragedy.[2] Henry Crease of the Little Rock Company said that he and Murphy "made a visit to that city" while the company pursued its way to Albuquerque. "The population is about 4,000, and it is certainly the meanest hole in existence. We had to keep in our saddles to prevent our horses from being stolen from us."[3]

Another member of the Little Rock Company, signing C. E. G., wrote on June 20 describing Santa Fe even more fully.

> Santa Fe takes the lead of all places I ever was in for gambling. It is filled with sporting characters, and even the women gamble. On one of the streets last evening I noticed in front of one of the houses a transparency with the names of the games that were carried on within. To gratify my curiosity I went in, and there sat an old Mexican lady and several other younger ones round a table with their cards. The betting was heavy. I can hardly imagine how this town is supported. The country around it is barren. At the north stands a snowcapped mountain, while the valley in which the town is situated is dry and sandy. The streets are narrow. In the morning this place is crowded with men, women, and children who come in from the country with articles for sale. A Mexican will walk about the town all day to sell a bundle of grass worth about a dime. They are the poorest looking people I ever saw. They subsist principally on mutton, onions, and red pepper. The proportion of poor to the rich is about a thousand to one. Groceries are very high here, but dry goods are about as cheap as at Little Rock.[4]

Others commented about the prices. Corn was selling for $2.50 per bushel, coffee, sugar, meat and bread were 25¢ per pound.[5] Albuquerque prices were equally high. Mules sold from $60 to $100. "Everything we want to buy is held at enormous prices, and anything we have to sell will bring next to nothing. One of the emigrants is offering his five-horse wagon and gear for $40. Flour is worth $7.50 per 100 lbs. Corn is $6 per fanaga (140 lbs.), sugar 25¢ per lb. Mutton $1 to $2 each.[6] These prices contrast sharply with those they had paid in Fort Smith where mules and horses sold from $40 to $60, corn 35–40¢ per bushel, bacon 5–7¢ per lb., and flour $5–6 per barrel."[7]

It was the common practice of these New Mexican towns to entertain the emigrants with *fandangoes.* These dances were welcome diversions after two months on the trail. The grace and beauty of the Mexican senoritas drew many comments in letters home. C. E. G. of Little Rock noted, "The Mexicans waltz beautifully and go through the Spanish dance to perfection."[8] Another Little Rockian wrote "the people treat the b'hoys well, and the way the native population waltz is a caution to cripples!"[9] At another point in the same letter he stated, "They waltz 'devinely,' and their dancing is 'dem foine'."[10] King in his diary of the Clarksville group noted that at Anton Chico he and several others "visited a fandago for a few minutes where we saw the Mexicans in their favorite national amusement, the dance; and I was much surprised to see with what ease and grace a 'peon' . . . would hand his signorita to the floor to engage in a gallopade or waltz."[11] Dr. Fagan of the

Little Rock company at a camp twenty miles from Santa Fe wrote, "The b'hoys are in the best kind of spirits, and we can go to a fandango every night or two, if we please. We frequently take occasion to make ourselves agreeable to the senoritas, and although there are none of us much distinguished for our gallantry among the fair sex, I assure you our efforts in this line have been eminently successful among the brunettes."[12] Having successfully completed what the engineer from Van Buren calculated as 840 miles from Van Buren and facing 1,500 miles by Cooke's route to San Francisco, it is understandable they should feel a little celebrating was in order.[13]

Fourth of July was the major festivity of the overland journey, and almost every group of emigrants celebrated the occasion in some fashion. Many of the Arkansans were somewhere along the Rio Grande on July 4, and they spared no effort to create an American birthday celebration. The Clarksville company took the initiative in planning and inviting the Little Rock and Davis (Van Buren) companies who were also camped near Socorro to join with them in a big celebration. A member of the Clarksville company had taken pains to secure a copy of the Declaration of Independence when the group had passed through Van Buren in April.[14] A committee planned the food, program, music and activities for the occasion. The groups joined together and purchased twenty lambs from a nearby rancho which were the basis for dinner. Led by a band, the companies marched through the encampment to the place of services. Rev. A. B. Bates of Clarksville offered prayers, Dr. W. F. Fagan of Little Rock read the Declaration of Independence, and Rev. J. B. Annis delivered the patriotic address. After this the Arkansans "drank to the health of our friends at home and (to) the prosperity of our country in an assortment of brands. One mess brought out some of the best Hollands (gin), another cognac, while your humble servant and a few others were lucky enough to find at the bottom of a truck some sparkling champagne, reserved for this occasion. At sunset we fired a grand salute, and in the evening we had a fandango, at which, by special invitation, there were present quite a crowd of the fair senoritas." Captain H. P. Dorsey (Helena) marshalled the men in firing a grand salute of four rounds.[15]

N. L. Birge of the Fort Smith company was among those who went to Santa Fe. He spent a week there, including July 4th, and in addition to mentioning the snowcapped mountains, he had this to say about his group's celebration of Independence Day: "I stopped a week in Santa Fe—spent the 'fourth' there with the boys, and such a destruction of 'mint juleps' would be surprising to anybody out of Arkansas."[16]

Internal dissension had come to plague many of the Arkansas companies, and most of them arrived in the vicinity of Santa Fe and Albuquerque factionalized and disorganized. Disagreement over which side of the Canadian River to take, the muddy quagmires, the lack of grass, hard feelings over camp duties and camp sites, disputes over policy and discipline and numerous other factors had taken their toll and accounted for much of the dissension.[17] But no doubt the unwieldy size of the Fort Smith expedition and the desire on the part of many to make faster time accounted for much of the animosity. Trail life produced tensions of its own, and most learned by trial and error that small parties of twenty men got along decidedly best and that three or four men to a wagon or mess was sufficient for safety and harmony and gave a better opportunity for water, wood, and grazing. Fear of the Indians had caused the emigrants to seek the military escort, but the peaceable behavior of the Indians emboldened many to "break off" and proceed as best they could. Added to these accumulated tensions, when they arrived in Santa Fe and no longer had the military escort, a number of weighty decisions had to be made. Which trail would they take? Would they continue with wagons or sell them and pack? What protection would they have beyond Santa Fe? The Arkansas groups made various responses to these challenging questions.

Writing about the Fort Smith company, N. L. Birge remarked in his letter dated July 23 that they had crossed the Rio Grande at Albuquerque and were 175 miles from Santa Fe.

> I suppose you will hear before this reaches you, that the Fort Smith Co. has long since been among the things that were. It was resolved into its component parts the other side of Santa Fe, and is now scattered in all directions. Some sold their wagons at Santa Fe and turned back; others intend going through with pack mules. Among the latter are Steinthal and Bennett. We left them at Santa Fe. I left Seaman's mess at Santa Fe and joined Bolivar Bennett's as also did Share and C. Sinclair.[18]

Mary Conway confirmed this information in a letter written on the Rio Grande, 20th July, 1849:

> We are all well and get along much better than you would suppose. We have necessarily had to undergo many toils and privations but have not suffered as much as I expected, for we have been blessed with good weather. . . . Our company was quite large but some got to disobeying orders and Captain Dillard resigned, which split the company all to pieces. Since then we have been traveling in a dangerous part of the country, where the Indians have been committing depredations on the whites, and they actually murdered two men within three miles of us. There are scouting parties out in all directions after the Indians. We had an escort of United States troops under Captain Marcy, as far as Santa Fe with us.
>
> "We expected the government would furnish an escort from Santa Fe to San Francisco; but, to our great disappointment, we will have no such protection. We have yet to travel a very great distance through a country much more dangerous than that through which we have passed.
>
> "Our disorganized company are getting together again, and in a few days will elect their officers and will then be better prepared to afford some protection. I expect we will stop about two weeks, soon, to rest and recruit our teams; they stood the journey very well until about 200 miles back, when they began to become jaded and lean."[19]

Writing a few days later from a camp 25 miles south of Socorro, Dr. Conway, Mary's father, gave more information about the Fort Smith company's reorganization.

> There are here now 25 wagons and about 80 men and the election of officers will take place tomorrow, after which we will proceed on our journey. The range is very fine here, and our teams are doing remarkably well, although

since we have been on this river (Rio Grande) our health has not been so good. It will take us about two months to get to San Diego on the Pacific coast. I send this by an express who goes to Socorro for blacksmith's tools."[20]

The Fort Smith company left the Rio Grande on August 3 and traveled over Cooke's wagon road to Santa Cruz, Tucson, the Pima Village, then down the Gila River and across the Colorado River to California.[21]

The Little Rock company also faced the same decisions and similarly divided into factions. Sam C. W. Lewis of this company wrote from Santa Fe on June 18 that Henry Crease and Jim Murphy had accompanied him to Santa Fe while the majority of the company went on to Albuquerque.[22] When Crease rejoined the main group a few days later, he, too, described the company as much divided, "some having packed while others continue on with the wagons."[23] Many of the Little Rock company sent letters back from Santa Fe, so the folks back home were aware of their safe arrival in mid and late June in the Santa Fe area, but also aware of the discord among the group. Excerpts from their letters indicate some of the problems.

In the Mountains 12 miles east of Santa Fe, June 17, 1849.—I am here among the pine trees upon the mountains. We do not expect to go to Santa Fe, but will leave the road here to go to Albuquerque. Our company is a good deal split up. About six wagons have gone on to Santa Fe. They except to sell their wagons at that place and go through, with pack mules, by the Old Spanish Trail. . . . When our party get to Albuquerque, 75 miles from this point, we shall decide whether we pack, or go with our wagons. . . .

E. D. Robbins[24]

Alden Woodruff writing from the same camp noted that his mules were "literally worsened by their jaunt," but he was optimistic that two or three days of rest would make them "good as new." He continued, "We intend to have our wagon tires cut and re-set on shrunken wheels tomorrow, and will leave for Albuquerque where we shall stay a week or ten days."[25]

C. E. G. commented on the many emigrants who were abandoning their wagons at Santa Fe to pack, but the majority of the Little Rock company were going to start with wagons, but take packsaddles and be prepared to pack if necessary. He noted they would take the Cooke route and "be at the diggings in about three months."[26] A short distance from Albuquerque, Sam C. S. Lewis decided to quit the company and join a group returning to Independence County. He and some comrades from Arkansas were prospecting for gold just beyond Albuquerque and were attacked by Indians at night. Harwick of Monroe County and Shaver of Hempstead County were killed by the Apache.[27] Lewis was in Little Rock on October 21.[28]

At Socorro, 180 miles from Santa Fe, the Little Rock contingent was comprised of "ten wagons and thirty men, not sufficient for our protection, but close to the Clarksville company."[29] The Little Rock emigrants esteemed the leadership of Captain Rogers of the Clarksville company and considered him "exceedingly well qualified to lead an enterprise of this kind." Consequently,

---

WASHINGTON
ROCKY MOUNTAINS
OLD OREGON TRAIL
Willamette River
OREGON
IDAHO
Snake River
WIND RIVER RANGE
Klamath River
Goose Lake
Mt. Shasta
LASSEN'S CUTOFF
Pit R.
BLACK ROCK DESERT
Goose Creek
Soda Springs
South Pass
Independence Rock
Sweetwater
Mount Lassen
City of Rocks
Raft R.
Bear R.
MORMON TRAIL
Lassen's Ranch
Truckee River
Humboldt River
GREAT SALT LAKE DESERT
Great Salt Lake
Fort Bridger
Feather R.
Donner Pass
Humboldt Sink
Sacramento R.
Carson R.
CARSON VALLEY ROUTE
Salt Lake City
SIERRA NEVADA
Lake Tahoe
NEVADA
Green River
San Francisco
Stockton
San Jose
San Joaquin R.
Owens Lake
UTAH
Sevier River
Monterey
Beaver Dam Wash
DEATH VALLEY ROUTE
LOS ANGELES TRAIL
DIVIDE
CALIFORNIA
FUNERAL MTS.
Death Valley
PANAMINT RANGE
CONTINENTAL
Mission San Fernando
MOJAVE DESERT
SAN BERNARDINO MTS
Los Angeles
Cajon Pass
ARIZONA
COLORADO DESERT
Colorado River
N
S
San Diego
Gila River
Pima Villages
Tucson
Guadalupe Pass
Altar
SONORA
BAJA CALIFORNIA
SIERRA MADRE OCCIDENTAL
J. W. AUDUBON'S ROUTE
ATLANTIC OCEAN
PANAMA
Callao
Rio de Janeiro
Valparaiso
Talcuahano
Santa Catarina Island
Straits of Magellan
Cape Horn

THE WAYS WEST
Caribbean Sea
PANAMA
Chagres
Chagres River
Cruces
Gorgona
Panama City
Bay of Pana
NORTH DAKOTA
Missouri River
SOUTH DAKOTA
MINNESOTA
WISCONSIN
ney Rock
NEBRASKA
IOWA
Courthouse Rock
Grand Island
Kanesville (Council Bluffs)
Platte River
MORMON TRAIL
OHIO
INDIANA
ILLINOIS
Fort Kearny
OLD
Big Blue R.
Little Blue
OREGON TRAIL
St. Joseph
KANSAS
Kansas River
Independence
St. Louis
SANTA FE TRAIL
MISSOURI
KENTUCKY
Arkansas River
Cimarron River
Grand Saline (Salina)
TENNESSEE
River
Fort Smith
OKLAHOMA
Rock Mary
ARKANSAS
Memphis
Mississippi River
Little Rock
ALABAMA
MISSISSIPPI
TEXAS
LOUISIANA
FRENCH COMPANY'S ROUTE
Austin
New Orleans
San Antonio
Galveston
Port Lavaca
Corpus Christi
Rio Grande City
Monterrey
NUEVO LEÓN
TAMAULIPAS

they chose to "remain with him until we get through the country of the hostile Indians." What made planning more difficult was the lack of reliable information about the route after leaving the Rio Grande. The Clarksville and Little Rock companies crossed the Rio Grande at Albuquerque. An unsigned letter from one of the Little Rock men described the river and the boat:

> "The river is from 400 to 700 yards wide, and very swift, with any quantity of sand bars . . . Our boat is 30' long and 8½' wide, and will pass anywhere for a good piece of workmanship. The material cost us $24. The Clarksville company and our own built the boat in two days, and we shall be able to sell it for $75 or $100."[30]

Another letter indicated they were among the very first to make the crossing, having been preceded by "some 70" which "we will probably overtake or pass within two weeks." This letter also stated the Little Rock group had made the trip through to Santa Fe two weeks ahead of Captain Marcy and were now "laying on our oars, making but from 10 to 12 miles per day to improve our teams before taking to the hills."[31]

The Clarksville company, according to D. Maclean, opted to "stick to the wagons as long as they can go."[32] But they too were not without their troubles for the journey down the Rio Grande was through heavy sand and there was little grass for feed, no shade, and no wood for camp fuel. The King journal entries while along the Rio Grande convey the hardships and the dissension created as a consequence of these privations. Sometimes the emigrants could buy wood from the Mexicans who packed it from the mountains on jacks.[33] To come upon a cottonwood grove and its promise of cool shade could lift the spirits of the emigrants. "Rejoicing over the prospect of a camp in a cottonwood grove, we were disappointed in one respect for the flies and ants were so numerous that it was impossible to rest either laying, sitting, or standing." Captain Rogers was sick and they had to stop the train after only five miles. Chaparral and mesquite were the principle growth. "The day's drive was very fatiguing and many of the steers gave out but none was left (behind). The subject of leaving wagons was in agitation, but no determination made with regard to what should be done." On July 15th "the captain made a change to small wagon," and the company left two wagons. "The company appears to be busy all day in regulating loads and throwing away all unnecessary stuff such as boxes and barrels, etc." The loose sand and the mountainous stony areas were "a continual drag for the teams. It was very distressing to one who wishes to get to California to look at the wornout oxen which were unyoked and left." The dust was awful and the emigrants hoped for rain but the "sun rose and blasted our hopes." At some points the road was so steep "we were compelled to hold our wagons with ropes to prevent them from turning over." These hardships increased tension and arguments for on July 17 "the council met at night and passed some resolutions of great importance concerning the changing of mess mates."[34] No other details are given, but it can be assumed that mess-mate switching was extensive and disrupting the progress and well being of the group.

King recounts another source of discord among the Davis party (Van

Buren) which was traveling with the Clarksville group. It seems that a few men in the Davis company stole seven mules below Socorro, and this had split the company for the men denied their misconduct, had not been punished, but could not explain the seven mules. The offended portion of the company took the blacksmith wagon and team which was the property of the entire company and left. H. H. Davis in a letter to Captain Rogers said he had foresworn both parties and he and his family would attach themselves to another company.[35] King maintained Davis "wished to clear his own skirts" after he found "his mode of traveling was not countenanced by any company or set of men that wished to do what is right."

The overloading referred to in King's journal was a mistake universally made by the forty-niners no matter the route taken. They discarded items at various stages as a consequence of some difficulty or obstacle imposed by the road. Those following the northern route began "throwing off" as they approached Fort Laramie. For hundreds of miles the trail was littered with every conceivable object, many of great value. The purpose was to switch to a lighter wagon or sell all and use pack animals. On the southern route, the casting off first occurred at Santa Fe and along the Rio Grande, to increase later in the desert crossings. Letters and diaries constantly refer to this overloading, and the experiences of the forty-niners were used by the emigrants during the following years to good advantage. Potter in his study commented; "the tragedy of it was not the loss of goods, but the loss of energy—most of the excess was hauled for hundreds of miles, constantly retarding the journey and weakening the teams, before thrown aside."[36]

A group from Helena, Arkansas, had arrived in Santa Fe on June 1 before any of the other groups. They had crossed the prairie in 62 days; "and out of that number (we) laid by 24, leaving 38 days in which we made the trip.... We are going to pack from this place. Twenty of us are going from Taos with a lieutenant who has been ordered to California as an aid to Gen. Smith. We expect to go north of the Old Spanish Trail, and will make the trip in 40 or 45 days."[37] This trip proved to be exceedingly difficult and after some 200 miles, they turned back to Santa Fe to take the Gila route. They were taken on board a steamer at San Diego on October 1, and told the story of their sufferings to a passenger from Helena who was bound for California.[38]

The Van Buren company rested and recruited at Albuquerque. Their dissension seemed to have been kept to a minimum. John Boyer, a member of the group wrote:

> "We have been two months coming to this point. Our company has enjoyed fine health. We have lost but two oxen of the company; some few seem to be pretty well broken down. Our mules are in about the same order as when we started. Good, hardy mules and horses are most to be preferred for the trip. Not a single wagon has broken down. You will notice that we did not see a single Comanche Indian and but few buffaloes. Numbers of antelopes were seen, of which we killed some; meat fine. And the road—I don't think so good a natural road of the same distance could be found anywhere—for days, just undulating enough to rest the teams.... From information here, we learn that Cooke's route is entirely practicable, being about fifteen hundred miles to San Francisco. We have determined to take this route. Some of our company will pack.[39]

With the formation of new units and the completion of preparations for the last part of the trip, the emigrants began to leave their second "jumping off" place. There was no departure schedule for the various groups leaving Santa Fe and Albuquerque, and each made its own arrangements. Many emigrants bemoaned the loss of the military escort and feared trouble from the Apache, Navajo and Utah Indians. Captain Marcy learned on his arrival in Santa Fe, contrary to what he and the authorities in Washington had believed, that the Old Spanish Trail did not go directly to San Francisco—indeed it was an impassable route for wagons. The only wagon route to California was by Cooke's or Kearny's routes to the Gila River. As we have seen, the Arkansas emigrants continued on their journey after a brief recruit. Marcy stayed in Santa Fe six weeks recruiting and gathering information about a return route to Fort Smith which would correct the error of bringing the gold seekers 300 miles north of Cooke's route.

In describing the Fourth of July celebration and noting King's journal entries July 10–17, we have gotten a glimpse of the emigrants' experiences along the Rio Grande. On July 21st they were ready to bid the Rio Grande good-bye. "No one is grieved at the idea, for you can't rest for the mosquitoes and other plagues, seemingly put here for no purpose but to annoy the Californians, for there is nothing else to annoy."[41] The "other plagues" were flies, scorpions and snakes. Caspar S. Ricks had joined the Arkansans at Albuquerque and continued with them to California. He notes in his diary that leaving the Rio Grande behind was "a source of general rejoicing to us. We had drank of its muddy waters so long that some in the company began to imagine they were getting as full of sand bars as the river itself. We hoped to bid adieu to the rats and mosquitoes which had been a source of great annoyance to us."[42]

After leaving the Rio Grande on July 21, Arkansas' Californians were to follow Cooke's Wagon Road across the Rio Mimbres and through Guadalupe Pass to the village of Santa Cruz through the Santa Cruz River valley to Tucson, across an eighty-mile desert *journada* to the Pima Indian villages where they intersected the Kearny Trail and proceeded west along the south side of the Gila across the Colorado River and through ninety miles of more desert to Carrizo Creek, Warner's Ranch, San Diego, or Los Angeles. The Arkansans tell their own story. Alden M. Woodruff, son of Little Rock's earliest newspaper editor, W. E. Woodruff, was only twenty one; yet, he wrote letters which rank with the very best of all the California letters and which chronicle the experiences along the southern route. After reaching California, he wrote a long letter describing the trip from Albuquerque to San Diego. It succinctly sunmarizes the trip and hints at the hardships and suffering they endured. Other letters follow which underscore particular incidents that Woodruff mentions.

Curtis Creek, California, February 6, 1850

I believe I gave you a description of our journey up to Albuquerque, where I wrote you last while in New Mexico. After leaving Albuquerque, we passed down the Rio Grande about two hundred and fifty miles, passing on our route several Indian villages, ranchos, and the town of Socorro, where there is a force of dragoons stationed. Socorro contains about five hundred inhabitants, but like all Mexican towns, is a dirty, filthy place. We lay by here one day to recruit our teams for a long drive to the next camp on the Rio Grande. We left the river about thirty-five miles above El Paso and took Colonel Cooke's trail (a very circuitous one) down through the state of Sonora, Mexico. Before leaving the river, we supplied ourselves with water for beast as well as for man, for a march of thirty-six miles on which we understood there was not a drop of water; but after marching about eighteen miles, we came to what is called Foster's Hole, a very large hole in a rock, capable of holding one hundred barrels of water. At this place we watered our teams and traveled on, passing a large valley covered with fine grass and wild peas. We struck camp on the plain when night came (without water), and next morning about nine o'clock made the spring, where we had good water but very little grass. We lay by here the remainder of that day and part of the next.

It was at that place (and the only one) that we saw Indians. Mr. Thibault had strayed off from camp, hunting, and fell in with three Apache. When he first saw them, they were riding at a fast gait and seemed to be on the trail of something, and did not perceive him until he hailed them and presented his gun. They halted and asked him in Spanish if he was an American. He replied that he was. The Indians said they were friendly to Americans, and one of them took him up behind and brought him into camp. The Indians were on the trail of a cow which had been given them by some emigrant and which some Texans had driven off some two or three hours before. We gave them a note to the Texans, saying that they had claimed the cow of us, and they rode off down the road at full gallop after them. About sundown they returned with part of the cow and a note from the Texans, saying that they had killed the cow before the Indians overtook them, and had bought part of it of them for a pistol, percussion cap, and some other little articles, which they showed us. They promised to return in the morning with mules and horses to trade. But when they came, there were so many wishing to trade (Davis's and the Clarksville, Arkansas, companies had arrived over night), and [they] were pulled and hauled about at such a rate, that they were frightened off and but very few trades made. If our company had been alone, we might have traded off our broken-down mules and horses, and have got good fresh teams again.

We left this place about three o'clock in the evening and traveled about twelve miles to the next water. We reached the Rio Mimbres next day, a distance of about twenty-five miles. Here I drank the best water I had tasted since I left home. It was equal to ice water. Next day we camped near Ojo de Vaca (Cow spring), where we lay by one day for the Lincoln company to overtake us. Here we made a great fire on a high hill, to get some Indians into camp to trade with, but none came. After leaving Ojo de Vaca, we traveled fourteen miles to the next camp, but in getting there we found that the water had dried up. We, of course, jogged along, hoping every mile to find water; but on we went until late at night and no water. Two of my mules gave out about eight o'clock, and I was obliged to lay by for the night. Some of the teams got to the spring that night but were not able to get water, there being so many teams ahead of them. I got to the place about nine o'clock next morning, but could get no water except for my own use. But luckily for us, some holes of water were found about a mile from the road. We, of course, kept it to ourselves until our animals had drunk their fill. We left this place for Dry Lake, about fifteen miles distant, and could get no water for our mules. Next morning we heard there was water about two miles distant, and immediately packed up and drove down, where we found a large well which afforded an abundance of water, such as it was. It was clear and cool enough, but tasted strong of decayed vegetation. We lay by here one day.

Nothing of any consequence transpired until we reached Guadalupe pass, the worst place for wagons to travel over I ever saw. It was almost perpendicular for two miles. We had to take off our mules and let our wagons down with ropes, etc. After getting to the bottom, we traveled down a canyon for some twelve miles or more, crossing a stream that ran through it some thirty-five or forty times in that distance. About the twenty-fifth [of] August we arrived at Santa Cruz, one of the frontier towns of Mexico. It was at this place that I traded off my pinchbeck jewelry* to very good advantage. For that which cost me about seventy-five cents, I got two and one-half bushels of unbolted flour, several pounds of sugar, and several other little articles. It was a long time before I could get the women to bring their flour to my wagon, but I finally devised a plan. Add. S. borrowed a fiddle and sat on the wagon pole and played, while I sat in the wagon and dealt out jewelry to the women for their flour and anything else that they had for sale. After we shut up shop, Add. and some of the boys invited the women out and had a fandango.

*This was cheap jewelry made of copper or zinc to imitate gold.

We left Santa Cruz and traveled down the Santa Cruz river. We passed through one of the most beautiful valleys I ever saw. All along the banks we found deserted towns, ranchos, and furnaces. The whole country abounds in rich gold and silver mines. But as soon as a town or rancho is built, the Apache tear it down and kill all the males and carry off all the females. The valley is covered with mesquite timber and is the finest grazing country (except California) I ever saw. We traveled down the river about one hundred miles to Tucson, where we lay by two days. There are two or three companies of soldiers stationed here to protect the inhabitants; but as soon as they go outside the town, the Apache drive them in again. They are like all Mexican soldiery. After leaving Tucson, the next seventy-five miles of our road to the Gila river was through a perfect desert. In the dry season there is not a drop of water and but little or no grass. But luckily for us, there had been several rains, and we found holes of water all along the road. And there was considerable young grass springing up, which helped amazingly; but it was only in spots that we found this. It was in the midst of this barren waste that we lost William Fagan, one of the best young men in our company . . .

It took us four or five days to make the Gila, when we found what little grass there was, eaten close to the ground. We found here the Pima Indians, represented by Lieutenant Emory as the most innocent and harmless race of Indians on the continent. We camped among them one night, and next morning we were minus our lead line; and almost every wagon lost some article from their wagon or harness. They might have been honest when Emory was among them, but they have learned bad manners since. We bought corn, fodder, wheat, melons, and such things from the Pima. They asked high prices in money, but a hickory shirt* would go as far as five dollars with them.

**A worker's shirt made of cotton twill.

We traveled down the river three or four days and found no grass— we had plenty of corn and wheat—but we soon learned how to find grass. We had to swim our stock over to the bars and islands, which were subject to overflow, and on some found plenty of fine grass. It was on this river that my best two mules (Pol and Bill) were ruined by getting mired in the quicksand. After my mules were broken down, I had to swap off both for one, leave my wagon, and pack. We traveled about twenty days down the Gila before getting to the crossing of the Colorado, when we crossed in a boat made by some people from Pope county, Arkansas. Burke Johnson was among them. We paid them $1.25 to cross our packs and had to swim our mules. Pierce lost his mule in swimming.

We left the Colorado and started into the Great Desert, and camped at the first well, about fifteen miles from the river. Here we had to tie up our mules without anything to eat except a few mesquite beans, and at twelve o'clock that night made out to get all our animals watered. The well yielded about a pailful every fifteen minutes. Next morn we drove our mules about twelve miles from the road, where we found plenty of beans. We gathered all we could, and after letting our mules eat their fill from under the trees, we packed up and started for the next wells, about twenty miles distant. When we got to the wells we found them dry. We wandered about hunting water until after dark, when we heard some one halloo. We went to them and found them to be Keats and mess, who had started before us in the morning. They had found some holes of water, which our poor mules waded into with a rush. We had to tie up that night without anything for our mules to eat, and next morning we made New river, about twelve miles distant. Here we found plenty of water and grass. There is something strange about this river. It had sprung up about six months before, and its banks were lined with fine grass, all the growth of a few months. We stayed here about five hours, and started for the next well (five miles), now a lake formed by New river; and after watering, started for the next well (a lake also), which we made about eight o'clock. We fed this night on beans which we had taken care to supply ourselves with at the river. We left next morning and made Carrizo creek that day, a distance of about thirty miles. Next day we made Vallecito. Here we found a little grass and plenty of sulphur water. We lay by here one day, and next day made San Felipe, where we had good grass and water. Here we all concluded that we would go down to San Diego and take the steamer; so next day we packed up and took a mule trail, which cut off some thirty miles, and camped that night at Santa Isabella. Here we had quite a feast on peaches and grapes. We lay by one day, and next drive made Santa Maria, and next evening, about eight o'clock, made the old mission of San Diego, five miles from the town, passing in the eve the rancho of Santa Monica. Next day we drove to within half a mile of town and camped, to await the arrival of the steamer. We were at San Diego five days before the steamer arrived, when we all took steerage passage. It went mighty hard. And in three days [we] were in San Francisco; and in a fortnight more we were in the diggings.

A.M.W.[43]

The emigrants expected to travel thirty-six miles without water once they left the Rio Grande. They left the river at 3:00 p.m. and continued traveling when night came. "Dark approached and as it grew darker, the road appeared to be alive with wagons and songs, for every man seemed to be doing what he could in the singing line. For some three hours we could not tell where we were going, only that we were in the road. . . . At 1 o'clock at night the train halted until day."[44] They then had to travel eight more miles to find water. Another day and night of such travel and the oxen were "famished for water, some fainting, as it were, and sinking down, which caused some considerable trouble to raise them." Then the Rio Mimbres, and "some of the finest water you ever drank."[45] More days of limited water found in pools, abandoned wagons and gear, and then a major elephant—Guadalupe Pass.[46]

F. J. Thibault of the Little Rock company kept a journal which has never surfaced but from which three excerpts were published in 1851 in the *Gazette.* His description of the Guadalupe Pass captures the fear, drama and victory of the Arkansas trekkers.

From the Journal of F. J. Thibault

July 31

We have now entered a pass in the range of mountains (Cordilleras) that have gradually been hemming us in for several days. Portions of them, that tower up in every direction, are covered with, to us, a new variety of oak and cedar—, others, more scantly covered, are showing their rough and uncouth rocky sides, bidding defiance to the adventurer. Several of us selected one most easy of ascent, and climbed to its summit—there to sit and view the mere speck of ground occupied by our train, and then let the eye range over the immense waste of plain, and the towering heights that sport with the clouds. One feels himself shrink before the Omnipotent power that created and rules this immensity of space. Our day's drive having been rather a rough and difficult one, we camped in a small valley, completely encircled by these mountain peaks—having made but 12 miles.

August 1

After proceeding through a short pass, had a good road for four or five miles, when we came to the brink of a descent, that would make the head swim to look down. This our wagons had to descend probably 800 or 1000 feet in half a mile, and to pass over the ground one would pronounce it for wagons impassable. We were obliged to take out a portion of our team, lock the wheels, and attach ropes both to the sides and back end of the wagon. Here in this intense heat, being jerked and dragged down this precipice I might say, for near half a mile, with the certainty of having to ascend to undergo a like process, our bottom was fairly tried. It was truly a terrific descent—one miss drive, and a wagon whirled to destruction! No one felt inclined to trust himself on the back of his animal for fear of performing a summerset over its head. To take a seat on the verge of this descent, and view this mountainous and broken landscape, would fill the beholder with dread, at the probable difficulties we will have to surmount before the mountain barrier can be passed. When I came abruptly to the brink of this frowning gulf, it was a sight that caused me to pause and gaze with admiring awe on a scene of black and terrible desolation, the like to which my eyes had never beheld. Well might the boys say, we have overtaken 'the elephant' at last. After making the descent, which was performed without any other accident save some pretty severe bruises and scratches, we camped in a small valley, with scarcely level ground enough for our wagons to rest upon for a long time. Our day's drive six miles with a day of hard work before us.

August 2

Made an early start, and after having accomplished a steep ascent, we descended to the same branch we had camped upon the night previous, followed it down for twelve miles, crossing it ever 100 yards. Some idea may be formed of the road from the fact of the mountains rising abruptly on each side, the bed of the stream being torn up by the torrents, and at places covered with large round rocks and deep deposits of coarse sand, that our wagons would sink deeply in. The scenery was truly grand—here the wild and romantic might find food for the imagination. Had I a more gifted pen, I could here use it to advantage. One might see towering rocks, like huge chimneys, with cavities where could be sheltered all the men in our train—other places where it appeared nature had been trying her freaks, by moulding these rocks into a thousand fantastic shapes. I quote the language of one of our larks, whilst expressing himself in relation to the pass, 'Boys, I don't know the exact meaning of the term Guadaloupe, but if it means the *devil's* pass it is well named, if not, it is miscalled.' In descending this creek, the enormous heights would confine us to the narrow limits of the stream, and for every few hundred yards a new scene would burst upon our sight. I would at times experience a degree of wild excitement—while gazing about me at the giant mountains and listening to the rush of waters, and the noise & bustle of the drivers of the teams, through this difficult pass.—And often I have stood on some commanding height, and wished that these friends we had left behind, might for a short space of time be transported to my side, that they might enjoy those lovely scenes of primitive nature, that lay stretched at my feet for miles and miles in extent.[47]

King's journal notes the Clarksville company only one day behind the Little Rock group. Moving into the canyon on August 3, he wrote, "the canyon where we camped was not sufficient in width for us to form a circle with the wagons, so we dropped in as we could." No guard was put out. Cliffs and mountains "close in on sides," and at places "you could not for your life, tell whether you could go at all or not. Sometimes I could see but three yoke of my oxen and my wagon, the other two yoke of oxen making the turn, carried them out of my sight." He judged the mouth of Guadalupe pass to be 100 yards.[48]

After leaving Guadalupe pass the emigrants took a local road to Santa Cruz which was somewhat south of the Cooke road. The Apaches had made disastrous raids in this area during the preceding two years and deserted villages and ranches caused much comment by the California emigrants. Wild herds of cattle were in the area as a consequence of the raids, and the emigrants were able to secure fresh meat for their meals. King commented extensively about the cattle hunts, the fine taste of the beef, and the drying of beef over the fire and "sacking it up" for the rest of the trip. Santa Cruz was a small Mexican village where the emigrants could trade for flour, sugar, dried peaches, eggs, chickens, beans, and molasses. Woodruff traded his pinchbeck jewelry and others shirts and blankets. The Mexicans lived in dread fear of the Apaches and Mexican soldiers were stationed both in Santa

Cruz and Tucson.

From Santa Cruz to Tucson was a distance of about one hundred miles through the lovely Santa Cruz valley. King commented on the deserted ranches, churches, and fine orchards of peaches, pears, apples and quinces—all green. The caravan met Mexican soldiers on their way to protect Santa Cruz.[49] Reaching Tucson in five or six days, the travelers laid by to rest and recruit their teams, to trade, and to prepare for the eighty-mile desert *journada* from Tucson to the Pima villages. The Arkansas groups were lucky in finding holes of water and some grass due to rain for ordinarily none was to be had. However it was fifty miles from Tucson that tragedy struck the Little Rock company with the short illness and death of William P. Fagan, the popular young physician.

Robert Brownlee writing to his brother Thomas in Little Rock recounts this sad event.

> It pains me to announce the death of Dr. W. Fagan. Fifty miles this side of Tucson he had been complaining, for a few days rode in the wagon, and as we had neither grass nor water, we were compelled to make a long drive to obtain both as man & beast stood in need of them. That night, August 22, he was taken with a bleeding at the nose and mouth, which reduced him very fast, and at a quarter to 9 o'clock next morning he died with his hand in mine without a struggle. He appeared sensible but said nothing nor made any request. Every attention possible was rendered him, as we had in our company Dr. Holt from Washington, Arkansas, who did everything in his power for his relief. We, in our destitute condition, intered him under a large muskite [sic] tree, and secured the remains of one as kind, obliging, and of as promising talents as ever started on this journey. The impression made on me that day over the grave when Mr. Thibault was putting up a prayer to the Giver of all goodness, will never be forgotten by me, and I think by more present. Tears were rolling down the cheeks of some who I believe never shed a tear before. The shock was severe as we all had so very fine health, to think we had buried one companion, and another about to depart. Mr. Thibault's black boy died the day after in the same encampment. As the train after burying Mr. Fagan were compelled to leave, I stayed and helped to inter Jordan about 100 yards from the former. From this Mr. Keatt's and Mr. Hunt's wagons started and reached water and grass next morning.[50]

Fagan's letters have been quoted above. He was well liked by the Little Rock b'hoys and had me a hit with the Mexican senoritas at the fandangoes. One other excerpt from a letter from his messmate, Henry Crease, when they were camped fifty miles beyond Santa Fe, gives a closer glimpse of his personality.

> Dr. F. and myself are cooks today and at this present writing he wants to know what I am doing in the wagon; my answer not being very satisfactory, he has dropped his tin cup and dish cloth and thrown the spade in the fire, and comes to see for himself. He is not at all satisfied, and very cooly remarks 'that every d—d bean would be burnt up, while the (?) wood would not make coals enough to bake bread.' I close at this.[51]

The Little Rock company made the *journada* in five days reaching the Pima villages and the Gila River. Just as Woodruff commented on the dishonesty of the Pima, so did others. King stated: "They look very innocent and pretending to be very honest, yet they will steal anything that is loose. We got in town and found their dwellings to be wigwams made of straw or sticks. Their clothing consists of a breech cloth, and sometimes a shirt, but not often."[52] Here the Indians brought produce such as melons, corn, and wheat into the camp to trade. Their prices were "very high." The groups recruited and made ready for the forty-five miles of desert which they then faced. "Some of our animals were weak in consequence of having no water and traveling 25 miles of dusty sandy road."[53] Brownlee's mess laid in thirteen bushels of corn and wheat for the desert crossing.[54] One diversion enjoyed by many of the Arkansans was fishing and bathing in the Gila. King said, "The boys were bathing all day in the river."[55] One of the Clarksville company had abandoned a wagon back on the desert; and after resting a day, some of the boys were sent to "bring it in."[56]

A non-Arkansas group which had come this route two months earlier during the dry season had a very different story to tell about reaching the Gila. John S. Robb, a correspondent with the St. Louis *Weekly Reville,* described his desert crossing to the Gila in this way:

> "From Tucson to the Gila river, a distance of eighty miles, there was not a drop of water, except what we carried with us, nor a blade of grass for our animals, and it required two days' travel to pass it; of course it was a journey of suffering. My animals were nearly exhausted, but personally I did not suffer as much as many others of the party. There were forty men in all, and some of them were forced to drink their own urine. One man of the party was found on the hills perfectly insane from his suffering from want of water. The last ten miles I became so faint I could scarcely sit upon my horse, and he was so exhausted that I could not urge him out of a walk. I struggled on, however, never despairing for a moment, and finally reached the river. Here men and horses were up to their middles in the stream, slaking their mad thirst, and thanking God that they had at last gained water. It was the most delightful draught of water I ever tasted."[57]

The journey down the Rio Gila was long and trying, requiring ten to thirty days depending on the condition of the company. Woodruff said they were twenty days in reaching the Colorado River. Water and grass were neither one plentiful on this desert plain. The emigrants learned to swim their animals over to bars and islands which resulted from the river's earlier overflowing.[58] The dust, heat and sand along this route were irksome and very fatiguing to both man and beast. King said of one of the sand storms, "it reminded me of reading of the sandy deserts of Arabia." He also wrote, "No one can imagine how disagreeable it is." The sand along the river was so hot, "almost impossible for a man to walk barefooted on it." The animals suffered great physical strain, and to relieve their strain and promote progress, the emigrants abandoned articles which had become superfluous, including stoves, chairs, tools, wheels, and even wagons. King wrote, "To see a fine wagon abandoned is a common occurrence here, and it does not seem to mortify a man's feelings to leave his property at all."[59] Abandoned wagons continued to increase and parties "walked carrying provisions on their backs."[60] There was sickness in the Clarksville company, "three confined and some complaining." No doubt heat exhaustion was taking its toll.

Conditions of short water and poor grazing necessitated the breaking up of companies into component messes to improve their prospects. Brownlee wrote, "Our company broke up by chance, as every mess would try and do the best in finding grass for the teams, and it so happened that McVicar's wagon and mess, which is composed of J. McHenry. R. Drew, S. Brownfield, W. Garrety, and their two black boys, and my worthy companion, J. Clark has been traveling in company."[61] The Clarksville company similarly divided into three parts.[62]

Not only did the animals suffer strain and collapse, but so did men's nerves. A murder in the Clarksville company occurred along this portion of the route. The King journal records in great detail the empaneling of a jury, the trial and the execution. It is a rare example of trail justice as practiced by the overlanders and given here in its entirety. George Hickey stabbed Elijah Davis around noon on September 5. Davis died in ten minutes and was buried at 5 o'clock. "The emigrants generally determined to arrest Hickey," and a Mr. Young, not of the Clarksville company, made the arrest. At 6 o'clock the horn was sounded at Captain Redmond Rogers' tent to assemble the emigrant community. Major John W. Patrick, acting as sheriff, and Captain Rogers, acting as judge, made a few remarks and the trial began. A. D. King read the writ of indictment against Hickey:

> Be it remembered that upon the 5th day of September, 1849, George W. Hickey having been charged and accused of committing murder upon the body of one Elijah Davis, in the state of Mexico, and the Department of Sonora, upon the day and year aforesaid, while upon his journey in the territory of California. He was put upon his trial by the Clarksville Company and other citizens of the United States of America on their journey to the said territory of California. And the said company and citizens aforesaid in view of their duty to their country, and at the special instance and request of Maj. John W. Patrick, of whose mess or family the said G. W. Hickey is a member, did proceed to empanel a jury, whose names are as follows, to wit: C. L. Street, Emanuel Speegles, John May, John C. Upton, A. M. Strayhorn, Thomas Johnson, L. R. Rolling, David Jamison, Reuben McFadden, John M. Davis, Samuel Groin and John Groin (Guion, Guin?).
>
> Witnesses for the plaintiff being called and sworn upon the holy Evangelish [sic] of Almighty to despose the truth, the whole truth and nothing but the truth; deposes and say: Yancey Harper, first examined deposeth and saith: 'Upon the 5th of September, 1849, I was sitting close to Davis and Hickey was standing close to Davis on the other side and they commenced disputing about Mrs. Lee and after a little bit one word brought on another and George W. Hickey threatened to whip Mr. Lee's son if he ever pestered him. Davis told him that he could not whip him where he was. Hickey said: 'As you take it up, I can whip you.' Davis rose to his feet, the damned lie was given and I do not know who passed it first.' (Here the prisoner asked the witness if Davis did not throw off his hat and roll up his sleeves). Answer: 'He threw off his hat, but I did not notice his rolling up his sleeves, if he did. Then Hickey struck Davis. Hickey made the first pass, from that they clinched; Thomas King and myself

jumped up and ran to them and said to each other that we would let them fight it out. It was not but a little bit till Davis threw Hickey and gave him enough. I suppose as much as he wanted. Hickey hallooed 'take him off.' We, King and myself, took hold of Davis and took him off. Then Hickey got up and we thought it was all done. King and myself were two steps off and Davis on the other side of Hickey from us. The next thing I saw, Hickey had his knife in his hand just making his thrust at Davis. Davis aimed to dodge his lick, but Hickey stuck his knife in Davis, under the left shoulder. It appeared like Hickey wanted to cut him again. I caught Hickey by the wrist and Hickey threatened that if I did not let him go he would cut me with his knife. By that time Davis was aiming for his gun. His gun was six or eight steps or perhaps, 10 steps off. He saw him get his gun and Hickey tried to keep me between him and Davis a little bit. I saw that Davis would shoot. I jumped out of the way. Hickey made towards a tree some four or five steps off and dodged under some limbs. Davis shot at him and Hickey dodged. By this time, Davis could not more than stand up. King and myself took hold of him, took him to a shade and laid him down. He died in 10 minutes after we laid him down. He died from the stab he received from the hand of Hickey.'

Question by the prisoner: 'Did you not notice me take my knife out of my pocket as I rose?'

Answer: 'I did not notice it. I further sayeth not.' Yancey Harper.

Thomas King next sworn, saith: 'I saw the first lick. Hickey struck the first lick; they clinched. Davis appeared very willing to fight him. Davis threw him and gouged him. Hickey hallowed and I and Harper pulled Davis off of Hickey. We got them apart three or four steps. I was standing between. The next I noticed Hickey was making his lick at Davis with his knife. Harper caught him just as he made the lick, but not in time to stop his thrust. Harper proceeded to let him go for Hickey swore he would cut anybody and friend that would hold him. By this time Davis got hold of his gun. He was so weak that he did not get his gun to his face to take aim, but held it towards Hickey and fired. Davis was so weak I laid him down. He died in 12 or 15 minutes. I believe the stab he received from Hickey was the cause of his death. The stab was on the left shoulder under the shoulder blade bone. Davis died. Hickey had killed him. This was about 12 o'clock, September 5, 1849. Hickey did not stay till he died.' And further this deponent saith not.—Thomas King.

James Lee on behalf of the prisoner, 12 years old, says: 'I did not see them fight. I was off on the other side of the cattle about 50 yards from Hickey and Davis when they fought.'

Question by the defendant Hickey: 'Please tell what threats you told me Davis made against me this morning when we went to water the cattle.'

Answer: 'I did not tell Mr. Hickey that Davis had made any threats against him. Davis made no threats against Mr. Hickey as ever I heard. Davis did not go with us to water the stock. He stayed to hunt a steer which was missed.'

Question by a juror: 'Did Davis come down to where you were herding the stock?'

Answer: 'He did.' And further this deponent sayeth not.

his
James X Lee
mark

George L. Patrick, a witness called by the jurors and being duly sworn says: 'I was at our wagons this morning when Hickey came up, he said he had had a scrimmage with Davis, that Davis had scratched his face a little, and that he, Hickey, had sent Davis to his long home, or he was in hopes he had, or words to that effect.'

Question by Hickey: 'Did I not say that I believed Davis intended to kill me?'

Answer: 'I heard you say, but I do not know whether it was at that time or not that he said that today. It was not long until news came that Davis was dead and Hickey said, when he heard it: 'Thank God!' It was not long until father came up and asked Hickey how him and Davis came to fight. He said they got into a quarrel and Da''is shot at him and he stabbed Davis. Father said that Davis was dead. Hickey then said, 'Uncle John, that's my whole heart's desire.' And further this deponent saith not.—G. L. Patrick.

John W. Patrick, sworn, says: 'I was at Mr. Rogers' tent when Hickey came to my tent. I stayed at Captain Rogers' tent until I heard that Davis was dead. I then went to my wagons. Mr. Hickey was there. I then spoke to him as my son above testifies. I told him he had killed Davis and it was an awful thing to take his fellow being's life and he ought to feel himself entirely justifiable. He said he did feel justified in the eyes of God and man from the threats Davis had made. He said Davis had taken his gun down there and he and Davis had had some words about the gun swapping and he said Davis had threatened his life and said he should not get to California. I asked him who he could prove these threats by. He said James Lee. I heard Mr. Davis ask Mr. Lee if he wanted the gun. Mr. Lee said, 'no, keep it.' This was this morning where they were grazing cattle and before the fight. And further this deponent saith not. Mr. Davis was a member of Mark Lee's family.—John W. Patrick.

After hearing all the testimony, the jury retired without hearing any law quibblers to get up a prejudice or a sympathy for the criminal and after having been out a few minutes they brought in the following verdict:

'We, the jury' find George W. Hickey guilty of the murder of Elijah Davis, and believe he should be executed. We would recommend that he be executed in the manner of military executions, shot, 12 guns be loaded, six with powder and balls and six with powder only and all of the men upon this encampment cast lots and the 12 that it falls upon be the executioners. The vote of the whole encampment to be taken with regard to his execution. Emanuel Speegles, C. L. Street, D. A. Jamison, Lewis J. Rolling, Thomas Johnston, J. M. Davis, John Guin, John May, A. M Strayhorn, Reubin McPhadden, S. R. Guin, J. C. Upton, Jury.'[63]

This verdict was rendered about midnight. The company remained stationary the next morning. After herding and tending cattle, the horn was blown at 11 o'clock a.m. to again assemble the encampment. The company was to vote on the verdict of the jury, and the yeas and nays were recorded by each man's vote and duly recorded in King's journal. Note Mark Lee, of whose family the victim was a member, did not vote; whereas the senior Patrick whom Hickey referred to as "Uncle John" voted "nay" while the junior Patrick voted "yea."

	Yeas.	Nays.
J. W. Patrick		1
John Willis	1	
Jerry Willis	1	
John Pearson	1	
Yancey Harper	1	
Thomas King	1	
—.—.Keely	1	
G. L. Patrick	1	
John White	1	
William Lockridge	1	
William Keillyn	1	
A. M. C. Robinson		1
C. B. Sartin	1	
W. Bailey	1	
William Harman		1
William Aikin	0	0
John Silor	1	
G. W. Turner	1	
I. N. Ward	1	
A. B. Bates		1
F. A. Hamilton	1	
P. Carr		1
Jasper Kitchen	1	
B. Phillips	1	
R. M. Thomas	1	
G. C. Shelby	1	
D. Speegles	1	
D. Henry	1	
R. Rogers	1	
T. C. Jarnagin	1	
J. F. Rollins	1	
William Young	1	
Thomas Riley	1	
James Logan	1	
William R. Rogers	1	
S. Campbell	1	
J. L. Prewitt	1	
William Holland	1	
Jacob Rogers	1	
H. Willis	1	
Alex Harman	1	
Joseph C. Johnston	1	
E. P Tatum		1
Abr. Guest	1	
A. P. Clark		1
T. J. D. Young		1
T. B. Price	1	
A. D. King	1	
M. Thompson	1	
William Henderson		1
John Johnson	1	
W. M. Campbell	1	
C. B. Street		1
H. G. Street	1	
John Barton	1	
W. F. Malory	1	
N. McConnell		1
Tom Porter	1	
Totals	46	11[64]

Sustained by an overwhelming majority, the execution was set for 3 o'clock p.m. John F. May was appointed to choose the place of execution. A site one mile away from the camp was chosen "so as to be out of sight of the women and children." King further noted the behavior and attitude of Hickey during these proceedings, and indicated something of his own thinking regarding the decision.

> All this time the poor criminal appeared to make light of their proceedings, as if he thought it was a hoax. Twelve men who had drawn lots were selected as a firing squad to execute the prisoner. Six rifles were loaded with powder and ball and six loaded with powder only. This was done so that the men of the firing squad would not know who had a loaded rifle. The rifles were stacked and Dave Logan was selected as the one to reach into the stacked rifles and hand them one at a time to one of the firing squad. Young Logan was first blindfolded before handing out the rifles (although if he had not been blindfolded he could not have told which rifles were loaded with powder and ball.) Dave did not like the job he had been selected to do, but he went ahead and performed his duty.

The men who had been on the jury were excused from drawing lots, as we did not think it fair to them after having served as a jury and convicted Hickey, to require them to act on the firing squad.

What made matters worse for Hickey was that he had wanted to come with us on the trip but was not financially able to do so and Davis, who was one of those big, generous-hearted fellows, told Hickey he could go along with him and help out what he could in the driving of a wagon for him, so Hickey accepted and came with us. Most of us thought that Hickey had shown ingratitude in killing Davis, after Davis had been kind and generous enough to bring him along and board him. Then again if Hickey had shown any remorse of conscience after he had committed the crime, there is no doubt the jury would not have voted to execute him, as has already been said, Hickey seemed proud that he had killed Davis and throughout the trial he seemed to take it as a joke and he evidently never dreamed that he would be executed till just a short time before it was done.

The following drew the lots as the executioners or firing squad: James Logan, T. C. Jarnagin, Jacob Rogers, Tom Porter, William Holland, B. Phillips, T. B. Price, N. McConnell, William Henderson, John Barton, I. N. Ward and G. L. Patrick.

When we were ready to leave for the place of execution, Hickey requested Thomas Hackney to let him ride his mule. Now young Hackney has a fine mule and he had fed her scraps from the leftovers from the camp and she is rolling fat and very swift and Hackney surmised that Hickey would probably run off with his mule and possibly make his escape, so Tom refused the request.

Just before the hour of execution arrived, the Rev. Mr. Gwin delivered a lecture and offered up a prayer. Then Hickey was marched out to where his grave had been made, in his every-day garb.

When the place of execution was reached Hickey was placed on his knees near the open grave and blindfolded. A white piece of paper was pinned directly over his heart. The firing squad then took their positions and at the signal of the 'Ready, Aim, Fire,' the 12 rifles were discharged and Hickey fell back dead. Four of the rifle balls had penetrated his breast.[65]

The second portion of the King journal at the University of Arkansas does not include the information after the names with yea/nay votes. Two pages, however, are missing from what distinctly appears to be original pagination. Fortunately, King's record is corroborated by John F. May, one of the jurors and lieutenant for the company. May noted:

> Hickey threatened to whip a boy traveling with the company and persisted in his annoyance of the boy until Davis interfered. A fight ensued. Hickey killed Davis. During the night a council was held, a military court formed and Hickey pronounced guilty and sentenced to death. A dozen men were detailed to a firing squad—six with loaded guns and six with blanks. A piece of white paper was pinned over Hickey's heart and the order given to fire. No one knew who had shot him.[66]

The Articles of Association for the Clarksville Company (Appendix B) made no specific provision for dealing with murder. The articles deal primarily with outfitting requirements, duties of officers, property, and general demeanor; however, Article 11 was something of an elastic clause. It empowered the council of thirteen men "to try any member of the association for any offence he may commit, and punish as a majority of them may determine." The council had stepped aside for a twelve-man jury—solid American jurisprudence practiced on the trail. Article 24 was an oath signed by every member to abide by the rules as they were written in the document and "such other rules as the council may adopt." Justice was stern and quickly determined. A brief statement of what had transpired was attached to a stake in a conspicuous place along the road for all passersby to see. In this manner, Foreman says the emigrants had filed a formal report of their actions to other emigrants. Two emigrants in different parties who came along the Gila route six to eight weeks later mention the notice in their journals—Cornelius Cox from Pennsylvania and Lorenzo Aldrich from New York. Aldrich wrote:

> The sentence of his companions was carried out by drawing from the party two men who loaded six rifles with ball, and six with blank cartridges, the murderer was placed at a distance of twenty paces, and the shot entering the region of heart, he expired immediately. They were both from Arkansas and between 25 and 30 years of age—the precise cause of the quarrel is not known.[67]

The Arkansans reached the juncture of the Gila and Colorado rivers at different times and in small groups having purposely divided themselves along the Gila to facilitate watering and grazing. The Colorado River was reported as beautiful but having deep swift currents. By mid-October the army was operating a ferry at the Colorado, but these early groups crossed in ways of their own devising. Brownlee's group of four wagons and seventeen men were first and "pretty much in the advance of the main emigration." Brownlee said he had not seen the "other boys" in three weeks. This group was at the crossing for three days where "we were every minute expecting an attack from the Yuma Indians about 75 strong, armed with bows and arrows, spears and knives. We closely guarded our stock and property and showed the *horse-eaters* that we were ready to fight as they were to attack. I can assure you we were in a tight place. They were as stout, able-bodied men as I ever saw, and as straight as a rush."[68] The Yuma ate horse flesh and were hostile toward the emigrants. Brownlee wrote his brother that they safely crossed the Colorado in a wagon bed, but "others along with us were loosing packs and mules, and one man sunk 4 times when we reached him in time to save his life."[69]

When Woodruff's group came along some days later, they paid $1.25 to some Pope County Arkansans to take their packs over on a boat they had built. Meanwhile, the packers swam their mules across and Pierce lost his mule.[70] King's portion of the Clarksville company reached the juncture of the two rivers on September 28. "Some men were detailed to gather grass and some to build a raft to cross the father of waters in California." Gathering forage (grass and mesquite beans) for the desert which awaited them after crossing the Colorado was an important task at the crossing. King noted the hostile appearance of the Yuma and their troublesomeness. "They killed a man yesterday below here. They can steal and us looking at them all the

Send Women to Johnson County

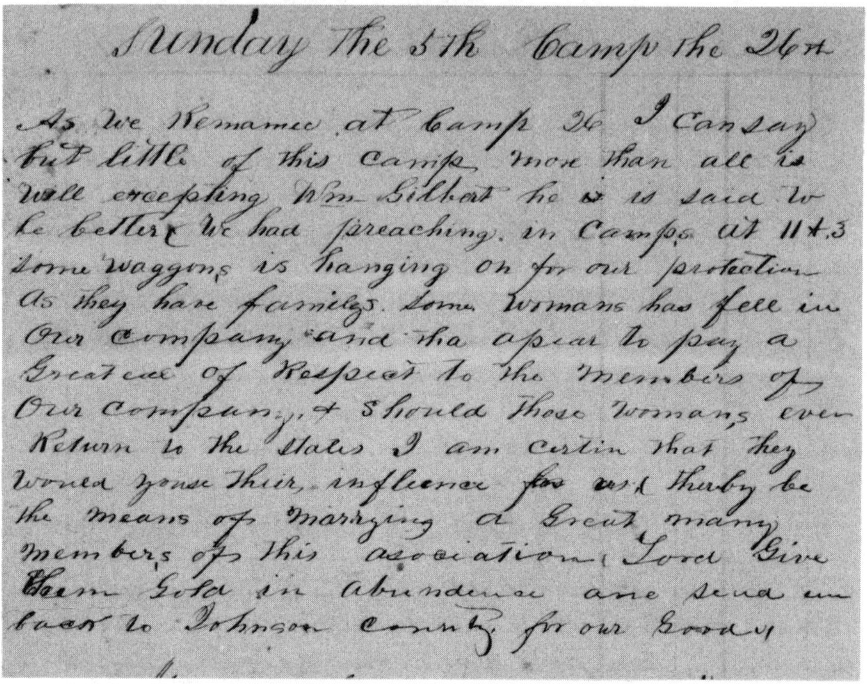
Sunday The 5th Camp the 26th
As we Remained at Camp 26 I Can say
but little of this camp more than all is
well excepting Wm Gilbert he is is said to
be better We had preaching in Camps at 11 & 3
Some waggons is hanging on for our protection
As they have familys Some womans has fell in
Our company and tha apear to pay a
Great deal of Respect to the members of
Our company, & Should those womans ever
Return to the States I am certin that they
would youse their influence for us & thereby be
the means of marrying a Great many
members of this association, Lord Give
them Gold in abundence and send em
back to Johnson County for our Good

from the journal of A. D. King, University of Arkansas Library—Special Collections.

Sunday the 5th Camp the 26th

As we remained at camp 26 I can say but little of this camp. More than all is well excepting Wm. Gilbert. He is said to be better. We had preaching in camp at 11 and 3. Some waggons is hanging on for our protection as they have familys. Some womans has fell in our company and they appear to pay a great deal of respect to the members of our company. And should those womans ever return to the states I am certain that they would youse their influence for us and thereby be the means of marrying a great many members of this association. Lord, give them gold in abundance and send 'em back to Johnson county for our good!

This note of levity from the original King journal, Illustration 2.

while. They were seen at all times of the day on a mound beyond the Colorado looking at us and our stock."

They had to move ten miles down the Colorado to the crossing and "commenced crossing" in the afternoon on the raft and "crossed til 2 o'clock at night." The Yumas were expert swimmers and were hired to help while "men who were not expert water men were engaged in cooking."[71]

The Conway family did not reach the Colorado River until October 24. The manner in which this date is so precisely pinpointed is interesting. Lieutenant Cave Johnson Couts was in charge of a military escort for Lt. A. W. Whipple's survey party for the Mexican boundary. Couts had earlier served at Fort Gibson and had friends at Tallequah and Fort Smith. He left San Diego on September 11 bound for the Colorado-Gila Rivers.[72] He encountered Brownlee's mess and J. J. Simmons advance Clarksville group about 75 miles east of San Diego.[73] He continued to meet numerous Arkansans, so many that he wrote in his diary: "If any are left in Arkansas, it is more numerously populated than I had anticipated." They bombarded him for informtion regarding the route and seeking advice as to whether they could make it on wagons. But these Arkansans also shared information about his friends back in Arkansas and about all those who were going to California. Young Mary Conway must have always been mentioned and Lt. Couts greatly anticipated the meeting. For three weeks he saved her a bottle of molasses and a lump of sugar. Finally the Conways and their ten children, including seventeen-year-old Mary, "an angel in such wilds," arrived at the Colorado on October 24 and remained until the 28th. On two evenings Mary and her mother "dined" with Lt. Couts.[74] The Conways were able to cross on the army operated ferry.

Having crossed the Colorado, the Arkansas emigrants then faced the long-dreaded ninety-mile trek across the desert in California where no water and no grass were expected. An earlier emigrant called this the "Sahara of the Americas."[75] The crossing was made in three to five days, the weary men and animals traveling in the early evening and late night. Temperatures ranged from 100 to 120 degrees Fahrenheit and combined with the sand and hot winds produced great thirst. J. J. Simmons' Clarksville group of twelve wagons moved ahead after crossing the Colorado and were in San Diego on October 12. Simmons described their ordeal:

> The balance of the company were left behind on the edge of the great desert. They were waiting to recruit their teams and to decide whether they would abandon their wagons. The party that came through suffered much from fatigue and thirst being on the desert 2 days and 2 nights, without water or grazing for their cattle. This distance was 99 miles and the sand in many places on the route was dry and loose, the cattle sinking into it to their knees.[76]

Simmons reported the loss of only one of his ten oxen. After meeting Lt. Couts beyond the desert and learning the road, water and grazing were good to San Francisco, his group was jubilant about making it with their wagons.

Woodruff wrote that his group fed the mules on mesquite beans and

---

The map on the following page is from the journal of A. D. King, University of Arkansas Library—Special Collections.

A Map of the
San Angeles
Mision de San Gabriel
Indian vilage
San monica
Sn Deigo
Port of Sn Deigo

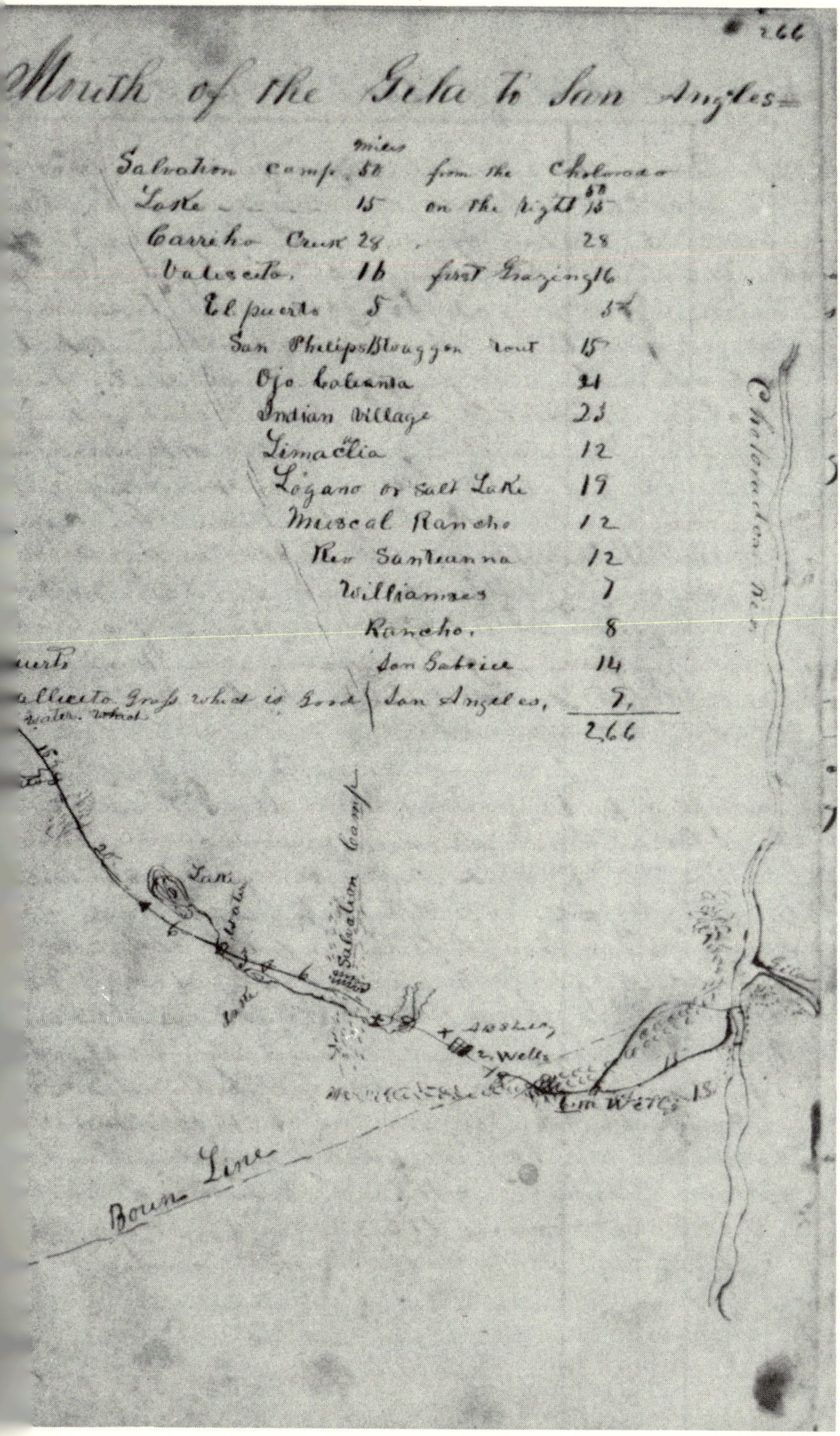

Mouth of the Gila to San Angeles

	miles		
Salvation camp	50	from the Cholorado	
Lake	15	on the right	50 15
Carriso Creek	28		28
Valiscito	16	first Grazing	16
El puerto	5		5
San Philips Bloaggon rout			15
Ojo Calienta			21
Indian Village			23
Limaclia			12
Logano or Salt Lake			19
Muscal Rancho			12
Rio Santeanna			12
Williamses			7
Rancho			8
San Gabriel			14
San Angeles			7
			266

found a water hole fifteen miles out which "yielded about a pailful every fifteen minutes."[77] Again loads and wagons were readjusted and more items were abandoned on the desert. The stench of dead animals in the hot air only heightened the fear they felt for the welfare of their own animals. As if all this were not enough reason for hopeless despair, one of the Clarksville groups had three bad cases of fever. Then forty-five miles beyond the first water hole or sixty miles out, they came upon an unexpected providence—New River. It was so called "from the cause of no water being there previously." The fall wet season accounted for the water and grass. This was an unexpected blessing, and the emigrants appropriately named it Camp Salvation. Unfortunately, Alfred Shelby and W. B. Howell, two of the sick men, died only hours before Salvation was reached.[78] King's map shows Camp Salvation and the graves (the x marks) of Shelby and Howell. The Clarksville group laid by at this oasis until October 12 enjoying the damp atmosphere, the cool mornings, and the cold nights. The weary stock recruited on the new grass and lolled about in the water.

After negotiating thirty more miles of desert they came to Carrizo Creek and then to the Mexican towns of Vallecito with its sulphur water and San Felipe where good water, grass, and fresh produce gave them respite from their harrowing desert experience. Brownlee said of their camp at San Felipe on September 16, "This is the first good encampment, we may lay by two days. . . . I am in good health—never better. Three pints of coffee at one meal, with bread and meat in proportion looks as if I enjoy myself after passing the great Desert. . . . Our teams are very tired. Clark and myself work six mules with a light wagon, carrying about 300 pounds load. After resting a few days to recruit, we can go as fast as the pack mules. No set of men were ever so provident as we have been—that is, have suffered in no way—got nothing stolen."[79] Compare the 300 pounds with 2,500 pounds wagon loads with which they had begun! Just beyond San Felipe at Warners Ranch the road forked, one direction led to San Diego (80 miles) and the other to San Francisco (700 miles). Some opted to go to San Diego and thence by ship to San Francisco which was risky "as the monthly steamer is always crowded."[80] Woodruff's group decided to ship from San Diego and they "packed up and took a mule trail, which cut off some thirty miles."[81] Brownlee continued with his wagons to San Francisco. Woodruff wrote from San Diego on October 4 of his arrival; he had located the other Arkansas boys and reported McVicar and Brownlee were the only ones in his party who kept their wagons all the way.[82] The Little Rock boys were in the diggings at Agua Fria on November 15, seven months after leaving Fort Smith.[83]

King described the experiences of the Clarksville group after making the desert. At San Felipe. they feasted on melons, peaches, and corn. Moving on overland toward Los Angeles, they came to Warner's Ranch where grapes and peaches (at high prices) and horses and cattle were plentiful. At Warner's, Mr. Johnson, D. A. Jamison, David McLean and others left with their wagons for San Diego to ship. The mule wagons set out the day before the ox teams. The others continued on through some Mexican villages where they found plums, wheat, corn and pumpkins. On October 29, they came to William Ranch in a "fine valley of land." William had an impressive "herd of 20,000 cattle and 1,500 brood mares and other stock and grazing horses besides." They laid by two days and their animals recruited on fields of fine oats. The fall rains had begun. On November 2 they camped on the outskirts of Los Angeles and went to the city, "the largest place I have seen in Mexico or Calif." They found J. May who had been in the advance party and spent time buying and trading. "J. May's large wagon sold for $135, one of Roger's wagons for $125, and Daniel Henry's for $90. All of which were well sold." The Arkansans were trying to sell and buy oxen—"selling the old for California cattle which are much larger than the American cattle." They spent a week in Los Angeles purchasing new teams and on November 10 began their march to Stockton and the gold fields.[84]

The Arkansans caught their first glimpse of the Pacific within ten hours travel from Los Angeles. About thirty miles from the city, the rains came and for four days they were unable to travel. In this interval, they were able to enjoy bear, which were very numerous, and deer. As a consequence of taking a wrong road, they went twenty miles down a mountain and camped on the shores of the Pacific. All day they had "heard her roar and groan as though she was in trouble about something," and that night "the roar and groan of the Pacific prevented some of the company from sleeping." King pronounced the Pacific "a great ocean" with crooked rocky shores and many shells and sea fowls. They waited for low tide and "in three places we went on the beach where the water is over in high tide." This must have been an exhilarating experience for landlubbers. They continued journeying along the shores of the Pacific until the 25th of November, and then turned northeastward toward Stockton. The next three weeks were spent in rain, sleet and hail storms, with ten inches of water in the wagon beds on occasion, and in a vain three-day search for all the horses which broke loose. On December 16 they found a letter left by William Collier instructing them to change their course from Stockton to Santa Cruz which was forty miles back east on the coast. No clue is given as to why they turned away from the gold fields. Probably they determined to wait out the wet season somewhere other than the mines. More days of rain and impeded travel and finally on December 11, their destination, Santa Cruz, California. For this group it had been eight months to the diggings rather than the projected six. Ironically they had begun their trip in April in the muddy quagmires of the Indian territory and arrived in the California wet season to endure torrential rains, flood and impeded travel.

El Dorado had been reached—now to find the gold.

Yuma Indian

by Sandford C. Faulkner, from the J. N. Heiskell Collection, University of Arkansas at Little Rock Library Archives.

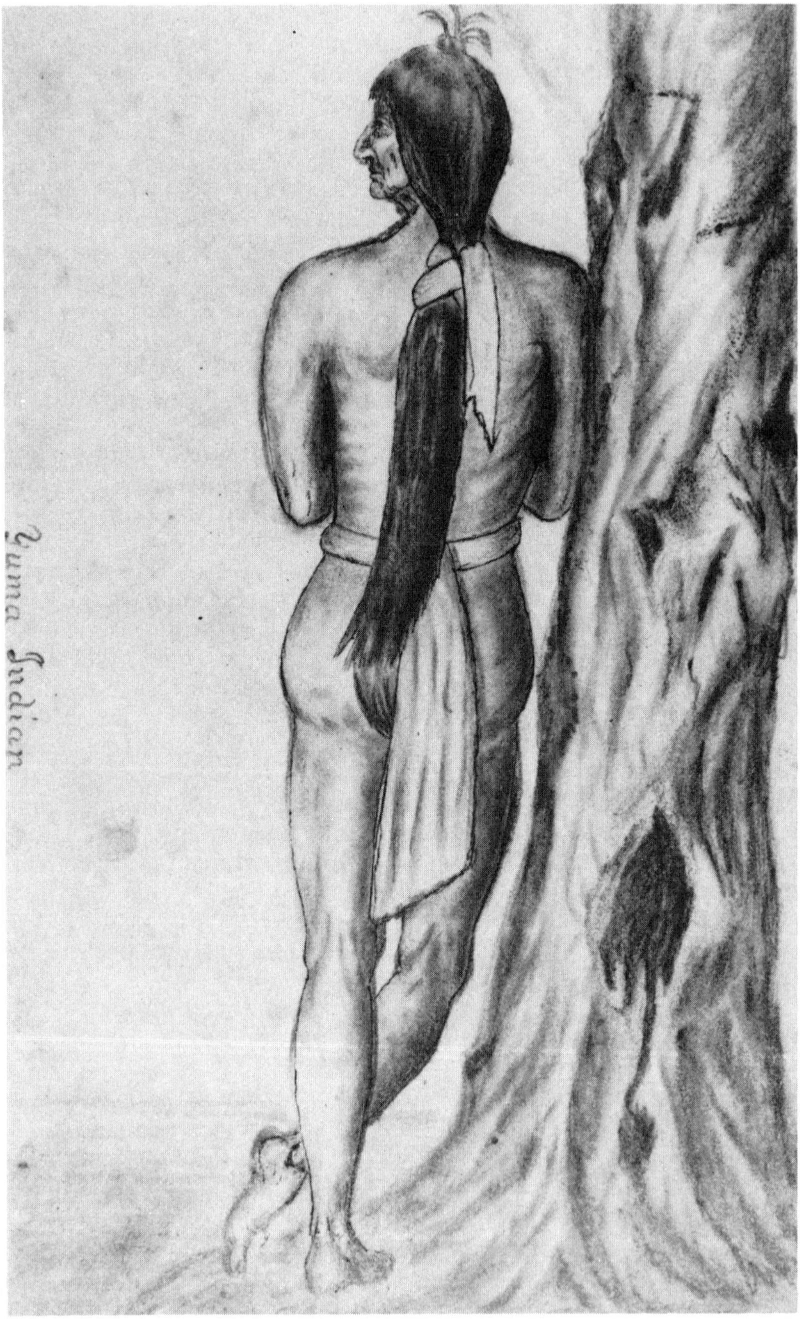

C H A P T E R V

The Cherokee Trail: Arkansas along the Northern Route

"And shall we Cherokee not take advantage of the times and be found trying to get to this glorious country?"

At the same time these Arkansans were experiencing the Fort Smith route, citizens of Fayetteville and northwest Arkansas in combination with the Cherokees and under the leadership of Lewis Evans pursued their more northern route from Fort Gibson to Grand River to the Verdigris, to Salt Fork, to Fort Mann, to Pueblo, to Fort Bridger, and on to the city of the Great Salt Lake. Arkansans trekked this route, later to become known as the Cherokee Trail, in 1849, 1850, and 1851. The Cherokees, like other emigrants, were letter writers, keeping their families, friends, and the *Cherokee Advocate* informed of their experiences. Their letters record their share of "elephants" along the trail and tell us much about Arkansans from the more northwestern portion of the state.

The Fayetteville Company and the Cherokee Company planned to rendezvous at the Grand Saline where it crossed Grand (Neosho) River in the Cherokee Nation on April 21, 1849.[1] The company was to organize and elect officers at that point. Over one hundred gold seekers left Fayetteville on April 20 and proceeded to the Grand Saline where they were joined by a small number of Cherokee from Tahlequah on April 23, which increased their number to 130 members, forty wagons and ten times as many oxen, horses and mules. Lewis Evans of Evansville, Arkansas, and one-time sheriff of Washington County, was elected captain; Thomas Tyner of Washington County was elected first lieutenant; Peter Mankin of Washington County was elected second lieutenant; James S. Vann of the Cherokee Nation and former editor of the *Cherokee Advocate* was elected secretary; Martin Matthew Schrimsher of the Cherokee Nation and maternal grandfather of Will Rogers, was elected commissary. The group was officially named the Washington County Gold Mining Company, but was called the Captain Lewis Evans' Company.[2] The names of 126 persons printed in the *Cherokee Advocate* were listed by county: 86 from Washington County, 10 from Benton County, 8 from Madison County, 15 from the Cherokee Nation, plus 5 slaves owned by the Cherokee, and 2 emigrants from Tennessee. Three of the Arkansans were women, Caroline Hail, wife of lssac Hail and the Freyschlag sisters, Hermina and Barbara, from Fayetteville. Three male Freyschlags were emigrants: Herman was the brother of these young women. Foreman recounts that Hermina was lately from Berlin and art and and music teacher at Miss Sophia Sawyer's girl's seminary at Fayetteville. Older citizens in Fayetteville related to Foreman that the Freyschlag sisters "walked all the way to California."[3]

The Evans' Company left Grand River on April 24 and one of the Cherokees who signed "Oo-cha-loo-ta" wrote on April 29 from Grand Prairie:

> Mr. Editor: For the gratification of those citizens of your country who have friends in this company on their way to the land of gold, I have snatched a few moments from camp duties to announce the safe progress for ninety miles from Tahlequah. . . . The company left the rendezvous on the twenty-fourth. The first day's travel was very difficult, owing to the heavy fall of rain a few days previous. The company had quite a foretaste of what they will have to encounter and overcome before they arrive at the auriferous mountains of the Sierra Nevada. Bogging down and prizing out of wagons was the business of the first day. Since, we have traveled and gotten along with less miring down, making short drives, which we did to enable a wagon to join the caravan which did not arrive at the rendezvous in time to leave with the company. We are all together now. From the appearance of the face of the country, and from reports of our contemplated route [which] we have had since we arrived here, [and] the yellow fever having broken out afresh with some of the company, the glittering fortunes which they are determined to accumulate are even now snuffed upon the western prairies. The laws which regulate [the company], and by which the company are governed, are few but good, though susceptible of improvement.
>
> The Cherokee portion of the company are thrown into a division together, and that hereditary disposition of clannishness, derived from their ancestry, is distinctly shown now. They are determined to stick together through weal or woe. Although they have left their country for a few months, nevertheless the fire of patriotic love burns with continued intensity of fervor for the future welfare, progress, and onward destiny of their country . . .[4]

They reached the Santa Fe Trail May 12 at a point on Turkey Creek about twenty-five miles east of the Little Arkansas River, and one of the company carved a large stone marker and placed it at the juncture of the two trails. On the stone was carved, "To Fayetteville, Arkansas, three hundred miles—Captain Evans' California Company, May 12, 1849." How we come to know this specific information illustrates well the communication system which developed on the trails to California. Eager to inform those back home about themselves, the emigrants devised novel means to transmit messages to those who would come after them along the trail. Using stones, bleached white animal bones, tree stumps, boards, oilcloth wrapped paper, and whatever surface presented itself, the emigrants left messages hoping that they would find their way to the intended destination. Foreman states they "gave their names, told of their health, of occurrences on the way, made helpful suggestions based on their experience, gave warnings of Indians to be guarded against, of bad places in the roads to be avoided, sent personal messages to be passed along to friends and relatives. This medium, extending for thousands of miles, became a sort of combination bulletin board, newspaper and post office that tempted travelers to constantly stop and read, and disseminated a great variety and volume of information, much of which was further broadcast by the press back home."[5]

Judge Hiram Davis of Fayetteville, a member of the Evans' Company, was one of the innovaters of this system when he placed a letter addressed to the editors of the *Daily Missouri Republican* at the base of the Arkansas stone monument. Other letters were added and the Arkansas marker became a "station" in the communication system. The series of messages were as follows:

Turkey Creek, May 25, 1849

Messrs. Editors: On our arrival this evening at this encampment on the Santa Fe route, two hundred and fifteen miles west of Independence, our attention was unexpectedly engaged by a monument, which bears upon its face the object for which it was erected. At the base of this rock we discovered a communication neatly folded in pasteboard and then in a piece of oilcloth, which corresponded to the inscription upon the monument, and which is intended for publication in your paper. The communication was written, it appears, by Mr. H. Davis in connection with the California company, who were the first to select and travel the route from Fayetteville, in Arkansas, to this point, the distance of which they set down at three hundred miles. Hoping that through the kind office of some returning traveler you may receive a communication thus thrown by the wayside upon the plains, so evidently calculated to the interest the friends of the emigrants in general and of Mr. Evans's company especially, we have concluded to run the same risk of trying to get to you, and through you to the public, a short letter of like nature.

"TO THE FIRST PERSON GOING TO MISSOURI: This letter will explain itself. I leave it at the foot of the 'Arkansas Monument,' hoping that while you curiously inspect the stranger who has planted himself in the forks of the road, you will find these lines and have the kindness to take them with you. If you go to St. Louis, hand them personally to Colonel Chambers; if not, lodge it in the first post office in Missouri. H. D."

"TO THE EDITORS OF THE REPUBLICAN: By giving a place in your journal to the following items, should this scroll fall into your hands, they will be read with much interest by many of your subscribers in Arkansas. Captain Evans's company of forty wagons and one hundred and thirty persons, mostly from WashingtonCounty, Arkansas, set out for California the twentieth of April, 1849, and took a route never before traveled. The company crossed the

Neosho at the Grand Saline, Cherokee Nation, and proceeded up between the two Verdigris, almost a due northwest course, until it struck the great road from Independence to Santa Fe, the estimated distance being about three hundred miles. No wagon had ever traveled this route before, and it was considered impracticable by some; but a better wagon road than we have made, I will venture to say, cannot be found west of the Mississippi river. The travel was on the divide between the Verdigris and what some call the West Fork, which we found to be exclusively of high, dry, rolling prairie slopes, offering no obstacles whatever to any number of wagons. The course leads over the headwaters of the two streams named, and [of the] Neosho, or Grand, river, which afford abundant water, timber, and grass at intervals of five and fifteen miles. Even at this early season (May 12, 1849) we have had plenty of excellent grass, and our stock are improving every day. At the place we struck the Santa Fe road, we found a grave where some hapless traveler reposes in the bosom of this beautifully carpeted land-ocean. Here we obtained a large stone and planted it in the fork of the road; and one of our cunning workmen cut these letters upon it, 'To Fayetteville, Arkansas, three hundred miles—Captain Evans's California Company, May 12, 1849,' to apprise the prairie traveler of a new road. From the best information, we struck the Santa Fe road some twenty-five miles east of Little Arkansas. On our route saw some deer, many antelopes, but no buffaloes; but from many indications, we know there are multitudes of them in this region at certain seasons. We had thought of continuing our route and course, and strike the Oregon road at the forks of the Platte, but find the grass will not justify it. Consequently we go directly to Bent's Fort, and thence take the nearest and best route for El Dorado. The company are in fine spirits and in good health—not one sick at this time. Nothing else could be expected of men who cook their food with buffalo chips, snuff the pure, bland breezes of the boundless plains, and [are] braced up with the lively hope that all the wildest dreams e'er wove in fancy's loom of ingots of gold and bags of dollars, will be realized beyond the Cordillera.

H. Davis"[6]

One of the Cherokees in the company, O. W. Lipe, wrote from the Grand Prairie on May 27 and gave more details about the experiences of the Evans' company.

> The greatest difficulty we had to the Santa Fe road was soft prairie in consequence of the rains. We arrived at the Santa Fe road on Sunday, the thirteenth instant, in twenty-two days from home. A question arose at that point what route to pursue—whether we should continue our northwest course to intersect the Oregon road at the South Fork of the Platte, or take the Santa Fe road to Fort Bent. The latter route carried; so we are now on a great highway and can travel twenty miles per day with ease.[7]

As Davis commented in his above letter, the decision regarding the route hinged on fear that there would not be enough grass on the Oregon road because more emigrants were using that route.[8] Lipe's expectation of an increased travel rate from twelve or thirteen miles per day to twenty was not to materialize due to another problem which caused extensive delays—loss of cattle. Note that he attributes the running away of the cattle to the presence of so many cattle carcasses strewn along the way.

> The first night on this road, the company lost fifteen head of oxen; and two nights after, on the Little Arkansas, forty-five more ran off; which has detained [us] now five days. Of the cattle, only twenty-one head have been found. Eight men are still in pursuit, which is the cause of detention, as the train delays for the purpose of those men to overtake us. How much more we shall be detained for those men to overtake us I cannot say, and have no idea that they will find any of the oxen....
>
> Among the oxen lost, Schrimsher has one yoke of steers he got of Delano; and his mate, George Keys, lost one yoke.... They started towards home, and probably will reach home if they are not stopped....
>
> Our cattle have done finely, and the cows give a good quantity of milk. I find cows very useful on the road and very little trouble. I think it would be difficult to leave them behind, as they will follow. I have taken off the yoke and confine them together by a pole and straps. As a general cause for the cattle running off after we took this road, is the immense number of carcasses of cattle which have died on this road, which seem to have died last winter.[9]

In addition to the strewn carcasses, he noted that wagons and tons of irons of every description were scattered along the road. "It seems as if the wagons are first left, and afterwards burned for fuel by others passing."

Lipe's letter also spoke of the good health and appetite of the group. "And above all, let me inform you that I am a great cook; beat the company baking biscuits." This was an accomplishment in that they were using buffalo chips for fuel. He indicated that all the Cherokees except Potter had killed buffaloes. "Any amount of buffalo calves could be caught, Daniel Gunter caught two when we first got to them, kept them tied all night, and then let them go in the morning. George Keys caught a young elk as we arrived at this encampment and will probably let it go in the morning." Other comments of general interest included the absence of Plains Indians and the unseasonably cold weather. "The weather was so cold for several days past that people travel wrapped up in overcoats and blankets." A wagon from Missouri with four persons joined the Evans' party at the Little Arkansas increasing the caravan to forty-one wagons and one hundred and thirty-four people.[10]

Eight days later on June 4 when they were forty miles west of Fort Mann, Lipe wrote another letter that he sent east by a trader bound for Independence. "The men who were in pursuit of lost oxen have returned without any. The whole number lost is forty-eight." Lipe felt the oxen were returning to the Creek Nation. This was an enormous loss and such news undoubtedly alarmed the folks back home. Lipe was correct about the animals returning home. They were seen at Elijah Hick's in the Cherokee Nation.[11]

From Fort Mann the Evans' company traveled to Pueblo where severe dissension resulted in a division of the company and the return of four wagons to Tahlequah and Arkansas. D. M. Gunter wrote his brother in Tahlequah of the troubles at Pueblo on June 22. When they arrived at Pueblo, at the base of the Rocky Mountains, some trappers convinced about thirty of them that they could not cross the mountains with their wagons. Consequently these thirty sold their wagons and what provisions they could not carry "at great sacrifice, one wagon selling as low as five dollars." These trappers then sold the emigrants mules for packing "at a very high price." Gunter noted that he refused to exchange his wagon and team for a mule and seven packsaddles. The packing part of the company included Gunter and James S. Vann, and they employed a guide by the name of Owens at seven dollars a day to get them to the "diggins" in sixty days.[12] The packers planned to go directly west across the mountains and make their way to Fort Bridger where they would pick up the Oregon and California Trail to Salt Lake City. The balance of the company led by Evans would continue with their wagons and follow a more northernly route from Pueblo, past future Denver, and thence to Fort Bridger. They crossed the South Platte, the Laramie, the North Park, the North Platte, and the Green River south of South Pass and then intersected the Oregon-California Trail. The Evans party were the first forty-niners to travel this route, and as a consequence it became known as the Cherokee Trail.[13]

The hardships of the packers are hinted at in this passage of a letter from one of the Cherokee packers, George W. Keys, which he wrote to this brother from "City of the Salt Lake, July 25, 1849."

> We have been about one month coming from Pueblo to this place, a distance of about one hundred miles over one of the worst roads in the West, with several large rivers to cross (we had them to swim and raft). In crossing Green river, there was one of the company drowned; he was from Benton, Arkansas, by the name of Garvin. Some of the party lost their guns, provisions, money, and saddles, which placed them in rather an awkward situation—one hundred miles from any settlement, with neither provisions, saddles, nor guns. After getting to Bridger's Fort, they fixed themselves up and have got to this place, where we intend to rest ourselves and recruit our animals, etc.[14]

Garvin could be James H. Gurin in the list of men from Benton County. O. W. Lipe in relating the same information to his wife used the name Garvin and added that he was sick and crossing the river on a raft made out of skins. The raft, Garvin, and all the baggage sank. The raft was made of skins because there was no timber. The Cherokee with the packers sustained no damage.[15]

In addition to these harrowing experiences, the packers learned upon reaching the crowded northern road that many of the gold seekers had died with cholera on the Platte. Among those dead were nine of fifteen Cherokees who had traveled the Independence route with Doctor Jeter Thompson. Among the Cherokee dead were Samuel Bell, Brice Martin and William Parks.[16] More will be said about this group later.

Back home in Arkansas the folks were reading about the terrible suffering along the northern route. The *Gazette* reprinted articles from the *St. Louis Republican* which were based on reports made by its correspondent at Fort Laramie. Epidemic cholera, shallow unmarked graves, dead animals, abandoned wagons and goods, and shortage of grass were always main items in these reports. The following is a gruesome example:

Scores have been passed which have no identity placed over their remains, and have not been enumerated in any catalogue. The graves that I saw had been dug up by the wolves; the bodies dragged to the surface, and the limbs and fragments scattered all around."[17]

An excerpt from a letter written by a U.S. Army officer at Fort Laramie was published in the same column as the above quote. It criticized the illustrious Senator Thomas Hart Benton from Missouri who was advocating the northern route for a national road to the Pacific. The officer considered this a sad mistake on Benton's part and urged southern congressmen to take advantage of the Memphis Convention to exert pressure on the national government to choose a more southern route.

> Fort Laramie, Aug. 2, 1849
>
> "I am convinced that a more southern route than this must be found to Calif. But people must believe what such a man as Benton says, without thinking about it; until it is proved by sad experience not be the route. . . . I regret that the southern leading politicians have not exerted themselves with the same industry that Mr. Benton has during the past summer, to have the Pacific route run from Memphis, or somewhere near that point. . . . I hope the members of the Memphis Convention will use all their exertions and be successful, and thus convince Mr. Benton that he is mistaken, at least for once.[18]

The Arkansas newspapers in the winter of 1849 and the spring of 1850 contain numerous editorials on the deplorable conditions of the northern route. These criticisms further served to recommend the southern route from Fort Smith to the 1850 emigrants. This will be further discussed in conjunction with the material on the 1850 emigrants.

The Evans' wagon party arrived at Salt Lake City about mid August. They too had lost one of their company, Thorp (Tharp?) from White river. It was noted that he "died from an old disease." After crossing the North Platte there was much sickness in the company, purportedly "mountain fever." Of the Cherokees, Lipe, Gunter and Schrimsher had been ill but were recovered. Lipe's letter indicated that the Cherokees "quit the company and went ahead" when they reached the Independence Road.[19]

When the packers arrived in Salt Lake City on July 24, they found the Mormons in the midst of a celebration commemorating the second anniversary of the entrance of the Mormon pioneers into the valley. The emigrants were completely unprepared to find such a civilized oasis in a spot so removed from "the States." They were impressed with the color and pageantry of the celebration, with the bountiful and varied foodstuffs, with the abundant provisions, and with the tremendous achievements of the Mormons in two years time. Repeatedly in diaries and letters from emigrants all over America, the Mormon accomplishment and the wonderful experience of relief and restoration which the weary gold seekers enjoyed while in Salt Lake City are recounted, The 1850 emigrants were to find the cost for these refreshments more dear. Perhaps a twist of fateful retribution for past grievances had a part in the Mormon pricing policies. Nonetheless, as Foreman states, "the California emigrants was a boon to the Mormons" who were able to market their excess produce, and the Mormons were a boost for the comfort and morale of the passing emigrants.

George Keys' letter to his brother the day after the celebration conveys something of the excitement and pageantry. Note the invitation to the dinner feast was extended to the emigrants.

> "City of the Salt Lake, July 25, 1849
>
> "Dear Brother: I avail myself of the present opportunity of writing you a few lines to let you know we are all well at present. We got here yesterday about ten o'clock, where we found five or six thousand Mormon inhabitants assembled at a feast or celebration, where they had met to celebrate the day of their arrival in the valley of the Great Salt Lake two years ago. This performance was very much like one of our temperance meetings. They marched around their shed several times, the band of music in front; then twenty-four young men in white uniform with swords in their hands; then came forty-four young ladies in white, followed by twelve old men bearing flags or banners. After speaking, singing, and parading around, firing cannon, etc., they sat down to as fine a dinner as you would find anywhere, which to us was not bad to take.[20]

The luxurious foods mentioned by the emigrants included beans, peas, potatoes, watermelons, radishes, beets, flour, milk, and butter. After three months of trail fare which included no fresh fruits or vegetables, it must have come as a welcome respite.

Salt Lake City marked another major decision point about whether to pack or to take wagons and which route was to be followed. Key's letter noted they were 800 miles from Sutter's Fort, and, incredibly, they hoped to reach there by September 1. Facing desert, loads had to be lightened; and emigrants often traded their heavy wagons for light ones built by the Mormons. Three routes were open to the emigrant. They could turn north on the Salt Lake Cutoff, going around the lake and intersecting the main route again at the two tall spires of rock known as Cathedral Rocks, and thence to the Humbolt. Or another choice was due west from Salt Lake via Hastings' Cutoff (1846), across the Salt Lake Desert and then to the Humbolt River. This route was not recommended by the Mormons as the season grew late and snow became a real threat on the northern routes, was southwest along the Virgin and Mojave rivers to Los Angeles. The Mormons wanted the emigrants to remain six weeks, work in the wheat harvest while their teams recruited, and then continue with a Mormon guide along the southwest route. One of the Cherokees, O. W. Lipe, having chosen the due west course and suspicious of the Mormons wrote: "There is no road from here to the [southwest] route; the emigrants will have to make their road and pay a Mormon one thousand dollars to show their way."[21] The members of the Evans' group divided taking the first two choices, arriving in California at different times as later letters indicate. The Mormons reported good news from California to the gold seekers, maintaining that the gold was abundant and that "any man that will work can make from one to three hundred dollars per day." Such news spurred some of the emigrants onward. Lipe remarked that some of them "leave here afoot, with provisions on their backs; others start with a pack or an ox or a cow. So you find some perfectly afoot. What a struggle for gold!"[22]

Westward from Salt Lake, the Arkansas and Cherokee emigrants were to encounter their worst elephant. Reaching the Humbolt River, they traveled some 250 miles along its banks in desert sun, wind and dust. At the Humbolt Sink, where the river mysteriously ended, the emigrants faced another decision about route. They could turn west and take the Truckee River route and cross the Sierra Mountains into California or continue south from the Sink and pick up the Carson River route and cross the mountains to the gold fields. Both routes had desert, canyons and mountains to traverse. Both took the gold seekers to Sutter's Fort or the new town of Sacramento which had grown up nearby. A third alternative was Lassen's Cutoff (1848) which left the Humbolt River soon after reaching it and made its way far north almost to Oregon before cutting back south to Lassen's California ranch. Cherokees took all three routes.

Early snows and a week long blizzard complicated these routes and cost

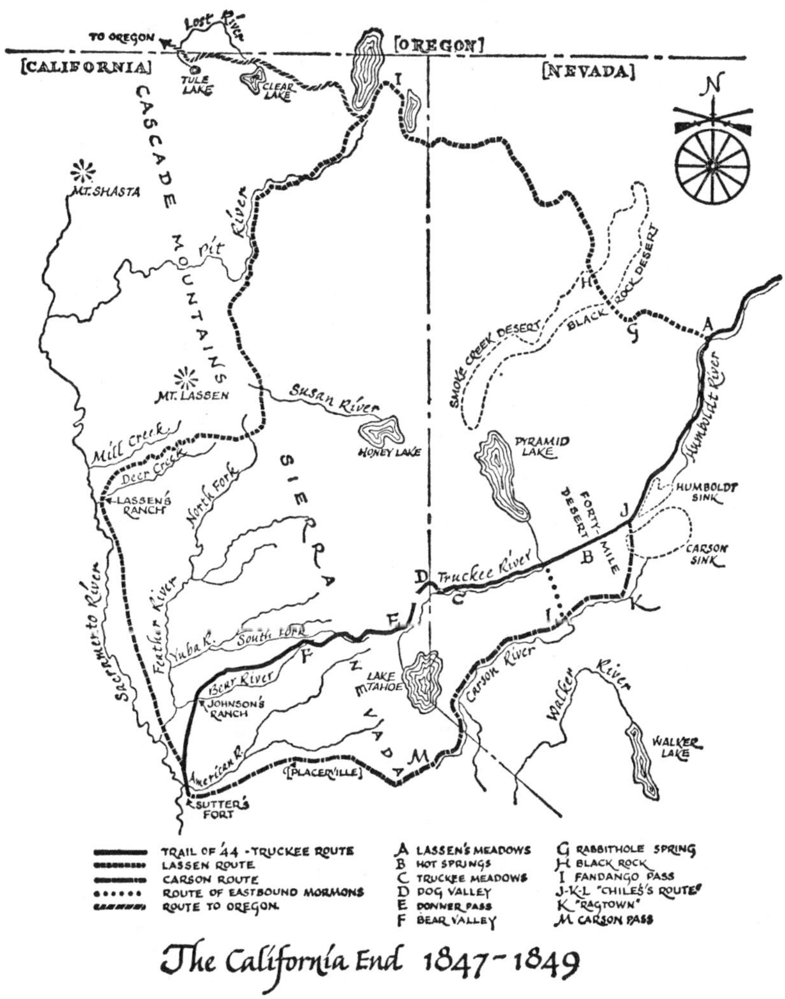

Truckee-Carson Routes

the emigrants equipment, animals, food, and for many, their lives. Reports of suffering and stranded emigrants and starving teams were received in California prompting the military governor, General Persifor F. Smith, to organize a relief party for emigrants on the Truckee and Carson routes in late August. A sum of $100,000 was authorized for relief purposes and command was assigned to Major D. H. Rucker. By mid-September the relief was ready when news of the emigrant suffering on the Lassen route caused Rucker to assign John H. Peoples to relief on the Lassen route while he took charge on the Truckee-Carson routes. Peoples was a civilian newspaperman from Texas who came to California via a southern route. Both men worked untiringly and heroically even when ill with mountain fever to aid the emigrants.[23] Rucker had been stationed at Fort Gibson and knew many of the Cherokees. He selected Senora Hicks of the Thompson party to help render aid and advice to the emigrants.[24]

The rescue parties began going out in mid-September. By early October heavy snows and rains made the roads impassable and buried wagons and animals like in mud. Then in late October the week-long blizzard came and covered the grass causing the mules and oxen to starve and freeze to death and leaving the emigrants stranded. Cherokee Jonathan Mulkey wrote home about his rescue by Senora Hicks:

> April 13, 1850
>
> We arrived here last December in the wet season with loss of all our outfit but two oxen; horses and cattle perished in the boggy soil. You have no doubt heard of the great mortality suffered by our emigrant party. James and myself had all the incipient stages of that dreadful malady, cholera, which so weakened us that we had to quit our own train and join another in order to procure the services of a wagoner, which took place on the 5th of August last; and we have never seen any of them since except Senora Hicks, who was employed by Major Rucker, of U.S.A., to meet the near emigrants, to afford the most unfortunate of them aid in getting through; we have never seen him since his return from that service; but we have no doubt of his doing well, as Major Rucker showed a great interest in his behalf. I had a long spell of scurvy which came near ending my life.[25]

Rucker's final letter in the series of rescue reports was December 1, 1849. It included this pathetic description:

> This afternoon Mr. Peoples came in with his party, hauling in the last of those whom he had left in the snow here his mules died, and who were in the rear of the emigration. A more pitiable sight I never beheld as they were brought into camp; there were cripples from scurvy and other diseases, women prostrated by weakness, and children who could not move a limb, all helpless as infants; in advance of them were men on mules who had to be lifted on and off the animals, so entirely disabled had they become from the effects of the scurvy.[26]

The next information about Evans and the group which remained with him is in a letter from Sacramento City from one of the Cherokees, Joseph Sturdivant, to his wife Ary.

"Sacramento City, November 20, 1849

"DEAR WIFE: I take this opportunity of letting you know where I am, and that I am well at this time but have been sick for the last three weeks. I have had a spell of sickness since I arrived here. Our company have all been sick but Carter; consequently we have not worked much. We have worked only two weeks, in which time we made some seven hundred dollars. McCay and Carter are now in the mines at work, and Williams and myself started this morning with four pack mules with provisions to them. They are about sixty miles from this place. I am now in camp with William Shores and Captain Evans, who arrived here about three weeks ago with about half of the Arkansas teams. The balance of the train (and my team with them) took the northern route on Humbolt river. I learn from Lieutenant Rucker, who has been with supplies to relieve the emigrants, that they had been caught in a snowstorm and have lost all the stock that belonged to the train. The government lost all of their mules and everything else except some beef cattle. So my team, wagon, and everything else are gone to the d——l, though small losses here are matters of small consequence, as money is very plentiful . . . I have got time to write but a short letter. I will write to you again in February, at which time I will set the time for leaving here. Judge Davis, who lives in Fayetteville, will leave here in February for home. By him I will send eight hundred or a thousand dollars, so that you can buy you a negro man. I sent you a trunk and buffalo rug from Pueblo, by Mr. Tiner (that lives up near Fayetteville); but have since learned that they were all killed by the Indians . . .

Joseph A. Sturdivant[27]

From this we learn that Evans and about half the party arrived around November 1, and the other half took the Lassen or more northern route. An interesting citation in one of the most famous of the 1849 journals of the northern route mentions the Cherokees. J. Goldsborough Bruff, captain of the Washington City Company kept a thorough diary and sketchbook. His company took the Lassen cutoff, and he cited in his diary on November 1 at his camp thirty-five miles above Lassen's that "some Cherokee" were searching for their lost cattle.

There were several other parties of Cherokees who went to the gold fields in 1849, and letters from them give a little more information about the Evans company. One was a pack-mule company from Fort Gibson led by J. N. A. Carter and A. M. Wilson which also included white men. This group took the southern route via Santa Fe and the Gila River and took only four and one-half months to reach the "diggins." Lovely Rogers, a mixed-blooded Cherokee touted by the editor of the *Cherokee Advocate* for his "intelligence and great scrutinizing observation" was a member of this group. His letter to William Shaw of Fort Gibson mentions "those" [Cherokee?] on the northern route "are getting in."

Tuolumne River, California, September 17, 1849

My Dear Sir: You no doubt will be expecting a letter from me long before this reaches you, and think rather hard of me for my long silence. You know that when we left Fort Gibson we expected to reach our destination in sixty-five or seventy days. I do not now recollect what grounds we had for making such calculations, but I know that: we were most sadly disappointed in (not) reaching here as soon as we anticipated. We were exactly four months and twelve days in getting to the diggings. We came through without any accident or trouble, but it was laborious, toilsome business all the time. We came through about as soon as any parties that came the overland route. Those that came the northern route are getting in. I have been informed that their provisions gave out before they got in and that they suffered a good deal; in fact, some of them came very near starving. The citizens of San Francisco contributed twelve thousand dollars' worth and sent to them. Persons that come any of the overland routes will earn all the gold they make . . .

"Myself and J. N. A. Carter and Shaw and two young men from Georgia are working together. We shall not return to Gibson until we make twenty thousand apiece. A man can make money here at anything, except doing nothing. I have never seen such a place to make money in my life. There is any amount of provisions at San Francisco and Stockton . . .

"You must excuse this very imperfect letter, for I have to write on my knees. Please write to me soon. I should like to have the *Cherokee Advocate* sent to me. Direct your letters to Stockton.

LOVELY ROGERS[29]

Another member of this packing company, George E. Grymes, also wrote to Shaw at Fort Gibson.

"Sacramento City, September 18, 1849

"Dear Sir: Pardon me for not having written before, as I promised. I have been waiting to hear from some of you and to see clearly what could be done before I wrote. I went to the mines immediately on my arrival at this place (July 1), (and) stayed there one week; left Bob (Robert Shaw) hard at it. To be candid, I could not stand it—rather would not—at that season. I came to this place, made some money for twenty-one days, returned to the mines (not where Robert was), was taken sick, and had to return forthwith. I have been sick ever since, and at this time am quite feeble. On Saturday last I went to Robert; he came back with me. He has done well—$1,100 to date. We leave in the morning for the Trinity river, two hundred and fifty miles up the river Sacramento, where we understand great things can be done. I hope so, and trust we may not be disappointed. F. Chisholm and J. Vann are here; Lovely and his party are at work on the Stanislaus river. I have not seen any of them except Chisholm and Vann; the colonel had left when we arrived. So you can judge how much we were disappointed on that score. But if I can get hearty once more, and Bob keeps well, we'll make something yet. Thousands of emigrants are still in the mountains with broken-down teams and cannot help themselves. Mr. Shaw, this is the most crazy place you or I ever saw. Everything is perfectly wild! Wild! Wild! God only knows the suffering there must be here this winter."

George E. Grymes[30]

J. Vann and C. Chisholm were of the original Evans' party and packed from Pueblo, but their route to California is not known.

Another group of Cherokees led by Dr. Jeter L. Thompson took the Independence route to California. There were fifteen in this group and nine were to die of cholera at the Platte River.[31] This tragic news was learned at the Salt Lake by the Evans' company. The Thompson company reached "the valley of the Sacramento on the 25th October, being on the journey six months and ten days." His letter from the Feather River Mines on November 1 made this comment: "Many we hear are still on the road all along for two hundred miles from the settlements in snow three feet deep."[32] So the Thompson party preceded some of the Evans' group who took the Lassen Trail and who were seen by Bruff November 1 near Lassen's.

Scurvy and cholera were two maladies often mentioned by the emigrants. Scurvy was a problem on both the overland trip and the sea voyage to California. It was caused by the lack of fresh fruits and vegetables and could cause death after a painful illness. The symptoms of scurvy were swelling and bleeding of the gums, followed by swelling of both legs below the knee, intense pain in the limbs, and finally the turning black of the limbs. The cure was fresh vegetables and fruits—not easily obtainable on the trip. Several diaries record emigrants eating wild cabbage and wild onions. It is no wonder that emigrants on the northern route rejoiced over the fresh edibles at Salt Lake City; while those on the southern route responded the same way to fresh fruits and vegetables obtained in the Mexican towns. The forty-niners were able to advise the emigrants in 1850 to add more dried fruit for warding off scurvy.

Cholera was the terror of the trail, a horrible disease which struck and killed without warning and caused the death of many gold seekers. When it struck a caravan, it created great havoc and almost uncontrollable terror. A peculiar feature of cholera is that there was no long drawn-out suffering. A single day ordinarily ended the strife in death or recovery. The victim would be wracked by cramps, then violent diarrhea and uncontrollable vomitings. Then came alternate chills and fever, and the victim turned blue. No one could touch the bedding where cholera had been. The terrible fear which it produced could cause devoted friends to desert the hapless victim or minister with heroic devotion. If the stricken one recovered, he would be in such a weakened state that the next few days were also agonizing. Cholera was wide-spread in the midwest in 1849 and even worse in 1850. Great loss of life occurred while emigrants were crowded together on riverboats or in outfitting towns, especially those in Missouri. The disease burned itself out as the emigrants pushed further west onto the sundried prairies and hills. Amazingly it skipped many trains.

Early estimates by H. H. Bancroft placed the number of cholera deaths in 1849 on the northern route at 5,000, but George R. Stewart's estimates are considerably lower at 750. Stewart did not consider the Cherokee Trail or the southwestern route from Salt Lake City to Los Angeles as part of the northern trail. He estimates 22,500 people started over the California trail and that 21,500 made their way into California almost equally divided among the three routes: Lassen, 8,000; Truckee, 7,000; Carson, 6,000. His total figure was based on figures cited by a St. Louis newspaper correspondent at Fort Kearny who signed "Pawnee."[33]

J. N. A. Carter of the Fort Gibson party returned in February 1850 and brought back many letters from members of the Fort Smith company to their friends and families which he took to Fort Smith for delivery.[34] Carter announced that he would lead another party to California along the Arkansas route as soon as the grass was ready.[35]

Quite amazingly, despite the suffering and hardship of the forty-niners, the fiftiers were making their plans to go to California.

C H A P T E R V I

The Golden Land

"This is a real paradise of a land."
"Mining is somewhat like a lottery,
there's a great deal of luck."

Most Arkansas forty-niners reached the gold fields in seven or eight months rather than the projected six. During these months of hardship on the overland journey, they had been sustained by their dream of wild riches. They were eager to be about the business of finding the gold. Many letters written by Arkansans during the first several months in California convey this initial sense of excitement for the beauty of the new land and for their safe arrival at their destination. The following excerpts capture their enthusiasm.

Asa Scarborough of Union County was one of the first to leave Fort Smith on March 12 with the Heath pack-mule company. They made the trip in four and one-half months and Scarborough wrote to C. F. Sargent of Eldorado.

Embarkadaro, Calif. July 29, 1849
[another name for Sacramento]

Dear Sir:

It is with gratitude to God who has spared my life to reach this place, that I hasten to inform you that I am still in the land of the living, and enjoying good health. I arrived here today, and reached the upper or dry diggins, on the 26th, forty-five miles above this place, and remained there one day and a half. I then came here to write a letter, as there is no mail from the mines to this place. I could write much, but the schooner leaves in two hours for San Francisco, and will arrive in time to put the letters aboard the mail steamer at that place. This place is 150 miles up the Sacramento River from San Francisco—it has sprung up since the mines have been opened, and now contains probably 50 stores, all canvas houses, with five exceptions . . .

No doubt you are anxious that I should have something to say about the gold in this country. I have not operated but about half a day, and I made an ounce. The success of miners is variable, from $5 to $50 a day—indeed I saw one man who made $100 one day; but that is by no means common. A fair average calculation is $20 per day, although there are thousands of men who do not obtain $1 a day the year round, in consequence of laziness and dissipation.

Nearly all the people here are friendly and sociable, and will tender their purse of gold to almost anybody that is destitute. Please read this letter to my dear companion and children if alive. I do not expect to return home until this fall come a year. I have come a long distance, and don't feel inclined to go home without making something . . .

Give my love to my family, and all inquiring friends. . . . I am the only representative that the State of Arkansas has in the gold regions, so far as I can learn.

Your friend,
Asa Scarborough[1]

Unknown to Scarborough, Tom Parsel of Little Rock, who traveled the Panamian route, arrived in San Francisco on July 29.[2] Earlier than either of these Arkansans, however, was W. W. Fowler of Fort Smith who arrived in San Francisco on April 13 having traveled across Mexico to Mazatlan and thence by water to San Francisco. Fowler wrote to J. R. Kannady, a Fort Smith merchant.

San Francisco, Cal., April 22, 1849

Friend Kannady,

You make think it strange to receive a letter from me at this place; but it is no more strange than true, that I am here. I arrived here on the 13th. I came across from Brazos Island, through Mexico, to Mazatlan on the Pacific Ocean; and at that place, I got aboard of a ship, came here in 28 day's sail.

Now I have been here at work one week, at $13 per day, and $12 per week for board. Everything is in proportion: whiskey 25¢ per drink. As for the mines, I cannot say anything about them, only what I hear from those that have been there; and they differ very much in their statements; but all agree that they can dig $15 or $20 per day; and from that to $100. I saw a man last week, who had been in the mines for 6 months, and says he averaged $50 per day; and he was on his way home, *satisfied.*

Now, sir, you cannot do better than to come here, and the sooner, the better; and if I can be of any assistance to you, I will be glad to serve you. If you should come, fetch your family with you, as you can live better and cheaper with your wife than you can without her. Washing is $6 per dozen. If you should conclude to move to this country, do not bring any more baggage than you can get along with, unless you can come by water; in that way you could bring a large amount of baggage.

I shall go to the mines in a few days, and shall not be at this place for several months, provided I can do better than I can here. (Undoubtedly he had hired himself out as a dock worker or some other type day laborer.)

There are several little towns starting up on different parts of the Bay; one at

Stockton, and one at Sutter's Fort. I will find out, if I can, the best location, and let you know.

Respectfully, etc.
W. W. Fowler[3]

The Reverend W. W. Stevenson, who had served as geologist for the Little Rock company, wrote from Los Angeles on November 27, 1849.

Dear Sir:

I am at last able to advise you of my arrival at this place (or near to it). It would be more labor than I can now bestow upon the subject to give you an outline of our overland trip. We have seen much, very much indeed, of men and things. My own mess have come through without any serious pain or privation except myself, who was very nearly out once, and that at the end of the journey, or at the point where we could begin to breathe the air of California. I am now with Thorn and family. It is probable we will remain near this some time. This is a real paradise of a land. Grass and oats are now springing up as in May in Arkansas. The orange, lime, palm, and olive are in my sight while writing. We cooked last night by a fire made of the olive tree (dead). Provisions are high, except meat. Beef is plenty and low. Wheat is worth $2 per bushel.

Wheat produces most abundantly. 50 bushels is regarded as an average crop. Gardening is carried on all the year. One crop is taken up and another planted. I have seen here as good cabbage as ever grew. In a word, nothing is wanting but time and labor to render the valleys of Calif. the finest part of the earth. The grape grows here in perfection, wine ferments without acidity, and they make brandy by the tun.

Say to all who may wish to come out to hold on a bit, so soon as I can it will be my business to write to many; but do not fail to say to all to hold on a little bit, especially those who may bring their families. Females bear the toil of the way much better than the males. I saw but one female grave, but many of the other sex.

Respectfully,
W. W. Stevenson[4]

In a second letter written to Jared C. Martin in January also from Los Angeles, Stevenson shares more information about the agricultural prospects for California.

We have been in California 2 months, and Robert and myself are boarding in a Spanish family among whom the Spanish language is only spoken. This place is some 500 miles below San Francisco, near the coast, which we reached after a travel of 8 months, completely tired out. Our mules were as much worn out as ourselves. The range is very fine, and the valleys look as fresh and green as May in Arkansas. From this place the mountains can be seen, covered with snow, some 30 or 40 miles off, presenting a beautiful picture when the sun shines brightly upon the tops. The land is well adapted to every kind of plant, and wheat is produced in great abundance. Corn, cabbage, turnips and beets grow well; in a word, every kind of vegetable that can be raised can be grown here at all seasons of the year. The cattle are of a superior kind, and the horses are very good. Sheep and goats are plenty, and afford superior food; but hogs to the inhabitants are rejected as food. No son of Abraham was ever more free from the sin of eating swine-flesh than are the Californians and even Mexicans here.

The agriculture of the country is most miserable, as these beings are about 300 years behind the time in everything relating to it. There is not one in 50 can read a word or know anything of the geography even of their own country.—The U.S. are only known as the place from which "los Americanos" come. With five good hands and the necessary implements, five years would be sufficient in which to realize a fortune. Many who own 100 cows do not make an ounce of butter, although it is worth $1 per lb., Irish potatoes $2 for 25 lbs., wheat from $5 to $12 for 240 lbs.

The people are a mixed race, and not one in a hundred is white. Some of the young girls are tolerably fair, but the mass are as dark as Indians. But their moral character is worse than their complexion.[5]

Robert Brownlee of Little Rock was very impressed with California. His first letter written from the mines on December 1, 1849, and two others in January reveal his enthusiasm and his desire for his Little Rock brother, Thomas, and Thomas' family to come forthwith to California.

Aqua Fria [Agua Fria], December 1, 1849

Dear Brother,

We have safely arrived, by the Southern overland route, at the end of our journey. This place we reached in good health and fine spirits on the 15th of November, and now, comfortably seated at our own fireside, I hasten to give you a few items of my short experience in the gold diggings.

The Mexican gold seekers had preceded us at these washings, and therefore we are hunting for their leavings. The gold is found in ravines leading to this stream, the 'Aqua Fra,' which is about the size of that well known rivulet in your city known as the 'Town Branch.' The gold appears to have accumulated here during the lapse of ages, by being washed down from the hills, and lodged in the crevices of the slate rock, and amongst the gravel at the bottom of the creeks.—Some of our mess on one day get more, and others less. The yield is by no means uniform; but none make less than $5 per day, (as every pan of dirt returns some of the dust,) while sometimes very large amounts are secured by a few hour's labor. On the first day, W. Garetty and myself were working within three feet of each other. I got but about $5 worth—Garetty found a crevice in the slate filled with mineral, and took out $70 worth. One piece weighed $13.25 . . . I shall not speak of the other diggings as I have not visited them. I only write you what I have seen myself. I advise you to come here forthwith. Come by the Isthmus route.[6]

A letter dated January 4 reported his success at packing provisions from Stockton to Agua Fria. This letter ended with, "I hope to see you all out here soon, as I believe this to be one of the finest countries in the world."[7]

Three more weeks of observation in California only underscored Brownlee's enthusiasm and he wrote to Thomas again:

Stockton/Jan. 27, 1850

Dear Brother,

My plan would be for you to come and establish a Ranche on some of the tributaries of the San Joaquin, say on the Stanislaus, about 25 miles from Stockton. The Stanislaus is a beautiful stream abounding in salmon ... Along the river are the finest farming lands ... The river is the great thoroughfare to the Southern diggings, and taverns and boarding houses established here would make money very fast. Any person who could have vegetables on his table could have as many boarders as he could accommodate, as the scurvy is very bad in the mines above. The only place of accommodation now to be had are tents scattered here and there along the roads. For one meal they charge two dollars. I am still packing, but I intend opening a store at some of the mines this summer. All the Ark. boys that I have seen are well. I have been at various diggings, and I learn that $8.00 per day to each man is a fair average of gold dug during the winter when ground is full of water. In the summer I know I will be much better.[8]

Brownlee was to remain in California as a merchant and later as a successful farmer.

Benjamin Wills of Saline County wrote to his wife from the mines at Agua Fria on January 6, 1850.

> ... I believe we are bound to do well if we can keep our health and are industrious. We have been at these diggings since December 5. In one month we obtained enough money to buy our provisions for the winter, and today we have a surplus of $300. ... The gold is here and plenty of it. ... I think that I shall be home by next Christmas.[9]

James B. Galloway of Little Rock in a lengthy letter to his wife related much information about the Little Rock boys. Note that Galloway and his group initially hired themselves out to replenish their resources and then bought shares in a mining venture. He also described for his wife the prospectors efforts to redirect the flow of a river by constructing a dam so that the rich river bed could be mined. Many Arkansans would be involved in such abortive efforts during the winter and spring.

Tuolumne River, 4 miles below
Hawkins Bar, January 6, 1850.

... we remained in San Francisco, several days, waiting to get passage on some vessel bound for Stockton. We at last secured passage on a small schooner, crowded so that we scarcely had a square foot to each man, and were seven days getting to that place. We made a stay there of three or four days—put a few things in a wagon, and started for Hawkin's Bar, where a little over 2 months ago, we pitched our tents for the first time in the gold mines. Our company consisted of Keatts, Crease, Pennington, Thibault, Lavenberg, Edwin Galloway, myself and two negro men. The evening of the day after we reached the Bar, we *hired ourselves* to a Mr. Henry, at ten dollars a day, and worked one week at that rate. The next week we worked on shares, and the week following Thibault, Keatts, Edwin, and myself, purchased the interest of Mr. Henry's two partners, consisting of one-half of the diggings, and we are now working the lot as a company. Our diggings are yielding more than any we know of on the river, i.e. from $6 to $16 each, per day, although our best and main diggings are under water. They have been in that situation since about a week after our arrival here. When the river reaches its lowest stage, which will not be until some time in July or August, we will endeavor to make every hour count. Then we expect to make two ounces per day to the man.

We have also been engaged for the last four weeks, with fifty men, in digging a race 1000 or 1200 yards long, for the purpose of diverting the river from its channel. When this work is finished, (which will be about the 10th of next month), we will be able to bestow our undivided labors upon our present diggings, until sometime in June, next, at which time the waters will have subsided sufficiently to enable us to throw a dam across the river, so as to force it from its present bed into the race. We then expect (the river being at its lowest and running through the race) to find a very large amount of gold in the bed of the river, below the dam. Keatts, Thibault, Edwin and myself own one share each in this work. The river was turned in this manner, at Hawkin's Bar, last fall, and those engaged in it were taking out large quantities of gold, when, unfortunately, the river rose upon them, after they had been at work but a few days, and swept from them the glittering prize . . . From our present prospects, we ought to make $10,000 each by this time next year, and no wild calculation either.

There are 6 to 8 of the LR company in this neighborhood, besides us. They have scarcely made expenses, having reached here several weeks after we did. The balance of the company are at other mines.[10]

Lovely Rogers, the mixed-blooded Cherokee packer along the Southern route, wrote from the Tuolomne River on September 17, 1849, that his mess of five would not return to Fort Gibson until they made $20,000 each.[11]

The Arkansans had split up upon reaching California and gone to the different mines. Writing from Weaver's Creek on February 23, 1850, which was above San Francisco, one M. G. D. who had packed from Santa Fe via Salt Lake reported a safe journey. He was working with L. T. Green and E. Day from Camden.

We have a very comfortable cabin, and have enjoyed fine health up to this time. The winter has been a mild but very wet one, and we have only been able to work about 2½ days per week since we arrived here, 20th November last (1849). These diggings are not so rich as some, but we can work here when the richer ones cannot be worked on account of high water, and even here we shall not be able to work the best ground, which is in the bed of the stream, for 2 or 3 months.

I can scarcely give you an idea of what I am doing, though I will be on the safe side and say that counting the working days only I can average $10 per day. I am told that the rainy season is nearly over. If so, I hope to lay up something before it sets in again. I fully expect to average $16 per day through the summer and fall, besides my expenses, which are very great. . . . Tell my friends who are most interested in me, that I am doing well, and expect to do better as soon as the waters fall, and hope to see them before long and to bring lots of gold with me. This is truly a poor man's country, and will be for years.[12]

In a letter to the editor of the *Fort Smith Herald,* M. W. Steinthal of the Fort Smith company wrote from San Francisco.

Friend Wheeler:

In accordance with the promise I made to you, I take up my pen to give you a description of this country, or rather my observations of matters and things. This undoubtedly is a great country—all former descriptions that I read in the papers in the U.S. fall far short of the reality. The mines, at present, appear to be inexhaustible. Every day new discoveries are made. I saw yesterday, myself, a *lump of gold,* weighing upwards of 23 pounds . . .

Now a word to those I left behind, who wish to come to this country. This is a good country for a daring, enterprising spirit, especially, if a man has some money and should meet someone to inform him how to act, but, without it a man is perfectly lost, and if he is not firm, *will soon yield to despair,* and become of little use.—I would sincerely advise every body who is doing well at home, to stay there, especially if they have families.

All the Arkansas boys appear to be doing well here and elsewhere in California. . . .[13]

The next letter is especially descriptive of the California scene. D. F. Shall was a former Little Rock merchant in partnership with Boileau. They had dissolved their business and gone to California in April 1850, arriving in Stockton May 26, 1850. His letter is to Gordon N. Peay, another Little Rock merchant, who undoubtedly decided against the California venture.

Stockton, Cal., 26th May, 1850

My dear old Friend—I have reached, you see, the region, the great centre of attraction, of all the world, and am as much bewildered by the novel and wonderful things with which I am surrounded, as a child is for the first time with its lap full of curious toys, or as old Rip Van Winkle was upon waking from his hundred years' nap. The climate and its two seasons—wet and dry;—the productions of the soil, wild oats, clover, red top, etc,;—the sparseness of the timber, and consequently the bare and waste appearance of the country;—the fine cattle, mules, sheep and dogs, the fleas and flies;—the magic growth of cities and towns;—as per example one year ago there were seven tents at this place, and now there are between 500 and 800 frame houses, with a population of about 6000, and increasing; the enormous price of town lots in the cities and the rents of houses—such a building as the old Recess [a saloon in Little Rock] would have rented last winter, in a good location, in San Francisco, at the rate of $100,000 per annum, and would bring now $3,000 or $4,000 per month—each monte table in such a house rents now in San Francisco for from $500 to $800 per month;—Gambling—the grand characteristic of the country—its usual prevalence, its legitimacy as a profession, being virtually recognized as such by an act of the Legislature, putting debts of this nature on the same footing with those contracted in any other way; the high rates of fare, even at the present time when every thing of this nature is reduced to one third or half what it was in the winter, $7 per day for instance at the best house in San Francisco, and here, where my lodgings cost me nothing, I cannot live decently for less than $3.00 to $3.50 per day—lodging alone is $1.50 per day; the fluctuations of the markets and their suddenness from one extreme to the other—as per example, domestics which were selling but a short time ago at 10 to 20 cts., are now worth 30 to 40 cts. per yard by the bale—in a short time they may be down as low as ever, or still higher, regulated entirely by the supply on hand and demand; if the supply is large, they must sell, because the risk from fire and value of money is so great—the common rate of interest is 8 to 10 per ct. per month, and has been as high as 15. Time is money here, and one month is about equal to twelve in the States. Next in wonders is the prodigality and dissipation of a very considerable portion of the miners, particularly of the young men; but last and greatest of all wonders, is the abundance of gold, the extent of the country over which it is scattered, broad cast, as it were—the profusion with which it is spent and the utter want of appreciation of the value placed upon it in the States. What think you of a boy, 8 years old, betting 200 ozs., of gold upon one card at monte, and winning it? It was certainly done by a Mexican lad in this place, who, having thus doubled his pile, left for home with his mother soon after. Axe handles are worth here at this time $2 each. Hickory shirts, each, by the doz., large size and superior article, only 62½ cts. Thus you see the contrast in prices caused by scarcity and over stock.

I am very much pleased with this place, and think I would like to live here. At this time the climate is delightful—far more so than any other I have been in since I reached this country—as far as San Fran. I would not be compelled to live there one year short of a million. The most desirable part of the country, as far as I can hear, from those at all acquainted with it, not only for salubrity of climate, but for agricultural purposes, is the valley around Los Angeles, and that around San Jose. In the former, grape of the most delicious kind, producing excellent wine, oranges, limes, lemons, figs, olives, clover, wild oats, etc., grow in great abundance, and the lands as rich as any in the world, and much of it so situated as to be irrigated, and a climate unsurpassed. In these vallies [sic] the stock raising business could be carried on more extensively and successfully than any other.[14]

One final letter indicative of these early appraisals of California was written by John B. Hockett of Fort Smith to J. R. Kannady. Written from Stockton on June 22, 1850, Hockett expressed gratitude for a safe arrival, but significantly understated the hardships of the overland journey when he wrote:

We did not find the trip out as pleasant as sleeping on feather beds, and riding in buggies, but were very well content to get through safe and in good time. We had to sell our wagons and pack through from the lower part of California. . . . It is not as easy to make money here as it is generally thought. Many persons are arriving here that wish themselves at home again—many who had made enough to pay their passage, are on their way home, but I am not so easily discouraged. I came here to make enough to live comfortably upon the rest of my days, and I will do it or die in the attempt.[15]

Since arriving in the mines in November, Hockett had made "a little over one thousand" with the prospect of enough to "do him," after his return home next fall.

If Arkansans' spirits and prospects were high during the initial months in California, they were so despite numerous difficulties that attended their life in the mines and towns. They arrived in California at the beginning of the wet season. Both 1849 and 1850 were unusually wet years in California and the rains plagued the miners and interrupted digging for long periods. The ground became spongy and the trail-worn wagons could not be used. The few usable roads ran parallel to the coast, and mere cattle trails served as interior roads.

Strings of pack mules could manage the mire and the rock and gullies beyond, but not wagons. Because packing was the only means of supplying the mines in the wet season, provisions were exorbitantly high and prices charged were unheard of back home. Almost all the Arkansans mentioned high prices and were apparently taken completely by surprise at this situation. Undoubtedly this had not been taken into account in their planning for the trip, and many had to work at various jobs to make a "grubstake."

In addition to the Shall letter quoted above mentioning the fluctuating markets, several Arkansans quoted specific California prices for the folks back home. Robert Brownlee in a December letter to his brother Thomas in Little Rock had this to say about prices and hauling charges:

> .... provisions are very high. Flour, sugar, coffee, hard bread, pork all $1.25 per pound. Clark and myself laid in our provisions at Pueblo (Los Angeles). At that place we got flour for $10 per hundred pounds; coffee 13¢. When I first came to the mines, I sold 100 lbs of flour for $87, but it has risen since on account of the bad roads between here and San Francisco. On account of recent rains wagons cannot be used, and all transportation is by pack-mules. It costs $50 to get 100 pounds of merchandise brought here from Stockton, a distance of 100 miles. I shall start down in the morning with mules, for the purpose of packing up provisions, I can make as much by that as I can by digging. I am getting $ per day for the loan of my jack-plane. This is the usual price for a day's hire of almost any sort of a tool. I was offered an ounce of gold for my chopping-axe, but I concluded it was best to hire it out for $ per day.[16]

In another letter written one month later, Brownlee, J. W. Clark. and W. E. Garrety were packing from Stockton to the mines at Agua Fria, a distance of one hundred miles.

> We get $75 per 100 lbs. We have 8 mules, and are about to buy as many more, if we can get them. Mules are worth $150.00 each.[17]

Alden Woodruff writing to his editor father on February 7 listed these prices for February, at Curtis Creek in the southern or lower mines but noted, "one month ago, these same articles were from 50 to 75 per cent higher than now."

The following are the prices here, since the 1st inst.

Pork	lb	75	Rice	lb	60	Pickles, sm. jar 5.00
Flour	"	60	Beef	"	37½	Pickles, lg jar 8.00
Sugar	"	75	Venison	"	40	Mud Boots $24 to $32.00
Coffee	"	75	Potatoes	lb	90	Coarse pants $16.00[18]
Beans	"	60	Molasses, bottle 1.50			

These prices are similar to those at Weaver's Creek in the northern or upper mines at the same time as reported by M. G. D. in his letter:

> . . . I will state the prices for a few articles, which are the lowest we have been able to buy at, counting cost and carriage:

Salt pork	70¢ lb	corn-meal	.50 lb	potatoes	.60 lb.
Flour	56¼ "	coffee	.45 "	onions	2.00 "
bacon	1.25 "	salt	.50 "	pepper	1.35 "
rice	.45 "	salaratus	1.65 "	molasses	$6 per gal
sugar	.75 "	beans	.50 "	vinegar	$4 " "

> Thus you will perceive everything is sold by the pound or gallon. We buy our supplies 40 miles below at Sacramento City, and pay 35¢ per lb., for hauling. I had to pay $5 per pair for 3 pr. of coarse negro shoes. Fine shoes & boots will not sell here. Coarse boots are worth from $10 to $40.[19]

Asa Scarborough from the upper mines complained in July 1849 about the extravagant prices paid for hauling to the mines.

> . . . They charge from $16 to $30 per hundred pounds; which makes provisions very high. A teamster gets from $300 to $400 per month for driving a team. A man gets from $10 to $15 a day for any kind of labor. A wagon & 4 mules or 2 yoke of oxen, are worth from $10 to $15 hundred.[20]

It is very easy to see why some of the Arkansans determined to make their riches by hauling rather than digging.

A listing of the prices current in Fort Smith in August 1850 will enable the reader to better perceive just how outrageous these prices seemed to the Arkansas gold seekers.

Fort Smith Wholesale Prices Current

Coffee, lb. 15–16¢
Tea, lb. 60–1.25
Sugar, brown 8–9¢
" , loaf 12½–16¢
Salt, per sack coarse 2.25–2.50
Salt, " " fine 3.00
Flour per 100 lbs. 3.00–3.50
Meal per bush. .62–1.75
bacon, per lb. 4–6¢
lard, per lb. 5–7¢
eggs, per doz. 10¢
butter, lb. 10–15¢
chickens per doz 1.00–1.25
fodder, per 100 bundles 1.25–1.75
onions, bush .75–1.25
whiskey per gal. .35–.38[29]

Just imagine paying 25¢ for a *glass* of whiskey when you could get a *gallon* for 35¢ back home! It was enough to break a drinking man's heart or pocketbook.

The camp stores were the first institutions of the mining camps. They served as the nucleus for the future town. The store could be a tent or a log cabin and its proprietor dealt in food, clothing, tools, blankets, liquor by the glass or bottle, and occasionally medicine. But just as importantly, the storekeeper extended generous credit and information. Like the taverns and inns of an earlier America, the campstores served as the social centers of the mines.

Sickness was another problem which marred the euphoria of many miners, including Arkansans. Scurvy had been a problem on the overland trip and continued to be so due to camp diet which lacked fresh fruits and vegetables. The mainstays of the camp diet were pickled or cured pork which was usually fried, beans, sourdough bread and flapjacks. Such fare was not what bodies exhausted by an overland journey or sea voyage needed. Then add to this poor diet long work days in the mines in water and wet clothing, and it is easy to see how illness was a serious concern. Scurvy, dysentery, malaria and bilious colic were frequently mentioned maladies. Mosquitoes, fleas, lice and contaminated water along with improper diet accounted for these diseases. Almost everyone fell ill sooner or later. One of the cures for scurvy if diagnosed soon enough was raw potatoes. Since potatoes varied in price from 60¢ to $1.50, they were considered too high to eat and used only for medicinal purposes. Vinegar was another medicinal aid and also extravagantly priced. A sick miner was of no use to himself or his partner and lost time was lost money. This helps explain the "health report" included in almost all letters. Henry Keatts, W. W. Stevenson, S. B. Bennett, Thomas Thorn, and Alden Woodruff were among the Arkansans reported ill in California.[22]

Young Woodruff had scurvy. In "a letter to a lady" in Little Rock written from the Curtis Creek diggings on June 29, 1850, he said:

> I have been doing tolerably well for the last two or three months, but it was hard work to make both ends meet during the winter. I have been laid up some 10 or 12 days past, with scurvy, so that I could not work, but am still able to walk about.[23]

George Evans from Ohio, who had met the Little Rock group outside of Tuscon at the burial of Dr. Fagan, was also diagnosed with scurvy, "the bane of these mountains." His diary entry describing his prescription is illustrative of the recommended cure for this disease and points out Evans' ingenuity.

> They advised me to get all the vegetables afforded by these hills and use them as long as I remain, but go to the coast at the first opportunity. To put their prescription into practice, I sent up the side hills and had some wild cabbage and a small wild onion brought down, and I purchased a bottle of lime juice and a few Irish potatoes. All these vegetables I use raw, with the juice of the lime, and most sincerely hope this change of diet may be productive of a cure. The cabbage found tastes like cress and resembles a plant the Germans in Ohio called kale. It makes a lucious salad with lime juice and a little sugar.[24]

It would have been interesting to know the sum he paid for the bottle of lime juice. In December he had paid $1.50 for a pint of vinegar![25]

If sickness and disease were not enough, there were landslides, cave-ins and related mining accidents which caused deaths. As time passed homicides and suicides would claim their number also.

Having reached California and faithfully made their reports back home, the gold seekers became eager to hear from their loved ones. For many it was a year before letters from home reached them. The Arkansans' letters contain poignant pleas for letters and papers. "I have not been able to get any letters or news from you since I left."[26]

Alden Woodruff in a letter written February 4, 1850, wrote:

> Dear Father—
>
> It is now almost 10 months since I heard from home. On my arrival in California, I was certain of getting a letter—but have not as yet received a single one. What is the reason you do not write?

And then two days later young Woodruff wrote again:

> I received your letter of 22nd October 1849, on yesterday, per the express. It only cost me $2 postage to get it; but that's nothing, for I was glad to get it at any cost. It is the first time I have heard from home since I left Fort Smith.

The senior Woodruff and his family must have been grateful to receive both these letters via the same mail and know their son had heard from them.[27] These were not the last of Woodruff's complaints. On August 6, 1850, he wrote:

> It is very strange that I do not get any papers, and stranger still, that none of the Little Rock folks have ever received a Little Rock paper. So, don't forget to send to 'Stockton, California.'[28]

The "express" Woodruff refers to were private mail carriers who took letters from San Francisco, port of arrival for most California mail, and delivered them directly to the miners at the various camps. The charges for this service were excessive, but the news-hungry miners were willing to pay and save themselves the trip to town. The mail steamers came twice each month to San Francisco and crowds of 500 or so lined up at the post office before the understaffed clerks had finished their 12 to 20 hours of sorting. Lines could continue for three days and places in line sold for $25. Getting mail to the inland post office was even more delayed. Added to this was the avalanche of miners mail, 50,000 letters home every two weeks, which had to be processed.[29] Many times the miners blamed the folks back home for laxness when it was an understaffed and poorly developed mail system which was at fault.

A seventeen-year-old New England boy, who became a merchant in California until his untimely death due to tuberculosis at age twenty-three, kept a journal of his trips from Stockton to San Francisco. Before opening his store, he ran an express to Sacramento and San Francisco. His description of "mail call" clearly indicates how important home ties were.

We got some 300 names to get letters for . . . I have just returned from below bringing some 50 letters . . . The postage on letters is 40¢, but we get $1.50 each . . . As soon as I come in sight of the "bar" on my return, the miners drop their tools and run to meet me, in haste to get letters from their dear friends at home. And those who are so unfortunate as to receive no letters, frequently *rate* their friends at home most severely, for neglecting so important a duty. And as they look upon their fellow miners (who are more fortunate) reading epistles of friendships and constancy penned in fine hand of female, frequently a tear comes unbidden to the eye, while the heart grieves at being thus forgotten by loved ones at home. But sometimes a letter bears a black seal, and I have been the recipient of such a missive, convulsively grasping a lock of hair it bore, uttering lamentations, and sobbing as only one can when he has lost "one" whose affection and happiness was closely entwined, and almost inseparable with his own.[30]

Thoughts and conversations about home can never be catalogued, but a few Arkansans penned comments about them. C. A. Cellars of Little Rock noted one such fond memory to the *Gazette* editor.

I sometimes imagine myself walking up Markham Street, and dropping in at the Anthony House to get a julip. Such luxuries as well as many others with which your city abounds are *non est* in these parts.[31]

The Galloway brothers from Little Rock, Ed and James, worked on New Year's Day with a special purpose in mind. Ordinarily work was not done in the mines on Sundays or holidays, but as James explained to his wife,

. . . we intended to appropriate the amount we might get to purchasing a present, when we reached New Orleans, on our return home. We took out nearly 5 ounces of beautiful dust, about $40 each. What shall the present be? Let me know. We also worked on Christmas, with the same view, but only got about $6 each.

This labor was viewed as individual and did not have to go into the partnership fund. In the same letter James mentions another favorite pastime for him and F. J. Thibault.

Thibault and I have many a chat about our wives and children. It is our greatest pleasure.

And then a final reassurance for James' wife:

I have not spent five dollars unnecessarily since I have been in the mines, and do not intend to do so.[32]

Not every gold seeker nor every Arkansan could echo Galloway's statement, for San Francisco, Sacramento, Stockton or Sonora were always alluring places to relax from mining and find liquor, gambling and carousing. San Francisco was often mentioned by Arkansans, and indeed this city came to personify the golden land. Arriving in San Francisco via

Panama in July 1849, Thomas Parsel of Little Rock described the city thus:

> San Francisco is a handsome little place, of about 2,000 inhabitants, where goods and provisions are as cheap as they are in Little Rock. This may seem strange when I tell you that money is as plenty as dirt, and that property & rents of all kinds are enormously high. One house about the size of Dr. Cunningham's rents for $150,000 a year, and others in proportion. Carpenters and other mechanics receive $16.00 per day, laborers $12. Lumber is from $400 to $500 per thousand feet.
>
> The reports from the mines are more favorable still. New & rich discoveries are made every day, and thousands on thousands are coming to work them. There are 170 large vessels lying here deserted by their crews.[33]

San Francisco was an exciting place to be throughout the 1850's. Overnight buildings would spring up and as quickly disappear due to fires which frequently swept through the city destroying both lives and property. Between January 1850 and June 1851 fires razed the city six times![34] A Little Rockian, John H. Ward, writing to Dr. Lorenzo Gibson from San Francisco on May 30, 1850, reported, "I had my pegs well set here, but this last horrible fire here has done me great injury."[35] Gold was, of course, the foundation of San Francisco even though the diggings were well to the east of the city. It was the major seaport and post office. Contrary to contemporary tales, the streets were not paved with gold, but rather unpaved. San Francisco was known for its gambling houses and saloons, and it was the ultimate place for a miner to kick up his heels when he had enough gold to afford it. The streets were thronged with a mixed and motley crowd which precluded a description of the so-called "typical" forty niner. The posturing gentleman, the dirty bearded miner, the newly arrived greenhorns, Mexicans and "foreigners" from all over made up the huge crowd.

Gambling was the preeminent pastime and descriptions abound regarding its excesses. Shall remarked to Peay, "The gamblers now being the monied men, and lavish with their dust, they are generally, as a consequence, the most influential characters in the State—they are the *bon ton* leaders of fashion and politics."[36] Ralph Beiber quotes John E. Durivage, correspondent of *Daily Picayune,* regarding gambling and drinking:

> There is no end to the gambling establishments here; one can hardly look to the right or left without seeing a faro bank, roulette or monte table, or a 'sweat cloth,' around which are an abundance of betters—and betting high, too. Morning, noon, and night, in fact during the whole twenty-four hours, gambling is carried on to excess. As a matter of course the quantity of intoxicating or exhilarating liquids, under the general and comprehensive term rum, daily consumed, is very great; and the emolument derived from the sale of the same, at retail, in small lots known as drinks or horns, is very considerable. Every glass of liquor is sold at *twenty-five cents per glass;* and as whiskey brings *$1,* and brandy but *$2* per gallon, it strikes me forcibly that the profits arising from the sale of the same must be very considerable. To say that the distribution of this deleterious compound has no visible effect, would be to depart from the truth.[37]

Monte or Mexican monte was a card game in which the players bet against the banker and his funds. The Mexicans had introduced the game in California and were especially adept at it. The Arkansans had encountered the game in the Mexican villages on their trip via the southern route. Alden Woodruff's letter from the mines at Indian Bar commented that the gamblers liked to have the Mexicans at their monte tables because they were *"the best betters at monte."* Continuing, he concluded,

> It is a fact, that a Mexican will bet on monte, all that he makes, and run the chance of loosing his *grub*. And there is another thing which is but too true—the Americans are not *slow betters*.[38]

Woodruff had been in Sonora the week before which undoubtedly prompted his comments.

Writing from San Francisco on May 30, 1850, John H. Ward of Hot Springs had this to say about conditions in the city.

> If you ask who have done well in California up to date—thus do I answer, a few merchants, a few lawyers who are more sharp than honest, a few gangsters, and *all* of the *prostitutes*. It is a tolerable country for preachers, some remain good and some turn gamblers, but passing few of the people who come to California are converted into the House of God. There are many good people here and also a few of the very worst.[39]

Shall also wrote about "the Wild and restless spirit of dissipation that prevails in the towns—wilder and more reckless, far more than an imagination had ever conceived—it soon sickens one with the country." Then philosophically he concluded:

> Here men exhibit the natural bent of their character plainer than they ever did before. If they had any of the rascal in them, here they show it; if any of the gambler in them, here they become confirmed gamesters; if they had a secret liking for brandy, here they indulge without restraint; if a fondness for lewd women, here they gallant and keep them in the most public manner.[40]

Women who were prostitutes were euphemistically referred to in the mines as soiled doves, ladies of the line, or sporting women.[41] California was very much a male experience, and of the few women who went, even fewer were in the actual mines. One estimate of the number of women who traveled westward in 1849 is 10% of a total of 50,000 emigrants—roughly 5,000 women.[42] But reliable statistical information is lacking. Interestingly, the absence of women was felt by many to increase the recklessness and lawlessness of the mining camps. There were actually attempts made back East to recruit women to move to California as a civilizing influence upon the situation![43]

Turning now from the more general impressions and problems which the gold seekers faced, let's look particularly at the diggings where Arkansans sought their fortunes. Map 5 shows the major rivers and streams, and the camps from which Arkansans corresponded are named. The region tributary from the San Joaquin River north to the town of Stockton was known as the Southern mines. Stockton was the county seat of San Joaquin County, one of the original twenty-seven counties. Stockton was the major supplier for the

N
S
Clear Lake
Sonoma
Benicia
Carquinez Strait
San Francisco
San Francisco Bay
San
PACIFIC OCEAN
THE GOLD COUNTRY

Deer Creek
Rich Bar
North Fork
Middle Fork
South Fork
Nelson Cr.
Bidwell's Bar
Downieville
Feather River
S I E R R A N E V A D A
Yuba River
Rough and Ready
Deer Creek
Long Bar
Nevada City
Grass Valley
Marysville
Hock Farm
Bear River
North Fork
Middle Fork
Lake Tahoe
Manhattan Bar
Georgetown
Mormon Island
Sutter's Mill
Coloma
American River
Weber Cr.
South Fork
River
to City
Sutter's Fort
Hangtown (Placerville)
Sacramento
Cosumnes River
Mokelumne River
Mokelumne Hill
Caloveras River
Stockton
Angel Cr.
Carson Cr.
Angel's Camp
Murphy's Creek
Mormon Diggings
Murphy's
Sonora
Jamestown
Woods Cr.
Wood's Creek Diggings
Sullivan's Creek
Stanislaus River
Jacksonville
Hawkins Bar
Tuolumne River
San Joaquin River
Merced River
Agua Fria
Mariposa
Mariposa River

Southern mines of the Mariposa, Merced, Tuolumne and Stanislaus rivers. Freighting, staging, trade, commerce, agriculture, and stock raising developed and grew making Stockton a fixed settlement. Some of the camps along these rivers from which the Arkansans wrote were Agua Fria, Indian Gulch, and Carson Creek on the Mariposa; Hawkins Bar, Indian Bar, Wood's Creek and Curtis Creek on the Tuolumne; and Murphy's Creek on the Stanislaus. Most of the Arkansas forty-niners were in the Southern mines as their route terminated in southern California. The region tributary to the Sacramento was known as the Northern mines. Arkansas correspondence was received from Weaver's Creek, [misspelling for Weber's] on the South Fork of the American River.[44]

Most of the camps grew up along a stream or on a hill and were nothing more than collections of tents or a few wooden cabins. Most of them have long since disappeared without a trace and their exact location can no longer be determined. To further complicate matters, the same camp names appear on other rivers. The Arkansas miners were careful to mention the name of the river in their letters. The Spanish names of the rivers and camps have beautiful translations which convey some salient characteristic. "Mariposa" is Spanish for butterfly, and at certain seasons of the year countless numbers of butterflies are present.[45] The Mariposa diggings were opened in the summer of 1849 and were rich and spectacular at first, but proved to be shallow and quickly worked out. The town of Mariposa was about eighty miles from Stockton and reached via the Mariposa Road which was impassable mud in the rainy season. The Mariposa Indian War, 1850–1851, was provoked when the miners intruded upon the lands of the Indians. A volunteer Mariposa Battalion of some two hundred miners fought the Indians who then signed treaties and agreed to live on reservations. The firm of Brownlee, Clark and Company in Agua Fria was sutter to the battalion.[46] Both were from Little Rock and had very early decided hauling and merchandizing were more profitable than digging for gold.

Agua Fria Creek was the main tributary of the Mariposa River. "Agua Fria" means cold water and reportedly the water stung and numbed the hands because of its cold temperature. Ordinarily a meandering creek, it became a swollen river in December when the winter rains came. The "town" of Agua Fria was a few miles west of Mariposa. Carson Creek was a short tributary of Agua Fria Creek.

Many Arkansans camped in the shade of huge live oak trees along the Tuolumne River. Little Rockian C. A. Cellers said of Indian Bar: "It is a beautiful spot surrounded on the East, West, North, and South by large and lofty mountains."[47] During the winter of 1850 the river camps along the Tuolumne were quite large, and thousands of miners were engaged in attempts to divert the river in order to mine the bed. The sad experience of the Arkansas Dam Company will be related shortly.

Various gold terminology was used. "Gold dust" was not a fine powder or dust, but was a general term for smaller particles of gold. Gold "flakes" were larger and rather flat particles. A gold "nugget" was a pebble-shaped piece which could vary in size and shape. See Illustration 2. An ounce of gold was valued at $16. A half ounce to an ounce of gold a day was generally regarded as the minimum required to keep a miner at work paying inflated prices for food and supplies and putting aside a little to get back home some day. Soil that was worth digging for gold was called "paydirt." A rich strike, which was impossible to keep secret, was called a "bonanza." In 1849 and 1850 the gold seekers were involved in "placer" mining, that is digging and panning in areas where alluvial deposits had accumulated—variously referred to as ravines, chasms, crevices, canyons, or gulches. *Veta madre* was Mexican for mother vein and became Mother Lode to the miners and loosely referred to the gold rich region of Central California.

The parcel of mining ground held by a miner or a company was called a "claim." The size of the claim varied at different times and different locations depending on the richness of the diggings. On Rich Bar in the Northern mines, the claims were 10-foot squares! Each miner was permitted one claim, and possession was signified by the presence of tools. Howard C. Gardiner's party at Hawkin's Bar on the Tuolumne learned this "mining law" the hard way. Someone "jumped their claim" because it was abandoned (toolless). "We had forfeited the claim through sheer ignorance. . . . We were howled with vexation. That claim afterward known as 'Gauly claim,' (after the miner who took it over) was the richest spot ever struck on Hawkins Bar and yielded thousands of dollars before it was exhausted."[48]

As we have seen, the men who went to California were from every walk of life, but none who could claim "gold miner" as a vocation. Beginning with a pick and shovel or jacknife or spoon, the forty-niners discovered for themselves the art of mining. The Mexicans had preceded the Americans to the mines and were already proficient with the primitive techniques of extracting the placer gold. By imitation, trial and error, the Americans progressed from one gold digging technique to another. They came to know by experience that red earth was more promising, that iron pyrites glitter, that gold shines evenly, that iron pyrite was gritty between the teeth, that gold smashed flat and did not shatter, and that gold was heavier than all the other materials among which it was found. Indeed, the latter knowledge was the key to devices such as the cradle or rocker, long tom and sluice box which were used to extract the placer gold. See Illustration 3. The rocker or cradle was a primitive portable device which had been used in Europe for three centuries. The following is a good contemporary description of a rocker from Geiger and Bryarly's journal.

> There was a little stream running along the deep hollow upon which they were working. There was about 50 men at work, & their average, I understand, was one ounce to one (ounce) & a half a day. They were using what they call the rocker. They are about the size of a common cradle with just such rockers. Half way upon the top is a seive upon which the stone & dirt is thrown, & a man rocks or jolts it with one hand & with the other pours water upon it. The fine dirt & sand is washed down in the bottom where there is clefts, (also called riffles) separated a foot apart & a few inches high, to catch the heaviest of the sand & with which the gold is mixed. When it gets full up to the clefts, a hole being bored in the bottom of each, the dirt & sand is drawn off in a pan & washed, by shaking, rubbing, & washing the dirt, stone, & gravel out, the gold remaining in the bottom. This is the most tedious part of the operation but yet it is attended with considerable interest. To one of these ordinary washers, four men generally work, one to dig, one to carry the dirt, the other to rock, and the last to wash.[49]

Tools for Extracting Gold

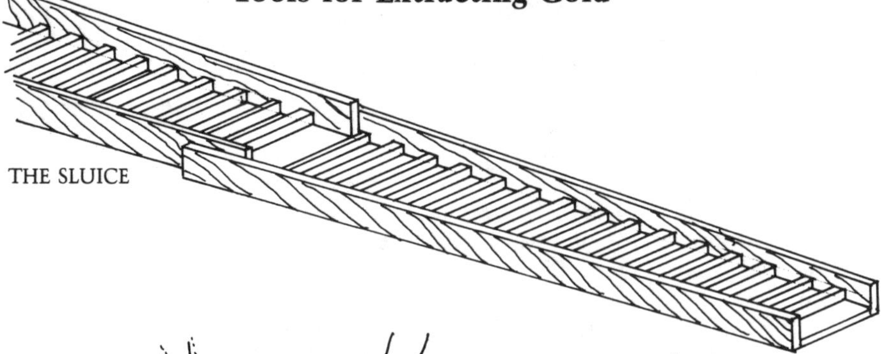

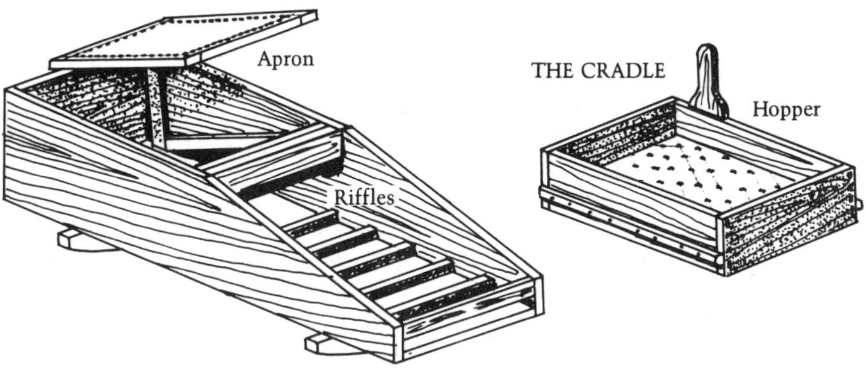

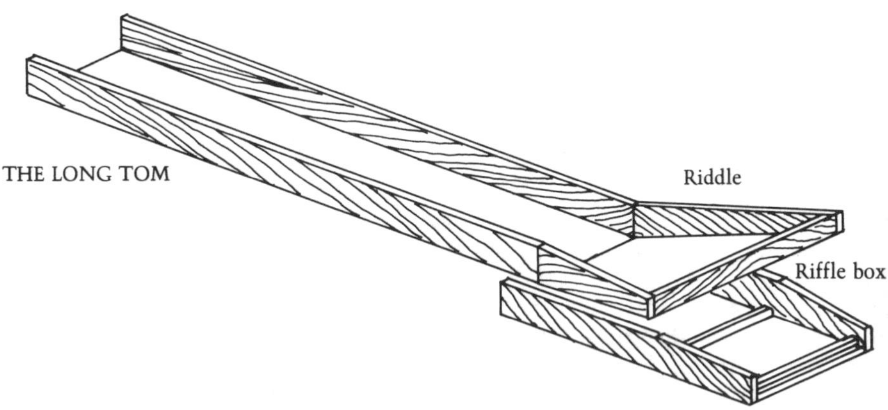

Brownlee used a rocker on the Agua Fria in November 1849, and wrote to his brother Thomas: "I have made a rocker, and day before yesterday we tried it on the dirt which had been washed by the Mexicans last year. We got *three ounces!* Yesterday we got but $8 worth. Tomorrow we may have better luck.[50]

The long tom and sluice box were perfections of the cradle and could process more gold-bearing dirt. Water was an imperative factor for all these techniques and became very crucial for claims staked far from streams. Consequently ditch-digging and flume-building were necessary for such claims. A flume was a wooden channel, sometimes supported on a trestle and used to convey water to a claim.

As the placer gold became scarce, the miners looked for ways to recover gold from solid quartz. The Mexicans used the *arrastra,* something like a grist-mill, where large stones crushed gold-bearing fragments of quartz. Alden Woodruff was involved in a quartz mining project at Indian Bar on the Tuolumne and left a vivid description of his opinion of the process:

> . . . "I have only one word to say about the quartz rock, and that is that it is one of the *greatest humbugs* that has ever been started since the mines were discovered; and has been the means, and will be, of breaking more men, than any one of numerous humbugs that have been, and will be, started in and about California. It is true, that there is a great deal of quartz that contains gold, but it will not pay to work it as present; it may do 10 or 20 years hence, when wages and provisions get lower.[51]

The difficulty of quartz digging necessitated mechanical mining companies and capital which the individual miner could not afford. Hydraulic and other large-scale mechanized mining was not to wait ten or twenty years, but began in the mid 1850s.

Whatever method was chosen gold mining involved far more work than most gold seekers had anticipated. The wonderful gold-washing machines lugged from the East were virtually worthless. Long hours of back-breaking work, many times standing in cold water and wet clothing, and rewarded by only enough dust to meet exorbitant expenses took their toll upon the gold seeker's enthusiasm. It is easy to see how many turned to trade as a quicker way to obtain riches. Others would become completely disillusioned and head for home, wiser maybe for their experiences, yet probably shamefaced that their gamble had not paid off.

An Arkansas experience which was well documented in numerous letters concerned the damming project on the Tuolumne River in 1850. It epitomizes the California experience of many Americans. As noted earlier, the fall of 1849 was unseasonably wet, and mining operations were delayed due to high water. In January a contingent of Little Rock men including Crease, Murphy, Bun Low, A. Cellars, Pennington and boy, the Galloways, Henry Thibault and F. J. Thibault had begun digging a canal to drain about a half mile of the river with the prospect of finding "millions of gold."[52] The dam could not be thrown across the Tuolumne until July or August when the water was lower. The numbers involved in this canaling project and the length of the canal were to significantly increase. In March Cellars wrote from Indian Bar with further information:

Next July we intend to drain this river, or a portion of it, by means of a canal about a mile and a quarter in length. We have a regular association, with President, Directors, Secretary, and Henry Crease of your city, being Treasurer, and George Henry of Texas, President. The following gentlemen from Little Rock, belong to the association; all expect to realize $5,000 per share. Wm. Pennington and boy, H. Keatts and boy, Thibault, E. G. and James Galloway, B. B. Low, Lavenberg, Henry Crease, J. Murphy (who is about leaving for Moccasin Creek, in search of the precious metal) and your humble servant—all of whom are in good health, and send their respects to all friends.

The last we heard of Alden M. Woodruff, he was at or near Wood's diggings, about 20 miles from this. McVicar, Brownfield, Brownlee, Clark, Haralson, Pearce, McHenry, and young Drew, I know nothing of. Parsels is in the mountains, 25 miles from here.[53]

On July 24, 1850, Henry Keatts wrote his brother James in Little Rock with further news about the project and the numbers involved:

We have had rather ill luck thus far, but, if I can regain my health, I will make up for it, so soon as the river falls, so as to enable us to realize from our canalling and damming operations on this river—and hope to bring home soon $3000 to $5000. It, however depends on the falling of the water. It has been on the fall for three weeks past—but slowly. We have suspended operations on our work for the last three weeks, but as soon as the water falls sufficiently, we are prepared to throw our dam across, and commence collecting the gold. I long to be at it. There have been 3 slaves sold in our company, within the last week—2 for $1000 each, and the other for $1,200. You can see, from this, what the repute is of our work. There are some 15 or 20 companies within 10 miles of this place. Not a foot of river is now vacant, that is practicable for canalling, and several *cainons* have been taken by companies, that will require years to complete, and at a heavy cost. The water will have to be conveyed in aqueducts the whole length of their operations.[54]

At about the time Keatts was writing, Alden Woodruff had moved from his Curtis Creek diggings to Indian Bar and joined the canal venture. In a letter to his father, he updated the project and news from "Our California Boys."

Indian Bar, Tuolumne R., Aug. 6, 1850

"As it is a very lazy time with me now, I can find time to write you a few lines. I moved from Curtis Creek to this place, about 2 weeks ago, and bought an interest in the "Arkansas Damming Co" for which I paid $200, and have been at work on it for the last ten days. If it should prove rich, I will make a pretty good haul; if not, I shall lose a whole season's work, and have to commence anew; and, what is worse yet, pass another winter in the mines. Nearly all the Little Rock Co. are engaged in the 'Indian Bar, and, Arks. Co.' So you see we are all together once more.... McVicar is here, and has put up a large trading establishment, eating-house, bakery, and *rummery,* and is doing a very fair business, *on a credit.* If the Damming Co.'s fail, he will be a broken merchant. Wm. Pennington and John Hughes have just opened a trading-house, and are doing a very fair business.

It will be about the 1st of Sept. before we will be able to work in the river, as it falls very slow, and has some 3 or 4 feet to fall yet to low water mark, and about 2 feet before we will be able to put in our dams. The river falls from 2 to 5 inches during the day time—it is just according to the quantity of snow that melts on the mountains each day.... The Indian Bar Co. sent out three men, this morning, for the purpose of hiring 100 men to work on their claim. They will put their dam in, in a short time. They have enough ground to keep 1000 men employed the whole season. We have about 10 days' more work to do, before we will be able to turn the water into our ditch. As far as our claim has been tried, it has proved to be very rich; and I think we will realize $3,000 to $4,000 to the share, (33 shares), if the rainy season does not come too soon.

All the boys are well, and in good spirits, and think they will go home this winter, with a 'pile.'[55]

The exuberant expectations of great riches met with sad defeat some time in September due to the unexpected rise in the water level of the Tuolumne. Writing to his wife, F. J. Thibault recorded the failure:

Indian Bar, Tuolumne R., Sept. 30, 1850

Dear Wife—All our hopes, founded on the Tuolumne river, have proved a failure. We had our work completed, and were just about taking out the gold, when it commenced raining, and made a complete wreck of all the dams on the stream.—Hundreds of men are completely ruined—deeply in debt and out of funds. Thank God Henry & I are comparatively well off. I have a few hundred dollars due me, and as soon as I am able to collect it, we will start for home....

I am fearful there will be a bad state of things prevailing here shortly, and I am anxious to get away.[56]

Young Woodruff also explained the loss:

...We were visited with a heavy rain the other day, which caused the river to rise and tear away all the dams across it, with but one or two exceptions. Our dam was not quite completed (having 2 or 3 days work to do), and was knocked into 'pi' at the very outset. We intend working out the banks and side—damming it, which we can do, and let the dam go until next year.—It is rather a sore lick on me, and has nearly broke me, but I can get up again by going to work. The Indian Bar dam is torn to smash, and but little will be done this year by them. I intend to make all the money I can this fall, buy shares in the Indian bar & Arkansas bar companies, and then *winter in LR* and return next summer. These are my present intentions. How they will turn out, *quien save* [*sabe*].

It would have made you laugh to have seen the long faces the boys wore, when the waters came down upon our works, which had cost us so much labor and expense. Shares were offered for a mere trifle. Some offered their shares to any person who would pay their debts.... I think I can shortly buy very cheap.

All the LR boys are well and in good spirits.[57]

The senior Woodruff in editorial comment upon this letter from his son praised the spunky spirit of the Arkansans:

. . . Our LR boys were not inclined to *give up* because of their misfortunes, but were in good spirits, and determined to *try aqain,* when we hope they will be rewarded by *better luck.* We do not like to see men give up, because they sometimes meet with misfortunes. The right way is to try again, and again, and never despair. Industry, preserverance and prudence, invariably lead to success, in all laudable enterprises; and we hope our friends from this portion of the State are yet destined to reap a rich reward for their labors and sufferings in the gold diggins of Calif.[58]

Nonetheless, it was Woodruff's editorial comment the week previous to Thibault's letter which conveyed his and many of the Arkansas Californians disillusionment with the golden land:

This sad state of things among that portion of our friends in Calif., who are engaged in mining and canaling the Tuolumne, for the purpose of turning the stream, is confirmed, by three gentlemen who returned last week, and who left that stream after the sudden rise of water which blasted all their hopes. They represent the works, which had been erected at great expense and labor, as entirely swept away, and a large portion of those engaged in those enterprises, as in a state of despondency, when they left. Some of them, however, we understand, had realized considerable gold before the rise came upon them; and, as the rise had come much earlier than usual, many were in hopes it would subside in time for them yet to reap some reward for their labor and sufferings . . .

(The three returnees) have seen as much of California as they desire and neither of them has any inclination to return thither. They represent most of the emigrants from Ark. as anxious to return home, and think that few who can raise the means to return, will tarry longer than the ensuing winter. The misfortune, however, with a large portion of them, is, that they have not the means. But few of them, if any, have been lucky enough to light upon any of these *big lumps* which the California and other interested papers are continually speaking of, to lure the too credulous adventurers from the States, to brave the dangers and privations, to say nothing of the expense, of a trip to that far-off region, where more than nine-tenths meet with nothing but disappointment and suffering. The experience of the past two years, we think, will deter such wholesale emigrations to that region, as have been hitherto witnessed.[59]

In a further report on this failure of the damming project, the *Arkansas Gazette* copied the following article from the *Pacific News* dated October 15, 1850:

"Mining on the Tuolumne"

By the rains some 3 weeks since, 36 dams on the Tuolumne river were washed away, or partially injured. But so great was the faith of those engaged in these works that the bed of the stream would pay, could they ever fairly get into it, that most of the companies went to work and repaired their dam; and now, many of them are testing the reality of their expectations. It is somewhat remarkable that of all the stream upon which so much labor has been bestowed this season, the Tuolumne alone has proved anything nearly as rich as the beds of the streams were generally supposed to be. This is rich without doubt, yet there is great difficulty in working the channel to advantage.... Should the rains hold off 3 or 4 weeks, a good deal will yet be taken from this river—enough to repay the miners, in a measure, for their long and constant labors on the banks, in the way of ditching.

Some of the companies, however, will not attempt to do anything further this fall, but wait for another season, when they hope to be so thoroughly prepared as to be able to commence operations early.

Now that the various damming operations off the rivers have been given up, as a general thing, the miners are looking about for winter quarters where they may be able, in part, to repair their misfortunes of the past summer.... The road from Stockton to the mountains is daily swarming with mule trains and wagons loaded for the mines, and unless the rains set in very soon, that whole region will be in much better condition to afford all needful supplies to the laborer, than it was upon the sudden coming up of the rains last fall.[60]

This damming catastrophe was responsible for yet another slang expression in the miner's jargon. "I have been damming a river," came to be a stock expression for having had bad luck. The Tuolumne experience underscored the note of disillusionment which had crept into the Arkansas correspondence from other quarters. David F. Shall writing to Nicholas Peay reported that he and Boileau had not found a "point to locate ourselves, nor any opening in any kind of business, that suits our limited means, and promises fair and safe profits." Further, he commented on unsafe travel conditions in California due to the $20 per head per month tax on foreigners which had led to horse stealing, murder, and highwaymen. He ended by congratulating Peay "for your good fortune in having changed your mind about coming with us." Shall recommended only married men who were dissatisfied with where they were and who wanted to make California their permanent home should come.[61]

This letter occasioned lengthy editorial comment by Woodruff who respected Shall's intelligence and reliability. Woodruff calls attention to intentional deception of gold seekers by various interested groups:

"We have since seen six or eight letters, written by other respectable and intelligent people from that quarter, all of which speak in the same terms, and point in most gloomy colors the situation and prospects of things in general in that quarter. These letters all unite in stating that the dissatisfaction is great and general, and that hundreds and thousands would most gladly return to the U.S., had they the means & opportunity of doing so, and are cursing their own folly for ever having left home. Some of these letter writers say that there are great numbers, whose interest it is to keep up the delusion in the U.S., that it will probably require much time to undeceive the people here, so as to check the flood of emigration, and prevent thousands from sacrificing comfort and good prospects at home, in exchange for disappointment, privations, sufferings, sickness and death in that disagreeable and unhealthy climate. Among those whose interests it is to promulgate exaggerated tales, are the numerous steamboat owners, all of whom have active agents, the real estate owners, all the owners of both sailing and steam craft employed in the coasting and interior trade, and all the traders, store-keepers, and a vast number of others, whose gains can only be continued by keeping up the existing excitement in the U.S., and whose present golden harvest would be ruined should emigration be checked.

That there is gold, and in large quantities, scattered through the country, there is, of course, no doubt, but if we will take into account the number of persons now in Calif., engaged in the business, it can be readily ascertained, by a short calculation that the aggregate amount of *all the gold* that has been thus far collected, would not be an average compensation to *all of them*, equal to the wages of common day-laborers in the U.S.!

The papers of Calif. continue filled with the most exciting accounts of new discoveries of gold, and the finding of lumps of five, and ten, and thirty, and one instance, a single block of over eighty *pounds*, of which one-half was pure gold!! These kind of tales have been so long and so constantly repeated, that we have lost all confidence in them, and we have yet to learn of any arrival of single specimens in the U.S., containing more than 25 or 30 ounces of the precious metal.

It is time, we think, for the public press of the Union to raise a warning voice on this subject, and to expose the exaggerations which are so industriously circulated. They have already lured thousands to their ruin and will, if not checked, lure other thousands to the same fate.

The national wealth, in way of lost labor and lost property in shipping and merchandise, has been injured and reduced ten-fold the extent of all the gold yet received from thence, and we believe that every dollar of all future receipts of the article will cost the nation, three, four, or five fold. The bubble, even there cannot be continued much longer, and general ruin will, of course follow the explosion of it.[62]

Extracts from other letters indicate that California had lost its sheen. Thomas Parcel was damming on the Merced River along with S. Brownfield and Jessup Mc Henry. Writing to A. J. Hutt, a Little Rock merchant, on August 4, he said:

How it (the damming) will turn out I do not know. I am in hopes to make enough to take me home—but, whether I do or not, I shall come home this fall for it is getting too unsafe to live in this country. They are murdering and robbing in every direction. There were fourteen men murdered and robbed within the last two weeks, between this and Stockton; and day before yesterday, two men had their throats cut and were robbed, only three miles from this spot. So you see it is very unsafe for a man to travel here especially if he has money about him. There are 500 men banded together at a place called Warner's Ranch in lower California, for the purpose of robbing the Mexicans on their return home.... So you can see what things are comming to in California. I firmly believe that in six months from this time, a man's life will not be safe, either on the road or in his bed, if he is known to have $100 in his pockets.

Do not think of removing to California. There are more broken merchants here than you ever saw or heard of. If a man can get a good run of business, and does not get robbed or murdered, he can make money; but the chances are 100 to 1 against him. I therefore give it as my special advice to my friends, not to come to California.[63]

Alden Woodruff in several letters commented on lawlessness and murders. A June 29, 1850, letter noted that "such outrages were becoming quite common in the mining region." The tax on foreigners in the summer of 1850 resulted in increased lawlessness of all kinds. On August 6, Woodruff wrote, "There has been during the last two months, about 100 murders (that I have heard of) committed in the Southern mines—some of them the most horrible that I ever heard of."[64]

The *Gazette* began studying the California papers for reports of Arkansas deaths. Two such reports follow:

"Murder of an Arkansian in California"

The following is copied from the *Sacramento Transcript* of the 12th June, for the information of the friends of the deceased.

Allen Thompson, from Arkansas, was murdered on Saturday night, 7th inst., in his tent, on Jackson Creek near the Mokulumne river. He was found upon the floor the next morning, with a ball hole through his head, and his body cut, in a horrible manner. An axe, which belonged to the deceased, was used for the latter part of the deed of blood. His purse, emptied of its contents, was left on the table, and from appearance the perpetrators of the crime sought only the gold. An inquest was held upon the body, on the 8th, and a verdict rendered in accordance with the facts.[65]

We cut the following article from the news received by the last arrival from Calif. The only person we know of, by the name of Simmons, who has gone to Calif., was Joseph J. Simmons, a respectable citizen of Conway Co. He, however, was a widower when he left for Calif., and we have not heard of his marrying since. We, therefore, hope he is not the individual referred to below, as having had the misfortune to kill a man who had persisted in insulting his wife. But, if the facts are as stated, we are not certain that he was not justifiable in the act, by the laws of God & man.

Murder at Hawkins Bar—The wife of a man named Simmons, from Ark., residing at the above named place, was annoyed by the repeated insulting advances and even threats of violence upon her person, by another man of the name S. E. Elmendorff, formerly of Penn. of which Mrs. Simmons informed her husband, who gave notice to Elmendorff, that if he persisted in coming about his premises, he would shoot him. Not intimidated by this warning, Elmendorff perservered, and at last taunted Simmons in his own house with his not having fulfilled his threat. Simmons immediately shot him with a pistol, causing his death in about 30 mins. Considerable excitement ensued. The friends of Elmendorff insisted upon hanging Simmons without a trial; but through the interference of others he was released from their hands, received a hearing before a legal tribunal, and was held in custody to await his trial at Sonora.[66]

In the absence of organized government, the miners called mass meetings, elected alcaldes, and established rudimentary civil and criminal codes. Juries were hastily corralled and justice was swift and often deadly. There was much evidence of anti-foreign sentiment.

Responding to many negative reports of persons whose veracity was unimpeachable, the *Missouri Republican* also began long editorial comment on the conditions in California and the intentional deception of Americans concerning the golden land.

From the *Missouri Republican*

One of the misfortunes attending to the discovery of gold in Calif., is, that the accounts which we have been in the habit of getting from there, in many cases, have been intentionally deceptive. It seems to have been the easiest matter in the world to find out the few who have been successful in picking up fortunes in the mines, or in acquiring large prospective wealth by speculations in town lots. But little is said of the thousands who have made nothing—who are there, without the means to get away—nor of the thousands who have gone down to an untimely grave. Private letters, it is true, tell something of this discouraging state of things. But these seldom find their way into the newspapers, and, of course cannot exert much influence upon the judgement of our excitable people. We are led to these remarks by the perusal of a letter from Sacramento City, dated in July, and written by a gentlemen whom we know to possess a discriminating mind, in relation to the Quartz Rock Gold. We think he went there with a view to operations in this rock for gold. He had traveled at the date of his letter some 800 miles, through the mining and mountain regions of Stockton, Sonora, and Mariposa, and up to that time he had been unsuccessful. . . . (Says yield, due to price of labor, would not pay to work quartz)

The writer says:

"I saw more long faces in my trip to the Southern mines, than I ever saw in my life, in the same length of time. The emigrants are arriving every day across the Plains, generally in good health, but much disappointed in the prospect for making money. There is plenty of gold, but it requires the hardest kind of work to get it, and the expenses are heavy. The climate is much better than I expected to find. St. Louis is well represented here: I cannot turn a corner without running against someone I have seen before.—Generally, very few intend to make a permanent settlement in this country."[67]

No doubt dissppointment, frustration, anger, defeatism, depression, embarrassment, moodiness and various combinations of several emotions and attitudes beset the gold seekers who had staked so much on their big gamble. No blanket statement can summarize the response of all Arkansans to their experience. Some made their "pile," others returned penniless; some considered the experience "worth it," others were embittered by it; some made their pile in mining, others made their fortune in merchandising, hauling, or keeping hotel, eating house or bath house; some died without ever again seeing Arkansas, others deliberately chose to make California their permanent home. How the venture ended for the majority of the Arkansans remains hidden in privately held letters or perhaps has been lost forever. But for some individuals there are records.

Redmond Rogers, captain of the Clarksville company, opened a trading house in Sonora and later another in San Francisco. He advertised in the New Orleans *Picayune* as a merchant in San Francisco. He was in California for over a year, leaving there on November 15, 1850, via the steamer to Panama, New Orleans and Little Rock, arriving in Little Rock the last of December. "Captain Rogers speaks very favorably of the health of those portions of California he has seen, and, we believe, is very well satisfied with the result of his stay there for over a year—but had not decided whether he would return, or not. That we think, depends on his better half."[68] Alden Woodruff returned from California in mid-1851, "wealthier only in experience."[69] Only twenty-one at his leaving, he had hoped to make $5,000 or $10,000 and return home to settle down as he was "very tired of this mode of life."[70] His father was eager to have him assume the editorship of the *Gazette;* and, despite his poor health at his return, Alden became junior editor much to his father's pleasure. "I, today, have the satisfaction of executing, in part, a purpose which I have long entertained and fondly cherished. It is the association of my eldest son, Alden M. Woodruff, with me in business, and his introduction to my subscribers as the editor of this paper."[71] Alden was not satisfied with his new vocation, however, and in eighteen months pursued other endeavors. Margaret Ross stated that Woodruff had three separate careers after leaving the *Gazette:* planter, steamboat owner/commander, and manager of the *Gazette's* job printing office. He died in 1893.

Thomas Parsel had been jailer before leaving for California in 1849. He returned in 1854 and took the job of deputy sheriff and crier of the United States Court which he kept until his death in 1887.[72] There are no clues as to whether he had made money or not.

F. J. Thibault in company with Henry Keatts, returned to his wife in Little Rock after almost two years' absence. No mention was made of his brother Henry Thibault who presumably stayed in California. F. J. Thibault kept a journal from which three excerpts were printed in the *Gazette* on January 31, May 9, and July 11, 1851. The complete journal has not surfaced.

Limus Armstrong of Johnson County was gone for eighteen months. Returning through Little Rock in November 1850, "he appeared to be in fine health and spirits, as he passed on, and we understand brought about $4,000 home with him . . . this is very good for eighteen months' labor."[74]

A notice in the *Gazette* on March 29, 1850, must have thrilled the soon to be departing 1850 overlanders. It read:

> The Fort Smith *Herald* states that a gentleman has recently arrived at that place from N. O. on his way to Calif., who states that he met at N. O. five returned emigrants from Calif., who went out last spring from Fort Smith. They started from Fort Smith on the 12th March, and made the trip to the mines by the southern route, in *S e v e n t y D a y s!* They were at the diggings five months, and each one brought back over $10,000 in gold dust![75]

March 12, five emigrants, and seventy days correspond to Asa Scarborough, S. G. Stanley, Jesse Owen, G. Ballard and J. H. Sellers who went with the Heath Pack Mule Company which was the first to leave Fort Smith on March 12 and did arrive in seventy days.

The Camden *Herald* reported that two of its citizens, Beam and Elliott, had returned after little more than one year, and "after *not more than six weeks of digging*" in possession of "a fraction over $5,000 apiece!" This amount was clear of all expenses and served as a catalyst for the 1850 gold seekers.[76]

William Gilbert of Johnson County returned via Panama in August 1850 with "*a big lump* of gold in its native state, weighing between 13 and 14 ozs." Gilbert had dug the piece himself and also showed "a handful of smaller pieces, weighing from $1 to $5." He told his audience he had been "well recompensed for his time and toils during his absence, but feels no desire to return there."[77]

Dr. and Mrs. J. W. Tappe of Little Rock returned after an absence of almost two years. They made the trip out and back by steamer and were reported in good health and spirits. The Tappes, "like every other adventurer who has returned, whom we have conversed with, are perfectly satisfied with California, and have no desire to return."[78] Young Jessup McHenry, also of Little Rock, returned to marry, but no comment was made upon his findings.[79]

Richardson, Joy, Cassey, and Beebe, of Crawford County who left in the spring of 1849 were back home in July 1850, but the paper indicated nothing regarding their prosperity.[80] Wiley Joy, however, in October gave notice to the *Herald* that he was "leaving for the land of gold, next spring," and wanted "to have a company of 25 or 30 families, who will fit themselves out well. He intends settling in California for life."[81] Winfrey, another citizen of Crawford County who went out in the spring of 1849, returned in October 1850 saying that "he had realized in California about enough to bring him home, and that he has no inclination to return there—and he also added, that he thought a large portion of the Arkansas emigrants would return during the ensuing fall or winter; if they were fortunate enough to realize sufficient from their labors to enable them to do so. Most of them were satisfied with California, but would be better satisfied to get home."[82]

The Reverend William Wilson Stevenson of Little Rock and his two sons were among Arkansas' forty-niners. The senior Stevenson was an early citizen of Little Rock, active in the Christian Church, in the first historical society, in the organizing of the town government, and in petitioning for statehood in 1836.[83] He married Maria Toncray Watkins, wife of the murdered Issac, in 1831; and sons John C. and Robert W., as older teenagers, and one negro servant accompanied him overland to California. Stevenson initially kept a hotel in Stockton, and Robert hauled, "making considerable."[84] Robert served several times as sheriff of Calaverous County while in California. Stevenson remained in California where he died in 1888 at the age of 91.[85] Maria did not join her husband in California.

Carl Jarnagin (Cal), a member of the Clarksville company, found the largest lump of gold reported by the Arkansans. He found it on his claim near Sonora; it weighed 23¾ pounds and was valued at $3,000. There is a picture of Jarnagin dressed in his finest, in the *Gazette's* tenth serial of the King journal in 1941. The picture was taken in the late 1860's, so Jarnagin must have remained in California.

John Hockett, along with his father, went with Dillard's Fort Smith company in 1849. John returned to Fort Smith in 1853 to drive a herd of 937 cattle back to California. Only 182 cattle survived the long drive to California. John was a rancher and farmer near Porterfield, California. When he died circa 1905, he owned 4,000 acres of land.[86]

Dr. John R. Conway and his family eventually settled in San Francisco after spending time in San Diego, San Gabriel (near Los Angeles) mines, and in the San Joaquin Valley. Dr. Conway practiced medicine, but also served as Surveyor of Los Angeles County.[87] Conway served the Confederacy during the Civil War as a surgeon, and returned to San Francisco after the war, dying in 1868.[88]

James McVicar, a Scotsman, and a stone mason, came to Little Rock in

1837 along with three other of his countrymen to work on the State House. He was very active in Masonry, serving as Grand Master of the Grand Lodge of Arkansas. In the Mexican War he served as quartermaster sergeant in Col. Yell's cavalry regiment which qualified him to serve as captain of the Little Rock and California Association. McVicar owned Lot 8 Block 32, presently part of the site of the Arkansas Territorial Restoration, which he did not sell when he went to California. His luck in California was not in mining but in trading. He opened a trading post on the Tuolumne River shortly after arriving in California. During his years in California, 1849–1869, he amassed quite a lot of property including town lots, ranch land, and mining properties.[89] He also served as Justice of the Peace in Mariposa County. He returned to Little Rock in 1856 at the age of forty-two to marry Amanda McHenry Miller.[90] He and Amanda lived in California until 1869 when they liquidated all their California holdings and returned to Little Rock.[91] It was upon their return that McVicar sold Lot 8 Block 32. They died shortly thereafter, Amanda on July 10, 1871, and James on September 18, 1872. James was buried in a perpetual care Masonic lot and Amanda at Calvary Cemetery.

Robert Brownlee, also a Scotsman and a friend of James McVicar, was probably the Arkansan most smitten by California. His "Dear Brother" letters quoted earlier convey his excitement for the new land and its prospects and his desire to have his brother join him. Brownlee in early 1852 made a visit to Scotland and en route visited Little Rock. In October he was again in Little Rock with his bride Annie Lamont, age 18, who four years earlier had nursed him while he convalesced from a mining accident which occurred in Saline County.[92] Brownlee and his bride, brother Thomas, wife and son then went via steamer to California, arriving in November of the same eventful year. Both families settled in Vallejo and went into farming and dairying. Eventually Robert would own 1,100 acres of prime wheat and barley land in Napa County. He was a well-known and respected early California settler. He and Annie had seven children and lived in "a magnificent two-storied home."[93] Brownlee died in 1897 at the age of 84.

For some then, California had been golden, for others a lost gamble. For California the effects of the gold rush were dramatic. Wrested from Mexico in 1847, the population of California was only 18,000 when gold was first discovered in 1848. Thousands upon thousands poured into California so that by the end of 1849 the population had swollen to almost 100,000, more than enough to qualify her for statehood. In Washington the pro-slavery and anti-slavery senators agreed to the Compromise of 1850 which admitted California as a free state and organized the rest of the Mexican session as a territorial government with no provision for or against slavery. President Fillmore signed the admission bill on September 9, 1850, making California the 31st state. This was nine years before Oregon, the original outpost on the Pacific of the United States, and sixty-two years before New Mexico and Arizona. By the boom year of 1852, the population had reached 250,000 and by 1860 it was 380,000. Contrast this with the 52,000 population figure for Oregon in 1860!

The peak of the rush in terms of mineral output and numbers going to California was 1852. More than $81,000,000 in raw gold was mined in California that year. The first seven years of the gold rush yielded $350 million worth of gold. Migrations continued until the Civil War, but after 1852 the settlers by far outnumbered the seekers. The placer deposits were exhausted, and sophisticated machinery replaced the individual miner. Of the 380,000 population figure for 1860, only 82,572 were listed as miners.[94]

C H A P T E R V I I

The 1850 Exodus

"And how many people will go this year?
I find no one calculating less than 2,000."

In order to follow the Arkansas forty-niners to California and recount their experiences, the excited preparations by even larger numbers of California emigrants in 1850 have been neglected. The towns of Fort Smith and Van Buren were again teeming with people who were outfitting, organizing, and waiting for the greening of the grass. True the accounts of suffering by the forty-niners had been recounted, but the papers accentuated the positive accounts and the glowing California prospects. All of the East was in a new fever of excitement, and the lure of California was even stronger than before. Estimates would determine that twice as many went in 1850 as in 1849.

The *Fort Smith Herald* reported:

> A great many persons in this neighborhood are making preparations to start for California in the spring. Also, we learn that there are a great number in the Cherokee Nation making ready for the trip. They will go the Fort Smith route.
>
> Letters have been received from several persons who left last spring, giving such glowing and flattering accounts of an abundance of the precious metal, that it has set the whole country around, in a feverish excitement, which can only be allayed by a visit to Calif. where everyone can have a chance at working out the yellow stuff.[1]

The Johnson County folks were especially eager to set out. Letters had been received from Captain Redmond Rogers, who led that county's forty-niners, which stated he was "making $140 per day, and expects to return next fall with a fortune of $100,000." A large train was preparing to go overland, but four gentlemen could not wait for green grass and a lengthy trip overland.

> Captain G. W. Patrick, William B. May, J. H. Johnson and Oliver Perry, all of Johnson County, arrived here (Little Rock) on the *Pennywit*, yesterday, on their way to San Francisco. They go by the Isthmus. These gentlemen ordered our paper forwarded to them in California. Captain Patrick paid his subscription in California gold coin, which was brought home by an Arkansian recently returned from El Dorado, with his pockets full of the same sort. We wish the Captain and his party the fullest measure of success.[2]

A testimonial by a Texan was considered noteworthy by the *Gazette*. Judge Mars wrote from California to a friend in Texas:

> "I want you to come to Calif., without any mistake of defalcation; if ever you regret the hour you exchange Texas for Calif., I will acknowledge myself more mistaken in my judgement of matters and things than I have ever before been during my sojourn in this sublunary sphere. Texas will do—you, I will acknowledge, can do pretty well in that country—but come to Calif. next summer, and use the same industry you have for the last four years, and you will not thank any any man for $25,000 to $30,000. This is fact not exaggeration. You can live as well, perhaps better than in Texas, enjoy uninterrupted good health, and be in a better climate than in any country on the American continent.
>
> In the San Joacquin Valley, 25 or 30 miles east of this there is little or no frost. It is now as green with oats as a wheat field—these are our common oats. Wheat and the small grains are indigenous to this country.
>
> I know a place up the San Joaquin Valley as beautifully situated for farming purposes as the eye would wish to rest upon—enough for 200,000 settlers, at least—the land as rich as the best of Grayson Co., the water as good as any in the world, and as cool and refreshing in the middle of summer as a man could wish. When these valleys are cultivated, the mines will be worked to advantage, not before.
>
> Come to California, if but to see it. It is not half the trip I had anticipated.[3]

The *Gazette* was also careful to keep its readers informed about the variety of goods being shipped from the East to California. Such an article conveyed a sense of the rapid growth and development that was taking place in California.

> The NY *Herald* publishes a list of articles exported from that port to California during the year 1849, and the first 2 months of the present year. It states that the amount of merchandise sent from NY alone will probably realize in that region not less than fifteen millions of dollars—a sum a little beyond the whole amount of gold received from California. In the list published by the Herald, parts of houses are numbered by the thousands. In building materials there are some large items. Over four millions of feet of lumber . . . over a million shingles . . . timber, dressed boards, laths, joists, brick.

Six hotels, ten complete stores, nine ten-pen alleys, 372 frame houses, 59 iron houses, seven portable houses, 29 galvanized iron houses, one large galvanized iron shop . . . Exports of brandy, liquor and bread have been large.

On comparing the list of exports for 1849 with that of the last 2 months, we find the increase very considerable. Boston too continues to send large quantities of almost every description of merchandise to the land of gold.[4]

The *Gazette, Herald, Arkansas Intelligencer,* and other Arkansas papers were teeming with announcements regarding the formation of groups, contact persons, and departure dates. As early as November 1849, a Fort Smith and Fayetteville organization was taking shape.

Ho! for California

Maj. Elias Rector, of this place, and Col. Matthew Leeper, of Fayetteville, will head a company for Calif. next spring, and will go the Fort Smith route. These gentlemen are old settlers in Arkansas,—men of high standing, and respectability. They have their outfits ready, and will start in the Spring.

Persons of good standing, desirous of making an overland trip to Calif. can have an opportunity of attaching themselves to this Company by sending in their names to the committee of correspondence. Messrs. J. R. Kannady, John F. Wheeler, Charles G. Johnson, Mitchell Sparks, Solomon F. Clark, Sam L. Griffith, and Thomas McCarron.[5]

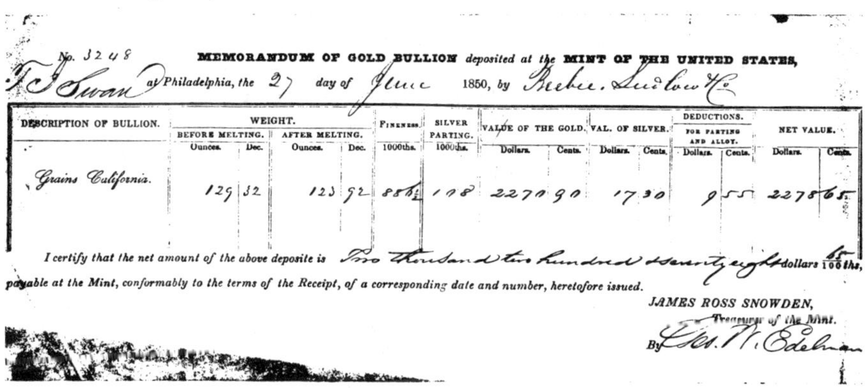

No. 3248 MEMORANDUM OF GOLD BULLION deposited at the MINT OF THE UNITED STATES, at Philadelphia, the 27 day of June 1850, by Beebee, Ludlow & Co.

DESCRIPTION OF BULLION.	WEIGHT. BEFORE MELTING. Ounces.	Dec.	AFTER MELTING. Ounces.	Dec.	FINENESS. 1000ths.	SILVER PARTING. 1000ths.	VALUE OF THE GOLD. Dollars.	Cents.	VAL. OF SILVER. Dollars.	Cents.	DEDUCTIONS. FOR PARTING AND ALLOY. Dollars.	Cents.	NET VALUE. Dollars.	Cents.
Grains California.	129	32	123	92	886½	118	2270	90	17	30	9	55	2278	65

I certify that the net amount of the above deposite is Two thousand two hundred & seventy eight dollars 65/100ths, payable at the Mint, conformably to the terms of the Receipt, of a corresponding date and number, heretofore issued.

JAMES ROSS SNOWDEN,
Treasurer of the Mint.
By Geo. W. Edelman

Gold Receipt

T. D. Merrick papers, Arkansas History Commission.

This notice was duly reported by the *Gazette* the following week.[6] Beginning in February 1850 the notices came pell mell in all the papers. The *Arkansas Intelligencer* reported the organization of a pack-mule company.

Several gentlemen in this neighborhood, experienced in frontier life, are organizing a company to leave this place, in the spring, for Calif. They intend to travel through the entire route with pack mules. By adopting this mode to transport their baggage, they expect to reach San Francisco in 60 days or less. As their company is not complete, a good opportunity is offered of those who desire to make such a trip. We understand that Messrs. John Winfrey, Earl Foster, and Benjamin Neil are appointed a committee to organize the company. Applications of admission must be made to them in Van Buren.[7]

Fort Smith also announced a pack-mule company:

Ho! for California

A gentleman of this place, of known integrity, proposes to take persons from Fort Smith to California for $200 each, paid in advance. The mode of conveyance will be pack mules, with a good substantial wagon to every ten men, so as not to be detained by sickness of men and animals. Should a man get sick the wagons are ready to haul him. The calculation will be for the wagons to travel 20 to 30 miles per day. Each man will be required to furnish himself with a gun, pistols, ammunition, etc.; also, blankets and clothing. All other things furnished.

Send in your names. If 60 good men will enter into the arrangement, we will start between the 1st & 15th of April.

Send your names to this office.[8]

J. N. A. Carter, who had gone to California in 1849, had returned to Van Buren in February and planned "to lead a small party, by the nearest and quickest route" back to California.

He will leave this place at the earliest date the grass will permit, and take a straight course over the mountains at the head of the Arkansas river, taking Bent's Fort in his route, and expects to go through in sixty days with wagons. He also expects to be in California six weeks to two months sooner than those who may go in any other expedition, and from the enterprising character, intelligence, and experience of Mr. Carter, we are fully assured that he will accomplish the trip in the time he promises.[9]

The *Intelligencer* assured its readers that anyone who wished to go overland to California would "have opportunities of falling in with parties at different periods in the spring . . . as several parties design starting from here, some with wagons, and others with pack mules—thus they can be suited as to mode."[10] True there were closely structured companies in 1850, but the more common practice was for emigrants who happened to gather at a given frontier point to associate themselves in small loosely organized groups. Probably they were responding to negative experiences of large groups as related by the forty-niners such as short water and forage, impeded progress, and incessant bickering. Small groups and loose organization also reflected confidence in a clearly delineated route, which necessitated no pilot and which had no serious Indian threat.

Little Rock began to stir in March when notice was given of a meeting to be held at City Hall on March 5 to consider "the propriety of organizing a company of emigrants to go the overland trip to California on pack mules."[11] No names were mentioned.

In April the groups started assembling in Van Buren and Fort Smith. Dr.

Potts and James Sewell, Jr., with ten or fifteen others from McLean's Bottom (Crawford County) were to be joined by W. M. Martin and a smaller party from Franklin County.[12] Dr. Harger of Fort Smith was to lead an ox-team company departing about May 1.[13] Col. Reynolds from Chicot County and his party with twelve or fifteen wagons left Fort Smith on April 16. They were to rendezvous at Fort Washita.[14] The vanguard of Captain Cotterel's party departed Van Buren in mid-April, also to rendezvous at Fort Washita. Two parties from Johnson County, one with pack mules and one with wagons also left Van Buren. Captain Robert Harris, an experienced mountaineer who had spent half his life in the Rocky Mountains, led a company of Californians from Washington and Crawford Counties. He planned to proceed directly up the Arkansas River and cross the mountains at its head thereby making a shorter trip.[15]

The next week's *Herald* reported "Emigrants are arriving every day, and our town looks quite lively." A group from Conway County, including T. T. Henry, S. A. Harris, J. H. Peel, and H. Byrd, had arrived; and the Johnson and Yell County boys, described as "real Arkansians, and of the right stripe" were expected. The Cherokees were also forming.[16]

The *Arkansas Intelligencer* published "the names of nearly one hundred emigrants who left the frontier during the week ending on the 26th. One train consisted of 13 ox wagons, 12 mule wagons, 1 carriage, 26 pack mules."[17] This group was to go to Fort Washita and thence on Marcy's 1849 return route to Dona Ana and then the Gila route. Fort Washita was a new settlement on the Texas Road which served as a rendezvous point for the 1850 emigrants who would cross the Red River at Preston and follow Marcy's "new road" 800 miles across Texas to Dona Ana. It was 157 miles from Fort Smith. Perhaps this was the group to which J. F. Simmons referred in 1852 when he recalled "183 men in our party in 1850" which left in mid-April.[18] Judge R. C. S. Brown of Crawford County, "one of the oldest residents in Arkansas," was "getting up a company" to follow the new Marcy route. Judge Brown was hailed as "an experienced frontiersman, one of our leading citizens, possessing great energy," and capable of raising an efficient company. He initially planned to depart on May 10, but he was "induced" to change his mind "in consequence of the earnest solicitation of many of the emigrants who were already assembled at Fort Washita on the 1st of May. They wanted Judge Brown to take charge of their expedition and leave on May 5. He did so, and the group departed on May 6.[19]

Doctor A. Bronson, Thomas Bronson, O. H. Smith, Green Suggs, and H. Rigney of Van Buren joined the Washita rendezvous.[20] Mr. Tanner and his party from Pine Bluff and Jefferson County left Fort Smith. The *Batesville Eagle* reported that companies of emigrants from Van Buren, Searcy, Marion, Izard, Fulton, Randolph, Lawrence, and Independence counties had departed.[22] The "Scott County boys" purchased their outfit from Bennett and Walton in Fort Smith and took the Fort Smith route.[23] Groups continued leaving in late May and early June from Fort Smith and Van Buren on their overland journey. On May 14, "a company of seventeen gentlemen, worthy citizens of Ouachita and Clark counties" left Camden for California via the Isthmus.[24]

It is regretable that names were not more carefully recorded for the 1850 groups. Many more Arkansas counties were represented that year and probably twice as many Arkansans made the trip in 1850 as did in 1849. More will be said of this shortly. The fire in Van Buren in early December, 1850 which completely destroyed the newspaper building, "not a type or sheet of paper being saved," robbed us of valuable records.[25] Without copying the names, the *Herald* noted the *Arkansas Intelligencer* had printed lists of emigrants leaving Van Buren.[26]

Fort Smith again aggressively put forward the Arkansas route as the only choice of a person with any discernment. Captain Marcy had returned from his escort of the 1849 emigrants by a route which shortened the trip some three hundred miles. Leaving Santa Fe, he traveled south down the Rio Grande to Dona Ana and then turned back east to Preston and then to the northeast to Fort Washita and Fort Smith. Dona Ana was located on the east bank of the Rio Grande, sixty miles above El Paso. It was fifteen miles below San Diego where Cooke's road left the Rio Grande. He made the distance of 894 miles in two months, including a two-week trail delay due to rain and high water. Dona Ana was the half-way point to the Pacific. The Fort Smith forty-niners completed the trip from Dona Ana to San Diego in two months, including two weeks of time spent on the Gila searching for gold. The Fort Smith Committee of Correspondence was most eager for Americans to have this information concerning a trip of only three months duration along the Arkansas route. Loss of time due to inclement weather and gold searching were deleted! They devised a very lengthy circular which the *Herald* published on February 16 with the request to newspapers throughout the United States to publish. It included recommendations by Captain Marcy, Colonel Emory and Captain Redmond Rogers as well as assurance to emigrants of being able to completely outfit themselves at good prices in either Fort Smith or Van Buren. The members of the Committee of Correspondence were J. R. Kannady, John F. Wheeler, Charles B. Johnson, Mitchell Sparks, Solomon B. Clark, Samuel L. Griffith and Thomas McCarron.[27] The circular is printed in its entirety in Appendix C.

One week later the *Herald* commented:

> "Look before you leap." Everyone of the Fort Smith Company have arrived safely in California without the *loss of a man*, and with scarcely any loss of property.
>
> "Is there any person so hardy, and so forgetful of his own safety and comfort, after hearing the manifold tales of suffering, and loss of property on the Independence route, that would risk himself upon it, when there is such a way open as the FORT SMITH ROUTE?"[28]

In a letter to Editor Wheeler, H. J. Share of the Fort Smith company said the trip would be very different for the 1850 groups, for "they will have a good well-beaten road to travel over, whereas we had to make and hunt our own way, clear through."[29]

Later still came this indirect advice:

> "A person who returned with Captain Marcy to Fort Smith from Dona Ana informed us that this road can be traveled by a blind man on a lame horse. Nuf Ced."[30]

The Fort Smith—El Paso route was to be the route adopted by the Butterfield Southern Overland Mail established in 1858.

Editor Woodruff in Little Rock published the Fort Smith circular and in a lengthy editorial entitled "Emigration to California" and subtitled "The Best Overland Route. Outfit, Etc., Etc.," he endorsed the Fort Smith route and Fort Smith as a rendezvous point for small parties. He could not resist saying, however, "emigrants intending going by way of El Paso, might save some distance by starting from Little Rock and traveling a direct course through Texas, over a good road, by way of Forts Towson and Washita."[31] When Marcy's return trip was publicized in September 1849, the *Arkansas Democrat* called it the "new Southern route" and encouraged the citizens of Little Rock to "look to it" and make Little Rock the staging point for the southern route.[32] Nothing had come of this, however. Woodruff made extensive commentary regarding the expense of the Isthmian route and concluded:

> By the overland route the actual cost of the trip is only the provisions consumed on the route—every article of the outfit, including wagon, team, etc. being worth their cost here when the end of the journey is reached. Many of the emigrants who went from Arkansas last spring, by the Southern route are now making fortunes with the team which took them through. The experience of all the late returned emigrants is in favor of the overland route. They say that when the overlander arrives, he is fresh, vigorous, inured to exposure, and qualified to endure almost any amount of hard labor of any kind. He can do anything—drive a team, delve in the earth, work the cradle, or walk forty miles a day, and thrive on it; while the passenger by the steamer and ships, are almost totally incapacitated for the very labors which he proposes to apply himself. Cooped up in little vessels, ill-ventilated and badly fed—the limbs becoming stiff and indolent, instead of being lithe and elastic, as they are by exercise on the plains—the emigrant when he gets to California, is indisposed to go to work, sick, it may be, for want of bodily and mental employments, and fully prepared to be a loafer, if he was not one before he started.
>
> We conceive, that viewing it in every possible light, the land route must be considered to be the cheapest and best mode by which California is to be reached; and of all the routes we believe the Arkansas route should have the preference. We give in another column the circular of the Ft. Smith committee, which plainly shows the superior advantages of the southern route. It is the best-known trail for wagons; and by pack-mules the trip can be made about as speedily as by the steamers.[33]

A number of Arkansans had chosen the Panama route, and all reported very negatively regarding their trip. Thomas Parsel went this route in the spring of 1849, and he described the trip in a letter to his wife written from San Francisco July 29, 1849:

> I left Panama on the 9th May on the schooner *Sylph,* being unable to obtain passage upon any steamer. I can give you no idea of the suffering and hardship endured upon the trip. The passage was 81 days, and the number on board the small vessel was 225. In the midst of constant rain and terrible storms, to which I was exposed, for I had to sleep on the open deck, with mouldy bread to eat and

foul water to drink, you may imagine that my situation was anything but pleasant. Many men would have given odds to have been in a warmer place below, of which you have heard. To stand on deck was to be drenched by rain and exposed to the pitiless storm—to go below was to be crowded into a dark, dirty, dismal hole with 150 men. But I am safely through although weak and exhausted, and will in a few days start for the mines.[34]

In February 1850 R. R. Moss of Little Rock was waiting in New Orleans to obtain passage via Panama. He answered an inquiry from Col. B. F. Owen of Little Rock concerning the advisability of taking his family via this route. Moss reported on the great numbers trying to go this route and the expense:

New Orleans, Feb. 15, 1850

Dear Sir—Yours of the 25th ult. I have just received, and with pleasure comply with your request. The route to Calif. by Panama, is the only one you could take with any degree of comfort to your family, and that, owing to the immense numbers going that way, is attended with difficulty and much expense; for each member of your family (cabin passage), it will cost you $380—and $50 to cross the Isthmus, and you would not be safe to start with less than $500 each. It is very difficult to get a through ticket in this place, and I am detained now, owing to that fact. Unless it is your design to locate permanently in that country, and even in that event to suffer many privations and inconveniences, I would advise you not to take your family. The expense of living in any part of California is enormous, and would consume all you could reasonably calculate to make to support your family.

Yours, respectfully,
R. R. Moss[35]

A final commentary on the Isthmian route was made by David F. Shall, former Little Rock merchant, to his friend Gordon N. Peay. Shall went to California via Panama in April 1850.

First and foremost, let whosoever wishes to come that route, get a through ticket, *or not come at all.* At Panama we could have sold our cabin tickets for $1200, and steerage tickets were sold at $550, and $600. The best time to leave New Orleans, to come this route, is from 1st Feb. to the 15th April. The latter is the date we left there, and there could not, as it turned out, have been a more favorable time selected. Those are the dry and healthy months of the year on the Isthmus. During the rainy season, the passage across there is almost inconceivably disagreeable. When we came over, it was, comparatively speaking, pleasant. A cabin passenger could not start with less than $600 or $700. He should have a strong medium sized traveling trunk with good leather straps, and a pair of saddle bags, filled with such articles of clothing as will suit the occupation he intends or expects to follow; summer and winter clothing are both needed here, but he should not bring much of either. What he does bring should be of the strongest and most lasting materials, and of colors to hide dirt—2 pairs of blankets, and particularly one umbrella. Bring no provisions. Have each package of baggage marked with name and destination. Cholera or dysentery mixture, Quinine, Blue pills, etc., will be necessary.

While passing through the tropic, live light, eat no fruit, drink no ardent spirits, and, on the Isthmus, drink as little water as possible, and keep out of the sun, etc., etc.

Be sure the steamer you leave N. Orleans on connects without delay with a steamer on this side, for, to be detained on the Isthmus will be found any thing but pleasant or safe, as far as health is concerned.[36]

The concensus seemed to be if a man was concerned about his comfort, his health or his pocketbook, he avoided this route.

An interesting account of a return trip to Little Rock from San Francisco via water is found in an extract of a journal of F. J. Thibault. He was a member of the Little Rock forty-niners. He described departing San Francisco on a "catch-penny trap" which, because they were "homeward bound," they were willing to risk. The venture took three-and-one-half months and involved much suffering, deprivation, delays and expense. One six-day delay became a pleasant interlude on the island of Granada where Thibault was impressed with the agriculture, cities, churches, cathedrals, hospitality, and costumes of the women. "Though our ladies would rather be brought to the blush in passing through this country, as the costumes of the ladies consist in a skirt similar to our own, but the person from the waist up is covered with a fine and thin texture, that merely reveals what it pretends to conceal."[37] The complete account is printed in Appendix D.

Of course, these negative water experiences only served to underscore the merits of the overland Arkansas route. The *Herald, Arkansas Intelligencer*, and *Gazette* in April began to report rumors "the Government intend sending out, early in June an expedition for the purpose of surveying the route from *Fort Smith* to San Diego and to select sites for the immediate establishment of *Military Posts.*" The Arkansas papers hoped Captain Marcy would be put in command "to go over the road again."[38]

Another inducement for the Arkansas route was reported May 17.

"Good News for Emigrants by the Southern Route"

The *Alabama* brings news from California, that in the Southern mines, in the district of San Joaquin, some of the rarest discoveries of gold deposits have been made during the winter, which were being worked with great success at the last accounts. Many large lumps, amongst which was one weighing 23 pounds, have been found at the Southern mines. The Fort Smith route leads directly to these mines, and it will be but a short time before those emigrants who have just left our frontier will be 'thar!'[39]

The same paper reported the emigrants on the Missouri route were "suffering greatly from want of provisions." The St. Joseph *Gazette* noted three thousand teams were congregated at that point, and corn was selling for $2 to $3 per bushel and flour $5 per 100.[40] The *Herald* reported and the *Gazette* copied:

"Missouri Emigrants going the Ft. Smith Route"

Mr. James, with 5 wagons and 15 or 20 men from Mo. passed through this place on Tuesday last, on their way to Calif. It was their intention to have taken the Indep. route, but hearing of the immense numbers, already in the neighborhood of Indep. & St. Jospeh, suffering from sickness, and want of provi-

> sions . . . they concluded to take the *Fort Smith route*, where they were certain of finding good pasturage, and good health. Hundreds will follow their example.[41]

In an article entitled "California Emigrants Coming Back," the *Arkansas Intelligencer* reported an aborted trip by Captain Smith and party from Rusk County, Texas. They had found the plains destitute of grass and crowded with emigrants, so they gave up their California venture.

> Capt. Smith and several other persons, citizens of Rusk Co., Texas, passed through this place on their return home from Independence, Mo., to which point they had traveled 600 miles, to start upon their overland trip to Calif. They state that after having fitted out at considerable expense, paying enormous prices for wagons and stock, they laid in 12 days provender for their teams, and went 120 miles on the plains, but finding it so bleak and barren, so destitute of grass, they thought it prudent to return before their provender was exhausted. They did so, sold out their outfit at Independence, and have abandoned the trip for this year.
>
> Thus, when they get back home in Texas, they will have traveled 600 miles to Indep., 120 on the Plains; 120 back to Indep. and then 600 home, in all 1440 miles, without having progressed one mile towards Calif.—They complain further of the money thrown away and time lost, in their goose chase.
>
> Capt. Smith says there are thousands who have started on the Independence route, and as more than half of them are inexperienced persons from interior Atlantic States, who have blindly embarked their lives and property in this dangerous enterprise, upon the persuasion of interested individuals, large numbers will perish.[42]

The point was very clear. Why would anyone in his right mind choose the Independence route when the Fort Smith route could be traveled all seasons of the year?

> Persons leaving here, in September & October, will reach Los Angeles, where they can remain during the winter, and as there is perpetual spring in that region, grass, wild oats, etc., grow in abundance, they can recruit their teams, and be ready, by spring to enter the gold mines, so as to make a good summer's work, and, if fortunate, be enabled to return to the States with a large amount of the dust.[43]

Again Fort Smith and Van Buren were alive with a flurry of activity as the California emigrants arrived "daily—hourly—" to complete their outfits. "There is not a house, room or even a shanty to rent in Fort Smith! Rents are higher in this place than in any other town in this state or even this side of California."[44] John Rogers, owner of the hotel in Fort Smith, decided to renovate his establishment in view of the prosperous conditions. He replastered, repainted, and refenced his premises. The *Herald* deemed it "the best hotel in northwest Arkansas. The beds and bedding at this hotel are always good, and the excellent pump in the center of the area of the hotel furnishes the chambermaids with the coolest and best water to place near the toilettes of the bedrooms."[45] A person who signed "Coleman" and claimed to be the Fort Smith correspondent of the *True Delta* wrote from Fort Smith on July 12, 1850, describing Fort Smith:

> . . . Fort Smith is on the south side of the Arkansas river, touching the western boundary of the State, where it joins the Choctaw country. On the north side of the Arkansas, is seen the S.E. corner of the Cherokee country . . . The town contains about 900 souls, who exhibit as great a variety of nation and race as one would deem could be found residing at any other place on the globe. . . .
>
> A late stroke of what the Dons call magic, converted Arkansas from a position as border State to the spot almost in the centre of the Union; that is, if Calif. is now in the Union, which is not likely to be the case. The result of this has been to make Fort Smith a thoroughfare for persons and goods from every direction. In the fall we see droves of mules and horses going down to Western Louisianna and Texas. In the spring large droves of mules arrive from Missouri, at Fort Smith, and having remained until the California emigration has departed, the traders go to Independence, Mo., to sell the remainder of their stock to the emigrants at that point; the time of the 2 emigrations allowing this to be done very readily.[46]

In the spring of 1850 an incident concerning Fort Smith's trade with the Indians temporarily replaced the gold rush as the major topic of conversation. Frank Weaver, a later editor of the *Fort Smith Elevator*, kept scrapbooks with information pertinent to the history of Fort Smith which he intended to write. He died before completing his task. In an article, circa 1920, entitled "Fort Smith Hub from which the Western Gold Seekers went into the Wilderness," he wrote about the 1850 rencontre between Editor Wheeler of the *Herald* and the Rev. Charles E. Pleasants.

> . . . The latter was a Philadelphian who had been living in the town about a year. He was a correspondent of the *New York Sun* and had furnished that paper with several communications in relation to events transpiring in this section. A short time before this occurrence, a party of Seminole Indians from Florida had passed through the town on the way to their new homes in the Indian Territory. In one of Pleasant's communications to the *Sun*, he intimated rather broadly that the local merchants had sold goods to the untutored children of the swamps at exorbitant prices, and that horse traders had also swindled them. For this Wheeler criticised him pretty severely in his paper. Pleasants retorted in kind, and then Wheeler wrote some more. The next time the now thoroughly irate gentlemen met there was an exchange of fiery epithets. Wheeler struck Pleasants with his cane, and the latter in turn shot Wheeler in the breast with a derringer. Fortunately for Judge Wheeler, he was carrying in his left arm a bundle of mail that he had just received at the post office, while in the breast pocket of his coat was a large pocketbook. These broke the force of the shot and saved his life. Owing to the prominence of the parties the affair occasioned much comment.[47]

We have seen throughout this account Wheeler's strong advocacy of Fort Smith and the Arkansas route, and this altercation further exemplifies the depth of his feelings.

Van Buren also had its champions. The *Arkansas Intelligencer* published "A Card" from John B. Ruddle of New Madrid, Missouri, on April 20, 1850, in which he commended the citizens and the service he had received while outfitting in Van Buren:

> A Card—The undersigned cannot take his departure from among the kind and hospitable citizens of Van Buren, without expressing voluntarily and unsolicited, his high regard for, and grateful acknowledgements to them for the kindness which he and his company of California emigrants have received during their sojourn in this enterprising and improving young city. During their stay, for the last ten or twelve days, they have had dealings with the merchants, mechanics, and others, in procuring outfits, and have found every article necessary for an emigrant, and upon terms that the most unreasonable could not complain of. He takes pleasure in commending the citizens of Van Buren to the emigrants rendezvousing on the frontier, to go upon the Southern route. Provisions, wagons, and goods of all kinds are abundant and cheap; the merchants are honorable and liberal, the mechanics industrious, punctual, and reasonable, and the citizens generally courteous and hospitable.
>
> His party comprising—of his immediate family 12, servants 5, with 4 others, in all 21, with six wagons and one carriage, will take up the line of march on tomorrow, with others, to join the rendezvous near Fort Washita, thence they will go upon Capt. Marcy's route to Dona Ana. His friends in *New Madrid, Mo.*, who intend going to Calif. by overland are earnestly advised to take the Arkansas Route.
>
> John B. Ruddle
> Van Buren, Ark., April 15, 1850[48]

Clarksville in the summer of 1849 had sought to inform prospective emigrants about its location and the success with which it had outfitted the Clarksville California Company of 1849:

> We feel it is our duty to give the public some idea of the flourishing city of Clarksville, more especially those of our subscribers living at a distance. Clarksville is 60 miles east of Van Buren, the county seat of Johnson County, and has a population of 500. At this place last spring, the largest California company that left Arkansas was organized here; they had their wagons made to order, and purchased all their oxen and mules at the very lowest prices—never, in no instance giving more than $35 per yoke for oxen, $60 for mules, and also purchased their entire outfit here at the lowest price—all this done without the least puffing or blowing about the matter . . ."[49]

The article went on to say that next year (1850) would be even better. Some of the advertisements appearing in the *Fort Smith Herald* are indicative of the commercial activity stimulated by the gold seekers.

> Gold Dust from California!
> or its equivalent, the article coined, will buy goods at #6 Commercial Row.
> W. B. Sutton & Co.[50]

Ho! for California

Just received, a lot of California hats, black and brown, and for sale by

W. B. Sutton & Co.[51]

Harness & Saddles

I am now making a large quantity of Heavy Team Harness, suitable for the California team which will leave this place next April, and will sell them at Cincinnati and St. Louis prices. Also Dragoon and Spanish saddles, just the articles required for such a trip.

Please call and see them.

John Gardner[52]

California Wagons

Eleven, two and three horse wagons, suitable for California emigrants, or for Farming purposes, for sale by

Bennett & Walton[53]

Bargains! Bargains! Bargains!
Charles and Brother
Commercial Row

Intend going to California in the spring, are now selling off their entire stock of DRY GOODS, GROCERIES, HARDWARE, CUTTLERY, IRON, CASTINGS, etc. at cost. . . .[54]

Ho! for California

Just received per steamer *Pennywit,* twelve dozen California hats of all colors and qualities, which we can offer for sale for cash.

J. & H. Beckel[55]

In Washington, Arkansas, merchant Benjamin P. Jett began serving notice in June that he was closing his business, obviously in order to go to California.

California Gold Dust!!

All persons indebted to me up to the 1st of January last, I earnestly require to make immediate settlement, as I'm *determined* to close up my business.

Benj. P. Jett[56]

The 1850 emigrants in Fort Smith also had available to them the services of Messrs, Smiths, Daguerreotypists. Wheeler wrote:

> They are doing wonders in the way of taking *pictures.* They understand their business, and their likenesses are true to life—can't be beat. Just walk in and look at their specimens, and if you are not constrained, before you leave, to have your *phiz* taken down, then we are mistaken. Their room is to be found over Messrs. Johnson and Grimes store.
>
> Prices range from $4 to $10 per plate.[57]

Emigrants in 1850 profited by the experience of the forty-niners who were not reluctant to advise those who came after them. One of the worst mistakes made by the earlier overlanders was using too-large wagons and carrying too many unnecessary provisions. The Fort Smith circular for 1849 had recommended 2500 pounds per wagon, whereas the general recommendation in 1850 was 1,500 pounds or even less. W. W. Stevenson of the Little Rock company advised fellow Arkansians to "take something like the clock wagon" and "not over 600 lbs."[58]

Woodruff copied from the *Missouri Statesman* the outfitting recommendations of "Mr. Helt, an old Santa Fe trader, who went out last spring." It is an excellent summation of forty-niner advice.

> *Wagon and team.*—A light two-horse wagon, well and strongly made, with what is called a 'drop tongue'—the tongue strengthened by a bar of iron along its whole length, and wrapped with hoop iron. Be sure to avoid a heavy wagon. For the team provide, if possible, old, well-broke mules—four years or over their spring; none younger.—If those cannot be got, get oxen. They stand the trip, if of the right sort and properly used, very well. Six mules or four yoke of oxen to a team, with three mules or good hardy ponies in addition to ride. If the team be of cattle, half of it with propriety might be milch cows. Indeed, they stand the trip better than oxen, and are cheaper here and sell for more in California. *The Load, Provisions, Etc.*—Take special care not to overload. A fatal error is often committed on this point. Have a light load—not over 1500 pounds and less if possible. For messes of four men, and that number to each wagon is all that should be allowed, take one barrel of crackers; 400 pounds of flour; 200 lbs of bacon (sides are preferable;) 40 lbs of coffee; 150 lbs. sugar; 15 lbs. of rice; a few lbs. of tea, pepper, and spice; a keg of molasses; a keg of vinegar; a few lbs. of candles; a 10 gallon keg to carry water; plenty of rope to stake out the stock and for other purposes; a mowing scythe is useless. *Tent—Clothing—Tools, Etc.*—Take three blankets for each man; a good tent; a few simple medicines; gun, elastic leggins for each man; (coats and bags of this material are useless;) an oil cloth to spread upon the ground on which to sleep is valuable; one or two picks; a shovel, (not spade;) two or three augers; saw; drawing knife; axe; hatchet; nails and such cooking utensils as common sense suggests. Trouble yourself with no tools to dig or wash gold with. They are plentiful and cheap in the mines. On the route, make it a matter of the first importance that the 'animals' are well fed and kindly driven, otherwise the very best will break down.[59]

The *Fort Smith Herald* reflected the spirit of excitement caused by the California emigration in its masthead. Prior to the fall of 1849, the *Herald* masthead was just plain print of the paper's name. From September 5, 1849, to March 30, 1850, the masthead showed a man on a horse blowing a bugle from which came "California Ho!" On April 6 and 13, the masthead was again plain. Then on April 20, 1850, the new dress of the *Herald* appeared representing the progress of California emigration through Arkansas. On one side a steamboat has obviously just arrived; and on the other, a locomotive on which it was hoped someday they would depart; and in the middle, the emigrants on their winding wagon train was pictured. The three masthead variations are seen in Illustration 5.

Three Fort Smith Herald Mastheads

So great were the numbers of Arkansans planning to go to California in 1850, that a note of concern began to appear in the papers. Would the state be depopulated?

> The *Arkansas Intelligencer* states that the large number of citizens in the surrounding counties who are making preparations to emigrate to California this spring, have awakened the apprehensions of some of our folks, who say the country will be depopulated. It is about to be verified that 'there will not be more than one man to seven women' left in the country. From all we can learn, between four and five hundred will go from Washington County. Many will go from all the surrounding counties.[61]

In another column in the same issue:

> A correspondent of the *Arkansas Intelligencer* writes that many of the best citizens of Fayetteville and of the surrounding country, are busily engaged in making preparation for the long journey to California; in the village there will scarcely be a husband left for the wives, or a beau for the young ladies.[62]

Senator Borland, who had been such an avid champion of the Arkansas route in 1849, came out as an opponent of Arkansans leaving for California. He feared the gold rush mania was draining Arkansas' population and causing real estate-values to decline. Borland strongly maintained these views and was able to persuade the war department to abandon Fort Smith in an effort to forestall the drain on Arkansas' resources. The senator's views and the response of newspaper editors, the Fort Smith merchants and some of the citizens follow.

Writing from Washington, D.C. on April 5, 1850, Senator Borland stated:

> "If our people could be induced with sober minds, and well regulated purpose, to look at home for work and wealth, instead of yielding to the

delirium of the day, and seeking both in a distant and inhospitable clime, I am very sure that they and the state would be incalculably the gainers, in all that makes life desirable and useful. If those of our friends who have gone to California, and are now there, driving ox-teams, digging ditches, crushing rocks, or washing sand in the Sacramento, with one half the labor and assiduity, they now display, to any one of the industrial pursuits among us, can there be a doubt, in any rational mind, that they would have realized as much pecuniary profit to themselves, while enjoying infinitely more personal comfort and social happiness—at the same time they were *building up the State?*

Let me in this connection present you one consideration: It is a simple calculation in arithmetic, and yet think of its results. Apart from the moral, social, and political influence (all so deteriorating) this draining (or driving) off so many of our population must have upon our State, consider, for a moment, the amount of money actually drained off at the same time. What is it? How many of our people have gone off in this way, within the last twelve months? I might say 2,000, and perhaps not overrate them, but I will say 1,000, and be within the bounds. Next, what amount of money, actual cash, did each one carry with him? An average of $200 is within, rather than beyond the sum. Here, then, in actual money (not paper, but gold and silver) is the sum of $200,000, a sum more than double the estimated amount of our whole State Revenue for the same period, and more than enough to pay the whole expenses of our State Government for two years! Add to that a very modest allowance for outfit, including horses, wagons, six month's provisions. etc.—say $150, to each man, and you have an aggregate of at least $350,000.

And how many people will go this year? I find no one calculating less than 2,000 which similar calculation will give for this number $700,000! This, added to the drain of last year, makes an aggregate of $1,050,000! *One million, and fifty thousand dollars!* in money and valuable property, drained off in two years! And to carry that away, we have sent off 3000 of the most active, intelligent and enterprising of our citizens! . . . How is she (the State) to be repaid? . . . Who expects *one-tenth* of these citizens, even should they survive the fearful encounter of hardships and disease, will ever return within our limits? It is the law of the world's nature, that its inhabitants ever travel westward in the course of the sun.

Solon Borland[63]

In a long editorial, Woodruff did not dispute Borland's figures, but suggested California had as much to offer as Arkansas, except the cotton interest, plus the added advantage of the gold mines. Woodruff responded to the statement about what men were doing in California—crushing rocks, etc.—and asked:

Why then are they in California? The correct answer is plainly suggested by the remark. Who is so blind as not to see that it is because in California the true measure of dignity is accorded to labor, while in Arkansas it is too often slurred at as disreputable! It is idle to attempt to disguise this fact, or to gloss it over with excuses. The evil is too apparent to be denied; and unless the false sentiment be speedily eradicated and a healthier tone take its place, the State is doomed to lament the loss of many of her most active and useful citizens.[64]

Again, on May 17, Woodruff editorialized on the effect of the emigration. He commented on the rush of people to California, the worship of Mammon, and the "great hurt" to the newer western states:

"We have accounts from some western States, attributing the depreciation in value of real estate and the stagnation of business" to this emigration. "We know of cases in Arkansas where farms have been forced into market, and comfortable clearings sold for a song, or abandoned by the settlers, for the purpose of enabling them to seek their fortunes in the land of gold."

... "In considering this matter, however, it should not be forgotten, that while one portion of our country is suffering a drain of its citizens, another portion of the same great country is receiving the benefits arising from the additions thus made to its population."[65]

Woodruff's philosophical "good of the nation as a whole approach" was not acceptable to Senator Borland. In May and June, Borland went beyond letter writing and appealed to the War Department to abandon Fort Smith. His appeal was successful, and General Matthew Arbuckle, commandment of the Fort Smith Garrison, was ordered to remove the garrison to Fort Gibson. The people of Fort Smith held a public meeting on June 25, 1850, to formulate a protest against the abandonment of the Fort.[66] The *Fort Smith Herald* was outraged and proclaimed:

"The withdrawal of the last company of Infantry from this post has left about half a million dollars worth of public property exposed.... The public buildings for Military purposes at this place are the finest, and best buildings on the Western frontier. There are two large elegantly finished brick buildings, two stories high, 40 by 100 feet covered with slate, a gallery on each side, two stories supported by pillars of brick. A large building, which was burned down in 1849, now nearly rebuilt, for soldiers quarters 65 by 60 feet, for two companies of men; the carpenter's work is already to be put together, and the brick made for the brick work. The large two-story stone buildings for commissary and the quartermaster stores, a brick guard house, and a stone magazine, all surrounded with a stone wall three feet thick.

"There are also two large stables on the public grounds capable of containing 200 horses, besides outhouses, &. The government purchased 300 acres of land of Capt. Rogers for the building of this post. The fort lies immediately on the line, partly in the State and partly in the Choctaw Nation. These improvements have been left to go to waste and destruction by withdrawing the last company of Infantry for Fort Gibson, where there are already three companies—and where there is no more use for them than there is here. The barracks at that place are built of wood, are old, and many of them rotting down.... The desires and caprices of two or three men were to be gratified and Uncle Sam has to foot the bill to the tune of several hundred dollars."[67]

Editor Wheeler was not inclined to be philosophic as was Woodruff, and concluded his protest article:

Some of our great men have expressed fears that in opening the road to California, it would have a tendency to depopulate the State, by drawing off its inhabitants with the gold mania. For the information of such persons, we would state that a few hundred persons have gone from this State to California, but, for every 100 who have gone, a 1,000 persons have come to the State, the past season has been immense, and we venture to say that the census rolls will develope facts in reference to this subject, that will astonish every Arkansian.[68]

The citizen protest was not without effect, for General Arbuckle was ordered February 12, 1851, to reoccupy Fort Smith by drawing a company from Fort Gibson.[69]

Interestingly another political question faced the citizens of Fort Smith at this time. A public meeting was announced for July 13, 1850, "to devise the best means of dividing the county, as demanded by public interest." The act of the General Assembly creating Sebastian County was approved January 10, 1851, by Governor Seldon Roane. It provided all that portion of Crawford County lying south of the Arkansas River and part of Scott and Logan counties would be known as Sebastian County, and Fort Smith was the county seat.

While the citizens of Fort Smith debated depopulation and county boundaries, the 1850 exodus was winding its way to California. Despite all the favorable publicity regarding the Southern route, several groups which left Arkansas in 1850 chose the Northern route. The Cherokee Emigrating Company left Tahlequah on April 22 to join Arkansans from Washington and Benton counties at the Grand Saline and proceed by the Evans-Cherokee Trail as the Cherokees of 1849 had done.[70] A group left Cane Hill in Washington County, Arkansas, on April 9 to rendezvous at the Grand Saline. James Mitchell II and William Quesenbury were along the party of twenty-four with six wagons which left Cane Hill. Both men kept diaries of their trip. The original Quesenbury diary is at Duke University, but it was published verbatim in the Washington County Historical Society's publication *Flashback* (1979). Quesenbury was a teacher at his own school in Cane Hill and a humorist who wrote under the name, "Bill Cush." He would be twenty-eight when he reached California. Mitchell's diary has never been published. It was made available to the Arkansas Territorial Restoration by Mrs. Frank Wait, and the author has been permitted to quote it extensively.

The Mitchell and Quesenbury diaries point out the problem and dissension which beset this group. They found themselves too early for grass and the Verdigris River was too high to ford requiring the construction of a buffalo-skin raft. The groups were slow in catching up to the rendezvous, and there was fear of Indian trouble on the part of some of the group. Mitchell was fifty-seven years old at the time of the trip. His writing style is terse. The two diaries are integrated to describe the experiences of these Arkansas overlanders via the Northern route.

Left Cane Hill, Washington County, Arkansas on the 9th April, 1850 on a trip to the gold diggings in California. Wm. Quesenbury and me together. Weather a cold wet day. We overtook our messes that evening that had started the day before in wagons. Our first camp about 34 miles from home near Bower's Mill.

10 Wed. A clear day with a little frost. Strickler and me got corn and fodder at Bower's Mill. Each of us paid $1. We took the wrong road toward Fort Gibson.

11 Thurs. In 3 miles got in our right road and could see wagons ahead who belonged to our company. We got to the Grand Salt works and intended crossing Grand River, but our company would not because they said the grass was too scarce when in my opinion the real cause was waiting for more company for fear of Indians. [They bought corn for feeding stock.]

12 Friday . . . We held our election at night. (J. T.) Craig and [Perry] Park were made our officers. [Consequently this became "Craig's Company."]

13 Saturday. A beautiful frosty morning. All appeared ready to cross Grand River. All appeared good humored and ready to assist each other. Our wagon was first over there being only 6 of them in all . . . only 24 men in company. . . .

16 a rainy, warm morning. We got to the Verdigris and attempted to cross, the banks being bad. Two of the wagons got over with great difficulty and had the offer of ox teams to help the rest of us over next morning if we would wait til morning. We waited and in vain.

17 Wednesday. Cold and cloudy. 60 men with ox teams were across the river in sight of us who offered to assist in crossing the river last evening and refused to help this morning unless we would join their company and pledge ourselves as honorable gentlemen to not leave it. This gave us double vigor, and we soon got over without assistance. The most of our men were in favor of remaining here till grass got better, and some of them went off 5 or 6 miles after corn and returned without any. Could not get it for $ bushel. I plainly see the main cause of the detention is waiting for more men to overtake us and go with us. . . .

20 Saturday. All made ready to start on our journey. The ox company started first. 3 men from Tennessee joined us which made us 27 strong.[71]

Mitchell became more and more provoked with the unnecessary delays which he saw as excuses "to wait for more company." A Cherokee runner overtook them late on April 20 and asked them to wait for the Cherokee party. Mitchell wrote:

I saw at once it pleased some of our leading men, and they were determined to wait for them. I determined to not wait and go on it being 8 days since we left the Branch on Grand River and only have traveled about 40 miles. We could have traveled in the same time 80 miles at least and our animals in as good a condition as they are and of had as much corn and provisions as we now have.[72]

Nonetheless Mitchell's company decided to wait for the Cherokees and sent men back to the river to see if they were yet there. Return Jonathan Meigs, son of the longtime Cherokee agent and husband of Jane Ross, daughter of Cherokee Chief John Ross, was with the Cherokee party. Women were also reported to be in the party. From Saturday evening until Thursday morning, Mitchell's party waited. They fished, bathed, traded with the Osage, and fussed about the delay. Mitchell's mess mates were Strickler and Robinson. Strickler, like Mitchell, "was strongly in favor of going on," but Robinson "appeared very angry at us and urged that we should bind ourselves before we went any further to continue with the wagon under any circumstances. We gave him a positive refusal without he were to bind himself also to travel a constant daily gate to the mines." To relieve the tension, Mitchell, Strickler and Cush went fishing. Mitchell noted "Robinson eat some!"

On Monday evening "the long looked for, great and much esteemed Meigs" arrived at the river and was waiting assistance to cross. The women reported to have been with the group had joined another company at Fort Gibson. One man from each mess was detailed to assist Meigs, but Mitchell "escaped this labor" and went fishing. With the added Cherokee group, their party was to number 49 men and 13 wagons. All but four wagons had arrived when they started on Thursday, April 25. The four overtook them on Friday evening. The entire party traveled together on Saturday and made 12 miles. Sunday they laid by, and on Monday a meeting was called and "more than half our company dropped off from us who we had been waiting for and who had sent us word to wait for them. But all this I anticipated."[73]

Quesenbury's diary also referred to the dissension. On the 20th he wrote, "I wish I had never heard of or been connected with the company." On the 23rd he wrote, "Lying by yet, eating up our provisions." At the meeting on the 29th, Quesenbury said, "Our same old crowd, except Shipley went on with us."[74] Elections were held at the meeting and the following officers were chosen: Clement Vann McNair, captain; Robert Harris, lieutenant; John Gott, sergeant of the guard; Alfred Cunningham, wagon-master; and John H. Wolf, secretary. The rules and regulations and duties of the officers were also drawn up. The sergeant was to mount the guard and visit them once each night; the wagon-master was to arrange the order of march; the captain determined travel and camp time and was in general charge. A committee of twelve was to punish minor offenses.[75] Probably thinking order had been established, the group moved out and made 20 miles that day, and traveled and camped well and "good humored" on the following two days. Mitchell served as advance scout and used the time waiting for the wagons to keep his "memorandums", to rest, and to graze his animals.[76]

The contentment was short lived, however, for approximately 100 Osages stampeded their camp on May 2 and drove off many of the animals which were later retrieved. Mitchell was not appreciative of the captain's handling of the situation and considered him unduly afraid. The Indians camped close by after the stampede but rode off the next morning. The majority decided to lay by until more company from behind came up, but Mitchell and his mess (Crum and Robinson) left the group and went on ahead where they joined some ox teams on May 5.[77] Quesenbury noted on May 4th and 5th there was talk of turning back, and he felt "suspense about the future, have no confidence whatever in any management, such as we have, of affecting anything."[78]

While they were waiting, they were joined on May 6 by Samuel Mayes, John Lowrey Brown, George Washington Adair, and twenty other Cherokees with twelve wagons, besides forty whites from Missouri and Arkansas. On the 9th twenty-one more men with five wagons joined the party, making in all 105 whites and Cherokees, including twelve women and fifteen Negro servants, and thirty-four wagons. Clem McNair was still the captain, and John Beck, Weatherford (Ludge) Beck, Brice Hildebrand, Joe Spears and Eagle and John Clark were among the Cherokee members of the party.[79] The larger group then traveled close together, and Quesenbury noted the "Cane Hill crowd are stationed on the outside seam of the line of encampment which is Wagon Master Cunningham's work." The spring was unusually cold with strong winds. Prairie dogs began to appear and the first signs of buffalo. Quesenbury remarked on camp signs left by Mitchell and Crum.[80]

Unfortunately dissension continued to plague this company—"pallets can't be made right nor anything else," wrote Quesenbury. There was some sickness which delayed travel, plus Merrill was caught sleeping on picket and had to be tried by the Committee of Twelve. He was found guilty, but his fine was remitted. McNair resigned as captain because of this decision, but he was reelected.[81] Finally at evening camp on May 16, when the company had reached the intersection of the Evans' and Santa Fe Trail, the decision was made to separate. Quesenbury recorded 18 wagons, including his, broke off and moved ahead. These wagons were using horses and mules and could move faster than the ox team. Return Johnathan Meigs, John Ross, Joseph Coodey, Ben Sanders, and John H. Wolf were among this advance party.[82] Clem McNair and John L. Brown remained behind with the ox team. Elections were held for the advance party, and John Wolf was elected captain, Robert Harris lieutenant, Buckner sergeant, Dennis wagon-master, and Craig secretary.[83]

Quesenbury now in the Wolf company noted they were fifty-nine men strong with sixteen wagons. His diary recounts their first meal of buffalo on May 17 and subsequent buffalo and antelope hunts, and prairie dog adventures, including his capturing one for a pet. As they progressed, they made plans to pack when they reached Pueblo. Meigs did not plan to pack. On June 4 Quesenbury said 23 men had signed an agreement to pack. When he listed the men; however, there were 36 names.[84] Quesenbury and three others went on ahead to Greenhorn, a Mexican village near Pueblo, to make preparations for switching the group to pack saddles. When they reached Fort Bent, they discovered Mitchell and Robinson had preceded them by one week. The preparations were extensive and time consuming. McNair's rear company, which had been joined by more Cherokees, overtook the advance party at Pueblo. J. J. May attached himself to McNair's wagon party, deciding against packing; while Return Meigs decided to pack. The cast-off items of the packers were consigned either to the river or to a huge pile which Quesenbury ignited with three tent poles when they left Pueblo at noon on June 15.[85]

So along the Evans route, Mitchell and ox wagons led by Captain Edmondson, Quesenbury and the packers, Wolf's remnant wagon group., and McNair's slower wagon company were stretched out for California.

Mitchell's diary from May 3, when he left the Craig company until June 29 when he and Quesenbury were reunited on the trail, recounted the use of buffalo chips for fuel, eating and killing buffalo and antelope, geological formations, vegetation, weather, absence of shade, prairie dog towns, river crossings, Indian encounters, and more squabbling among the emigrants. While he was away on advance guard duty, Robinson, the owner of the wagon, threw out Mitchell and Crum's possessions and joined another broken mess.[86] Mitchell loaned his pony to a man in exchange for hauling some of his things. Mitchell then had words with the man because he used the pony to hunt during encampments rather than permitting the pony to rest. For punishment, Mitchell's mess was given the toughest morsel of meat when the divide of the kill was made! On May 31 Mitchell was at Bent's Fort where he could stand on the old walls and see snow on the Rocky Mountains. He passed the base of Pike's Peak on June 7. On June 12 they made a tedious crossing of the swift South Platte River using canoes and rafts which they fashioned. They supposed their crossing to be 40 or 50 miles above where Evans crossed in 1849. They then crossed the Laramie River and entered the Laramie plains, intersecting the Evans trail on June 21 and rafting the North Platte on June 27.

Building rafts and crossing so many rivers had, of course, slowed their progress. On June 28 Mitchell and fourteen others "left the train and determined to try and get to the mines sooner than the wagons could go." Even so, they too had many little creeks to cross which were part of the mountain drainage system. On Saturday morning, June 29, as they were saddling to start, Mitchell's group was surprised by a loud yell. Two men came toward them—Cush (Quesenbury) and Buckner.[87]

After traveling two days with the pack-mule company out of Pueblo, Quesenbury, Buckner and Riley Buchanan decided on June 17 "to make a start for California." Riley rejoined the packers on June 22, and Quesenbury and Buckner continued on alone. Quesenbury's entry on June 25 clearly revealed his loneliness. "I have thought more about home since last night than I have during the same period of time since I left. I dreamed of home last night. Saw friends, but this morning sorrow returned and 'The voice in my dreaming ear melted away.' " Quesenbury was following Captain Edmondson's (Mitchell's group) newly cut trail and using their discarded rafts to cross streams. Quesenbury overtook Edmondson's train on the 28th and learned that Mitchell and his party of 14 had only two hours before struck out on their own. Quesenbury and Buckner "resolved to follow their track and overtake them." They tracked until dark, made camp, and left the next morning "by the first peep of day." They saw smoke, shouted and were answered by Mitchell. Completely unreflective of his joy, Quesenbury states: "came up and found Mr. Mitchell and our friends." But Mitchell better caught the essence of the meeting when he wrote: "I have never seen a man more glad than Quesenbury appeared to be when he came up with us." Together they crossed the gap in the great divide.[88]

They were in a "barren, destitute country" with bad prospect for grass and water. When water was found, it was very alkaline and unpalatable for man or beast. Quesenbury noted on July 4: "The Glorious Fourth! Dry times with us."[89] It was dry from the standpoint of water as well as liquor. Continuing through the mountainous region, they reached Green River where grass and good water were plentiful in the river bottom. Quesenbury using his spyglass spotted a canoe across the river and swam across to procure it for their crossing. They attached logs to either side of the small canoe, and in seven trips succeeded in crossing their packs, losing only one pewter plate.[90] They camped with "plenty of mosquitoes and horseflies" in attendance and the next day camped within two miles of the Independence route.

Both diarists comment on the heavy wagon traffic on the "great trail" as well as the number of dead oxen, horses and mules. Mitchell said they passed "60 wagons in 17 miles." Quesenbury wrote: "The Emigrants seem to mind their own business. They never take the trouble to raise their heads or speak as we pass them."[91] Both men spoke disparagingly of Fort Bridger as resembling "a strong horse pen" or "a picketed horse lot." When they reached Weber River, they found a sign warning them that if they took the left-hand road to Salt Lake, they would have to pay a toll to the Mormons who had recently opened the new road. Dead animals along the road and in the water gave them added incentive to pass numerous wagons and make their way on to Salt Lake City. The toll charge was ten cents for each animal and seventy-five cents per wagon. Quesenbury noted "Mitchell and Crum cleaned up for a decent entry into the Mormon City. I will be more modest and pass through so quietly that I will be unnoticed."[92]

Quesenbury stated he was disappointed in the city, but Mitchell thought it "the finest valley for farming that ever I saw." He was impressed by the irrigation ditches and the length of the growing season. They remained three days in Mormon City, replenishing supplies, shodding horses, buying wheat in shieves for fodder, visiting the gunsmith, getting baking done, and having tin cans made. Mitchell and Quesenbury spent a night with Old Chan, the miller and dined on "fine peas, a little butter, good light bread, and milk." They enjoyed another back-home treat—they burned a candle and sat up till midnight! They wrote letters home and went to the post office to mail them on Sunday, July 15, but were told the postmaster was one of the preachers for the day, so they must wait until 12 o'clock to post them. Quesenbury and Mitchell decided to attend the church meeting. The postmaster was preaching "which amounted to nothing but sickening praise of the Mormons and a recapitulation of their sufferings." Brigham Young also preached and then announced "no more flour was to be sold under 25 cents a pound." They mailed their letters and left.[93]

They made their way across the Salt Lake Desert River using a guidebook they had purchased from the Mormons which they soon discarded as worthless. They crossed a couple of more Mormon "toll concerns." Grass was almost nonexistant and the water filled with alkaline deposits. Mitchell said they "traveled 63 miles in two days and till late at night without grass."[94] There were numerous wagon trains, packers, and dead animals to impede their progress. On July 25th they nooned on the headwaters of the Humbolt in a wide beautiful, grass valley. They camped early that evening to avail the animals of good grazing. Both men commented on their delectable curlew supper on the 26th. Mitchell's diary ends on July 27 with them continuing down the then-narrowing Humbolt River Valley, but Quesenbury's continued another three weeks.

The Humbolt River in Nevada, sometimes called Mary's River, received its name from Fremont in 1845. The river was muddy and putrid and barely able to sustain life. Grass was only to be found growing on islands in the river, and the emigrants had to swim and cut grass for the animals; or if not too marshy, swim the animals to the bars to graze. Digger Indians, whose main diet was roots, lived along the river. They had gained a reputation for thievery. The emigrants continued 250–260 miles along the rivers length until it mysteriously disappeared in the "Sink," or sand. Ware's *Emigrant*

Guide said of the Sink: "It is a low marsh, surrounded with bulrushes and saline incrustations and emits a most disagreeable effluvia; the water cannot be used for man or beast."[95]

The emigrants suffered greatly along the Humbolt, and Quesenbury highlights those sufferings. It was not possible to hold a course close to the river because the banks were a quagmire due to a hot spring melting the heavy winter snows and flooding the valley. The good grass which had been reported in 1849 was nonexistent in 1850. At one point Quesenbury wrote they got "bothered about the road which branched out in all kinds of circles, cross forks, high cuts, etc. Found the right track came in over a ridge, struck the river."[96] They had to cross the river on a wagon body ferry. "The water is bad, causing our horses to urinate continually." His pony named "Dog" mired several days in a row. They took various "cuts" seeking grass or an easier passage. Dead animals were strung along the way all the way to the Sink. At one nooning, he swam the river to cut grass which required six trips to retrieve and required their lariats. Trains were constantly passing as the emigrants pushed on to the Sink. They were plagued by mosquitoes along the river which did not "let up" til after midnight. Dead stock began to be reported in the water.

When they reached the Sink, they had to choose between the Carson or Truckee River routes. Choosing the Carson route, they faced forty miles of desert before reaching the Carson River and the last 100 miles to California. The forty-mile stretch had to be crossed without forage and water, and men and animals both were pushed to the limits. One writer said, "Had the Humbolt Desert been ten miles broader, probably only a small fraction of the emigrants would have lived to reach its western side."[97] When the emigrants sighted the sand, they began to discard wagons, beds, furniture, and every conceivable item in order to cross the desert. Quesenbury wrote, "The destruction of property from wagons, down to every article of an outfit has been immense. Vast quantities of animals lie dead on the road. Some are dying, some standing."[98] Quesenbury parched coffee and baked bread on an abandoned stove. He recorded something not mentioned in the 1849 accounts—a water wagon charging a dollar a gallon, and then another charging 75 cents a gallon. They asked every man they met how far it was to the river and no two agreed. "The sand continued heavy and deep til we reached the Carson River which was just at moon down." There were trading establishments where the emigrants could buy flour and beef. "Grass thieves" sold grass for 25¢ a bundle. "I counted today since we left the sink four hundred and fifty-four dead horses."[99]

Along the Carson River they could rest and recruit and prepare for the last leg of the journey to the mines. The water and cottonwood shade were so welcome. Quesenbury also picked up a very good pair of boots from an abandoned wagon. He had abandoned his at the Sink where they stuck in the mud. He bought dried apples from another emigrant who was making his pack lighter. Quesenbury learned from Wacooli, a slave of Rollin Ridge's, who was in Rector's group, that the Rector party had taken the Truckee route a day or so before. On August 20, Mitchell and Strickler decided to go on by night toward the mines and better grazing. Quesenbury chose instead to make camp and rest his animals. They divided the provisions. "I went and talked with some Illinoians about a hundred and fifty yards off; then came back and laid down beneath the pines, solitary and alone—the first night I have been so, since I left home,"[100] The next day the entry read: "My birthday. I am now twenty-eight years old." Neither Quesenbury nor Mitchell would find a fortune. Both returned to Cane Hill—Cush to become editor of the *Southwest Independent* in Fayetteville and Mitchell to farm.

The Cherokee and Arkansas group which Mitchell and Quesenbury left behind them on the trail had continued to have dissension and regroupings. Clem McNair resigned his command at the end of June when they reached the Evans' Trail, and Cherokee T. F. Taylor took command. A Captain Oliver and his ox train, including more Cherokees, joined them, and they proceeded to the left of the Evans-Cherokee route. They crossed the North Fork of the Platte on July 3 and Green River on July 19. At Green River they abandoned their wagons and prepared to pack and reached Fort Bridger on June 27. At Fort Bridger they become part of the stream of emigrants on the Oregon Trail. On July 31 they reached Salt Lake City but remained only until August 2. They traveled another seventy-five or eighty miles and then laid by with many other emigrants to recruit the animals in preparation for the ninety miles of salt desert. Here disaster in the form of cholera struck the overlanders. Return J. Meigs "took cholera about three or four o'clock the same afternoon and died at nine o'clock the same night." Russel, Huss, and Gabriel Martin succumbed in the next several days to the dread disease, and Clem McNair, Jack Hildebrand and a black man recovered.[101] The sickness slowed the train and caused dissatisfaction. McNair's, May's, Martin's and Dr. Barber's messes pulled out of Captain Taylor's company leaving 33 men in that company.[102]

This group camped on the Humbolt on September 4, some five weeks after Mitchell and Quesenbury had been there. John H. Wolf wrote of this camp:

> No bread for more than a week and very little meat. No flour to be had for love or money—we cut grass and packed it to our horses to feed them on the Desert; at four o'clock this evening we started. Continued down the waters of Mary's River (Humbolt) which at this place spreads out and resembles a large mill pond. We crossed the river and traveled until midnight when we stopped until morning where we fed the grass to our horses which we had been packing for them . . .
>
> Early this morning we found at daylight that we were near the last waters of the River fairly out on the Desert which is a sandy plain for which reason traveling over it is very slow. We suffered more crossing this desert than we have since leaving home, and we saw more property destroyed on this plain, waggons [sic], horses, mules, and cattle than we had yet seen in crossing over the same number of miles.[103]

Wolf reported the death of Talbot Bean while crossing the desert and noted "nearly all of us took the diarrhea." From Carson River, they were 100 miles across the Sierras to California and another 150 miles to Sacramento. Captain Taylor wrote from Sacramento on September 27, that he had gone there alone with none of his animals surviving. His company had scattered "in order to get along. I don't know what I will do. If I had the money I had when I left home I should return as fast as steam would bear me via the Isthmus."[104] A letter from John Wolf on November 27 indicated he and a group of Cherokees had erected cabins on Feather River below the juncture of the Feather and Yuba rivers.[105]

One other group which went the Northern route was that of Major Elias Rector. Rector was born in Virginia and moved to Arkansas as surveyor in 1825 and to Fort Smith in 1837. He was appointed by President Jackson as U.S. Marshall of the Indian and Arkansas Territories in 1830. He held that post until 1846, and he was a much respected citizen. Major Rector and Col. Matthew Leeper, an attorney from Fayetteville, had announced in the autumn of 1849 they would lead a company to California over the Fort Smith road followed by Marcy the previous spring. For reasons unknown to us, they instead left Fayetteville and followed the northern route that Evans and the Cherokees had followed the year before. Major Rector's wife, Catherine, kept a diary during her husband's absence which will be quoted extensively in a later chapter. Catherine noted her husband left Fort Smith on April 3, and he did not leave Fayetteville until the latter part of April.[106] Rector regretted the decision to take the northern route, but he told Catherine in a letter from Fort Smith on May 18 "it was too late to look back." The *Fort Smith Herald* reported on the same day Catherine received her letter:

> We are informed, by a good authority, that the company of California emigrants that left Arkansas, to go on the northern route, split up on the Verdigris River, and have taken different routes. The prairies, on the frontier of Missouri, are represented to be entirely destitute of grass—nothing but a bleak waste. This party has had some difficulties with the Osages. It is thought that owing to the want of grass, and other difficulties, that a portion of the company will endeavor to turn across and fall into Captain Marcy's road.
>
> If this company had taken the advice of friends, they would have been, by this time, *five hundred miles upon the Southern, or Fort Smith road.*[107]

David V. Spring, a member of the Rector company, wrote to Editor Wheeler from Fort Kearny describing their journey:

> Fort Kearny, May 24, 1850
>
> Dear Sir:
>
> I am fortunate enough, after a long and tedious drive from Fayetteville, since the 20th April, to arrive here safe.—We are all well, and have generally enjoyed good health. I think, also, we are all in good spirits, as men could possibly be, after dragging through so many mud holes, and over such bad roads. Before we arrived in Fort Scott, the roads were rough and very heavy, after leaving these, up to West Point, 45 miles, part of the time we had pretty fair road, the remainder, however was as rough as could be . . . Then to Santa Fe road, a firm road, but mountainous, either hard pulling or holding back all the time. In short a worse road I have never seen. Grass—scarce . . .
>
> You know I have always been in favor of the F S route, and now I can assure you, that I am doubly so. . . .
>
> This is one of the most miserable places I ever saw . . . there is neither wood, nor soil upon which to raise vegetables; a few huts built entirely of mud, ditched around. This is Fort Kearny![108]

The next word from the Rector party came from Mark L. Evans at a point "three miles west of the summit of the South Pass, June 26, 1850." He wrote about the poor road, the scarcity of wood and water, the number of streams to ferry, and the exorbitant ferry charges. The ferry at the Upper Platte charged five dollars per wagon and four dollars for each yoke of oxen. At Green River the Mormons charged ten dollars per wagon. He also commented on the tremendous number (5,000) of wagons ahead of them. Many emigrants were abandoning their wagons and goods and packing. The "destruction of property" bewildered him. He noted diarrhea had plagued the company on the Platte. His group had pulled ahead of Rector, Leeper, Spring and Ledford as well as some of the Cherokees. "All well when we left them. . . . Many have exhausted their provisions and will evidently have to suffer in the extreme. Many are going by Salt lake, but we will take Sublette's cut off, and save some 200 miles or more. . . . It is taxing on us to have to take our horses two or three miles off (the road to graze) and guard them all night. . . . We think we will get through by the 15th of August."[109]

David Spring wrote his brother Dr. N. Spring of Fort Smith a long letter after they reached California on August 16:

Nevada City, California
August 23, 1850

Dear Brother:—

After a long, tedious, tiresome, and sickening journey, I have at length made landing at the place above written. I know but little of the country, as I only arrived at the first diggings on the 16th inst., making my journey through from Bentonville, eight days less than four months. I wrote to you from Fort Laramie which you have doubtless received. There Col. Leeper left us as we were throwing some wagons away. We were there three days. Here we struck the Black Hills, the peaks of them were covered with perpetual snow. . . . Here I left that enormous big wagon; sold my horse for a stout spring wagon, getting $40 to boot. We then struck across the Black Hills, still up the north Platte, heavy sand and rough hills. 125 miles from Laramie, we crossed the Platte at the Mormon Ferry, at $5 per wagon, $1 for each mile. After crossing, we filled our casks with water and watered our stock, for there is no good water for 30 miles. Eleven miles from the crossing we came to Poison Spring, and from the amount of dead stock which lay around, it has a good name. 19 miles from here we came to Willow Spring, the only good water you find to Pacific Spring west of the South Pass, which is distant from Willow Spring 150 miles. . . .

(Spring then talked about sickness.)

John Taylor was very sick; came near dying, and was not able to do much for 900 miles. In fact, we had him to haul for 600 miles. Past this side of Laramie, Riley Sprague was taken at night, or about half an hour after dark. I left him between sundown & dark well and hearty, laughing with the boys. One hour after this, I was called from my tent to see about him, and had he been a stranger and I passing by, I would have said he had been sick for 2 weeks. His eyes were sunken, his voice very feeble. (Spring said it was congestion of the brain) . . . He lingered in this way for 2 days & died June 20, 1850 . . . (They had to bury him) It is a dreary, lonesome place. We had simply to wrap him in a sheet and throw the dirt over him, without any boards to keep the dirt from his body. I know it was as well, but I assure you it will make the blood run chill in any human heart to have such a task to do. Next Evans was taken, then Cox, the wild Irishman, and Taylor, all sick, so there was all the labor of gearing, driving, and attending to mules thrown upon Hart, Neal and myself . . . Maj. Rector came near loosing two of his hands.

2 days travel from Laramie, cholera came up with our train, and was represented as being very bad behind us. I thought I had seen enough sickness, and I told the boys to use a limber whip, and you may guess they did, for in the next three days, we passed over 700 wagons. We were then clear, high & dry from the cholera.

This contingent of the Fayetteville party passed Col. Leeper at the head of Sweetwater River. Spring feared Leeper was experiencing many difficulties, and would not get through with anything. Continuing their trip from Willow Spring, he wrote:

. . . You pass (from Willow Spring) through the South Pass to the Pacific Spring; from this to Big Sandy, 25 miles no grass. At Big Sandy, fill your casks with water for the first desert, which is 63 miles. . . . We had nought but a desert all the way through. Green River is a rough, bad stream to cross . . . From Green River to Bean River, 50 miles, rough, heavy roads; in the beautiful valley of this river, you find good grass, the first you get on the road. Then to Soda Springs which cover 1½ to 2 miles square. . . . They gurgle up and sink back and always keep up a beautiful boil. Then to Fort Hall road, then Salt Lake Road, then Hot Spring Valley (which was 950 miles from Laramie) So on an average for 26 days, we made 36½ miles per day. Then to the Humbolt the beginning of sorrow . . . From the head to the sink of this stream is at least 350 miles, and not one inch of the distance agreeing with the description which Fremont, Myers, Ware and others have given it. So far from it that instead of being a beautiful valley clothed with blue grass, herds grass, clover, etc., in most parts, it is a miserable sterile waste—a soft ashy earth, which will admit the feet of mules from five to 25 inches in depth. You are seldom, if ever, out of the sight of a dead horse, or ox, and at night when you are drinking your coffee and eating your leather hoecake, you can have the pleasing reflection that the coffee is sweetened, and the bread shortened with the odorous orange water of dead animals, for every few hundred yards you could see them dead in the only stream of water we had. The Sink is awful. 75 miles above we threw away every wagon we had. Only one as a company wagon, and packed through, finding our mules too weak to bring them in . . . We came the Truckey river route from the Sink, because no one had scarcely traveled it. It is about 75 miles from the Sink through the desert without one drop of water; and about 95 miles without one blade of grass. After getting on to the Truckee we had good grass, good pure water, and air uncontaminated by carion . . . Fifty miles you travel up this river. Then it is 100 miles to the nearest mines.

Your affectionate brother
David V. Spring[110]

Note they had made the trip in "eight days less than four months," which was considerably shorter than some of the forty-niners' seven or eight month trips. Marked roads and lighter wagons had profited the 1850 groups.

Two half-blooded Cherokees, Rollin and Aeneas Ridge and their slave Wacooli, were in Rector's group. In a long letter to his mother written about six weeks after their arrival in California, Rollin described their experiences from Fort Laramie to Yuba. Rollin had a very picturesque style, and his letter is an excellent summary of experiences along this northern route. It complements the information in the Spring letter and in Quesenbury and Mitchell's accounts. The letter is given in full in Appendix E, but several excerpts illustrate his descriptive powers. Referring to the tolls and purchase of supplies from the Mormons, he noted it "shelled" the money from him. The "Mormon Guide, a little book consisting of four small leaves," cost 50 cents. His meals without meat cost 37½ to 50¢ per meal and would have been a dollar with meat! One final expense of his Mormon visit was not mentioned by the other Arkansans who visited Salt Lake City. "I went to the printing office in the city and bought one of their little newspapers with my name, arrival and departure in it, and sent it to you by the Mormon mail. I paid 75 cents for this."

The dust was especially loathsome to Ridge as they approached the Humbolt.

> ... We waded thro' mineral dust ... sometimes up to the horses' knees, but commonly four or five inches deep. This we did every day from morn 'til night thro' clouds of dust, whose poisonous particles made sores in the nose and ears and for myself affected my throat dreadfully. You have no idea how terrible it is to bear, this dust. Continually, not for a mile or two, but for hundreds of miles, filling your eyes, ears and throat! At night you are not free from it. You cannot shake it out of your blankets, and every time you turn over, light clouds of the precious incense greet your senses.
>
> ... We could not comb our heads; it would have taken two days to have combed out the dirt that got into them in one—so that our heads looked like old mops which had scrubbed floors from time immemorial ... After a day's travel each individual every night, looked like he had been rolling himself over and over in the dirt, head and ears, and had taken pains to see how perfectly hateful to the sight he could become!
>
> Our best friends would not have known us. If we had, in the plight ridden thro' the neighborhood of Fayetteville, driving our long, bony legged mules and horses (which the buzzards were beating their drums for, as old black Peter would say) before us, the sense of the ludicrous would have been so supreme—our long solemn faces helping it off too—that the boys would have hooted at us as we passed by and the hilarity of the spectacle been without bounds. ... Poor Humanity! to what miserable passes will it put itself for money.

Ridge also commented on the water wagons from Salmon Trout River which met the emigrants on the western edge of the forty-five mile desert stretch beyond the Humbolt Sink. Trudging through deep sand and intense heat:

> We couldn't carry enough water in our canteens to quench our thirst for any length of time; besides the sun shone so hot that water became so warm as to be an emitic ... Nearly dead, we met some wagons ... with barrels of the precious liquid which they sold to us for a dollar a gallon.

> I never supposed, til I got to the desert, I should have to pay for so common an article as water. But those wagoners made thousands of dollars by selling it. . . .
>
> Horses lay dead . . . every fifty yards thro' the desert. The stench was in every breath we breathed . . . It was as tho' we had been standing with our noses to a piece of carrion![111]

Major Rector wrote Captain Rogers of Fort Smith from Sacramento on September 6, and the *Herald* published this excerpt:

> The trip was long and unpleasant—one, on account of the bad route. There was much suffering on the way, by the emigrants, and from the accounts daily received, the suffering has increased. The grass and water, on the road, especially on Humbolt river, was of the worst quality—in fact on that river, for near 300 miles, there was a greater destruction of property, than on any other part of the road. *There is not a man who came the northern route, that will return that way;* and it is the opinion of most persons that *THE ROUTE CANNOT SUPPORT ANOTHER IMMIGRATION.*[112]

No doubt Editor Wheeler regretted the suffering of his friends and fellow Arkansans who had chosen the northern route, but he could not resist an indirect "I told you so." More of Rector's experiences are recounted through his wife's diary in the following chapter.

One other Arkansas emigrant who traveled this route, possibly in Rector's or Mitchell's party, was Robert Little of Crawford County. In a letter to his wife he said:

> I reached here, Cullomia, [Coloma] Upper Calif., on the 4th of Aug., after a tedious and long journey with many privations and hardships on the way. I lost both of my horses 100 miles short of the end of my journey, and had to travel the rest of the way on foot. I traveled 300 miles on 4 lbs of flour, 1 lb of rice and 1½ lbs of bacon and had to swim the Humbolt river and cut food with our knives to feed our stock, such a scarcity of grass. We traveled down the Humbolt river 200 miles and had always to swim to get food for our starving animals, and sometimes could get none for them at all. We had to cut their grass which grows in the middle of the river, below the surface of the water and many have been drowned in trying to get food enough to keep their animals from perishing.[113]

The *Arkansas Gazette* copied material from the New Orleans *True Delta* based on a report from "a gentlemen direct from California." His account corroborated the suffering on the overland Oregon Route, and indicated relief had been organized in San Francisco and Sacramento to aid persons still east of the Sierras as of late November, 1850. "It is believed 5,000 emigrants have lost their lives this past season due to hunger, thirst, cholera and any number of other afflictions." This reporter indicates the greatest suffering was on the Truckee route [Rector's] and primarily attributable to the "scarcity of grass for stock which caused them to give out."[114]

The number of emigrants in 1850 doubled so that 45,000 made their way to California including more women and children.[115] Greater numbers went via the regularly established Panama route. There are no estimates for how the emigrants were divided among the routes. One thing is clear, those Arkansans who used the southern route got along with much less difficulty than those on the northern route.

Judge R. S. C. Brown, recently Cherokee agent, led a group of one hundred fifty emigrants, including Cherokees and Arkansans, from their Fort Washita rendezvous on May 6.[116] T. T. Henry of Conway County was a member of this group. When they arrived at Dona Ana, the halfway point on July 7, Henry wrote to Editor Wheeler:

> Dona Ana, July 7, 1850
>
> Mr. Wheeler—Dear Sir: In compliance with the promise I made you, I now am proud to say, that I have had as pleasant a trip so far, as I anticipated, to this place. The mule teams that left Fort Smith when I did reached the vicinity of El Paso, in fifty-four days, including all detentions on the road, the ox teams arrived 6 days later. All the Texas emigrants, are now in the valley of the Rio Grande, recruiting teams, together with those who came from Arkansas. The number is something over 500, that are on the southern route that Capt. Marcy returned by last fall, turning into El Paso from the Waro mountains. As for the road, I can say, without the fear of contradiction, it is the best that can be found in the world. *No bad mountains from Fort Smith to this place.* The emigrants are crossing 20 miles above Dona Ana, and taking Cooke's route. We found water at all the watering places, Capt. Marcy gave, except the Mustang Pond and the Cotton Wood Spring, which makes a stretch of 71 and 36 miles, without water. But the road in these places is smooth and firm, and by being prudent can be made with ease. I believe this route is bound to be the best route to the southern mines in California, and if the Ark. emigrants get along well as they have thus far, they will make the mines in *four months and a half with ox-teams.* There is considerable stir here in regard to the Gila mines, 200 miles from here. Some of us expect to halt a while, and see what the prospect is. It is said that we can make 3 ozs. per day by stopping there; if this be the case, we can afford to pass the warm weather there.
>
> T. T. Henry[117]

J. F. Simmons of Crawford County was possibly a member of the Judge Brown group. In February 1852 he had returned and planned to lead a group to California. In announcing his intentions and outlining his proposed route, he recalled his first trip in 1850. Note that he says there were 183 men in his party, and that they too found no water at Mustang Pond.

> Gen. Clarke—I have been requested by a portion of my neighbors, to make known, through the *Intelligencer,* the route and some particulars of the trip which I made to Calif. from this place in the spring of 1850. As there is a company about to organize in this county, which will start from Van Buren in March next, and others who might desire to join them, I will trouble you with a few lines.
>
> This is called the *Southern Route,* via 'Marcy's road,' from Van Buren on the Ark. river. It lies through the Choctaw and Chickasaw nations, to Preston, on Red River, in Texas; thence to Georgetown, the westmost settlement on the route. From here to Preston, it can be traveled at any time (before grass), because

provender can be purchased of the Indians. If we get to Preston or to Georgetown by the first of April, we will find plenty of grass and water. Grass appears a month earlier about Preston than it does on the Arkansas. In 1850 we found grass and water abundant on this route, all the way from Van Buren to El Paso, with the exception of one place—Mustang Pond, and in this vicinity we could have found it a short distance from the road.

I believe I can go through now and find an abundant of grass & water, although we will start a month earlier than we did in 1850, which will be about the 15th March next. By the time we get to Preston the grass will be sufficient. It is a pleasant route, and the climate, healthy. Out of 183 men in our party in 1850, only three were sick, one of whom died, whilst you know the northern route can be distinguished by a stranger, from the graves that mark the whole route.

The trip can be made to Calif. from Van Buren, with wagons, in four months, and with pack mules in much shorter time. I have traveled this route and expect to travel it again, believing it to be the best route for overland emigration. Persons wishing to go in our party, must make their arrangements to start from Van Buren on the 15th March next.

Respectfully yours,
J. F. Simmons[118]

Another group of Arkansans arrived at Dona Ana on July 29, Charles Clark and R. B. Ross wrote regarding this group:

Dear Parents.

I take this first opportunity to write you a few lines to let you know that we are at present in the land of the living and well at that. We left Fort Smith on the 17th day of May and arrived here on the Rio Grande on the 19th day of July and laid by eleven days on the road ... (See dear reader how much better is this route!) We made the distance from Fort Smith to the Cross Timbers by ourselves. There we overtook W. M. Holt and co. numbering 70 men. We traveled with them to El Passo [sic]. When we got there the ox teams were past praying for. Billingsley was unable to take us any further and we had to join in with Mr. Stinkard to get along. Our men now consists of old man Stinkard, Lafayette Byron and myself. At El Passo, flour is worth from $6–8 a hundred. We have meat & coffee enough to do us until San Diego where we expect to stay this winter. The distance from here is 850 miles and from there to the gold mines 500 miles. We will leave this place the first week of Aug., with 45 men and 8 or 9 wagons, all drawn by mules. We are all in good health and better spirits, and have flattering news from Calif. Old Mr. Stindard is so fat that the whole company grease their wagon wheels with his shadow. If we have no bad luck we will be in Calif. in 8 weeks from the first of August. Excuse this miserable scrawl, it was written on the banks of the Rio Grande under the shade of a willow tree.[119]

Before detailing some of the experiences of the 1850ers in California, another aspect of the Gold Rush deserves mention. What of the women who stayed behind? What were their impressions of the Gold Rush? Was it for them the great adventure or the great endurance?

CHAPTER VIII

The Women Who Stayed at Home

"Oh, California,
the thought of thee makes me sad."

"Oh, miserable California,
I wish you never had been heard of!"

How did the wives and sweethearts who stayed behind view the California Gold Rush? How did they fare while their menfolk were away? Regretably there are few public records of their opinions and feelings. The letters from their husbands were very personal and treasured and undoubtedly not considered for public viewing. Sometimes passages with references to the members of the company or descriptions of the route were given the papers for quoting, but the personal passages were not shared. A few private letters have been made available to the author, and even reading them more than one hundred fifty years later, one feels as if she has made an intrusion or eavesdropped.

Catherine Duval Rector, wife of Major Elias Rector, of Fort Smith beautifully captured in her diary the woman's perspective of the Gold Rush.[1] The Rector's lived in relative ease on a plantation two miles from Fort Smith. Their home was a two-story, white-washed log house with rooms twenty feet square containing immense fireplaces. The rooms were separated by an eighteen-foot hallway. Goodspeed described their home as "princely."[2] Catherine's diary is a marvelous record of the everyday life of the more affluent in early 1850's Arkansas. Among the many topics about which this diary provides excellent information are social life, child rearing, education, slavery, courtship, sewing, gardening, preserving, whitewashing, special events such as Tom Thumb's visit to Fort Smith or the exposition of the

from the Fadjo Cravens Collection, UA at Little Rock Library Archives.

Elias Rector **Mrs Rector**

magnetic telegraph, and women's reading material.

Catherine began her diary on Monday, March 11, 1850, about three weeks before Major Rector left. The Major was in Fayetteville making final arrangements. Some of the preparations which she mentioned included making needle books (cases) for the servants to take on the trip, attending a large dinner party where "nearly all the ladies and gentlemen of the garrison" were in attendance, and having "a great many gentlemen to dine" in their home. Major Rector was expressing his appreciation "to his friends, or some who had been very kind to him in getting ready for California."

Catherine was three months pregnant at the time of his departure and already the mother of children aged twelve, six and two. She expected her husband to be away for two years. Some of her diary entries reveal the trepidation she felt. In the diary she refers to her husband as "Maj. R."

March 13

I feel low spirited and depressed in feelings. Have I not enough to make me feel so?

March 18

Maj. R. appears very miserable about his business. It seems most everything goes wrong with us. But why despair? We have many blessings to be thankful for.

March 20

As the time approaches for Maj. R. starting for California, I feel dreadful. I can scarcely realize it to myself that he is going, but the dread reality is approaching.

March 22
Oh, California, the thought of thee makes me sad. All the gold in the mines cannot prevent me from having sad forebodings. Will I ever see Maj. R. again? Oh, what a journey and to be absent *so long!* It appears impossible.
March 27
Cut out two flannel shirts for Major Rector.
March 28
The day of the dining. How I dreaded it, but I believe it passed off well. Only to think, this time next week I shall be all alone, a widow, nominally, if not forever. I cannot realize to myself that he is going.

Major Rector was to rendezvous with Col. Matthew Leeper in Fayetteville, fifty miles from Fort Smith, and then their company would depart from there.[3] On April 1 the Major's wagons started to Fayetteville. Catherine recorded that she felt wretched in bidding the servants goodby and dreaded the next day when Major Rector would leave. Business detained him, however, and Catherine wrote:

April 2
Maj. R. expected to leave for California this afternoon. He went to town and did not get back until too late to start. I felt like a criminal that had a short reprieve from execution. But tomorrow, tomorrow is the agonizing day!
April 3
Maj. R. started this morning. How utterly wretched I felt in bidding my dear Husband good bye for two years, perhaps forever. How little we appreciate a blessing until deprived of it. Oh, God, our Heavenly Father, bless and protect him and prosper him in his undertaking, preserve his life and mine until we meet again, is the sincere prayer of his devoted wife. Give me fortitude to bear this time. The poor children cried like their hearts would break. . . .

Rector was in Fayetteville until late April, but he did not return home during the interval as Catherine hoped. She received from him and wrote to him long letters; their contents are not revealed in the diary. In one letter he requested her to purchase some items in Fort Smith and send by Mr. Sutton's wagon. She did not specify the items. A letter received on April 30 indicated he was leaving the next day—probably April 20–22. Her first letter from him after leaving Fayetteville came on May 18 and was written from Fort Scott.

May 18
He does not write in very good spirits. He says he expects to see more suffering on the road than he has ever seen in all his life. He says that it appears the whole world is going to California that road. He says there is no corn to be had and very little grass. How the poor animals will suffer. I am so sorry that he went that road, and as he says, it is now too late to look back.
May 22
How often do my thoughts turn to thee, my poor husband. Whenever I take a cool drink of water, then I think of you and wish you had it for I know how you enjoy good water, and I am afraid among your other suffering that will be one of the greatest.

Little Jimmy, her two-year-old, was very sick with chills and fever and Catherine had to send for Dr. Spring. "Oh what a week of anxiety I have had. Poor little fellow. He has suffered so much." Johnny, her six-year-old was missing his father. Catherine noted on the 23rd "he talked so much about you this morning. He asked me if you had come home. He said he dreampt you had." The twelve-year-old daughter, Harriet Amanda whose nickname was Shingo, had contributed her share to Catherine's maternal woes. On May 11, Catherine noted, "I had quite a difficulty with Shingo about whipping one of the little servants."

> June 3
>
> Two months since Maj. R. left him home. How much he has suffered in that time and how much more he will have to endure before he reached California—God only knows.

From June 9 to November 11, Catherine made no entries. Her baby, a daughter named Kate, was born during that interval on September 22. Catherine probably received letters from her husband. She did know of his safe arrival in California for on November 8, the *Fort Smith Herald* published a letter from Major Rector to Captain Rogers. It was dated Sacramento, September 6.[4]

In her diary entry for December 15, Catherine noted that she had read a letter published in the paper from David Spring, a member of her husband's company, which described their trip to California. It was dated Nevada City, California, August 23, 1850, and was very long requiring two and one-half columns to print. The letter, quoted in the previous chapter, details the route taken, the miles covered, sickness, death, and the ordeal of the desert. Catherine wrote, "How much they did suffer! I am now looking so anxiously for a letter from Maj. Rector."

December 1850 was especially cold in Fort Smith. On the 8th all Catherine's vinegar jugs broke, and the dining room was deluged with vinegar. The breakfast table had to be set in the parlor. Eleven hogs were killed on the 17th and the carpets shaken on the 20th. On the 24th, "the children returned from school to dinner bright and joyous in anticipation of tomorrow, Christmas Day." No word came from Rector until New Year's Day 1851.

> January 1
>
> Anything but a happy new years to me. I received a letter from Maj. R. this morning and a very handsome ring from him, made of the California gold. He writes very discouragingly about his prospects. He thinks of returning in the Spring. I did not think he ever would return unless he succeeded, but he is miserably homesick now.

There is another skip in Catherine's diary from January 6 to March 1 during which time her younger sister Susan, who lived with Catherine, was married to Major Page and moved into Fort Smith. The diary is devoted to everyday affairs, social calls, sick children, and disappointment about not hearing from her husband.

March 3

Done nothing today but nurse and read.

March 6

Done nothing nearly all day but nurse and am heartily sick of it. (Jimmy was sick.)

March 10

I sent to the post office expecting to get a letter from my dear husband. But, oh, how disappointed was I. Did not get any. I felt wretched all day.

March 13

The baby had a severe attack of the croup in the night. Better this morning. Jimmy very sick I sent for Dr. Spring. . . . So disappointed I did not get a letter today.

March 14

Jimmy very sick again this morning I sent for the doctor. He was better when he came. He thinks it is an intermittent fever he has. He told me to give him quinine. Poor little fellow. How I hate to give him medicine. He begs so hard. "No mama, no, no!"

March 16

What a strange disease. The children one hour apparently at the point of death and next well.

March 18

I don't know what I shall do for potatoes to plant. There are none to be had. Cut out carpet rags. Thought of you my dear husband to night, looking at the bright moonlight knowing you have light-night, but my thoughts were melancholy.

March 18

I have done nothing else but nurse this week. Mr. Rhym (hired by Major Rector before he left to help with the plantation) has been trying everywhere to get Irish potatoes, both scarce and dear. . . . I felt very low spirited this evening. I feel my great responsibility as a mother.

When Dr. Spring came to check on Jimmy on March 20, he had news for Catherine from California. Dr. Spring had seen a man just from California who had seen Major Rector. "He was well but fretting about home. He did not know whether he would be at home this spring or next. I do hope he will come this spring." The children were better, and she was taking walks with them. All the peach, pear and fruit trees were in full bloom. Still Catherine received no letter. Then on March 29 Major Gaines, a family friend from the Garrison, called on Catherine to tell her that he had seen a man on the steamboat that had seen Maj. Rector and that *he would be home in May.*

Catherine, however, longed for a letter of her own.

April 3

This day one year ago Maj. R. left for California. How many changes have taken place. Poor fellow, he has suffered more than any one. I wish he was at home. I sent to the post office expecting to get a letter from him. But how sadly disappointed I was. I then walked over to Mrs. Dillard's.[5] I heard that she had received a letter from her son. I thought I would hear something in that, but Mrs. Dillard was not at home.

April 4

Mrs. Dillard was kind enough to come over and read her son's letter to me. He spoke of Maj. R. as broken very much in appearance and from the tone of his letter, unfortunate. Oh, miserable California, I wish you never had been heard of!

Rather than sparing only herself the knowledge of California, she would spare the world knowledge of California!

Added to Catherine's anxiety about her husband was the problem of being pressed for cash funds. On March 11, "Mr. Barnes called to get money to pay his workmen for building the chimneys, but I had none for him." Then on April 5, Mr. Watterman, the peddler came to the Rector home. Catherine wrote, "I would not let him open his pack, for I have no money to buy anything."

Meanwhile, the corn and melons were being planted, "Fanny had a colt," and Catherine churned "29 lbs of butter." Little Kate was not very well, but Jimmy and Johnny were well. Catherine noted, "They are so much company to me. May I bring them up on the way they should go." Still no letter from Maj. R.

Catherine had several social callers on April 9. Of the visit Catherine wrote:

Our conversation was of California. Mrs. Polk said David Spring had written that if he was out of the country, he wished it might go to the D____. I feel almost as wicked about it as David. It is wrong I know, but I wonder if I shall ever see my husband again. I trust in God I may.

April 10

I do hope I may get a letter today. I had such a dream of Maj. R. last night. I thought he had returned home, him and his servants and they all looked so badly. Maj. R. looked so unhappy and wretched. Doomed to disappointment again—no letter today.

April 12

I heard a boat this morning. Could not help thinking Maj. R. might be on it.

April 14

Another mail day, but I suppose I am to be disappointed again . . . No letter. Oh misery!

On April 15 Catherine and the children went into town to stay a few days with sister Susan and make the visitation rounds among friends. It was there on the morning of April 18 while she was still in bed that she received a note from Captain Rogers informing her that "a gentleman had just arrived from New Orleans and said Maj. R. was there and would be at home in a day or two. So as soon as the carriage could be got ready, I came to make preparations to receive my dear and long absent husband."

April 19

Very busy cleaning up to receive my dear husband.

April 20

My beloved husband arrived about 12 o'clock. Oh! delighted we were to see him! He was completely overcome. Oh, my heart was full! He looks better than

> I expected to see him. A year's absence makes a great many changes. My heart raises in thankfulness to Almighty God for his safe return home to his family.

The 21st was a day of social callers paying their respects to Major Rector. Mrs. Dillard was among the callers inquiring about her son John. The following day Rector's homecoming presents arrived from New Orleans. There were "beautiful bonnets" for Catherine and Shingo as well as "pretty dresses," and for sister Susan, a "beautiful ring." The diary then recounts a round of visitors to see the Major and celebrate his safe return. On the 24th their guests brought champagne and ice with them. Catherine served fresh strawberries on these occasions.

A housewifely note intrudes itself into the celebrations. "Busy all day arranging and fixin Maj. Rector's clothes. Brought the side board out of the parlor to put his things in."

As for Major Rector, his California gold experience had not been successful. He went into town several days the first week home and on the 27th "had one of his old spells of low spirits." Rector did not find a fortune; in fact, he probably suffered reverses as a consequence of his venture in California. Another skip occurred in Catherine's diary from May 6 to September 1, 1851. On September 4 she makes her last reference to California and the finanicial woes which Rector suffered as a consequence. The Major had been to town where he met Judge R. S. C. Brown, the former Cherokee agent who led a group of one hundred fifty Cherokees and Arkansans to California in 1850. Judge Brown

> . . . had received letters and remittances from California. Maj. R. expected the same, also he thought Judge Brown ought to have given him some of what he had received as he had given him money to bring him home from California. Maj. R. was cursing the world! I told him he had no one to blame but himself. I thought that as he had gone so far from home, underwent so many hardships, and knowing the necessities of his family, he would have been more careful of his money.

Let's hear it for women and having the last word!

The author has seen no letters written by women to their husbands. There is clear evidence the men pined for these letters while in California, and clamored at the post offices in expectant impatience to receive letters from home. They remain quietly hidden in attics or have been destroyed.

Some private letters written by husbands to their wives have surfaced. The author was graciously permitted by Mrs. Charlie T. Davis (Sonny) of Little Rock to see private letters written by members of her family who were among the Clarksville gold seekers. Sonny's grandmother, Sue, was a Johnston. Joseph E. Johnston in a poignant letter to his wife Malinda was explaining why he had not come home in two years as promised.

> Sonora, California
> May 18, 1851
>
> Dear and Ever Beloved Wife,
>
> I once more take my pen in hand to inform you that I am in good health and have been ever since I wrote you before, which was in the middle of last month.

I received your kind favor (letter) the other day, dated February 19, 1851 and was glad to hear that you was all well. . . . (Here he gives account of many in the Clarksville Company and how well they were doing).

I expect everybody will make a fortune but me, and it does appear that I am doomed to hard work and poor pay, all the days of my life. It has rained here all spring so that we could not work, and is raining today, and looks as though it would rain a month. However, I am not out of heart, neither do I wish you to think that I am disposed to grumble. Such is not the case, for I know the gold is here whether I ever get it or not, so I live in hope. Even if I have to give it up in despair, I am in just as good heart now as I was when I first began . . .

My Love, you must not think hard of me, or take it so much to heart for my coming home this Spring, for I am sure you know I would not of stayed away from you if I had not of thought it was for the best. I do want to make a little before I come home if possible, and if I can't, after giving it a fair trail, I will try and be satisfied anyhow. However, let that be as it may, let me make much or little, stay long or short, my love for you is, and forever will be the same. So do try and not make yourself uneasy about me. You may rest assured that there is nothing on earth that would give me more pleasure than to see you and be with you, but as that cannot be just now, nothing else gives me more pleasure than to hear that you are well and satisfied. So I hope you will try and be content with your lot, and I will try and do the best I can to make you comfortable, and try to get home as soon as possible. But all these things you know without me to tell you.

Give my love to Father and tell him I was glad to hear from him. . . . I hope he will forgive me for not coming home in two years as I promised. I can make no excuse only I did want to make some money before I come home. . . .

I will set no time to be at home myself for fear I might disappoint you again, but you may rest assured that I will be there as soon as I possibly can. I hope you will not fret about me, for I will not suffer. Do all you can to make the children learn their books and everything else that will tend to their best interests. Tell them I will bring them some pretty books when I come home, if they will learn them well.

Give my love to Father and my brothers and sisters, Puss, John and all the rest, and receive for yourself the best wishes of your loving husband. Please write soon

Joseph C. Johnston

Johnston returned to Arkansas at some point after that and left his brother Thomas in San Francisco in charge of their properties. Thomas was writing Joseph at Dardanelle asking for his full power of attorney and giving an account of their business. It shows to ongoing problems of fortune hunting in California.

San Francisco
October 18, 1855

Dear Brother,

I received yours of the 15th July. I answered it some time ago. John T. Boyer left here on the fifth of this month for Arkansas by way of New York. He intends to return with his family in the Spring.

(Here follows paragraph requesting title bond and power of attorney.)

We have compromised with Ham & Hathaway by selling them a lot and getting some money. I paid $700 borrowed money and $600 to Boyer, $200 to the lawyers and I have enough left to pay taxes which will be $300 or $400. So I am out of debt and have got a brick warehouse on one of the lots that I sold which is full of grain, which will enhance the value of the balance of the lots 25%. The house, of course, belongs to Ham & Co. and I have got more ground than we had at first, but I have (dearly?) earned all that I have gained. I have had three lawsuits, been in prison and been swindled out of over $2,000.00 in the compromise, besides the squatters and the lawyers fees. The lawyers fees alone is between $600–700.

All my funds is exhausted. I have not worked one month since last March. Times are a little better. I have worked three days this week and am out of a job, so if you have more loose cash than you know what to do with, you may send a little over this way. I think our title is good except the state's revisionary interest—that is often ninety nine years. It goes to the one that purchased the states sale. I want to buy it in if I can as the lots won't sell for near their worth without the states interest.

Write soon. I have not heard from Jack since I wrote to you before. Give my respects to all.

Thomas Johnston

Another worried husband, John H. Ward from Hot Springs, was concerned by letters from his wife that she was in some financial difficulties and that some of his debts had not been paid. He was writing to Dr. Lorenzo Gibson of Little Rock to take charge of these matters.

San Francisco 30th May 1950

Dear Gibson,

(Here follows a long description of San Francisco and California which was quoted earlier.)

When I left home I was owing in my neighborhood about $670. I sold to John Brown a Negro boy named Charles for $800. I received of the $800–$100 in hand and left Mr. Cummins vested with full and legal power to close this sale of the Negro, to receive the remaining $700 and to pay my debts with it. Now I learn by letters from my wife that up to the last of February, some of these debts were still unpaid. These debts are disturbing my wife. I want them paid. I left in Mr. Cummins hands a note on my friend Mr. Keats for $150. I wish this last sum paid over to my wife forthwith. I sent from New Orleans to my wife about the 25th of February last a certificate of deposit for $100 on the Canal bank at New Orleans. Now will you be so kind as to look to these matters for me. My debts must be paid at any sacrifice, but first of all must my family be comfortable. Will you see and confer with my wife, and serve me in these my wishes. I *am at a great distance from my family, and I have written to Dr. Lorenzo Gibson. . . .*

John H. Ward

P.S. I have written to my wife and if she is in Little Rock, you will please stop her letters in Little Rock.[6]

Letters to the wife of another Arkansas emigrant, J. Rankin Pyeatt, who traveled with Captain Evans' Fayetteville and Cherokee company in 1849, described the trail experience, squabbles, dust and hardship as others have already done. These letters also describe a husband's anxiety and concern for his family and his earnest desire for his wife and children to join him in California. The quotations are from letters written after he reached California on October 20, via the Carson River route. He and his young son Andrew, his brother, Porter, and several others from Fayetteville built a cabin for the winter on the Consumnes River about thirty miles southeast of Sacramento.

His first letter from California was dated November 11 and described conditions, prices and prospects in California. He was especially impressed with the cost of lumber. His own trade must have been saw-milling, for he made this proposal to his wife Elizabeth:

> . . . This is the best business that I know of. A good saw mill would clear from five to eight hundred a day. If I had a good seat (location) and plenty of *timber* I would like to build one in this country—if Elizabeth and children were hear [sic]. What do you think of this prospect? If you and the children will come, I think in a few years I can, with your help, make enough to do us the balance of our days. There are many ways to make money, in a word, anything a man could go at he can make and if he will be industrious and saving, he can in a few years make enough to do a common man his lifetime. . . .
>
> We will start to the city (Sacramento) in a few days to get our provisions. I hope to get some word from you then for I have not heard from you since I left home. It would do me good to see a few lines from you, but it would do me a heap more good to see you and the children. But will I ever see you again in this world? I hope I will, but should I not, will we meet in heaven? I leave you to answer this question. For my part, I am determined to try, through the help of God, to get there. May the Lord help us all to do our duty toward Him and our fellowman.
>
> To the subject of your coming here, not to live here, longer than two or three years, for I don't like the country well enough to live here any longer than I can get enough to do us our lives. I don't want you to come by land for it is too great an undertaking. The dust is enough to kill anybody.
>
> . . . If you will come let me know as soon as you can and I will make preparation for that purpose so that I can go after you next fall and direct you how to fix for the trip. You will please let me know as soon as you can, for if you come I want to select a place and build a house.
>
> . . . Nothing more at present, but remain your affectionate companion.

A month elapsed and still no word from home reached Pyeatt.

> December 9, 1849
>
> Dear Companion, Children and Friends,
>
> Having not heard a word from you since I left home, I have become very anxious to receive something from you. It would do me more good than anything I could think of . . . You may think you know how anxious I am to get a letter from you, but you know nothing about it, nor cannot know unless you were in the same situation that I am in, having been absent about 8 months and

not having heard a word from you. I have no doubt but you have heard from us several times, for I have written six letters to you from different points. Why I have not gotten a letter I cannot tell unless they are directed to San Francisco. This place is so far distant (200 miles) from that, we can't get letters from there.

We made arrangements with a merchant to lift our letters out of the (post) office there and bring them to Sacramento City for one dollar extra on the letter.

Pyeatt then went on to describe for Elizabeth the difficulties of mining—working in water and having to take time out to cook meals!

. . . I have offered to give one dollar a day for to have Andrew's any my cooking done, and couldn't get it. At that, this may look like giving a large sum, but we could make from $1.00 to $1.50 an hour a piece, and it takes longer than this to get a meal cooked. *Hear* [sic] *you may see the need of a cook and housekeeper.* (Author's italics).

. . . The last I wrote you, I wrote on the subject of your coming hear [sic]. I again mention this subject. If you and the children were here, we could make enough to do us in a few years and then go back to where we could enjoy it, for I don't think this country will be a pleasant country to live in for some time yet, as there is nothing like farming or orchard making here . . . The most of the people have gone and left their families and went back as soon as they can get enough to answer their purpose. There are but few permanent settlers, and therefore, for the most part of the inhabitants are transcient [sic].

. . . I will try to send you some money if I can get a safe chance, which I think I can in the Spring . . . Judge Davis is agoing back I think next Spring, and if I can get to see him I will send you some.

The next of Pyeatt's letters was dated February 17, 1850. Still he had not heard from Elizabeth or any of his friends from home. He faithfully reported on conditions in California, Andrew's health, the rain, and selling the mules and oxen.

. . . Andrew and myself will have about on[e] thousand dollars when we divide the money that we got from our oxen, and if I could get a good chance, I would send it to you, but I don't know any at present. I will be at home next winter if I am alive, unless you come here before that time.

I would like to have you and children hear [sic]. I have not had a letter from you or any friend. Why not, I can't tell. Some of our friends have got some. It did me good to hear about you, but it would have done me much more if I could have got a letter from you or some friend. Why I have not gotten any, I can't tell unless you have not written any.

Send the children to school all you can. If you lack money, borrow if you can and I will pay as soon as I get home. I would write more, but I have a chance to send to the city and get it off by the first mail, and if I miss this chance, it will be one month before I have another chance, and the men that are a-going to the city won't wait for me to write all I want to write, so I must close my letter.

May the Lord be with you and bless you and keep you from all sin is the sincere prayer of your affectionate husband, father and friend.

John R. Pyeatt

Some time after this February letter, Pyeatt received letters from Elizabeth, for young Andrew writing to his mother in April said "Poppa has gotten two letters from you." Andrew had deep affection for his baby sister Mary and worried that she would forget him while he was gone to California.

Pyeatt's next letter reveals Elizabeth's negative response to his invitation to come to California.

> . . . As it respects your unwillingness to come here and your request for me to stay till the object of my journey is accomplished, that I cannot think of staying longer than this winter. When I think of the children and your society, the Church Sunday School and the society of friends, gold has no attraction to keep me longer.
>
> I expect to start home as soon as the rainy season sets in, which will be sometime in November and will be home the last of December or first of January.
>
> . . . I would like for you to write oftener and tell me about the children, whether they have forgotten me and if they are learning anything with their present teacher. In particular, I would like to know if Mary Adaline has forgotten me.

Pyeatt received other letters from Elizabeth, his brother Peter and friends. His next letter to Elizabeth on September 26, finds him answering the question, "John, just how much have you made in California?"

> . . . Your request to know how much I have made, I am ashamed to tell you, having made so little. I am at a loss to go home with so little, and feel like trying it this winter if I can see any good prospect. This I will try for 5 or 6 weeks and if I do not find a prospect in that time, I will start home.
>
> I am sorrowful to learn that so many of our neighbors are in such a way about California (planning to go). I would just say for the satisfaction of my neighbors that 19 out of 20 would be glad to be at home but cannot get there for want of money and I would say (to all our friends) to stay where they are until I get home and I think I can put them out of the notion of coming here.

Pyeatt had repeated the cycle of many gold seekers: borne the toil of an overland trip, evidenced much enthusiasm and a sense of promise for the gold country, suffered homesickness and anxiety, faced disillusion, disappointment and embarrassment, and was ready to return to Arkansas. The final of the ten Pyeatt letters is fragmentary and undated and included messages to various family members. It had this message about his homecoming plans:

> Andrew and myself will start there unless we see some good prospect to make something, then we will stay till spring, but the prospect must be good. It grieves me to think about staying longer than fall, but duty to my children and you, my companion, prompts me to stay as long as spring if I can make anything worthwhile by it.[7]

Pyeatt and Andrew returned to Arkansas via Panama. Andrew died on the return trip making the entire experience one of heartbreak for the Pyeatt family. Brother Porter had drowned while in California.

Judge Hiram Davis of Fayetteville was a member of the Evans' company in 1849 which blazed the Cherokee Trail. The Davis family permitted two of his letters to his wife Elizabeth to be published in *Flashback*. These letters mention many of the Fayetteville gold seekers by name, detail some of their squabbles, and note there were 130 members of the company. A dozen men in the party turned back at Pueblo, fearing the company could not make it to California that season. Davis, in the June 1849 letter, was reassuring Elizabeth that all was well and warning her not to believe everything these returners said about the company.

> The true reason I apprehend for their return is *homesickness*, for I assure you, my Dear Elizabeth, I have had enough of that myself to last me the balance of my life, but still I hope I have enough of self respect and firmness of purpose not to abandon an undertaking that I regard with so much favor . . . I pray you therefore to rest contented as to my success and safety, and give no heed to rumors to the contrary, as I doubt not they will be abundant and highly exagerated. I expect we have come the best route that could have been selected. . . .
>
> It may be some time before I have have a chance to write to you again my dearest Elizabeth, but I shall think of you none the less—I fear too much. I am too full to say more than to advise you to take good care of your sweet little self until the return of him that loves and adores you above all things in heaven or earth. The dear children, say many kind things to them for me and don't let them forget they have a father. Write.
>
> Your affectionate
> Husband Hiram[9]

In another letter written almost eleven months later, in May 1850, Davis described the rigors of prospecting in the mountains in rain and snow, the labor of damming a river to change its course, and the difficulty of getting mail and supplies. He said he had not seen a newspaper or a woman in many months and had doubts whether he would recognize either one should he do so! He was amazed at the numbers who continued to swarm to California:

> In the name of heaven, let no person you can influence even come to this wretched country. I have heard but one opinion expressed by all considerate men, and that is that gold can never pay a man for coming to this country. A few honest men have made fortunes digging gold; speculators in lands, town property and provisions and gamblers have done the best, but the large mass have more than worsted their condition by coming here.

From this letter we also learn that Elizabeth was, unknown to her husband and possibly to her, pregnant at the time he embarked on the golden journey.

> I am very anxious to hear from you as my last dates from home come up to your November [1849] letter only, at which time I was delighted to learn all things were well with you. If I could receive your February letter and learn of your confinement, its happy termination and the result you so kindly

> predicted, and that I much anxiously desire, the measure of my happiness would be full to overflowing.[10]

Mrs. Rector, Mrs. Johnston, Mrs. Ward, Mrs. Pyeatt and Mrs. Davis and thousands more like them had been left at home to carry on with the business of living and rearing children while agonizing about the safety of their loved ones who had gone to see the elephant. What sum of money it would have taken to keep a woman and her family for one or two years is not known. If the husband had left expecting to refurbish the household accounts with money from California, and none had been forthcoming, the situation was probably desperate. With various degrees of reluctance, these women supported their husbands' great gamble for riches. But Catherine's "Oh, miserable California, I wish you had never been heard of!" more aptly expresses the viewpoint of the women.

C H A P T E R I X

California Fever Subsides

"Stay home! Don't come to California!"

"California is the greatest curse to
this country that could probably befall it."

What reports did the 1850 emigrants make concerning their California venture? William Quesenbury acted as the *Fort Smith Herald's* California correspondent and in a long letter to Wheeler bemoaning having received no letters and no papers, Quesenbury reported:

> Sacramento City, California Jan. 29, 1851
>
> ... Not a single Arkansas man who came to this country either last year or this year, has made 1/10 part of his anticipations. Newspapers are constantly teeming with accounts of gentlemen returning with "piles" but no Arkansian excepting Alexander McKissick of Benton Co. can make this boast—and he is not inclined to do so, as Dr. Dean, who will leave here in April will testify, that he has been afflicted with the worse case of "piles" that ever came under his notice.
>
> ... Being your correspondent, you may regard me as "my brother's keeper." I am sorry I can give you so little information respecting my fellow Arkansians. They are scattered all over the country. Many of the Cherokees who came over the plains last season are wintering near Macosumne about 35 miles from here. Col. Leeper, Dr. Dean, Alex McKissick & several citizens of Wash. Co., are at the same place. Maj. R. & Judge Brown invest Stockton. The last I saw of Black, Harris, and the Lee's Creek delegation, was on the Macosumne near Col. Leeper.
>
> Advises friends to say home & *not* come to Calif.[1]

In another letter four months later, Quesenbury told Judge Jesse Turner of Van Buren.

> Sacramento City, May 31, 1851
>
> I have mined none since I have been here (he had been sick for several months after his arrival). I took a shovel, pick and pan . . . through the gulches prospecting. I suppose I mined . . . a dollar or so, which when I returned to the city some gentleman stole . . . When I left home an idea prevailed that in the mining country a man might dig anywhere he pleased and find gold, but they might as well go a duck hunting in the uplands as to endeavor getting the dust away from the streams in the dry season.[2]

The *Herald* in a column entitled "Arkansians in California" reported this synopsis of the news:

> Letters from California have reached us recently from some of our own citizens, who represent the state of affairs generally in no very encouraging light. Judge R. S. C. Brown of Crawford Co. writes us from Stockton February that the prospects are not sufficient to induce him to remain, and that he would leave as soon as he could close some business arrangements. He mentions that Maj. Rector of Fort Smith, will start home about the first of April.
>
> Hamen Mitchell from Stockton Jan. 27, 1851 advises friends *not* to come to California says none of Arkansians doing as well as they expected. David Shall merchandizing in Double Springs. Rector, Brown and Gen. Blackburn in good health.
>
> Regarding new gold fields called "Gold Bluffs"—Son of Col. Logan of Ark. informed him they were richest yet & thousands flocking to them. Logan said it was Nordheimer, formerly of Fort Gibson, who first discovered their location.[3]

The *Arkansas Gazette* published an article from the New York *Day Book* which cast California in a very negative light:

> "The California Swindle"
>
> Capt. Whitney (recently returned from California) expresses the same opinion we often express in the *Day Book*, that Calif. is the greatest curse to this country that could probably befall it. It has been built up on misrepresentation and lies, and will one day come back upon us like all curses, to worry & vex us to death. Not one in a dozen can get money to come home with—and the laboring poor, of which there are great numbers, are worse off than our poor Irishmen here, and have no prospect of ever being any better, unless their friends send them money to come home with.
>
> Notwithstanding all this, our newspapers, nearly everyone of which is interested, our steamboat owners, our shipping merchants, and our transportation line runners, are using all their influence to seduce more victims to their ruin, for the sole purpose of getting passage money.[4]

W. C. May, a member of the Clarksville forty-niners, did not give a flattering view of the mines, but his overall favorable impression of the land and climate of California was unmistakable. Note he attributes the improved quality of life to the arrival of wives who were joining their "enraptured husbands" in their new home. Writing to Editor Woodruff, he said:

Sacramento City, Cal. Ap. 15, 1851

Mr. Editor—I came from the mines to this city in Nov. last, since which time I have been trading in provisions; and, notwithstanding I have not made my 'everlasting fortune,' yet success to some extent has attended my exertions.

Trade is, and ever has been, since I have been in this country, very fluctuating. The prices current cannot be depended upon for 24 hours, and the reason is obvious. A number of vessels with their cargoes may arrive at the same time, and the prices of the articles with which they are freighted, decline, but should an article of merchandise become scarce in consequence of the non-arrival of vessels at their appointed time, immediately that article is made one of speculation. Trade is not so flush in this city as formerly, in consequence of the great majority of miners having gone to the Northern 'diggins.' So great was the rush from the Southern to the Northern mines, during the months of Jan. & Feb., it was thought the former would be depopulated.[5] The past winter has been unusually dry—but little rain has fallen in the valleys, and but little snow in the mountains, in consequence of which, the miners have remained in the mountains to work in, what is termed, the 'dry diggins.' During the month of March a great quantity of snow fell and blocked up the passes in the mountains, and hence they are cut off from supplies. Reports say nearly all the mules have perished and many of the men suffered severely.

I have nothing flattering to write with regard to the mines. But few are making money.... There is more pilfering and stealing carried on here than any other part of the civilized world.... Grand larceny is, by law of the State, considered a capital offense.

In the cities, society is improving rapidly, and this is very easily accounted for; for on the arrival of every steamer, more or less wives are welcomed to their new homes by their enraptured husbands.

This is the most delightful country on the continent. The valleys are the most beautiful—the soil the most fertile—the mountain water the most pure—the climate the most salubrious—ah! if we poor swines, gold hunters, had our wives and little ones here, we would ask for no better homes on earth.... Capt. G. W. P____, is or was at San Jose. I have not heard from him for some weeks. Our mutual friend, D. M____, is in this city, making money as usual.[6] He expects his family this fall. I know not when I shall return to Ark; but hope to give many friends a hearty shake of the hand there before another April.

Mr. Editor, can't you send us a few copies of your valuable paper? It would be heartily welcomed here by its old readers. You shall hear from me again soon, when I hope to be able to make my letter more interesting. 'Til then adieu.

W. C. May

Editor's note:

Our paper has been sent regularly to the writer, as well as to others, at Sacramento City. Its failure to reach them, we suppose, is attributable to the irregularity of the mails.[7]

Word came from a member of the Little Rock forty-niners, W. H. Pennington:

Indian Bar, Tuolumne, April 20, 1851

... Mining now is rather a slow business—all the old diggins are very nearly exhausted. There has been no new discovery in the Southern mines worth noticing. The banks of the Tuolumne, have been dry a great deal, the last winter. Miners have been driven from the mountains and dry diggins on the river for the want of water. The season has been very dry. We have had more rain within the last week than during the whole season previously. The rain has been sufficient of late to give water in the dry diggins and I presume they are going tolerably well. The water, however, will soon give out, so the dry season will soon set in. I think this is the last rain we will have this season. I have traveled a good deal of late over the mines, and I am of the opinion that the miners as a general thing, have been making but very little over their expenses.

... All of your friends, so far as I know, from Ark. are well and doing about as usual. Indian Bar is going to be a stirring place this season. Some half dozen bars, a ten pin alley, etc., etc.[8]

In addition to the poor reports from the mines, news came of terribly destructive fires and earthquakes in the southern part of California. W. C. May described these "convulsions" to William Woodruff.

Sacramento City, Cal. 1st June 1851

Mr. Editor—Calif. seems to be subject to convulsions of different natures.

Only one month since, and the Crescent City, the beauty and pride of the State, was reduced to ashes by the devouring flames, and 15 millions dollars worth of property, accumulated by continued persevering labor, was destroyed, after which, and within a few days of the same time, the greater part of the beautiful little city of Stockton was also burned, the loss of which is estimated at 1½ millions of dollars.

A short time later, or about the 12th of last month, all the Southern part of the state was visited by an earthquake. This, however, has been no new thing for the last two years; but, what is singularly strange about it is, that notwithstanding several shocks have been felt in the Southern part of the State, and even for some distance north of San Francisco, yet we have been entirely free from it in this city. The hearts of the farming community were made glad a few days since by the fall of a good day's rain (a thing unknown before here at this season of the year), than which nothing could be more desirable, after the dry winter and spring.

On the 19th of last month, the Democratic Convention, consisting of 176 delegates, met at Benicia, for the purpose of making nominations to fill the different state offices:

There follows list, etc____[9]

"California Items" continued as a column in the *Gazette,* and death lists, property losses, crimes and trials involving Arkansans were dutifully reported. The Sacramento *Placer Times* reported the death due to diarrhea of Jacob Sexton on October 30. This could be the J. Sexton in Mitchell's group. W. A. Vincent, age thirty, died of cholera on November 12.[10] On a happier note, the *Sacramento Times* reported on April 16, 1851, that J. H. Ward of

Arkansas had been instrumental in preventing a robbery. The *Gazette* made the following report:

> Capt. J. Headington Ward, of Ark., was the means on the 12th of April, of preventing an attempted robbery at Sacramento City. Having got item of the plot to rob 'the palace,' near the Tehama Theatre, he proceeded to the spot with the knowledge and approbation of the District Attorney, and when the burglars, under cover of the night, attempted to enter the house he discharged both barrels of a double barreled gun, killing one of the men and seriously wounding another. Capt. Ward immediately gave himself up to have the affair investigated.[11]

From Sonora in the Southern mines came news of a disastrous fire which "consumed the city" and caused $1,000,000 worth of damage. Editor Woodruff "extracted from a long list of principal sufferers the Arkansas friends and acquaintances" he recognized:

Boyer and Patrick	$4,000
M. B. Street	8,000
J. H. Ward	15,000
J. Street & Company	8,000
Arkansas House	4,000[12]

Amazingly as each spring came, small emigrating parties from various towns in Arkansas announced their intentions to leave for California and invited others to join them. Certainly the numbers going were greatly diminished, but year by year Arkansans continued to move westward. With an eye toward the 1851 emigration, the *Fort Smith Herald* as early as June 1850 agreed to join with the *Arkansas Intelligencer* in making available the pertinent details for prospective overlanders. Note the later day Chamber of Commerce approach to their concerted effort:

> We agree with the suggestions of the editor of the *Van Buren Intelligencer* in reference to the union of effort of the citizens of Van Buren and Fort Smith, in sending forth all the information relative to the overland California emigration next spring. There should be an united effort on the part of the citizens of the whole state, to make known the advantages of the route through this state. As long as gold is found in so great abundance in California, so long will the emigration continue, and the only thing necessary, for Arkansas to have a large portion of this emigration pass through her territory, is to place reliable information before the public, that is calculated to direct the emigrant aright.... Then let us work. 'Take a long pull, a strong pull, and pull all together.'[13]

On October 31, 1850, an organizational meeting was held at the Presbyterian Church in Fort Smith to adopt measures to facilitate the emigration via Marcy's Dona Anna route. The following resolution was adopted:

> *Whereas*, it is the opinion of this meeting that the spirit of overland emigration to California is likely to continue, and that the best route to that region is that

> leading from this place, commonly known as 'Marcy's and Cook's Route,' and that it is our duty to furnish any information respecting this route as may be collected, to make it better known to those intending to emigrate, and to furnish such other aid to the same as may be found necessary.[14]

The meeting also appointed a committee to get citizens of Van Buren and Little Rock to cooperate "in prompting a cause so important to Arkansas." The committee was also to prompt the Arkansas state legislature to bring to the attention of the War Department in Washington the "need for a general line of military posts" along the route. A series of new forts were built in the following year and the emigration picked up again in 1852.[15] One of the new posts was to be known as Fort Arbuckle in honor of General Matthew Arbuckle. He was not privileged to see the project completed, for he died June 11, 1851, of cholera at the age of seventy-five. He was buried at Fort Smith with military and Masonic honors.[16]

The number of emigrants in 1851 to California along all the overland routes was barely a trickle. The California Trail had seen 45,000 in 1850 and was down to barely 1,000 in 1851, and the Southern routes were similarly unused.[17] The Fort Smith group, which had been promoting itself since fall, reported a meeting at Clark's Hotel in February, and a pack-mule company led by Eli G. Collier (who had been before) and James Johnson announced it would leave Fort Smith on March 18.[18] There were no other references in the Arkansas papers for 1851 groups. The general concensus seemed to be that the great California hoax had been uncovered. The *Gazette* in January noted James Maddox of Dardanelle had returned from California on board the *Umpire No. 2.* He "reports an immense reaction in the emigration to California, there being five on their return to one going out."[19] The *Fort Smith Herald* concurred, with an editorial in the *New Orleans Picayune* which cast the California experience as a great hoax:

> If we judge at all from the tone of the Western papers, there will be no overland emigration whatever this year. The intelligence from the Plains within the last 6 months—the representation of hundreds who have returned in worse condition than when they started, and of the many who have returned in bad health, and dying, have satisfied the people that it is much better to stay home and do well than go off on any such wild goose chase. They can form their own conclusions now, from the representations of their associates and friends, and credence no longer given to the overstrained & glaring falsehoods put forth by interested sources in California.[20]

And so, one would think the California saga ended in 1851. Not so! The Arkansas papers in 1852 were again alive with excitement and reports of great numbers preparing to cross the Plains. Van Buren, Fort Smith, and Little Rock reported much activity. This 1852 revival of enthusiasm and numbers in Arkansas correlates with a similar phenomenon on the northern routes. The overwhelming characteristic of the 1852 emigrants was different, however; they were settlers. Many entire families were among those going West to buy land, to buy a home, or to work at steady wages. These emigrants, who would find a permanent home in California and Oregon, were lured by land and opportunity, not gold. The 1849 and 1850 gold rushers were overwhelmingly male, but from 1852 until the Civil War women comprised an increasingly greater percentage of the western emigrants.[21]

> The following are representative notices from the 1852 papers: *California Notice*—A meeting will be held at the court house, in Van Buren, on Sat. (21st inst.) by a number of persons who intend to go to California overland, on Marcy's route. The object being to organize into a company and fix upon date of departure.
>
> Persons at a distance wishing to unite with the company, are invited to attend or correspond with a committee that will be app't at the meeting for that purpose, from whom they can obtain all the necessary information.[22]

The *Fort Smith Herald* elaborated on the foregoing:

> As there will be a large emigration this spring, over Marcy's route to California; we have obtained form Mr. Merrill, of Crawford County, a gentleman, who has been to the land of gold, and returned, and designs going there again in the spring, a few suggestions, and directions for emigrants, that we think will prove of importance to those intending to emigrate overland this spring. A large company is forming in Crawford and Sebastian counties, and will leave in April for California. To all who are desirous of joining the company, we would advise them to be in Fort Smith by the 15th of April. But here is the directions of Mr. Merrill. He says:
>
> 'The proper time to start for California is about the 20th of April—the grass becomes good by that time—the roads good—and the streams down, so they can be forded.
>
> Oxen are better than mules, are much lower, the latter being much lower in California than the former. Oxen will bring from $100 to $150 per yoke. They stand the trip as well as mules, can travel as fast, and are much easier taken care of while on the road. Each team might take a yoke of milch cows, to furnish milk on the road, and will bring more in California.
>
> As there are a great many persons, who are going this spring, who are not acquainted with the proper *outfit*, necessary, a few hints may not be thought amiss. Four men to a wagon, is a proper mess. Let each man take 150 lbs of bread stuffs, 75 lbs bacon, dried fruit, rice, pickles, etc. which will be quite sufficient for the trip. Four men forming a mess, $100 each will be quite sufficient to furnish an *outfit*—and by taking ox-teams, they will realize twice the amount when they get through.'[23]

Note the outfit requirements were lighter than for either the forty-niners or the fiftiers.

Citizens of Arkansas were kept informed about the progress of this 1852 group by a correspondent of the *Fort Smith Herald* who was located at Fort Fillmore, New Mexico. On June 19 the correspondent wrote:

> The emigrants from Arkansas bound to California, are rolling in handsomely, all well and hearty. Not a death or accident has happened to the two parties just in—vis: Capt. Gilbert's and Capt. Cathay's companies: the former reached here 2 days before the latter. The River (Rio Grande) being very

high, the whole have to cross at Macilla, a Mexican town just below or south of the line, in a flat built a day or two since, at this post, and cut across to Cook's trail, joining it at a spring named after the colonel.

Most of the boys have called upon me, and we have had a real good talk over Arkansas affairs.

P.S. I have hardly time to say another word, but must. Some weeks since, the Mexican population of New Mexico, tried to get up a pronounciamento, but it was nipped in the bud by assembling six companies of soldiers at Albuquerque. Since then, all seems to be quiet, Indians and Mexicans.[24]

Editorializing on the strength of the 1852 emigration, Woodruff apologized for the excessive prices charged by a few Little Rockians for emigrant supplies. He also invited the emigrants to consider Arkansas as a home.

The emigration to the Southern portion of this State, Louisiana, and Texas, during the past fall, has been unusually large, and the tide which flows daily through our streets indicates that the volume abates but little, if any. On the opposite bank of the river are encamped near fifty wagons, with, probably, not less than 250 souls. Each night, for a fortnight, there have been, on an average, not less than 25 wagons encamped there, and, notwithstanding two hand ferry-boats have been constantly plying between the shores, the hourly accessions to the number makes the diminution scarcely perceptible.

In extenuation of what we understand has been the experiences of those who have traveled thus far into the State, we would say, that the country through which the emigrant has come, should not be taken as a fair sample of our lands; nor the treatment of a few harpies who stand by the way-side, exacting enormous rates for every article the emigrant is compelled to purchase, as a fair criterion by which to determine the character of the people.

The season for traveling is far advanced, and we fear that before many of the emigrants now on the road, reach their new homes in more distant portions of the south-west, the nipping frosts and cold piercing blasts of winter will be hard upon them. The natural roads, too, over which they will be compelled to pass, owing to the heavy rains which have fallen almost daily for several weeks past, and the immense travel which has preceded them, will be much cut up and rendered almost impassable. To such as have not made purchases, and who are not bent on reaching points beyond the limits of this State, we would say, that, within her borders lie thousands of acres of as choice lands as are to be found beyond. The crops of the past season were never more abundant, and a generous and hospitable people stand ready to welcome the emigrants to a home in their midst.[25]

Tragedy came to the 1852 group from Conway County. A large party which included many women and children met with unspecified sufferings and many deaths. The *Gazette* reported the distressing experience.

"Deaths of Arkansian Emigrants to California"

We have been politely shown, by John Quindley, Esq., one of the Representatives from Conway County in the present Legislature, a letter from his son, Mr.

John S. Quindley, dated Los Angeles, Calif., 27th Oct., 1852. He has been a year or two in Calif., and, hearing of the distressing situation of the party who emigrated from Conway County, in April last, went out 200 miles on the route and met and accompanied the survivors in to Los Angeles, where they had just arrived when he wrote. He gives the following lists of deaths which had occurred among the emigrants from Conway County:

Mrs. Mary Higgins, wife of H. H. Higgins

Mrs. Eliza Stinkard, wife of J. J. Stinkard

Mrs. Eleanor Wellborn, wife Wm. Wellborn & daughter Hon. J. J. Simmons

Miss Sarah Jane Reynolds, daughter of P. D. Reynolds

Capt. Wm. Craig and his brother Peter Craig

Henderson Murphy

The last three named leave widows, and some of them orphans, who accompanied them on their long and distressing trip to Calif.

The writer adds, that he had seen all the residue of the emigrants from Conway County, and that they are bore unmistakable evidences of their sufferings on the journey.[26]

George Stewart's study indicated six new roads were opened in 1852 for the last leg of the journey into California. All went to a different town in California and all had trail promoters. But the old story of starvation, overworked animals, short supplies and relief parties was again acted out.[27]

This incident is not to be confused with the infamous Mountain Meadows massacre which occurred in September 1857. On this occasion seventy men, women and children with forty wagons and seven hundred cattle departed from Carroll County for California. They were led by Alexander Fancher who had made the trip on two previous occasions. The Arkansans were joined by Missourians which swelled their number to 137 persons. The Fancher caravan passed through Salt Lake City where they found the Mormons reluctant to sell them supplies at any cost. The Mormons were having trouble with the United States government regarding their practice of polygamy, and they believed the United States Army was about to attack them. While encamped at Mountain Meadows, southwest of Salt Lake City, the Arkansans were attacked by Indians and Mormons disguised as Indians and led by John D. Lee. For three days the Arkansans held off the attackers and agreed to surrender when John Lee promised them safe passage. They were murdered instead with the exception of seventeen small children who were kept in Mormon homes until returned to relatives in Arkansas. The possessions of the emigrants were parceled out among the attackers.[28]

Evidence that Arkansans continued to go to California in 1853 is provided in the writings of C. F. M. Noland. Noland was an Arkansas lawyer who wrote humorous stories for the New York *Spirit of the Times* under the penname "Pete Whetstone." His regular correspondence to that journal was signed "N. of Arkansas," and two of his letters in 1853 mention the California emigration:

Batesville, Ark.
Feb. 16, 1853

My dear P.

. . . .

A great many of our citizens are bound for Oregon and California—real substantial men—excellent citizens—carrying their families with them. They will do well, I think and hope; they can do well here, many of them, but I presume they wish to do better. I think I am about as near to the setting sun as I ever wish to be.

Signed N.

Batesville, Ark., April 3, 1853

My dear P.

. . . Oregon and California have drawn heavily on us this season. Well, an overland journey to the Pacific is an undertaking to a stout and robust man, but to see young women without children, and women with young children in their arms, and women who are going to do well for their country, and that, too, before the dog days come and go, starting to California, excites my sympathy. They have stout hearts, and buoyed up by the love of husbands, parents, and sweethearts, there can be no such word as *fail* in their volcabulary.

Signed N.[29]

For many Arkansans, the California experience was clarified and summarized in 1853 with the appearance in their town of the "Panorama of California." The Panorama was an exhibit presented by Dr. T. F. Chambers. It reconstructed the overland trails to California, depicting rivers, mountains, plains, passes and often mentioned place names. It must have also depicted life in the mines and the California camps, towns and cities. The Panorama was exhibited at the State House in Little Rock July 2, 3, 4, 1853, and it undoubtedly made its way to Fort Smith, Van Buren and other Arkansas towns. The *Gazette* was very complimentary of the Panorama:

> The most of our citizens had an opportunity of seeing this excellent Panorama on Thursday, Friday, and Saturday nights of last week. It was well worth seeing—and we have seen none that were not highly delighted, as well as greatly instructed, by their visits to the exhibition.
>
> All the returned Californians with whom we have conversed, pronounce the work correct. And from examining it, one can get an idea of the mode of getting to Calif., as well as living after getting there, which cannot be got from the mere reading of descriptions of the country.[30]

Quite appropriately, this same issue of the *Gazette* noted the return from California of Captain John Dillard, leader of the 1849 Fort Smith company. He had been in California four years, but "Dillard does not look a day older than when we met him first in 1846; though he has heard some *big thunder* since that time."[31]

Measuring the California experience is not a simple task. The legacies the Gold Rush were good, bad, ambiguous, and individual. Much energy, excitement, freedom, and speculation was associated with the experience. Some understood their moment in history; others had a more limited vision. A. D.

King captured the drama of the moment as his party left Clarksville:

> The parting is indeed sad as we leave old Clarksville and start on our long and tiresome journey to far off California to the land of gold. I know that perhaps many of us will never reach the gold fields and that some of us will be buried along the trail and that our graves will be unmarked and forgotten, but a man will take great risks and desperate chances for money. It has always been thus and always will be. Anyway, we are taking the chance and will trust to the Lord to see us through.[32]

For many, California served as a symbol of hope and happiness, only to become a synonym for disappointment and failure. The *Gazette* speculating on the number of California fortunes wrote:

> It is calculated that out of every hundred persons who have gone to Calif., fifty have been ruined, forty no better than they would have been had they remained at home, five a little better, and four something still better, and one has made a fortune.[33]

Some were embittered by their experience, others were broadened and ennobled by theirs. Lorenzo Sawyer was a lawyer from Wisconsin who made the overland trip to California. He felt "expanded" by his experience and considered the trip "worth it" whether he found gold or not, whether he stayed or returned. Sawyer wrote:

> I have crossed the broad continent of America from shore to shore, have seen its magnificent lakes and rivers, have traversed its almost illimitable plains, have stood upon the Rocky, and other mountains, where the eye could take in a circle of perhaps three hundred miles diameter. I have been upon the desert and again upon the Sierra Nevada, have seen human nature under a great variety of circumstances, and in every stage of development from the most degraded specimens of the American savage to the intellectual and polished European race. I feel that I have a more enlarged, a more comprehensive view of the works of nature, a more accurate conception, and a nicer appreciation of their beauty and grandeur. I am sensible that I have obtained a more thorough knowledge of mankind, of their character, their energies and capabilities, of the motives and springs that govern human actions. In short, I feel that I am better acquainted with the world, my fellow man and myself, and I am thus far satisfied with my enterprise, though, in some respects it may not turn out as favorable as I could wish.[34]

Writing in the 1870s and 1880s, Mark Twain and Bret Harte presented the Gold Rush as quaint comedy and sentimental melodrama.[35] Their red-shirted miner was made to appear a fool; yet there is little of the fool in these Arkansans who staked their very lives on what they perceived as an unprecedented opportunity to strike it rich. That most failed and came to feel "foolish" or as if they had chased a wild goose did not make them fools in their dream or in their search. For most, seeing the elephant had been a sadder but wiser experience.

Arkansas was not depopulated by the Gold Rush, indeed it more than doubled its population in the decade of the 1850s. Arkansas towns also experienced growth as the table indicates.

Population Growth		
	1850	*1860*
State	209,897	435,450
Fort Smith	880	1,532
Little Rock	2,167	3,727
Van Buren	404	979

Based on U.S. Census figures.

Texas before and after the Gold Rush had the greater attraction for Arkansans. In 1860 only 2,000 Arkansas natives lived in California, whereas 11,000 lived in Texas.[36] The Gold Rush eased Arkansas beyond its frontier status by shifting the frontier to the West coast. All of America's frontiers had experienced a shifting in population; Arkansas' appeared more dramatic since it was concomitant with the Gold Rush.

The Gold Rush did not have the positive impact on Arkansas which contemporaries envisioned. True, the state's taxable property increased to $100 million during Governor Elias Conway's administration (1852–1856), but Arkansas did not become the hub for Western migration.[37] State leaders continued to press for a railroad to California routed through Arkansas. In November 1852, outgoing governor, J. S. Roane in addressing the necessity for a California railroad pointed to the advantages such a route could bring and urged Arkansas to press for the choice of a middle, as opposed to a northern or southern, route through Arkansas.

> If she [Arkansas] hesitate [to act on the railroad], the mighty wave of emigration, wealth, enterprise and refinement, now rolling westward, will break upon our inhospitable shores, and circling around us to the north and south westward keep its way . . . and leave our State a neglected waste amid prosperity.[38]

Indeed the railroad route did bypass Arkansas, and the state has remained one of the poorer states in the Union.

For the nation as a whole the Gold Rush had dramatic effects by providing a supply of specie, opening a new frontier, creating a new state, expanding a system of transportation and communications, and necessitating political compromise on the slavery issue. The fifties were generally a prosperous decade for the United States.

Beyond the individual, state and national significance of the California Gold Rush, it also stands out in American history as a great venture in individual freedom. A man or woman with minimum requirements could literally set out in pursuit of a golden dream. Electronics, mass transportation and corporate organization limit such individual ventures in our day to pursuits of the mind. The Gold Rush evokes nostalgia for a type of freedom, for a sense of adventure that has no place in the imminent 21st century.

A P P E N D I X A

1850 Census of Products and Industry

COUNTY	Name	Business	No. of Employees	Mo. Salary*	Item	No. of Items	Total Value of Items*	Cost per Item
BENTON	Bacon & Powlison	Carriage Makers	3 males	$25	Wagons Carriages Ploughs		$1,000	
CRAWFORD	John Gardner	Saddler & Harness	4 males	$25	Saddles	300	$2,300	$ 7.66
			1 female	12	Harness	200	$1,600	8.00
JACKSON	George Graves	Blacksmith	3 males	$25	Ploughs	100	$ 500	$ 5.00
		Wagonmaker	3 males	25	Wagons	12	480	40.00
	Andrew Poole	Saddler	3 males	12	Saddles	100	1,000	10.00
					Bridles	200	200	2.00
	James J. Waddill	Tanner	2 males	25	Skins	400	1,600	4.00
		Shoemaker	1 male	18	Boots & Shoes	500 prs.	950	1.90
JOHNSON	Louis F. Eubanks	Blacksmith	2 males	$12			$1,300	
	Hiram S. White	Saddler	4 males	12	Bridles	30 doz.	540	$ 1.50
					Saddles	20 doz.	1,300	5.42
	John M. Turner	Shoemaker	2 males	30	Boots & Shoes	500 prs.	700	1.40
	Isaac King	Wagonmaker	2 males	22	Wagons	24	840	35.00
	William K. Lewis	Blacksmith	1 male	10			500	
	Thomas Shatswell	Blacksmith	2 males	10			500	
	A. W. Peacock	Saddler	1 male	18	Bridles	4 doz.	62	1.29
					Saddles	60	900	15.00
PULASKI	George Metzger	Shoe & Bootmaker	2 males	$20	Boots & Shoes	200 prs.	$1,600	$ 8.00
	Kamer & Dooley	Coach & Wagonmakers	4 males	20	Coaches & Wagons	15	2,000	133.33
	George J. Leschr	Bootmaker	3 males	20	Boots & Shoes	300 prs.	2,000	6.67
	E. D. Gray	Bootmaker	2 males	15	Boots & Shoes	100 prs.	700	7.00

COUNTY	Name	Business	No. of Employees	Mo. Salary*	Item	No. of Items	Total Value of Items*	Cost per Item
	D. C. Corley	Blacksmith	2 males	$18	Farm Tools Horseshoes		$ 700	
	A. G. Dinny	Blacksmith	4 males	18	Farm Tools Horseshoes		1,200	
	Henry Snyder	Blacksmith	2 males	18	Farm Tools Horseshoes		635	
	John Lewis	Blacksmith	4 males	18	Farm Tools Horseshoes		1,655	
WASHINGTON	W. H. Blackburn	Blacksmith	4 males	18	Farm Tools Horseshoes		585	
	J. L. B. Haygood	Blacksmith	3 males	18	Farm Tools Horseshoes		1,200	
	Abner Davidson	Blacksmith	2 males	18	Farm Tools Horseshoes		960	
	Mark Bean	Blacksmith	2 males	18	Farm Tools Horseshoes		700	
	B. E. Woodruff	Wagonmaker	8 males	10	Wagons Plows	75 100	6,750 700	$90.00 7.00
	Peter VanWinkle	Wagonmaker	8 males	10	Wagons Plows	75 100	6,750 700	90.00 7.00
	J. R. Cate	Wagonmaker	2 males	10	Wagons	10	800	80.00
WASHINGTON	Eli Kelly	Saddler	2 males	15	Harness Saddles	25 sets 75	250 1,125	10.00 15.00
	N. B. Wilcox	Shoemaker	2 males	12	Boots & Shoes	700 prs.	1,500	2.14
	G. B. Anderson	Blacksmith	3 males	18	Farm Tools Horseshoes		700	
	William Hubble	Saddler	1 male	$30	Saddles		$ 600	
YELL	John B. Howel	Blacksmith	2 males	16	Farm Tools		1,500	
	Manson Young	Saddler	2 males	20	Saddles		800	

Prepared by Jackie Daugherty of the Arkansas Territorial Restoration's Research Staff from information in the *1850 Census of Products and Industry.*

*Rounded to whole dollars.

APPENDIX B

Articles of Association

ARTICLES OF THE LITTLE ROCK AND CALIFORNIA ASSOCIATION

Art. 1. This company shall be composed of not less than fifty, nor more than one hundred men.

Art. 2. This company shall have the following officers, to be elected by ballot, to wit: a captain; two lieutenants, (1st and 2nd); and orderly sergeant, and a commissary.

Art. 3. The duty of officers shall be commensurate with, and in every respect equal, in power and authority, with volunteer officers of equal grade in the service of the United States, except that a member of the Association may appeal from the judgment or order of the commander in case of tyranny or oppression, (if supported in the appeal by five members of the company,) to the decision of the Company—voting by ballot.

Art. 4. The duty of the Commissary shall be—to purchase provisions for the company while on the route; to employ guides; to purchase mules and horses for the general use of the Company while enroute—These offices to be performed at the request and of the Company. It shall be his duty, moreover, to keep all the accounts of the Company, of a general character, subject to the inspection and approval of the commander.

Art. 5. In case of death or resignation, or refusal, at any time to serve, of any officer selected by the company, the highest in command shall cause an election to be held to fill the vacancy,—which shall give all the power and authority to the officer thus elected that his predecessor held under the first election.

Art. 6. There will be a clerk appointed by the captain, whose duty it shall be to keep a journal of each day's journey, and note the company's camping ground each night, and record all events and circumstances as they may occur.

Art. 7. Every member of the association binds himself to provide the following articles, and be with them at Fort Smith, on the last day of March, 1849, to wit: 100 lbs. bacon; 125 lbs. flour, 25 lbs. coffee, salt, pepper, etc., in proportion. Other articles of provision may be taken, if desired, but the above specified ones must not be neglected. He shall also provide 5 lbs. of powder and 12 lbs. shot; one rifle or shot gun; pistols and knife. Owing to the scarcity of provisions in California, and from the nature of the expedition,—and, moreover, that we may be better prepared for the privations in the land of gold—the committee deem it advisable to adopt wagons, instead of pack mules. Every member shall, therefore, provide himself, or contribute his quota toward providing a good substantial wagon with four good mules; and this wagon shall not carry over 2,000 lbs. Every mess, consisting of not more than six, shall have a good tent, axe, saw, drawing knife, two or three chisels, augur, mattock, and a spade or shovel. These instruments will be found very convenient on the route, and of essential service when the emigrants arrive in California.

Art. 8. It shall be the duty of the Commissary to see that every member of the association provides himself with the above mentioned articles, and to report such member or members as fail to do so to the captain; whereupon his or their names shall be stricken from the roll and dismissed from the company.

Art. 9. Any member who may sicken, or become unable to perform the duties on the route of a member of the Association shall be sustained and assisted by his fellows, under the orders of the chief in command.

Art. 10. It is hereby agreed that any person wishing may subscribe his name, and be represented by his friend; and that servants may be permitted to accompany their master or his friend, being under the charge of such master or friend; but amenable to the orders of the company.

Art. 11. The route proposed for the company is: To proceed from Fort Smith to Chapman's trading-house, four miles above the north fork of the Canadian River, crossing the south fork two or three hundred yards above the mouth of the north fork; from thence to Edward's trading-house, on Little River; from whence directly between the north and south forks of the Canadian River, affording, at all seasons of the year, excellent grazing for stock. The streams rise in the neighborhood of Santa Fe, and often run so close together that they both can be seen from the same point, and is an unerring and natural guide to emigrants on their route; being on the dividing ridge which is as level as could be desired, and abounds with springs the entire distance. From thence the company will proceed on the route traveled by Gen. Kearney, to the Sacramento or San Joaquin, as may prove most advisable; which will be determined by the character of the face of the country, and such information as may be obtained of a reliable nature, and the knowledge of such guides as may be procured at the Company's expense. It is expected that every person who has determined to go has made up his mind to endure the hardships of camping out and attending to his horses, wagons, etc., but we are well enough acquainted with such a life to be able to say that those who have made the experiment, heretofore, have uniformally become of robust constitutions, and increased much in flesh.

We, the undersigned, members of the "Little Rock and California Association", do approve of the above rules and regulations for its government, and do bind ourselves as men, and do pledge our honor as gentlemen, each one for himself, to obey, enforce, and abide by them.

Printed in *Arkansas State Democrat,* February 9, 1849.

ARTICLES OF THE VAN BUREN CALIFORNIA ASSOCIATION

Art. 1. The officers of the said Association shall consist of a Captain, three Lieutenants, four Sergeants, and four Corporals—a Secretary, Treasurer, a Wagon-master, and Council of Administration.

Art. 2. All officers, except the Wagon-master and Council of Administration, shall be elected by a majority of the Association, to hold office until the Council of Administration may deem a new election necessary.

Art. 3. The Wagon-master shall be elected by the Council of Administration, whose duty shall be the immediate supervision of the progress of the wagons and teams during the march, acting always under the orders of the Captain.

Art. 4. The Council of Administration shall be constituted as follows: Every non-commissioned officer and private shall be numbered from No. 1, to the end of the list; and the first numbers, 1, 2, 3, 4, with the Captain, who shall be the presiding officer, shall compose said Council, until one week after the departure of the Association from Van Buren. Every week thereafter the highest number shall retire from the Council, and the highest number not yet in the Council shall fill his place, and so in rotation to the end.

The numbers shall be obtained by a draft, a record of which shall be kept in a record by the Secretary.

Art. 5. The Captain shall have full command and authority; and shall be supported in same, by the officers and Council of Administration.—The subordinate officers shall at all times hold themselves subject to the Captain.

Art. 6. The Secretary shall preserve a record of the proceedings of the Association, and shall keep an account of all monies paid into the hands of the Treasurer, and disbursed therefrom. He shall also serve as clerk at all meetings of the Council of Administration, and of the Association.

Art. 7. The Treasurer shall take charge of all monies paid into the Treasury of the Association, and pay all orders drawn upon him when such shall be signed by the Secretary, and counter-signed by the Captain.

Art. 8. The Council of Administration shall examine the character and equipments of candidates for membership and shall have power to receive or reject the same, as in their judgment they may deem best. It shall impose all necessary assessments, and shall make all necessary appropriations of the funds of the Association.

It shall have power to try all persons for drunkenness, violence of the peace, and other criminal conduct, and to impose penalties for the same, which shall be enforced under the authority of the Captain.

It shall be empowered to purchase, at the cost of the Association, a traveling forge, a medicine chest, and a cable; said property to be under the charge of the Council, and the joint property of the Association, to be disposed of at the end of the journey for the benefit of the same.

It shall be the duty of the Council of Administration, at any time, upon the written request of seven members, to call a general meeting of the Association.

Art. 9. The proportion of members to the wagons and teams shall be as follows: each wagon capable of bearing 3,000 lbs., and hauled by four yoke of oxen, or six horses, or mules, shall be appropriated to the use of no more than five persons, but each wagon shall not be loaded with more than 2,500 lbs. Each wagon capable of bearing 1,500 lbs., and hauled by three yoke of oxen or three horses, or mules, shall be appropriated to the use of no more than two persons, but shall not be loaded with more than 1,200 lbs.

Art. 10. Each person shall be provided with more than one gun, four pounds of powder, eight pounds of lead, one five gallon cask, one spade, one pickaxe, one-hundred and seventy five pounds of bacon, one-hundred and fifty pounds of flour or crackers, five pounds of salt, and two pounds of soap.

Art. 11. Each wagon shall be provided with one axe, one augur, one chisel, one gimlet, one drawing knife, ten pounds of iron, three gallons of tar, one stable lantern, one extra yoke of oxen, or mule, or horse.

Art. 12. No members shall be expelled from this Association, except by the unanimous vote of the Council of Administration.

Art. 13. These articles shall not be added to, diminished, or altered, except by a vote of two-thirds of the members of this Association.

Art. 14. Each person, before he can be admitted into this Association, shall sign these Articles, and pay five dollars into the Treasury.

Art. 15. Five members shall be elected to serve as a temporary Council of Administration, until the Association departs from Van Buren. Said Council shall superintend and direct the organization of the Association: shall inspect the wagons, equipments, and outfits of the members; and see that the conditions of these articles are complied with before their departure from Van Buren; and shall perform the other duties imposed upon the Council of Administration by these Articles.

Printed in *Arkansas State Democrat,* March 16, 1849.

ARTICLES OF THE CLARKSVILLE AND CALIFORNIA MINING ASSOCIATION

We, the undersigned, being about to emigrate to California, for our mutual protection and safety, and to give us weight and character in the country to which we are going, hereby agree to be governed by the following rules and regulations.

Article 1. Our company shall be styled, "The Clarksville and California Mining Association."

2. There shall not be received into this association more than 50 wagons, and not more than 10 of which shall contain families. The families are to be deemed private property, and weighed in as part of the load.

3. Each wagon shall be capable of bearing 3000 pounds, but shall no carry more than 2000, and shall be provided with four yokes of oxen, or six mules, one five gallon water cask, one axe, two shovels, one pick-axe, one auger, one chisel, one gimblet [sic], one drawing-knife, twenty-five pounds of iron, three gallons of tar, one extra horse or mule, fifty dollars in specie, and cooking utensils for at least 5 persons, including a tin-cup for each person.

4. There shall be not less than three able bodied men to each wagon.

5. Each and every person belonging to this association, shall, on the day of starting, be provided with one gun, four pounds of powder, eight pounds of led, [sic] one hundred pounds of bacon, and one hundred and fifty pounds of flour, ten pounds of salt, and two pounds of soap.

6. Each wagon and team, must be in Clarksville, on the morning of the 25th day of March, A.D. 1849, provided and armed as above required, ready for the journey.

7. The officers shall be, one Captain, one engineer, four lieutenants, one commissary, one treasurer, and one secretary.

8. It shall be the duty of the captain to divide the company into four divisions; to regulate all movements of the company, and to preside at all meetings of the officers.

9. There shall be a council, to consist of the captain, the engineer, the four lieutenants, the commissary, the secretary, the treasurer, and four members to be elected by the association, making in all 13 persons.

10. It shall be the duty of each lieutenant to take charge of a division.

11. The council shall appoint three persons to act as inspectors of wagons and teams; said council shall also have power to try any member of the association for any offence he may commit, and punish as a majority of them may determine.

12. There shall be a committee appointed to purchase a traveling forge, anvil, &c, to be used in common by the association, also a spy-glass, quadrant, and a field compass.

13. It shall be the duty of the engineer, to take charge of the sappers and miners, and spy company, together with the spy-glass, quadrant and compass. He shall daily take notes of the country and thus incidents of the journey.

14. It shall be the duty of the inspectors, to examine each wagon and teams, and to report the value of the same to the Council, and to see that each wagon has not more than 2000 pounds on it, at any one time and that it is accompanied with the articles specified in article 3.

15. It shall be the duty of the commissary to see that each wagon carries sufficient provisions for its mess, and to appoint a deputy to each wagon, whose duty it shall be, to apportion provisions, so that the commissary may make a weekly general report to the council.

16. It shall be the duty of the treasurer to receive, safely keep, and pay out monies belonging to the association. He shall pay no order unless it be signed by the Captain, and attested by the secretary.

17. It shall be the duty of the secretary to keep a record of all proceedings had in the council, and of all moneys received and paid out.

18. No wagon shall have more than one gallon of spiritous liquors to accompany it, and that only to be used, when permitted by an order from the commissary.

19. No gambling shall be permitted among, or by members of this association, under any name or device whatever.

20. The company or association shall travel six days and rest on the seventh, except when in the opinion of the council, there is a scarcity of wood, water, grass, or provisions.

21. Every wagon, horse, mule and ox, with their equipage, shall be valued into the association, and credited to the person delivering the same, and at the end of the journey, all property shall be valued out and each person shall receive the same property he put in, if it be in existence, if not, he shall receive a *pro rata* dividend from the association. Each horse, mule, or ox, to be well shod, and their owners to have with their wagons one extra set of shoes for each, and none of them are to be received into the association, unless they first shall have borne inspection.

22. All articls [sic] not heretofore specified in articles 3 and 5, shall be deemed private property, and a tax shall be assessed from time to time, on the whole amount of both public and private property sufficient to cover the joint expenses of the association, and in order to further this, each man, previous to starting, shall deliver to the secretary a list of all the private property he may have in the association, together with the value of each article.

23. No member shall be expelled from this association, unless by a unanimous vote of the council.

24. All persons joining this association, shall sign their names to these rules, and take the following oath, to wit:

I, ______, do solemnly swear, in the presence of Almighty God, and these witnesses, that I will be governed by the rules of this association, and such other rules as the council may, from time to time adopt, and that I will endeavor to promote the harmony, and advance the interests of this association, to the best of my knowledge and capacity, so help me God.

25. These rules shall not be altered or amended, unless by a vote of two-thirds of all the members of the council.

As there are doubts in the minds of some, with regard to the ability of oxen to perform the trip, Redmond Rogers hereby pledges himself to furnish means out of his private funds to purchase mules, that can complete the trip, provided the foregoing rules are adopted, and, that he be given a lien upon the wagons and mules so purchased, for the payment thereof.

Printed in *Arkansas Gazette* February 15, 1849.

APPENDIX C

1850 Fort Smith Circular

To the People of the U. States

CIRCULAR

of the Fort Smith Corresponding Committee.

Owing to the many misrepresentations and false statements published about the FORT SMITH ROUTE TO CALIFORNIA, and the alleged sufferings of those who tried that route, last spring, the Committee deem it their duty to correct the false impressions made upon the public mind, by these misrepresentations, by an array of facts that are incontrovertible. The Committee have no design to make statements of their own, and endeavor to palm them off for truths upon the public, but will present the testimony of men who are disinterested, honest, and entitled to the fullest credit. If the *Fort Smith Route to California*, does not possess superior advantages over every other, according to the observations of scientific men, then we are willing to lay down our pens and say no more on the subject.—We wish every person to examine for himself, and make up his mind in accordance with the testimony adduced. In the first place, as regards the country from FORT SMITH to DONA ANA, *over one-half the distance to the Pacific*, 894 miles—it has been surveyed and marked by Capt. Marcy, 5th Infantry, U.S.A., a gentleman who is entitled to credit, and his character as an officer stands high. An extract from his report, was published in our former circular, and is now before the public. After giving a description of the country over which he traveled with his train, he sums up the whole and says:—

"Hence it will be seen that from DONA ANA to FORT SMITH, a distance of 894 miles, our road passes over smooth and very uniformly level ground, crossing no mountains or deep vallies, and for FIVE HUNDRED MILES upon the eastern extremity, runs through the heart of a country possessing GREAT NATURAL ADVANTAGES."

Capt. M. made the trip from Dona Ana to Fort Smith, in two months, with the same train of mule and ox teams that he had taken to Santa Fe, besides he was detained in one place 14 days by a norther, and high waters, the whole distance, being 894 miles. The distance, he says, can be shortened at least 50 miles, and we learn from other reliable sources, that the distance can be reduced to 800 miles.

The *Fort Smith Company* left the neighborhood of Dona Ana between the 4th and 12th of August. A part of the company, made a trip to search for a gold mine reported to be on the Gila, the other part of the company with the wagons, traveled slowly, in order that those who were out on the hunt for gold, might be enabled to overtake them; and notwithstanding this delay, they all arrived at San Diego in two months from the time they left the Rio Grande. On the 16th of November, *Mr. S. Bolivar Bennett*, one of the company, writes to *Mr. Walton*, of the house of Bennett & Walton of this place, informing him of his safe arrival at San Diego, and says: "I have been here over one month, waiting for a vessel, the other part of the company having gone on with their teams by land."—Had this company traveled immediately along, without detention, they would have arrived at San Diego, on the Pacific in 40 days. Capt. *Marcy* says he can reach Dona Ana from FORT SMITH in FORTY-FIVE DAYS. If, therefore, the distance to Dona Ana, can be traveled in 45 days, which is a difference of 13 degrees of longitude from Fort Smith, the distance from Dona Ana to San Diego, should be made in a much less time, it being only 10 degrees, and over equally as good ground, according to the account given by Lt. Col. Cook, of the U.S. Dragoons, who traveled over this route in 1840, with the wagon train, belonging to the command then under Gen. Kearney. He says:

> "From the high valley of the river I ascended to the *table land* of Mexico, by an almost insensible slope over smooth prairie. For 150 miles on this smooth level table land, which is studded with isolated hills or mountains, I journeyed without any difficulty, passing over but three hills in two cases, I know; in the third, I believe unnecessarily; I then, unexpectedly and suddenly, arrived at a great break off to a lower level of country, the descent to which was very broken and rough mountains for fifteen miles. I found, however, that I had at that moment fallen into an old wagon trail, which led, I was told, from Yanos. I was able to get my wagons through, following a stream all the way, and descending in the 15 miles possibly a thousand feet."

Thus we see that the greatest descent on this route is only 1000 feet, in 15 miles. Compare this with the abrupt, and almost perpendicular ascent of the Sierra Nevada, which is about 7500 feet, and we find that this descent of 1000 feet dwindles into nothing. Upon the top of the Sierra Nevada, snow was encountered on the 4th of August, by a party, 20 to 30 feet deep; and in descending the mountain, the wagons were let down precipiced by means of ropes, and trees were lashed on behind to keep them from overturning.

Mr. Redmond Rogers, a gentleman of experience and possessing a great deal of sagacity and good sense, and withal a man of undoubted veracity, writing to his friends in Clarksville, in this State, from San Francisco, says, that he arrived in that country with all of his wagons and teams, and LOST BUT ONE OX, on the whole route, and found grass and water in abundance. He commanded the Clarksville company, fitted it up mostly at his own expense, had from 20 to 25 wagons, and left Fort Smith about the first of last April, and traveled to Santa Fe, thence down the Rio Grande to Cook's route, about 300 miles out of the way, and notwithstanding this excess of distance traveled, he and his company reached San Francisco in safety, and are now doing well, as we learn from his letters and those of others. Mr. Rogers sold five of his teams, in California, upon which he cleared $5000. This we learn from a gentleman of undoubted veracity.

The Little Rock Company traveled over the same road, arrived in safety, and all the members of it are now at the mines doing well. Numerous letters have been received from the members of the company by their friends, giving a description of their journey and their arrival in California. One of them, in a letter to a friend from San Francisco, says:

> "We sold our mules at San Diego, and took the steamer for this city. There were four hundred passengers on board; and although we had a hard time of it on the land route, there were not three days on the whole trip so unpleasant as the three we spent on board the steamer."

Nature seems to have marked out this route for the GREAT OVERLAND ROAD from the valley of the Mississippi to the Pacific ocean. The whole distance from FORT SMITH TO SAN DIEGO, on the Pacific, can be traveled without crossing a single mountain, and this cannot be done upon any other route now known. There is NO SNOW to be encountered, which is a consideration of vast importance to the emigrant.

The desert, lying between the mouth of the Gila and the mountains, which has been the greatest obstacle to the emigrant, has been supplied by Providence with a river of pure water, running through the centre of it, as if to accommodate the emigrant with a place for him and his cattle and horses, to quench their thirst and afford him a camping place to rest. The full account of the discovery of this river being in the midst of this desert, will be found in the annexed letter of Col. *Emory*, who is on the ground; running the line between Mexico and the United States, to Col. Abert, head of the topographical bureau. We ask the people of the United States to give it an attentive perusal, as it is entitled to the fullest credit, he being the gentleman who made the reconnoisance of the route, on the Gila, in 1846, under Gen. Kearney.

The discovery, by Capt. *Marcy*, of the route from Dona Ana to Fort Smith, obviates all the disadvantages the emigrants had to encounter last spring in traveling a distance of 300 miles out of the way. Now, the road is direct, and connects with Col. Cook's road at the Rio Grande. No delay is now necessary. All the emigrant will have to do is to be well prepared—"then go ahead."

We expect that a command of U.S. Troops, will be dispatched in the early part of the spring to make further reconnoisance on this route, with the view of shortening the distance at the points designated by Capt. *Marcy*, and to plant Military Posts on the road, for the protection of emigrants. *Fort Smith* is now the Depot, for the landing of troops, supplies, munitions of war, &c., for Forts Towson and Washita, as it is the highest, and indeed the nearest point of navigation for these posts. In a year or two, we are very certain the Government will land all of her military supplies at this place, for the posts on this road and on the Rio Grande.

Col. *Emory*, in his letter to Col. Abert, says: "Seeing vast numbers of emigrants now, (20th of August is the date,) coming over this route, most of whom, as they inform me, have no other guide than my report." Again he says:

> "The existence of water must soon be followed by the growth of grass; and, if the river continues, the route by the Gila, now much traveled, will stand fair to rival all overland routes to California. It is probably the only route within the limits of the United States that can be passed in the winter, and the one upon which will concentrate the winter travel to the Pacific."

Here is the testimony that cannot be doubted, and proves that THIS ROUTE will "rival all overland routes to California," and is "the only route within the limits of the United States that can be passed in the winter."

We defy the world to contradict, successfully, these statements. They are based upon the observations of gentlemen of the highest standing in the U.S. Army, men who have no interest but to serve their country in any capacity they may be called upon to act, and having no "abiding place," they must certainly be actuated in such cases, by disinterested motives.

We feel confident that a company with wagons can reach San Diego on the Pacific, with ease, in 80 days, and with pack mules in 60. There can be no doubt of this, and if any one should doubt it, let him make the calculation and he will be convinced. But, it is not necessary for a company to go by the way of San Diego, as it is out of the way. The road traveled by the emigrants at present, does not go nearer than 50 or 60 miles of that place. It is now plain and well beaten, by the numerous emigrants that have passed over it the present season.—Steamers make the run from San Diego to San Francisco in 3 days, and to Monterey in less time. Thus it will be seen that a company can reach San Francisco from Fort Smith in 75 or 80 days.

The FORT SMITH ROUTE is accessible from all parts of the United states, east, west north and south. Steamboats are running regularly from Natchez, Vicksburg, New Orleans, Cincinnati, Louisville, Memphis, St. Louis, Napoleon, the mouth of the Arkansas river, to this place. Emigrants can find the means of conveyance at any time from any of these ports, and after arriving here, can be supplied either in this place or in Van Buren, 5 miles below on the river, with every thing necessary for an outfit, at prices lower than can be purchased in any of the cities, and shipped to this point.—This was abundantly tested by the emigrants last spring.

Newspapers throughout the United States are respectfully requested to publish the above, with the annexed letter of Col. *Emory.*

J. R. KANNADY,
JNO. F. WHEELER,
CHAS. B. JOHNSON,
MITCHELL SPARKS,
SOL. F. CLARK,
SAM. L. GRIFFITH,
THOS. McCARRON,
Committee of Correspondence

Fort Smith Herald, February 16, 1850.

APPENDIX D

Extract from Journal of F. J. Thibault on Voyage from San Francisco to New Orleans

Reached San Francisco on the morning of the 6th October. Upon inquiry, I ascertained that there would not be a steamer before the 15th, and our chance for obtaining a passage on her, very doubtful. The ship *Powhattan*, Capt. Hopkins, that had been advertised to sail on the 5th was in the act of hauling out—consequently, we had but little opportunity of ascertaining her accommodations. We were homeward bound, and would risk the venture. It would have been better for us had we have remained a month or six weeks, than to have embarked on this catch-penny trap. Here we were detained until the 9th. on which day we left the golden gate, a stiff breeze blowing at the time from the North. Being the prevailing wind at this season, it was supposed we would probably make the port of Panama in thirty or thirty-five days. The wind held steady for about 9 days, a good studding sail breeze that enabled us to make about 1,500 miles to the South, during which time one of our fellow-passengers was found dead on his cot in the morning, no one knowing the hour of his death. He was soon sewed up in the remnant of an old sail, with a bag of rocks to his feet, placed on a plank at the gangway, the Union Jack (the flag of our country), spread over him for a winding sheet. At a given signal, the plank and corners of the flag are seized by two seamen, and raised to an angle, sufficiently to cause the body to slide off, and with one [s]plash he was resigned to his watery-grave. About this time the wind had become baffling and finally died away; or had we a wind, it was invariably a head one, from which we could profit nothing. I would here mention, that in fitting out these vessels, the least possible pound of ballast they dare start with, or the fewest number of casks of water for an average passage, as both costs considerable in San Francisco, is the plan which these swindlers adopt. It is a well known fact, that a vessel with an insufficiency of ballast, is not only unsafe, but incapable of carrying sufficient sail to profit by a favorable wind. As the weather became calm, we endeavored to while away the time fishing—many fish were taken, mostly of the Trigerfish, some Dolphin, and occasionally a Porpoise. Here we lay for about one month, about the 16th degree of North latitude, torturing the sails into every possible shape to invite a breeze. Many events both of a serious and amusing character transpired during that time—among other things the consigning to the waves of another of our fellow-travelers, who had mortgaged a farm to get to California, was taken sick on arriving there, borrowed funds to return, had gotten thus far on his way to his family and the rest is told.

No one but those who have experienced it, can imagine with what anxiety we would sit on the bulwarks, and watch the cat's-paw as it came on, ruffling the glassy surface of the great Pacific. We finally made the southern coast of Mexico. Our provision became almost unbearably hard, we were likewise placed on an allowance of water, two quarts being rationed out to each man, for all purposes. Had you any desire to get a cup of tea or coffee, you were compelled to crowd up to the galley, and deliver a like quantity of water to the cook, who after tasting it to prevent salt water from being wrung in upon him, would throw it into the coppers to boil. In due time we would crowd to the centre of attraction, and get the beverage—always bearing in mind that the last comers came off minus. Two quarts of water may be deemed sufficient by those who have never made the trial, or have crouched beneath any little projection that might afford a protection from the scorching rays of the sun, that was melting the pitch from the seams in the deck. I have heard $2 freely offered for one cup of water, without being able to obtain it. After receiving our coffee, we had the privilege of descending to the table, that was spread out with salt-meat and hard-bread—the meat affording an opportunity of having your thirst increased, in proportion to the consumption. You can have but little idea of the confusion attending the rating out the water to 200 souls. Not anticipating anything of this description, we were unprepared with vessels to receive it—some with an old bucket, others with coffee-pots, pans, jugs, or any thing that they were fortunate enough to stumble upon.

To add to our store of comforts our ship was well stocked with an insect known to California as miners, causing me to ascend to the main top with my blankets to avoid them, to the no small peril of my bones, being frequently disturbed at night and obliged to descend on deck by the squalls that would last just long enough to throw us all in confusion and are over. We at length made the southern coast of Mexico, one degree north of Tehuantepec, we stood in until within 15 miles and then sent a boat off to shore, it returned at 10 P.M., reporting not being able to land owing to the heavy surf running at the time. Several natives made their appearance on the beach inviting them to land—cocoanuts in abundance. The Capt. upon the request of the passengers came to the conclusion of running for the port of Tehuantepec to re-water the vessel. We anchored within 1½ miles of an abrupt eminence, there is a strong current making to the Southwest, and the breeze having died away was the cause of our anchoring to hold on to what we had already made. Next morning the 22d of November, the boat and 10 passengers started for the beach to ascertain if possible the bearing of the above named port. Shortly after they left us a heavy norther sprung up causing us to fly before the gale under double reefed top-sails at the rate of 10 knots an hour—farewell fellow passengers, you are abandoned to your fate, be it for weal or wo! If they were able to make the lee of a point of land for which they were making when last seen, they might possibly land. The passengers opposed the Captain in wishing to abandon them, he represented to us that they had taken the boat contrary to his wish, and that under the existing state of things he did not feel justified in remaining, or in other words, standing off and on. We had a heavy blow most of the day and night—the Captain shaping his course for Realejo, it came down in force upon us about 3 P.M., shaking the "kinks" pretty well out of us before day. The scenery along the coast of Guatemala, as viewed from the vessel, is of the grandest description—the mountains towering up their broken peaks far above the clouds. We would sit for hours at the time gazing on the beauty of the varying landscape. There is a strip of level land bordering the coast and extending to the mountain base, of considerable width, that I would judge to be cultivated, as we can occasionally get a sight of the natives along the beach. On the 1st of December we were told, should we not reach the port of Realejo that day, we would be curtailed in our rations one half. Fortunately we anchored off the entrance of the harbour, received on board our pilot and entered the port on the 2d. We were soon surrounded by the natives in their Bungoes with the most delicious fruits—pine apples, banannas, oranges, &c., &c. We engaged some natives to take us up to Realejo for one dollar each—a distance of three leagues, in their boats that are dug out of a single tree and capable of containing 40 to 50 persons. Gladly we bid farewell to the ship *Powhattan,* (I will acknowledge the corn, for once, "I was caught, I owe you one.") Realejo we found to be a small and filthy place, affording but little attraction to the traveler. I visited the ruins of what was said to have been a very fine and large Church that was represented to have been destroyed by Pirates upwards of two hundred years since. At this place we obtained ox-carts, with truck wheels for the transportation of ourselves and baggage to Granada a distance of 140 miles at the moderate rate of $6 per man, six persons to a cart, or should you prefer it you can procure horses or mules for eleven dollars, but most of us preferred the cart on account of our baggage, proceeded as far as Chinandega on the same day a distance of 9 miles from Realejo. This we found to be a most lovely place, regularly laid out at right angles, each building having a garden attached, the different enclosures being separated by walls, I might say, rather than hedges of the Cactus. The deep green of the orange might be seen mingling its shade with the plantain, banana, lemon and flowers and fruits of the greatest variety, with here and there the tall stem of the cocoanut shooting its diminutive head far above below constructed buildings which consist of a single story, most substantially built of brick, both burned and unburned, and plastered inside and out; the eaves of the root that are covered with tiles project far over the walls affording protection to the street walker from the rain.

We reached Granada on the sixth day, having traveled by easy stages through the following places Chichigalpa, Leon (the capital) Pueblo-nuevo, Nagarote, Materas, Managua, Masaga, and Granada, which is situated on the Lake of Nicuaragua. I will briefly state this is one of the finest countries in an agricultural point of view, it has ever been my privilege to pass through. The cities are well laid out and substantially built, with most magnificent churches and cathedrals, many of which I visited. The hand of Friendship and Hospitality was extended to us by the Natives, frequently meeting us in the streets and bidding us welcome. They expressed a great desire that we would settle among them, and made many inquiries respecting the construction of the canal. I consider them to be a fine, intelligent race of people—extremely neat and most scrupulously clean in their attire. Though our ladies would rather be brought to the blush in passing through this country, as the costomes of the Ladies consists in a skirt similar to our own, but the person from the waist up is covered with a fine and thin texture, that merely reveals what it pretends to conceal. There are decidedly two distinct races of people here, the descendents of the Castilian, and the aborigines. A system of Peonage exists similar to that of Mexico, the dark skins doing the drudgery. I found these people highly incensed against the British on account of their treatment of them in the occupation of the port of San Juan and in proportion as they extolled the character of the North Americans they condemned that of the English. At Granada we were detained six days awaiting a favorable wind to cross the lake, it being so boisterous at the time as to make it dangerous to attempt it sooner. Our mode of conveyance was in a large open boat propelled by "native oarsmen." They likewise carry sail as far as Don Carlos or the foot of the lake at which place we dispense with our masts—depending upon our oars in descending the San Juan river by which the lake empties itself into the Atlantic.—The distance from Granada or Don Carlos or the entrance of that river is 90 miles—from that point we descend the river to San Juan distant 110 miles—from Don Carlos, it is a narrow swift stream abounding in rapids. The forest along its margin is dense beyond description—the cheering rays of the sun are entirely excluded, where monkeys, parrots and mackaws scramble about in their wild gambols. Arrived at San Juan on the morning of the 5th day after leaving Granada, 44 of us having been crowded into this open boat independently of the crew that numbered 10, being exposed to the rain both day and night. On reaching this place we were met on the beach by the British Sergeant and is *Jamaica Negroes* and politely requested to fork over our fire-arms; that brought us all standing. We thought the matter over whether it would be better to turn in and whip them or comply with their request. The latter plan was adopted as they proposed to receipt to us for them and become responsible for their safe delivery on leaving port. In the harbor was a small brig bound to New Orleans; but as the child that has been badly burned generally avoids the fire, we begged to be excused, remained here one day when the British Mail-steamer arrived bound for Chagres, upon which we embarked the same day, and I am in duty bound to say that were were most gentlemanly and courteously treated by the officers, who took pleasure in affording us any information they were in possession of. Arrived at Chagres on the 24th of December—three steamers in port—two of them full—the *Georgia* still selling tickets for New Orleans at $100, being $25 above the published rates. Many who were desirous of procuring steerage tickets were informed that there were none for sale—that it was full, and as long as a man could be raised who could possible command a sufficient sum to procure a cabin ticket they sold them, and then opened for the sale of steerage tickets for $60. As long as that price could be obtained they demanded it and finally I was informed, sold them for $40. Those who had purchased for the first cabin fared but little better than the steerage passengers—several lives were lost going off to the steamer in small boats, the sea running high at the time, the boatman demanding $3, for his fare, and should a native boatman be caught demanding less, he was jumped and beaten. An incident of the kind occurred whilst we were there. We left his most loathsome of all places on the 24th of December—a heavy rolling sea caused the vessel to labor considerably for the first few days. Three of our companions died before reaching Havana at which place we arrived on the 30th. The fare on this vessel can only be fully known by those who travel upon her. Had we a desire to see a fellow-passenger we were compelled to appoint a place of meeting, so densely was this mammoth vessel crowded. Just think of 1340 passengers thrown together on one craft! . . . Men would die and the first information of the fact would be to make way for the body to be thrown overboard. And what did our cabin ticket entitle us to? Some very good provisions I will admit if we were fortunate in being good hands at the grab game, also a soft plank with our own blankets for a bed.

On arriving at Havana, instead of finding the *Ohio* to carry us to New Orleans as our tickets called for, we were told the *Falcon* would arrive in the space of a day or two in her stead and that we must allow our baggage to be placed on board a lighter and await her coming; for the authorities would not suffer them to land our trunks. This we positively refused to do and remained on board until the arrival of the *Pacific.* It was then represented to us by the captain of the *Georgia* that arrangements had been made with the *Pacific,* who informed us that no arrangement had been made with that vessel. We returned to our vessel and coolly determined to remain on board until some provision was made for us: After a while our very worthy Capt. Porter U.S.N. condescended to inform us that we would be received by the *Pacific* upon which we took up our quarters. Shortly after the leaving of the *Georgia* for New York, the *Falcon* arrived, bound for Chagres, and refused to take us on board. We immediately called a meeting of the passengers and appointed a committee to wait on the American Consul to redress our wrongs, which was effected by his having the *Falcon* tied up until she was released by the agent of Law's Line at Havana, who chartered the Pacific for our benefit. I would ask the American public if this state of things is to continue until these gentlemen are satisfied that there are no more to fleece? Are American citizens traveling in vessels under the immediate patronage of our government, and commanded by Naval officers, to have their pockets picked and robbed of their hard earned gains? Assuredly we must not murmur or speak above a whisper—why that is Capt. Porter, U.S.N.! After we had been detained 6 days at this place we finally got off as above, and in due time reached New Orleans. I will merely remark in conclusion that we were well treated by the Capt. of the *Pacific,* who informed me there was double the number of cabin passengers, as represented by the list obtained from the Georgia; and he could not be satisfied by the imposition until he had a rope drawn across the vessel and his mistake was evident. There was another fraud practised upon this Captain, who I am pleased to say treated us respectfully.

Arkansas State Gazette and Democrat, January 31, 1851, p. 3.

APPENDIX E

Rollin Ridge Letters

Yuba City, Oct. 4, 1850

Dear Mother: It is with pleasure that I sit down to relieve what I know must be your great anxiety to hear from your wandering children, torn as they are from you, and cast, as they so well can feel each morning that they rise, and each night that they lay down, on a strange and distant land. Believe me, it is no ordinary thing to come to California, as the thousands that sight here in the midst of all its wealth can testify.

I am wasting golden hours in giving you what I intend shall be an accurate account of everything connected with us and our interests in this vagabond land. You have, I hope, received letters from me giving an account our our journey as far as Fort Laramie.

After we left Fort Laramie we traveled 150 miles. Then finding that the grass was growing from thin to thinner, and from thinner to perhaps none at all, we concluded to abandon our wagon and pack. This conclusion as the events proved saved us the miserable alternative of walking over the Sierra Nevada with our packs upon our backs.

It was at Deer Creek, a tributary to the North Platte, where we packed. From Deer Creek to the Salt Lake we encountered the roughest road you can conceive, thinly provided with grass all the way; for 50 miles at a time no grass and no water. A large portion of the way was through sand and alkaline ground. Before reaching the Salt Lake a road turns to the right which is called Sublette's cut-off, saving some distance in travel. We should have taken this "cut-off", which avoids Salt Lake, but we were compelled to go by the Mormon City to get provisions—of which we were nearly out—although we had purchased frequently from those who, following our example in abandoning their wagons, were glad to sell a part of what they were forced to leave.

We resolved to pack very light, because I saw plainly at an early day in our journey that it would be nearly as much as any horse or mule could do to carry his own body to California over such a road with such subsistence with out adding a heavy load on to his own weight. With this view, we threw away, at one fell swoop, all our clothing, except one pair of pantaloons, one pair of drawers, etc. with a change, reserving also our overcoats. We threw away all our meat except enough to last us, as we thought, to the Salt Lake, which it did not. We threw away no flour at all, but had only enough at the start to last us to the Salt Lake, owing to the fact, I suppose, that we did not eat as much of the bacon as we should have done had we not been fonder of the flour. All our cooking utensils, save a coffee pot, mill, and a frying pan we abandoned of necessity.

Of all the cooking from that time till we reached this country—why, it fills me with horror to think of it! We had to mix up our dough in a pan, generally in a sandy and dusty place with the wind filling the pan all the time with the said sand and dirt and then bake it in the frying pan; which process consisted in burning the outside, and leaving the inside a "gaub" of sticky stuff full of the pure grease! Bah! it used to give me a fit of the utmost loathing after I had eaten it.

To give you an idea of it: after traveling over wide sand plains, traversed here and there by steep mountains all day at times to relieve our wearied beasts, having walked many hours, fatigued, worn out, nearly dead, we reach our "camping" place, tug away with our tired hands and legs in "fixing" the horses, in fetching water and wood, both of which we would frequently be compelled to walk after a mile or more, (owing to the non-proximity of the grass), then at last to sit down, faint and hungry to strong fat meat that tasted like rust and a piece of bread that made the stomach retch at every swallow, was anything but comfortable! Yet appetite was so strong the stomach, though it loathed, still called for more.

Sometimes we were able to buy from a wagon crackers and bread baked in ovens, and then—do not think I am exaggerating—we would feel a thrill of unbounded happiness at our good fortune in getting them.

But I am consuming too much space—yet I don't know how to do justice to my task without writing on, in the same strain. Pshaw! There's no use trying to tell anything in a letter. It would take me a week's hard talking, face to face. But still, you must have some inkling.

To speak briefly, we got to the Salt Lake. Aeneas and myself and Wacooli having rode 200 miles through clouds of dust every day when we were scarcely able to sit our mules, were burned up with *"mountain fever"* and suffering excruciating torture—yes, excruciating is the word—from pain in our backs that seemed to enter the very spinal marrow!

But we never said "die". We encouraged each other with manly words, but still journeyed on, performing all our duties as tho we were fully able to do so. Wacooli had no reason to complain of us. We put no more on him than on ourselves. We all worked equally hard and suffered together.

But that mountain fever! I will describe it fully when I get home. Believe me, we thought of home then, with its soft beds and kind friends, while thro' the long hours of the day we sat, pale and weak, on our poor jaded mules, or hung our aching heads over their necks to see if change of posture could for a moment alleviate our agony—but that is all past.

When we reached the Mormon City, we had all our animals with us except "Beach" which was fast failing and which we "swapt" for a "Snake poney", a very good one. All our animals were failing. We concluded to recruit at the Salt Lake, both ourselves and our beasts. It was necessary to have them shod also. We had long before thrown away our shoes and nails.

After much trouble questioning the Mormons, we found a range for our mules and the Snake poney. My gray poney I had turned into $35 in the city. We put our animals on this range to do the best they could.

We then took our perambulations thro' the city to satisfy our curiosity and I assure you our hunger, too. One or two meals in the course of our rambles of good, cool milk and light bread with butter and cheese, made us in love with the place for the time. We paid 37½ to 50 cents for such meals. After doing nothing but eat for several days we at last appeased our hitherto insatiable hunger for wholesome food, and prepared to lay in our supplies for California.

We had then no provisions whatever of any kind, except a few pounds of flour. To our astonishment we found that there was not a pound of bacon in the whole city, except what the immigrants brought in their wagons and sold to the citizens for their own use, parting with it in this manner because they intended to pack from the Salt Lake.

What was to be done? We had to buy fresh beef and cure it ourselves. According to the "Mormon Guide", a little book consisting of four small leaves and which they sold to us for the reasonable sum of 50 cents, the distance to Sacramento could be traversed by pack mules in 25 days or 30 at the fartherest. We calculated on this basis and cured beef to the amount of 90 pounds. We had intended to get more than that weight but when cured, the beef did not turn out to our expectations, and then it was too late to procure more. This beef costs us 12½ cents per pound, fresh.

You must excuse me for the desultory mode of writing. If you were in California, eating your head off, as everybody here is in danger of doing at $18 per week, and afraid, as I am every minute, that some chance of making money will pass me by forever, you would appreciate everything that I write, however badly written, and take a letter, not as a matter of course and elegance, but as an accommodation. He that writes a letter in California, unless a perfect loafer, I pronounce an exceedingly accommodating man and one entitled to the great gratitude of his friends.

We bought, in the way of supplies, 150 pounds of flour at 25¢ per pound. It had been sold to the immigrants immediately preceding us for a dollar a pound and even two in some instances. Our better fortune, which I thought bad enough, was owing to the harvest then in.

Our expenses all along the road had been heavy: 25 cents at every bridge over a mudhole; $5.00 per wagon over the different rivers we ferried—where we always found white men ready and if necessary backed by the Indians; and $2.50 for a pack mule or horse—when we had no wagon.

The Mormons even charged toll on the 44 miles of the road to the city. We paid $4 per horse for shoeing all round—God save us! It "shelled" the money from me. Besides all this, I had to do a great deal of riding in and out of the city getting provisions and "seeing to things" as the Yankees say.

My meals, without meat, cost me from 37½ to 50 cents per meal, with meat they would have cost me one dollar each. Baiting my mule $1.50. Why didn't I walk? Because I had to let down bars of fence for six miles from the range to the city and I couldn't pack beef on my back, and I couldn't walk to the mill, 18 miles and pack back flour upon my back. But I grow prolix.

After everything was finished, the mules recruited somewhat. I began to think there was danger of the grass drying up at the farther end of the route if I stayed longer. So I went to the printing office in the city and bought one of their little newspapers with my name, arrival and departure in it, and sent it to you by the Mormon mail. I paid 75 cents for this.

Now comes the tug of war. We expect to reach Sacramento in 25 days. We expect to eat dried beef, which is very good; to sleep without a tent, which is not good; to cross a desert, which is worse, but we expect not much more hardship.

We left the Salt Lake then, about the 15th of July. For 150 miles after leaving the Mormon City we had excellent grass and excellent water. After which, the entire distance may be characterized as a vast desert, through this desert it is only possible for the hardiest animals to pass, by means of the food and water found in the oases, which are made to last them thro' the more barren parts.

The weather was quite tolerable, altho' warm 'til we were some 200 miles west of the Salt Lake. Then, for several days it was very hot, and for two days insufferably severe. At the middle of the day it did seem that death must overtake us in spite of all we could do. If we laid down with our blankets over the sage bushes—which grow along the route to California from 2 to 3 feet high—the heat steamed up from the baked and cracked earth into our bodies and seemed to burn our very livers. If we stood up, the sun rays fell fiercely upon us.

There was no refuge, no shade and no water, except brackish, worse than none, to cool our raging thirst. So much for the first of these days. The second was like unto it only "more so." We had found no water, and 12 o'clock obliged us to stop and rest our horses which were utterly unable to travel on account of the heat. You will have some sense of the heat and thirst which consumed us, when I tell you our tongues hung out of our mouths as is the case with dogs!

When our animals had rested somewhat we rode and drove slowly along under the dreadful beams 'til sunset and coming shadows relieved us. But our thirst was unquenched, and almost past bearing. It was just dusk when, coming down the slant of a hill, we found gushing out of a hollow, a trinity of beautiful clear springs which united their waters 50 to 60 feet below!

We all dismounted, in the utmost haste, and ran to the water with parched lips, when lo! it was so perfectly brackish that no stomach could endure it for a moment! Two days, then, we had of awfully hot weather, without a drop of water that could cool our thirst!—We did not get water fit to drink until after travelling 35 miles the next day.

If the weather had not been so intolerably hot as to prevent all possibility of moving beyond a snail's pace, during every part of the day, and at mid-day all possibility of moving at all, we should not so have suffered. These sufferings from thirst were greater or less until we gained the Humboldt. I must observe also that the water was so bad as to act as a severe purgative after eating the bread mixed by it.

For 50 miles east of, and up to the Humboldt river, we waded thro' mineral dust—saleratus, salpetre, sulphur and what not—sometimes up to the horses' knees, but commonly four or five inches deep. This we did every day from morn 'til night thro' clouds of dust, whose poisonous particles made sores in the nose and ears and for myself affected my throat dreadfully.

You have no idea how terrible it is to bear, this dust. Continually, not for a mile or two, but for hundreds of miles, filling your eye, ears and throat! At night you are not free from it. You cannot shake it out of your blankets, and every time you turn over, light clouds of the precious incense greet your senses.

It often made my hands break out in large sores. I have seen this dust to thickly rising from a road that you could not see a horse 40 yards ahead—perhaps not so far; you could not even get an outline or glimpse of him. There was no use to try to avoid it, it rose with every tramp of your horse inside or outside the track, directly into your face. It was a light as the finest powder of any kind, and was often carried by little whirlwinds, sometimes in huge columns so high that you could hardly see the tops of them! Isn't truth stranger than fiction? I confess I stand astonished to this day at that sight.

At the head of the Humboldt we were still several hundred miles from Sacramento. Our provisions had become so short that we expected to suffer inevitably, perhaps to starve (game being at that time very rare) before we should be able to gain California.

We accordingly put ourselves on rations until we learned that on the westward side of the desert there were provisions which were sold cheap. Learning this, it then became our object to reach that side of the desert as speedily as possible.

It was an absolute necessity for us to do so.—We hurried on therefore our jaded animals to their utmost. Poor things! How faint they grew, and watery eyes and weary, as they grunted at each touch of the spurs or lash of the whip which drove them forwards.

All the way down the Humboldt, a distance of at least three hundred miles, the whole face of the earth was covered with a strong white and yellow substance called alkali, I believe, and the water being so strongly mixed with it as even to partake of its colors, we were continually drinking alkali or whatever poisonous substance it is, into our systems.

No wonder that strange spasms would seize us, and unaccountable fits of debility and exhaustion! Indeed, at this period of our journey our fatigue was so great that we were sometimes taken with blank despair of ever reaching our goal, or gold. Our knees would give way under us as tho' they had no oil; and we seemed to have a set of long, awkward, and unwieldy frames. Locomotion of the slightest kind was a task.

Our animals were suffering in the same way; stiff, and trembling in the joints at every unusual exertion up and down hill. Then the dirt, how can I pass it by! It was utterly impossible to keep clean. We were dirty as the filthiest, lowest, most contemptible, white Indian or "nigger" you ever saw.

We could not comb our heads; it would have taken two days to have combed out the dirt that got into them in one—so that our heads looked like old mops which had scrubbed floors from time immemorial. I tried once to get a comb to the skin of my head and barely did, but I had to lift the comb straight out of my hair, it being impossible to draw it thro' downwards.

After a day's travel each individual every night, looked like he had been rolling himself over and over in the dirt, head and ears, and had taken particular pains to see how perfectly hateful to the sight he could become!

Our best friends would not have known us. If we had, in the plight, ridden thro' the neighborhood of Fayetteville, driving our long, bony-legged mules and horses (which the buzzards were beating the drums for, as old black Peter would say) before us, the sense of the ludicrous would have been so supreme—our long solemn faces helping it off too—that the boys would have hooted at us as we passed by and the hilarity of the spectacle been without bounds.

I have seen packers pass us on the road whose appearance was so exhilerating that I leaned back in my saddle and very nearly killed myself with laughter! But when some poor ragged devil, who started with a most megre outfit under the expectation that it was only necessary to reach California to be a rich man—came riding along on his gaunt old steer, which was fully able to run a race with a snail, drubbing the poor old beast at every step to get him along, I confess my mirth was such that gods and men might have envied me! Poor Humanity! to what miserable passes will it put itself for money.

Here comes a man one day, driving one ox hitched to the fore wheels of his wagon, with a horse, or rather a faint resemblance of one, pulling in front of the ox, the man beating and banging them along when they looked as though they could not stand up another day. Having lost their teams by 'poison water' or thro' Indian theft, such were the straits to which men were reduced by degrees, 'til finally they were forced to take packs on their backs and put it thro' "footback".

Passing over much that is interesting, I must hurry on to an end. We arrived at last at the "Meadows", as they are called, viz: a large prairie bottom of the Humboldt, covered with tall fine grass and divided into green plats by deep sloughs of the river. Here, we were a day's journey from the Sink from which point the Desert commences.

The "Sink" derives its name from the singular circumstances that the river is there absorbed by the sands of the desert, and is forever lost sight of. The Meadows afforded the only grass and thousands of people with wagons and mules and horses were getting grass with which to cross the Desert.

We spent a day getting ours, which we cut with a scythe, and then packed over one slough after another on our shoulders, waist-deep in water for a half mile or more to dry land. It was a severely hard day's work for a poor fellow already worn out with travel. We had to cut enough to feed our horses once at the Sink and once in the centre of the Desert.

When we started from the Sink into the desert, and had travelled about an hour—we started near sundown, expecting to do thro' in a night—we were suddenly arrested by a slough that had but recently burst out, perhaps, and was so deep we were unable to cross it. Thereby, we were put off our course by 15 miles and, worse than that, detained all night at the entrance of the desert.

We were obliged to give to our horses the grass designed for the middle of the desert, and so leave them without substance entirely through. The water in this slough was unfit to drink tho' many did drink it.

On the morrow we started, compelled, contrary to our better judgment to travel 45 miles without water or grass, thro' deep sand and under the intense heat of the sun. We, with our animals, suffered extremely with thirst and hunger—for we were constrained to eat up the provisions which we had provided for the passage when we fed our grass to the horses.

We couldn't carry enough water in our canteens to quench our thirst for any length of time; besides the sun shone so hot that the water became so warm as to be an emetic. We traveled on, and on, and on, 'til within 13 miles of the Desert, when, nearly dead, we met with some wagons from the Salmon Trout river with barrels of the previous liquid which they sold to us for a dollar a gallon.

I never supposed, 'til I got to the desert, I should have to pay for so common an article as water. But those wagoners made thousands of dollars by selling it.

Some poor fellows, who were destitute of money, could get no water at all; many of them, too, who were afoot, it being refused them, even when they begged for it. Many were jogging along, with tears rolling from their eyes.

Horses lay dead, I think I can safely say, every fifty yards thro' the desert. The stench was in every breath we breathed. Thro' the entire desert, it was as tho' we had been standing with our noses to a piece of carrion!—It was so, without exaggeration. I shall never forget it. It made me sick and wretched as I never have been before, and pray God I may never be again.

Fort Smith Herald, January 25 & 31, 1851; published in Washington County Historical Society's *Flashback,* Vol. 28, No. 1, February 1978.

APPENDIX F

Groups

These lists are reconstructed from newspaper listings, diaries, journals, and correspondence. None of them are complete for records were not precise and smaller units, stragglers and independent-minded Arkansans are not recorded. Spellings of the same name varied among the correspondents. Francile Oakley included a partial listing of some 1849ers.

1849 Groups

Clarksville and California Mining Association

Officers

Redmond Rogers, Captain

A. D. King, Captain

John May, First lieutenant

Members

Adams, Bill
Aiken, William
Annis, Parson J. B.
Ashley, John
Bailey, W.
Barton, John
Barton, Miss Mary
Bates, A. B.
Campbell, S.
Campbell, William
Carr, P.
Clark, A. P.
Collier, William
Cravens, Jordan E.
Chrisman, Jobe
Cudd, James
Davis, Elijah
Davis, J. M.
Garner, Enoch
Garner, William W.
Garner, Wyatte
Garrett, Lem
Gilbert, William
Grace, John
Guest, Abra
Guion (Guin), John
Guion, Sam R.
Hackney, Thomas (17)
Hamilton, F. A.
Harman, Alex
Harman, William
Harper, Yancey
Henderson, William
Henry, Daniel
Hickey, George
Holland, Gilbert B.
Holland, William
Houston, John
Houston, Robert
Howell, W. B.
Jacobs, Isom
Jacobs, Stokely
Jamison, David A.
Jarnagin, Cal.
Jarnagin, Tom
Johnson, Hardin
Johnson, Harvey
Johnson, J. W.
Johnston, Joseph C.
Johnston, Thomas
Keillen, William
Kelly, N.
King, Tom
King, Hanna Patrick, wife
Kitchen, Jasper
Latimer, Rev. Robert
Lee, Mark
Lee, Nancy Hickey, wife
Lee, James (12)
Lee, Martha (small)
Lockridge, William
Logan, David (17)
Logan, James
Logan, J. L. C.
Lowther, Robert
Malory, W. F.
May, William
McConnell, N.
McLean, David
McKeever, Wiliam
McPhadden (McFadden), Rubin
Mitchell, Dr.
Murphy, John
Owens, Parson
Owens (wife)
Patrick, John W.
Patrick (wife)
Patrick, Mary Lee (7)
Patrick, G. L.
Payne, Bryant
Pearson, John
Philips, B.
Porter, Tom
Porter, William
Prewett, I. W.
Perwett, J. L.
Price, T. B.
Riley, J. C.
Riley, Thomas
Robinson, A. M. C.
Rogers, Jacob
Rogers, William H.
Rogers, William R.
Rolling, Lewis R.
Rollins, J. F.
Sartin, C. B.
Shelby, Alfred B.
Shelby, G. C.
Shropshire, Johnson
Siclar, John
Speegles, D.
Speegles, Emanuel
Strayhorn, A. M.
Street, C. B.
Street, C. L.
Street, H. G.
Tatum, E. P.
Thomas, R. M.
Thompson, R. M.
Turner, G. W.

Upton, J. C.
Wallace, John
Wallace, Robert
Ward, D. N.
White, John
Willis, Henry
Willis, Jerry
Willis, John
Wilson, Hugh
Young, William
Young, T. J. D.
Slaves of Captain Rogers:
  Ben, blacksmith
  Dan, blacksmith
  Jane, cook
  Charles
  Marcus
  Henry
Others from Clarksville:
  Houston, Maj. John S. (via Panama)

Captain Lewis Evans' Company
(Fayetteville Gold Mining Company and Cherokees)
Officers

Lewis Evans, Captain
James S. Vann, secretary
Thomas Tiner, first lieutenant
Peter Mankin, second lieutenant
M. M. Schrimsher, commissary

Arkansas Members

Bean, John J.
Bean, Oscar
Blackburn, Bur
Blake, James
Callahan, George
Carnahan, James
Carnahan, John
Carter, James
Carter, John
Cartwright, James L.
Chew, Joseph
Cline, John R.
Colville, Andrew
Colville, James
Crawford, A. A.
Crawford, A. B.
Crawford, J. S.
Crawford, William
Crosby, Nathan
Crosby, Wiley
Crumley, George
Crumley, Kidrick
Cunningham, Dr. W. R.
Davis, Judge Hiram
Devin, James
Devin, Matthew A.
Dickinson, James P.
Edmiston, A. E.
Edmiston, J. T. ("Thomps")
Epperson, Robert
Evans, Alonzo G.
Evard, (Avard), E. H.
Freyschlag, Barbara
Freyschlag, Christian
Freyschlag, Edward
Freyschlag, Herman
Freyschlag, Hermina
Garvin, James H.
Goddard, William
Hail, Caroline
Hail, Issac
Hand, Boly
Hand, John
Hastings, J. W.
Hoge, James M.
Hoge, William
Holmes, Calvin H.
Holmes, Cuthbert
Holmes H. P.
Ingram, James
Ingram, John
Irwin, James
Irwin, William
Jackson, David C.
Kellum, J. P.
Kimbrel, T. J.
Lewis, John
Lewis, Nathan
Mallet, William
Marrs, Squire B.
Matthews, J. M.
Maxwell, Thomas
McClure, George
McCullock, James L.
McCullock, Dr. Samuel
McKenney, James
McKey, George
McRoy, H. J.
Morrow, Hugh
Morrow, James
Morrow, William
Murphy, Issac
Myers, James
Nathan, George
Newman, John
North, George C.
Pierce, James
Powers, John
Pyeatt, A. B. T. (boy)
Pyeatt, J. Rankin
Pyeatt, H. Porter
Sanders, Benjamin
Sanders, John
Simms, Fred P.
Shores, Hiram
Shores, William
Shuler, Gus A.

Shuler, Leonard
Slover, Enos
Stokes, ______
Strickland, Jacob
Sumner (Summers?), Hiram
Sumner, John A.
Tharp, Nathan
Tiner, Aaron
Thomas, James A.
Van Hoose, John
Wham, John M.
Waits, Allen
Waits, Joe
Whitley, B.
Williamson, Robert
Wilson, Rev. Wm. (Horse)
Woodruff, Wyatte F.

Cherokee Members

Coleman, R. L.
Gunter, Daniel M.
Harlin, N. R. N.
Keys, George W.
Keys, Richard N.
Lipe, O. W.
McMaster, J. C.
Mulkey, Jonathan
Mulkey, Jonathan
Mulkey, James
Potter, Sam
Rattlingourd, Josiah
Smith, Walter J. B.
Sturdivant, Joseph
Williams, Robert
  Five Negro slaves

Little Rock and California Association
Officers

James McVicar, Captain
Henry Keats, first lieutenant
James Murphy, second lieutenant
A. M. Woodruff, orderly sergeant
George B. King, commissary
W. W. Stevenson, geologist

Members

Brownfield, S.
Brownlee, Robert
Cellars, C. A.
Clark, John W.
Crease, Henry
Drew, R.
  Servant
Fagan, Dr. William P.
Galloway, Ed
Galloway, James B.
Garretty, W.
Goddard, C. E.
Haralson, J.
Howell, Philo
Hunt, ______
Lewis, Sam C. W.
Lavenberg, ______
Lowe, Bun B.
Joiner, J. J.
  Boy
McHenry, J.
  Mingo
Pierce, U.
Pennington, William
  Two servants
Quigley, ______
Robbins, Elijah D.
Stevenson, John
Stevenson, Robert
  Servant
Thibault, F. J.
Thibault, Henry J.
  Jordan
Tucker, Dr. Wood
Others:
  E. W. H.
  Add. S.

Other Little Rock Gold Seekers

Abbage, M. (via Panama)
Conway, Dr. John (Fort Smith group?)
Conway, Mrs. Mary
Conway, Mary (romantic heroine)
  Nine other Conway children
  One female servant
Parsel , Tom (via Panama)
Tappe, Dr. and Mrs. J. W. (Via Horn)
Thorn, Thomas
Thorn, Mary (wife)
Thorn, Thomas A.
Thorn, Catherine A.

Fort Smith and California Emigrating Company
Officers

John J. Dillard, Captain
Sid B. Bennett, first lieutenant
F. G. Ake, second lieutenant
H. J. Share, third lieutenant
John Boyer, secretary
T. M. S. Goodkin, treasurer
Cyrus Hall, quartermaster
William Rogers, wagonmaster

Members

Beebe, ______
Bennett, George
Birge, N. L.
Goodman, ______
Goodkin, N. B.
Harrison, Bird
Ransom, ______
Richardson, ______
Seaman, J. W.

Bledsoe, ______
Campbell (blacksmith)
Cassey, ______
Chandler, (man)
Chandler (wife)
Chisholm, Finney
Dickinson, ______
Few, ______
Hockett, John B.
Hockett, ______
Humphreys, ______
Joy, Wiley
Kaulk, ______
Murry, Gordon
Nordheimer, ______
Shear, ______
Sinclair, Clay
Steinthal, M. W.
Tarver, Charley
Tob,
Winfrees, ______
Others from Fort Smith:
Hudspeth, J. M. (via water)
Wedsworth, J. N. (pack mule)

Van Buren California Association
Offices

Captain
Three lieutenants
Four sergeants
Four corporals
Secretary
Treasurer
Wagon-master
Council of administration

Members

Barnes, W. W.
Bell, Eli
Bell, H. W.
Black, James
Blewman, A.
Carver, John T.
Christy, A. P.
Craig, E. T.
Cunard, T. P.
Davis, James W.
Dyer, George S.
Forsman, James
Farris, Washington
Godard, John
Hartgraves, John
Hatty, John W.
Haygood, James
Howell, H. B.
James, John
Kelley, Moses
Low, Harvey
Low, William
McCurry, Robert
Minnes, John
Morse, Jesse
Newton, T. M.
Newton, Wilson
Perkins, P.
Price, D. C.
Price, Joseph
Pryon, N. A.
Roman, Asa
Renshaw, J.
Shannon, J.
Snyder, C.
Stevenson, A.
Stinnett, James
Talkington, A. A.

Van Buren California Emigrating Company
(Pack Mule Company)
Rules and Regulations Committee:

Bell, Hiram W.
Davis, J. W. B.
Lasater, J. W. D.
Marsh, Thomas
Miles, Samuel

Correspondence Committee:

Bishop, E. B.
Green, J. J.
Johnson, Thomas J.
Marean, J. P.
Ogden, John B.
Scott, Charles G.
Wallace, Alfred
Wilcox, Henry

Van Buren
(Later Pack Mule Company)

Old Maxwell, leader

Batesville Company

Cain, G. N.
Carey, R. S.
Dennis, W. H.
Durnal, H.
Eubanks, W. W.
Hughes, Thomas
Hughes, W. C.
Magruder, Lloyd
Martin, James
Pelham, Dr. James E.
Searcy, W. B.
Stone, John
Ward, Eli
Woodward, Joseph

Fort Gibson Party
(Arkansans and Cherokees)

Leaders

J. N. A. Carter
A. M. Wilson

Members

Chisholm, Finney
Cordrey, S. B.
Grymes, George E.
Rogers, Lovely
Scott, Thomas
Shaw, Bob
Wilson, A. D.
Wilson, G. W.

Fulton County Emigrants

Adams, Ervin
Adams, Peter F.
Hutchinson, Thomas J.
Irwin, Hiram
Reynolds, Benjamin
Wolf, George W.

Heath Pack Mule Company

W. H. Heath, Captain (Illinois)

Arkansas Members

Ballard, G.
Owen, Jesse
Scarborough, Asa
Sellers, J. H.
Stanley, S. G.

Helena Company

Officers

H. P. Dorsey, Captain
W. C. Stephenson, Lieutenant

Members
(68 men)

Biven, R.
Bukes, F.
Fulkes, F.
Heslip, Dr. A. J.
Hurd, J. B.
King, Dr. H. G.
Locke, J.
Martin, Hugh
Moore, J. T.
Price, R. H.
Remington, _____ and mess.
Russell, A. C.
Shell, J. C.

Hempstead County

Blevins, Allen W.
Bruce, R. H.
Cribbs, Joseph
Roberts, J. G. (Green)
Macey, Hiram

Camden

Beam, _____
Dey, E.
Elliott, _____
Green, L. T.
Seawell, S. F.

Izard County Emigrants

Adams, Jacob
Adams, P. H.
Adams, E.
Easton, Dr. N.

Johnson County Pack Mule Company

Armstrong, Lynus
Harris, John
Whiteside, William B.

Marion County Emigrants

Jefferson, R. A.
Jefferson, Thomas D.
Jefferson, W. P.
Young, Jesse

Saline County
(Probably in Little Rock Company)

Donahoo, Calvin
Guess, ______
Harrison, Isaac
Hutchinson, ______
Magruder, Lloyd
McAllister, ______
McCarty, ______
McCarty (son)
Thornton, ______
Vandergrift, ______
Vandergrift (son)

Dr. Jeter L. Thompson's Cherokees
(Traveled Northern route)

Adair, John Lynch
Bell, Samuel
Blythe, Elijah
Buffington, William F.
Bushyhead, Dennis W.
Clark, Tom
Henry, James
Hicks, Charles
Hicks, Senora
Markham, ______
Martin, Brice
Old Joe, a Negro bullwacker
Parks, William
Purley, ______
Tully, Judge

Western Rovers
(Camped at Sulphur Springs, includes Arkansans)

Officers

John L. Bass, captain
E. C. Bolinger, second lieutenant
M. E. Cole, first lieutenant
Hilliam K. Newman, third lieutenant

Sergeants:
R. J. Featherstone
B. Lack
C. L. Martin
W. P. Ware

Corporals:
Henry Hart
Elam Morrison
L. H. Humphreys
William Skinner

Members

Allen, L. J.
Anderson, John S.
Bennet, G.
Biffle, William D.
Boardman, J. H.
Bowden, H. B.
Bullock A.
Burton, V. B.
Carson, D.
Chase, J.
Clapp, P.
Claudet, C.
Clough, James P.
Clough, Hike
Cochran, Sam T.
Cole, James
Crossman, O.
Crouch, James
Davis, Benjamin
Davis, William C.
Day, John G.
Downs, Henry
Eaton, J.
Edson, J. H.
Edward, J. A.
Ewing, John
Fant, S.
Fant, William B.
Figgin, W.
Freeman, John
Fulligun, P. W.
Goodson, Joseph
Gorman, Robert
Gore, A.
Gill, L. B.
Harvey, James
Harvey, Thomas C.
Hague, ______
Hays, David
Hill, L. H.
Hopkins, W. A
Hurst, S. W.
Hurst, Joseph
Jennings, R. F.
Jones, F.
Jones, J. F.
Joyce, William W.
Killingsworth, J.
Kyle, R. G.
Lanier, R.
Leahe, J. J.
Magaw, I.
Macall, W. P.
Maltbey, J. R.
McClain, W. H.
Millner, J. H.
Mitchell, J. J.
Mitchell, J. W.
Morgan, O.
Neeley, W. C.
Newman, Thomas
Paxton, J. R.
Phillips, B.
Quisenberry, J. H.
Rendale, J. R.
Riley, J.
Rowe, T. K.
Stanley, C. G.
Steel, Z. D.
Stentell, Samuel E.
Stephens, ______
Stewart, J. M.
Stith, F.
Wallace, T.
Whatley, H.
Whatley, W.
Wheeler, Thomas O.
Williams, William G.
Young, William W.
Young, William

Others

Fowler, W. W. (Brazos Island through Mexico to Mazatlan, ship to San Francisco)
Harwick, ______. Monroe County (Killed at Albuquerque)
Hudspeth, J. M.
Johnson, Burke. Polk County (Died enroute)
Latta, Robert H. Washington County (from Mexican War to California)
Ward, John H. Hot Springs (via water)

1850 Groups

Judge Brown's Company
(Rendezvous Fort Washita)

Judge R. S. C. Brown, leader
Company of 150 Cherokee emigrants (no names)

Holt Company (Fort Smith?)
(70 Men)

W. M. Holt, leader
Byron, Lafayette
Clark, Charles
Ross, R. B.
Stinkard, "Old Man"

Mayes' Company
(Joined McNair's on Verdigris River)

Samuel Mayes, leader

Members

Adair, George Washington
Bell, Deveareaux Jarrett
Bell, Juliette
Brown, John Lowrey
Busheyhead, Daniel
Busheyhead, Edward W.
Byers, Zeke
Fields, Richard
Goss, Gen
Goss, Will
Holt, Charley
Holt, William
Lasley, Sam
Mayes, George Washington
Mayes, John Thompson
Rattlingourd, Looney L.
Shelton, James
Simcoe, Bose
Terill, Lige
Trott, Ben

McNair's Company
Officers

C. V. (Clem) McNair, captain
Robert Harris, lieutenant
John Gott, sergeant of guard
Alfred Cunningham, wagonmaster
John H. Wolf, secretary

Members

Baker ?, W. G.
Bates, Manley
Bean, Talbot
Beck, John
Beck, "Ludge"
Black, ______
Blake, ______
Brewer boys
Buchanan, J. Riley
Buckner, ______
Canon, ______
Carter, ______
Clark, Eagle
Clark, John
Colston, Bill
Colston, James
Coodey, Joseph
Coodey, Sam
Coodey, Susan
Crain, J. T.
Crum, George
Dean, Old Man
Dennis,
Dick, Sam
Drew, Richard
Elders, William
Forrester, Wiley
Gonder J.
Harkins, ______
Harry,
Haygood, James
Hays, Henry
Hildebrand, Brice
Hildebrand, Jack
Holt, William L.
Jennings, George
Jennings, Willitt
Looney, Bill
Martin, Gabriel M.
May, J. J.
May, Peter
May, William

McCurdy, ______
McDaniel, Charles
McQuorter, ______
Meigs, Return Jonathan
Merrill, ______
Merrill, Margaret
Mitchell, James
Nave,
Nevins, Jefferson
Nevins, John
Old Palmer
Oliver, William
Patilla, ______
Park, Perry
Peck, J.
Pierce, Jim
Potts, E.
Prescott, Henry
Puser, John
Pyeatt, Jim
Quesenbury, William (Cush)
Reece, J. M.
Rick,
Riley, Samuel
Robinson, ______
Rogers, ______
Rose, ______
Ross, H.
Ross, John
Sanders, Ben
Scott, Margaret
Scott, Sanford
Sexton, G.
Shaw, John
Shipley, Houston
Shipley, Jess
Smith, Tom
Spears, Jo
Strickler, ______
Taylor, Thomas
Terrill, Bet
Timberlake, Arch
Wafer, D.
Williams, Hamp
Williams, Jo
Williams, William
Wilson, Arch
Woodward, Bill
Woodward, Tom
Yates, ______

Rector's Company
(Fort Smith, Fayetteville, and Cherokees)
Leaders

Major Elias Rector
Col. Matthew Leeper

Members
(90 men)

Burrell (Rector's slave)
Cox, "the wild Irishman"
Dean, Dr. C. W.
Evans, Mark L.
Gillett, Caleb
Hart (slave?)
Harvey (Rector's slave)
Ledford, ______
Lumpkin, W. H.
McKissick, Alexander
Neal (slave?)
Pollard, Dr. T. T.
Ridge, Eneas
Ridge, Rollin
  Wacooli
Rutherford, Archibald
Smith, Auchey
Spring, David V.
Sprague, Riley
Stout, Moses
Stricklin, Jacob
Taylor, John
Yell, Clinton
Yoes, Jim and mess

Cane Hill (Washington County)

Allen, Johnathan, captain
Barker, Bud
Barker, John
  Peter, slave
Burrow, Isham
Burrow, Jarrell
English, Matt
Fagon, ______
Funkhouser, Allen
Gray, William
Hagood, James
Hodges, Anson
Hodges, Howell
Latta, A.
Latta, Jack
Latta, Sam
Marson, Richard
McKay, Dave
McKay, Tom
McPhail, John
Nidever, Jack
  Peter, slave
Shannon, Frank
Spencer, Hiram
Spencer, Issac
Whinery, Josh

Chicot County

Col. Reynolds
Party with 15 wagons

Conway County

Byrd, H.
Harris, S. A.
Henry, T. T.
Peel, J. H.

Franklin County
William Martin, Captain
Members

Allstodt, John	Martin, Reuben	Smith, Miles P.
Hicks, Jackson	Perry, _____	Teague, Jos.
Hudson, Jeremiah	Smith, J. W.	Tillman, _____

James Fork Settlement (Crawford County)
(Pack Mule Company)

Hackett, Jeremiah	McDonald, Allen	Stephens, Barry

Jefferson County

Alexander, P.	Goacher, W. J.	Ward, G. W.
Anderson, John	Hudson, G.	White, D.
Brunet, James	Lineberger, Jacob	Woodsome, John
Brunson, Dr. A.	Norwood, J.	Woodward, W. W.
Brunson, Thomas	Rigney, H.	Colored:
Davis, W.	Smith, O. H.	Albert
Frederick, William	Stockton, Dr. N. H.	General
Gillespie, Dr.	Suggs, Greene	Pompey
Green, J. B.	Treadwell, J.	

Johnson County

Pack mule company (no names)
Wagon company (no names)

Lawrence County

"Group of about 45" (no names)

McLean's Bottom (Crawford County)

Cravens, Samuel	Severe, James	Thirteen others
Potts, Dr.	Sewell, James J.	

Scott County

Logan, Col. (his two sons among group)

Van Buren Party
(Pack Mule)

Cotteral, S.	Neal, Harvey	Winfrey, Richard

1850 via Isthmus

Boileau, Alex (Little Rock)
Johnson, J. H. (Johnson County)
May, William B. (Johnson County)
Patrick, G. W. (Johnson County)
Perry, Oliver (Johnson County)
Shall, Dr. F. (Little Rock)
"Seventeen gentlemen" (Ouachita and Clark Counties)

Others in 1850

Harger, Dr. (Fort Smith)
Maddox, James (Dardanelle)
McFarlane, J. L. (Crawford County)
McFarlane, N. (Crawford County)
Simmons, J. F. (Crawford County)
Tanner, Dr. (Pine Bluff)

1852
Hempstead Emigrating Company
Officers

Old Man Thompson, leader
Col. Burrough, leader
W. M. Holt, teammaster

Members

Burrough (brother)
Burrough (son)
Butler, Dr.
Butler, Mrs.
Hillman, Ura
Logan, Bill
Johnson, John G.
Parish, _____
Parish, _____
Polly (mulatto cook)
Twelve others unnamed

1853

English, Old Mrs.
Ferguson, William
Gardner family
Rieff, Martin
Rieff, Polly Alexander
Rieff, Matilda
Rieff, daughter
Rieff, son
Stout, M. C.
Stout family

1854

Johnston, John I.
Johnston, James
"Number of other emigrants"
1200 cattle

Company outfitted by Johnson and Grimes

Sparks Company
(Outfitted by Mitchell and Sparks of Fort Smith)
Officers

J. H. Sparks, in charge of train
O. F. Rogers, captain
R. Plunket, Wagonmaster

Members

Armoser, W. E.
Arzhandt, C.
Ball, L.
Bell, G.
Bell, H.
Birnie, C. A.
Blucker, _____
Chaplin, H.
Cook, _____
Costello, T.
Czliax, A.
Dutch, _____
Euper, A.
Heckel, W.
Henry, W.
Jones, Mont
Kanady, H.
Lane, L.
Long, Jim
Lowe, B. B.
Mitchell, P. D.
Neal, Dick
Niphong, T.
Norton, P.
Plunket, Bob
Plunket, Ike
Plunket, R.
Plunket, W.
Rector, Thomas Hines ("Judge")
Rhodes, I.
Ross, Adam
Sawyer, F. M.
Smith, Ab
Smith, I. or J. A.
Smith, M.
Smith, W.
Sprout, John Wooten (?)
Taylor, J. H.
Tedcum
Wallin (?)
Wheeler, John
Wheeler, Theodore
Wheeler, William
Williams, I. or J. P.
Williams, N.
Zork (?)

Chapter I

Footnotes

[1]Grant Foreman, *Marcy and the Gold Seekers* (Norman: Oklahoma, University Press, 1939), p. 9.

[2]*Fort Smith Herald*, September 5, 1848, p. 3, col. 3.

[3]*Fort Smith Herald*, October 11, 1849, p. 2, col. 4; *Arkansas State Democrat*, October 13, 1848, p. 1, col. 2; *Arkansas Intelligencer*, October 14, 1848.

[4]*Batesville Eagle*, October 19, 1848.

[5]The *Arkansas Gazette* bemoaned the president's long-windedness as "inexcusable and abominable" but nonetheless printed his address in its entirety—two and one-half complete pages in a four-page paper! *Arkansas Gazette*, December 21, 1848, p. 3, col. 3.

[6]Goodspeed, *Biographical and Historical Memoirs of Central Arkansas* (Chicago: Goodspeed, 1889), p. 384; Margaret Ross, *The Arkansas Gazette: The Early Years* (Little Rock, Arkansas Gazette, 1960), p. 180 ff.

[7]Kevin Starr, *Americans and the California Dream, 1850–1915* (New York: Oxford University Press, 1973), p. 51 uses this term.

[8]*Fort Smith Herald*. For non-footnoted information on the history of Fort Smith see Ruth B. Mapes, *Old Fort Smith* (Little Rock, 1965) and William J. Butler, *Fort Smith* (Little Rock: International Graphics, 1972).

[9]*Fort Smith Herald*, September 5, 1848, p. 3, col. 3.

[10]*Fort Smith Herald*, September 27, 1848; *Arkansas Intelligencer*, October 7, 1848, p. 2, col. 5.

[11]*Fort Smith Herald*, November 22, 1848, p. 2, col. 5.

[12]Ibid.

[13]*Fort Smith Herald*, November 29, 1848, p. 1, cols. 2 & 3.

[14]*Arkansas State Democrat*, January 5, 1849; *Arkansas State Gazette*, January 4, 1849, p. 2 col. 3; *Arkansas Intelligencer*, February 10, 1849; *Cherokee Advocate*, January 29, 1948, p. 3, cols. 3 and 4; *Southern Shield*, February 24, 1849, p. 3, col. 4.

[15]*Arkansas Banner*, March 20, 1849.

[16]*Arkansas Gazette*, December 8, 1848.

[17]*Arkansas Gazette*, January 4, 1849, p. 2, col. 2.

[18]*Arkansas Gazette*, January 18, 1849, p. 2, col. 6.

[19]Ibid.

[20]*Fort Smith Herald*, January 17, 1849, p. 2, col. 2.

[21]There are questionable aspects regarding the King journal. In 1941 Steve H. Logan, son of David Logan, a seventeen-year-old member of the Clarksville company, published the King journal along with photographs and drawings in twenty-four serial installments in the Sunday magazine section of the *Arkansas Gazette* beginning January 19. Logan said the original journal was in his possession. Logan clearly indicated the journal was kept by King "and others." The complete original journal has not surfaced, but the second portion of the original is at the University of Arkansas, Fayetteville. The second portion logged the Clarksville gold seekers' trek from Socorro, New Mexico, to California and included the time July 6 to December 22, 1948.

Captain Randolph B. Marcy was in charge of the military escort for the large number of companies (one of which was the Clarksville company) leaving Fort Smith in 1849. Marcy kept a journal and made his report in the form of a journal. His topographical engineer, Lieutenant J. H. Simpson, also filed reports and maps. Grant Foreman in 1939 published *Marcy and the Gold Seekers* which included Marcy's journalistic report of the trip from Fort Smith to Santa Fe where he left the emigrants and then six weeks later began a return trip to Fort Smith.

The problem arises when comparing the first half of the 1941 Logan-*Gazette* version of the King journal with Marcy's report in Foreman's book. Vast portions of the material cited as part of the King journal are verbatim in the Marcy report. The closing entry in the first half of the Logan-*Gazette* version indicates that there are several handwritings in the journal and that Marcy, King, Simpson and two Indian guides, Black Beaver and Rover, all exchanged notes, reports, maps, stories, etc. for their journals. Without the original first half of the journal to verify multiple handwritings, the question must be raised whether Logan edited and embellished the King journal by using the Marcy-Simpson reports and Josiah Gregg's *Commerce of the Prairies* or whether King himself, as the entry indicates, freely made use of all the reports and journals being kept by those about him and from which he was permitted to copy or "swap" information. As the second half of the original reveals, King was not without writing ability and descriptive skills, but he was certainly not as flowery as Lt. Simpson who even outdid Marcy in eloquence.

A further intriguing discrepancy bears mentioning. Marcy engaged Black Beaver, an Indian scout and interpreter, while at Edwards Trading Post. The Logan-*Gazette* version says Captain Redmond Rogers hired Rover as an interpreter. Marcy does not mention Rover, but the King journal frequently mentions both Rover and Beaver. King's final entry in the first half of the journal acknowledged that Rover had kept most of the journal to that point. Beaver remained with Captain Marcy at Santa Fe and Rover, after about a week, returned to Santa Fe and took with him, according to the final entry, King's journal of the trip to that point. King deemed the journal safer in Marcy's keeping. Were there two well-educated Indians attached to the same company? Did Rover pen many of the wonderful stories recounted by King but not by Marcy? These stories deserve to be in print, but until the first half of the journal surfaces, their authorship and date remains uncertain. The reader should bear this in mind.

When using material from the first part of the journal, I cite both Marcy as reported by Foreman and the Logan-*Gazette* version. When using material from the second half of the journal, I reference the original. If the second half of the *Gazette* version is used, it is substantiated by other letters or diaries.

[22]*Arkansas Intelligencer*, January 27, 1849, p. 2, col. 3.

[23]*Arkansas Intelligencer*, February 10, 1849, p. 2, col. 3.

[24]*Arkansas Intelligencer*, February 10, 1849; March 17, 1849.

[25]Copied from the *Arkansas Intelligencer* by the *Fort Smith Herald*, February 21, 1849, p. , col. .

[26]*Cherokee Advocate*, February 12, 1849, p. 3, col. 3.

[27]Owen C. Coy, *The Great Trek*, (Los Angeles: The Powell Publishing Co., 1929), p. 229. Buford had made his trip from Fort Gibson to Santa Fe in July 1848 and reported the distance as 650 miles. His route was published in the *Fort Smith Herald* November 8, 1848.

[28]*Cherokee Advocate*, February 12, 1849, p. 3, col. 3.

[29]Ibid

[30]Ibid

[31]*Arkansas Intelligencer*, April 7, 1849, p. , col.

[32]*Cherokee Advocate*, May 7, 1849.

[33]*Fort Smith Herald*, March 21, 1849, p. 2, col. 10.

[34]*Fort Smith Herald*, April 4, 1849, p. 2, col. 2.

[35]Mary Medearis, ed., *Sam Williams: Printer's Devil* (Hope, Arkansas: Etter Publishing Co., 1979).

[36]*Batesville Eagle*, January 30, 1849, p. 2, col. 2.

[37]*Batesville Eagle*, November 30, 1849, p. 1, col. 4.

[38]*Batesville Eagle*, January 30, 1849, p. 2, col. 3.

[39]Ibid., February 13, 1849, p. 2, col. 4.

[40]Ibid., May 24, 1849, p. 2, col. 3.

[41]*Arkansas Intelligencer*, May 12, 1849, p. 2, col. 1.

[42]Foreman, *Marcy and the Gold Seekers*, p. 21.

[43]*Fort Smith Herald*, March 14, 1849, p. 2, col. 1; also *Arkansas Gazette*, November 15, 1849, p. 3, col. 3.

[44]*Arkansas State Democrat*, January 26, 1849 and *Fort Smith Herald*, January 31, 1849.

[45]*Arkansas Intelligencer*, April 28, 1849.

[46]*Arkansas Intelligencer*, March 17, 1849, p. 3, col. 3.

[47]Letter from Lovely Rogers, *Cherokee Advocate*, January 7, 1850.

[48]*Arkansas Gazette*, March 1, 1850, p. 2, col. 5.

[49]*Arkansas Gazette*, May 17, 1849, p. 2, col. 3.

[50]Ibid.

[51]*Arkansas Gazette*, October 4, 1849, p. 2, col. 3.

[52]Howard C. Gardiner, *In Pursuit of the Golden Dream* (Massachusetts: Western Hemisphere, Inc., 1970), p. 299.

[53]*Arkansas Gazette*, April 19, 1850, p. 2, col. 6.

[54]Pat Etter's *Bibliography of the Southern Route* has information on Gregg, p. 31.

[55]*Fort Smith Herald*, December 28, 1848; p. 3, col. 3.

[56]*Fort Smith Herald*, November 1, 1848; *Arkansas State Democrat*, November 17, 1848.

[57]The Cooke report was published in 1848. See Pat Etter's *Bibliography of the Southern Route*, p. 16.

[58]Emory's report was published in 1848 and is annotated in Etter's *Bibliography*, p. 28. Foreman discussed Cooke & Emory, pp. 293–94.

[59]*Fort Smith Herald*, July 26, November 8, 1848; *Arkansas State Democrat*, August 4, November 10, 1848.

[60]Joseph W. Ware, *The Emigrants Guide to California*. Actually Ware had never been to California and said so. He hastily compiled and published his guidebook to take advantage of market. A fairly good map was included. See George R. Stewart, *The California Trail*, New York: McGraw Hill 1962, p. 222.

[61]*Fort Smith Herald*, January 17, 1849; January 24, 1849.

[62]*Arkansas State Democrat*, October 27, 1848.

[63]Francile Oakley, "Arkansas' Golden Army," MA Thesis published in *Arkansas Historical Quarterly*, Vol. VI, No. 1, 1947, discusses Borland's activities and cites *Senate Journal* and *House Journal* references pp. 10–17.

[64]Ibid; *Arkansas State Democrat*, February 16, 1849.

[65]*Arkansas State Democrat*, February 9, 1849; *Arkansas Intelligencer*, February 17, 1849; *Fort Smith Herald*, February 14, 1849.

[66]*Senate Executive Comments*, 31 Congress, 1 session, no. 12, p. 2; ibid, no. 64, pp. 169–170; *Arkansas State Democrat*, February 23, 1849; *Fort Smith Herald, February 14, 1849.*

[67]*Fort Smith Herald*, February 28, 1849, p. 2, col. 5.

[68]Foreman, *Marcy and the Gold Seekers*, pp. 124–25 reports this from the War Department, Adjutant General's Office, Old Files Division. All of these signers did not go to California. The signers included merchants, newspaper men, hotel keepers, steamboat captains, lawyers, farmers, and artisans.

[69]*Arkansas State Democrat*, April 6, 1849.

[70]Ibid., April 20, 1948.

[71]*Arkansas State Democrat*, July 21, 1848; January 5, February 9, 16, March 2, April 6, 13, 1849; *Arkansas Intelligencer*, February 17, 24, March 3, 1849; (Washington) *National Intelligencer*, January 26, 30, 1849; *New Orleans Daily Picayune*, February 14, 1849.

[72]Ibid.

[73]*Arkansas Banner*, February 21, 1849, p. 2, col. 7.

[74]*Arkansas State Democrat*, April 27, 1849.

[75]*Arkansas State Democrat*, May 25, 1849, p. 2, col. 3.

Chapter II

Footnotes

[1]*Fort Smith Herald,* November 29, 1848, p. 2, col. 2.

[2]Copies from *Arkansas State Democrat* in *Fort Smith Herald,* January 3, 1849, p. 1, col. 4.

[3]*Fort Smith Herald,* January 24, 1849, p. 4, cols. 3 and 4.

[4]*Arkansas Intelligencer,* February 10, 1849, p. 4.

[5]*Fort Smith Herald,* September 13, 1848.

[6]*Fort Smith Herald,* April 4, 1849, p. 2, col. 3.

[7]*The Arkansas Democrat,* March 16, 1849, p. 2, col. 4.

[8]*Fort Smith Herald,* February 7, 1849, p. 2, col. 1.

[9]Ibid.

[10]*Fort Smith Herald,* February 14, 1849, p. 2, col. 1.

[11]*Arkansas Democrat,* February 16, 1849.

[12]*Fort Smith Herald,* February 28, 1849, p. 2, col. 6.

[13]*Arkansas State Democrat,* March 16, 1849, p. 2, col. 4.

[14]Ruth Mapes, *Old Fort Smith* (Little Rock: Pioneer Press, 1965), pp. 23–24 quotes this Louisiana emigrant's letter in *Fort Smith Herald,* March 28, 1849.

[15]Written March 16, 1849 and in *Arkansas Banner,* April 3, 1849.

[16]*Arkansas Intelligencer,* March 17, 1849, p. 3, col. 4.

[17]*Washington Telegraph,* January 31, 1849, p. 3, col. 4, February 7, 1849, p. 3, col. 6.

[18]*Fort Smith Herald,* March 7, 1849, p. 3, col. 4.

[19]*Arkansas Intelligencer,* April 7, 1849, p. 2, col. 1.

[20]Quicksilver or mercury was commonly used in washing to hold the free gold particles.

[21]*Arkansas Intelligencer,* April 7, 1849, p. 2, col. 1.

[22]*Arkansas State Democrat,* March 16, 1849, p. 3, col. 3.

[23]Ibid., March 23, 1849, p. 2, col. 3.

[24]*Arkansas State Democrat,* April 6, 1849, p. 2, col. 1.

[25]*Arkansas Gazette,* March 8, 1849, p. 2, col. 1.

[26]*Fort Smith Herald,* March 14, 1849, p. 2, col. 2.

[27]Ibid.

[28]*Fort Smith Herald,* February 28, 1849, p. 3, col. 5; March 5, p. 3, col. 5.

[29]*Fort Smith Herald,* March 28, 1849, p. 3, col. 3.

[30]Foreman, *Marcy and the Gold Seekers,* p. 129 quotes "Random Collections," Fort Smith *Elevator,* September 12, 1902.

[31]Written in Fort Smith March 16, and printed in *Arkansas Banner,* April 3, 1849.

[32]*Arkansas State Democrat,* March 16, 1849, p. 3, col. 3.

[33]*Fort Smith Herald,* March 14, 1849, p. 2, col. 3.

[34]*Fort Smith Herald,* March 28, 1849, p. 2, col. 1.

[35]Ibid.

[36]Ibid., April 4, 1848, p. 2, col. 1.

[37]*Fort Smith Herald,* March 28, 1849, p. 2, col. 1.

[38]Foreman, *Marcy and the Gold Seekers,* p. 17.

[39]Frank Weaver, "Hub from which the Western Gold Seekers Went into the Wilderness," *Fort Smith Historical Journal,* Vol. 11, No. 2, September 1978, pp. 58–59.

[40]*Arkansas Intelligencer,* January 27, 1849, p. 2, col. 3.

[41]*Fort Smith Herald,* April 11, 1849, p. 2, col. 1.

[42]*Arkansas Gazette,* February 1, 1849, p. 3, col. 5; repeated February 8, p. 3, col. 1;

February 15, p. 3, col. 1; February 22, p. 4, col. 1, March 1, p. 4, col. 1. *Fort Smith Herald*, February 21, 1849, p. 4, col. 1.

[43]Foreman in *Marcy and the Gold Seekers* suggests that California was a little-known country and the government was planning to send troops west and construct and occupy posts. This gave a military air to the venture and prompted a surge of patriotism among American men who sought to serve their country and get free transportation to California. This author found no reference to such motivation in the Arkansas records.

[44]The Articles of Association for the Little Rock, Van Buren, Fort Smith, and Clarksville companies may be found in Appendix B.

[45]Ibid.

[46]Ibid.

[47]Fort Smith circular in *Arkansas Gazette*, January 4, 1849, p. 2, col. 3.

[48]Ibid.

[49]Hastings, *Emigrants Guide*, p. 142.

[50]*Arkansas Gazette*, March 15, 1849, p. 2, col. 1; *Arkansas Democrat*, March 23, 1849, p. 2, col. 3; March 30, 1849, p. 2, col. 3.

[51]Ibid. March 30, 1849, p. 2, col. 3.

[52]William F. Pope, *Early Days in Arkansas*, (Little Rock: Fred Allsopp, 1895), p. 290.

[53]*Arkansas Intelligencer*, April 14, 1849, p. 2, col. 2.

[54]Ralph Bieber, *Southern Trails to California in 1849* (Glendale, California: Arthur Clark Co., 1937), p. 43 based his estimate on a summary of the source material available to him.

[55]Ibid.

[56]*Arkansas Democrat*, March 16, 1849, p. 2, col. 4.

[57]*Arkansas State Democrat*, April 27, 1849, p. 2, col. 4.

[58]Copies from *Baltimore Sun*, May 22, 1849 in *Fort Smith Herald*, June 27, 1849, p. 2, col. 4.

[59]*Arkansas State Democrat*, April 27, 1849, p. 2, col. 4.

[60]*Fort Smith Herald*, September 26, 1849, p. 2, col. 2.

[61]*Arkansas Gazette*, February 22, 1849, p. 2, col. 3.

Chapter III
Footnotes

[1]David Morris Potter, ed. *Trail to California: The Overland Journal of Vincent Geiger and Wakeman Bryarly* (New Haven: Yale University Press, 1945), p. 187. The introductory quote is found in Geiger's diary.
[2]*Fort Smith Herald*, March 13, 1849, p. 2, col. 1.
[3]*Arkansas State Democrat*, April 6, 1849 has Dent's preliminary report.
[4]*Fort Smith Herald*, March 14, 1849, p. 2, col. 2; March 21, 1849, p. 2, col. 6.
[5]*Fort Smith Herald*, March 28, 1849, p. 2, col. 1.
[6]Marcy was an important pathfinder for Oklahoma, New Mexico and Texas. In addition to his numerous reports, he wrote two books about his experiences. *Fort Smith Herald*, April 11, 1849; Foreman, *Marcy and the Gold Seekers*, pp. 145–147.
[7]King journal, April 11, 1849 in *Arkansas Gazette*.
[8]Foreman, *Marcy and the Gold Seekers*, pp. 54, 142–143.
[9]*Arkansas State Democrat*, April 27, 1849, p. 2, col. 4.
[10]Ibid.
[11]Ibid.
[12]Ibid.
[13]Bieber, *Southern Trails*, pp. 44–45 describes these two alternatives.
[14]*Arkansas State Democrat*, March 16, 1849, p. 2, col. 4.
[15]*Arkansas Intelligencer*, May 7, 1849, p. 2, col. 2. Council Grove was one hundred and fifty miles west of Independence and the final rendezvous and organization point before striking out across the prairies with great trepidation about the Indians. See Josiah Gregg, *Commerce of the Prairies*, p. 10.
[16]Foreman, *Marcy and the Gold Seekers*, pp. 212–213.
[17]Foreman, *Marcy and the Gold Seekers*, p. 191.
[18]*Fort Smith Herald*, April 11, 1849, p. 2, col. 2.
[19]*Southern Shield* (Helena, Arkansas) June 2, 1849, p. 2, col. 2.
[20]*Arkansas State Democrat*, June 1, 1849, p. 2, col. 4.
[21]Ibid.
[22]Ibid.
[23]Ibid.
[24]*Fort Smith Herald*, June 6, 1849, p. 3, col. 4.
[25]Ibid.
[26]Ibid.
[27]Ibid.
[28]Ibid., col. 5.
[29]*Fort Smith Herald*, June 13, 1849, p. 3, cols. 3 and 4.
[30]King journal, May 9, 1849, in *Arkansas Gazette*; Foreman, *Marcy and the Gold Seekers*, pp. 234–35 quotes Lt. Simpson's report with exact wording but dated June 15.
[31]King journal, May 17, 1849, in *Arkansas Gazette*.
[32]*Arkansas Gazette*, March 1, 1849; Foreman, *Marcy and the Gold Seekers*, p. 170.
[33]King journal, June 10, 1849, in *Arkansas Gazette*. This is not in Marcy's report.
[34]Ware, *Emigrant's Guide*, p. 10.
[35]Foreman, *Marcy and the Gold Seekers*, p. 58.
[36]*Fort Smith Herald*, March 21, 1849, p. 2, cols. 6 and 7.
[37]King journal, April 19, 1849; in *Arkansas Gazette*.
[38]King journal, June 13, 1849, in *Arkansas Gazette*; Marcy's journal, June 15, in Foreman, p. 233.
[39]Ibid, March 22, in *Arkansas Gazette*; Simpson's report p. 216 in Foreman.
[40]King journal, May 25, 1849.

[41]Gregg, *Commerce of the Prairies*, p. 383.

[42]King, June 11, 1849; Gregg, *Commerce of the Prairies*, p. 381, King journal, June 12, 1849, in *Arkansas Gazette; Marcy* in Foreman, p. 230; Gregg, *Commerce of the Prairies*, p. 381.

[43]King journal, May 24, 1849, in *Arkansas Gazette*, not in Marcy.

[44]King journal, April 13, May 24, 1849.

[45]Ibid., July 5, 1849.

[46]*Arkansas State Democrat*, September 7, 1849. This was reprinted from the *Arkansas Intelligencer*.

[47]King journal, April 25, May 5, 1849, in *Arkansas Gazette*. Marcy's journal does not include these emigrant adventure stories.

[48]King journal, April 18, in *Arkansas Gazette*. Marcy did not begin his journal until May 1.

[49]King journal, June 7, 1849, in *Arkansas Gazette;* Marcy's journal, June 8, in Foreman, p. 225.

[50]*Arkansas State Democrat*, June 1, 1849, p. 2, col. 4.

[51]Ibid.

[52]*Fort Smith Herald*, June 6, 1849, p. 3, col. 4.

[53]William F. Pope, *Early Days in Arkansas*, p. 290.

[54]*Arkansas State Democrat*, September 7, 1849, letter reprinted from *Arkansas Intelligencer*.

[55]King journal, May 24, 25, 1849, in *Arkansas Gazette*. This specific emigrant experience is not in Marcy.

[56]King journal, June 5, 6, 7, 1849, in *Arkansas Gazette*.

[57]King journal, in *Arkansas Gazette*. Her picture is in Article 13.

[58]King journal, listing of emigrants before journal record began.

[59]*Arkansas Gazette*, March 15, 1850, p. 2, col. 4.

[60]Grant Foreman, *Marcy and the Gold Seekers*, researched this information (pp. 143–144) and the tragic romance of young Mary is scattered throughout his book. J. H. Atkinson in the *Arkansas State Democrat Magazine Section*, September 22, 1963, pulled Foreman's information together in an article entitled, "Romance and Tragedy Highlighted the Trip to California during the Gold Rush Days."

[61]King journal, May 9, 1849, in *Arkansas Gazette;* Simpson's report, June 15, in Foreman, p. 235.

[62]King journal, May 22, in *Arkansas Gazette;* Simpsons's report, May 23 in Foreman, p. 215. Rock Mary is in western Oklahoma and still bears that name.

[63]King journal, June 25, 1849, in *Arkansas Gazette*.

[64]Ibid., June 27.

[65]Foreman, *Marcy and the Gold Seekers*, pp. 366, 368, 393; *Cherokee Advocate*, December 3, 1849, p. 2, col. 1.

[66]Ibid., p. 306.

[67]*Arkansas Banner*, August 6, 1850, p. 2, col. 7.

[68]Foreman, p. 338.

[69]King journal, April 30, in *Arkansas Gazette*.

[70]Ibid., May 5.

[71]The possum bellies according the King were a large dry hide stretched under the wagons. May 30.

[72]Ibid., June 20.

[73]Foreman, *Marcy and the Gold Seekers*, p. 248.

Chapter IV

Footnotes

[1]Lt. Col. Philip St. George Cooke had opened this first wagon road to California during the Mexican War in 1846. It left the Rio Grande at Dona Ana, went through Guadalupe Pass, then on the Tucson, the Pima Villages and the Gila. General Stephen Watts Kearny and Lt. Col. W. H. Emory left the Rio Grande north of Cooke's road and then continued west along Gila to Pima Village where it joined Cooke's. The Kearny-Emory Trail was for pack mules.

[2]*Fort Smith Herald,* October 3, 1849, p. 2., col. 2.

[3]*Arkansas Gazette,* October 4, 1849, p. 2, col. 3.

[4]*Arkansas State Democrat,* August 31, 1849, p. 2, col. 4.

[5]*Fort Smith Herald,* October 3, 1849, p. 2, col. 3.

[6]*Arkansas State Democrat,* September 28, 1849, p. 2, col. 3.

[7]*Fort Smith Herald,* March 28, 1849.

[8]*Arkansas State Democrat,* August 31, 1849, p. 2, col. 4.

[9]Ibid., October 5, 1849, p. 2, col. 4.

[10]Ibid.

[11]King journal, June 23, 1849, in *Arkansas Gazette;* Marcy's report p. 245 in Foreman.

[12]*Arkansas State Democrat,* August 17, 1849, p. 2, col. 3.

[13]*Arkansas State Democrat,* September 7, 1849, reprinted from *Arkansas Intelligencer.*

[14]*Arkansas Intelligencer,* April 14, 1849, p. 2, col. 2.

[15]*Arkansas State Democrat,* September 25, 1849, p. 2, col. 3; October 5, 1849, p. 2, col. 4; *Arkansas Intelligencer,* September 29, 1849.

[16]*Fort Smith Herald,* October 3, 1849, p. 2, col. 2.

[17]A majority of the Fort Smith company had prevailed over Captain Dillard and taken the north side of the Canadian. When it was found to be mud and hard going, the company recrossed the Canadian and stayed with the escort. *Fort Smith Herald,* June 6, 1849, p. 3, col. 4.

[18]*Fort Smith Herald,* October 3, 1849, p. 2, col. 2.

[19]*Arkansas Banner,* September 25, 1849, p. 2, col. 5.

[20]Ibid., October 2, 1849, p. 2, col. 3.

[21]Ibid., May 14, 1850, p. 3, col. 4.

[22]*Arkansas Banner,* August 14, 1849, p. 2, col. 5.

[23]*Arkansas Gazette,* October 4, 1849, p. 2, col. 3.

[24]*Arkansas State Democrat,* August 17, 1849, p. 2, col. 3.

[25]Ibid.

[26]Ibid., August 31, 1849, p. 2, col. 4.

[27]Foreman, *Marcy and the Gold Seekers,* p. 270.

[28]*Arkansas State Democrat,* October 26, 1849, p. 2, col. 3.

[29]Ibid., October 5, 1849, p. 2, col. 4.

[30]Ibid., September 28, 1849, p. 2, col. 3.

[31]Ibid

[32]*Arkansas Gazette,* September 6, 1849, p. 2, col. 3.

[33]*Fort Smith Herald,* October 3, 1849, p. 2, col. 2.

[34]King journal original, July 10–July 17.

[35]Ibid., July 23.

[36]Daniel M. Potter, ed., *Trail to California: Overland Journal of Vincent Geiger and Wakeman Bryarly,* p. 49.

[37]*Southern Shield,* July 21, 1849.

[38]Ibid., December 22, 1849, p. 2, col. 2.

[39]*Arkansas State Democrat*, September 7, 1849, p. 3, col. 4.
[40]Foreman, *Marcy and the Gold Seekers*, pp. 292; 339–341.
[41]King journal original, July 19.
[42]Owen Coy, *The Great Trek*, p. 240. Coy says Ricks wrote the diary, but Pat Etter, *The Southern Route—1849 Journals*, p. 44, notes there is no evidence to sustain the claim. The typescript of the original manuscript is in the Bancroft Library.
[43]*Arkansas State Gazette and Democrat*, April 26, 1850, p. 3, cols. 2 and 3.
[44]King journal original, July 21.
[45]Ibid.
[46]Near where Arizona, New Mexico and Sonora converge and where the emigrants crossed the Continental Divide.
[47]*Arkansas Gazette*, July 11, 1851, p. 2, col. 5.
[48]King journal, original, August 3 and 4, 1849.
[49]Ibid., August 16.
[50]*Arkansas Gazette*, November 22, 1849, p. 3, col. 2.
[51]*Arkansas Gazette*, October 4, 1849, p. 2, col. 3.
[52]King journal original, August 25, 1849.
[53]Ibid., August 31.
[54]*Arkansas Gazette*, November 22, 1849, p. 3, col. 2.
[55]King journal original, September 2, 1849.
[56]Ibid.
[57]Ralph Beiber, *Southern Trails to California*, p. 218, copied from *Weekly Reveille*, October 8, 1849.
[58]*Arkansas Gazette*, April 26, 1850, p. 3, col. 3.
[59]King journal original, September 14.
[60]Ibid., September 25.
[61]*Arkansas Gazette*, November 22, 1849, p. 3, col. 2.
[62]King journal original, September 26.
[63]King journal original, September 5, 1849.
[64]Ibid., September 6, 1849.
[65]Ibid.
[66]Diary of John F. May, Fort Smith Library. This is not an extensive diary.
[67]Cornelius Cox, "From Texas to California in 1849," *Southwestern Historical Quarterly*, Vol. XXIX, pp. 201–202; Lorenzo Aldrich, *A Journal of the Overland Route to California and the Gold Mines*, p. 56.
[68]*Arkansas Gazette*, November 22, 1849, p. 3, col. 2.
[69]Ibid.
[70]*Arkansas Gazette*, April 26, 1850, p. 3, col. 2.
[71]King journal original, September 28–October 1.
[72]Foreman, *Marcy and the Gold Seekers*, p. 303.
[73]Brownlee's letter in the *Arkansas Gazette*, November 22, 1849, p. 3, col. 2; Simmon's letter, Ibid., December 20, 1849, p. 2, col. 2.
[74]Foreman, *Marcy and the Gold Seekers*, pp. 302–306.
[75]Bieber, p. 228.
[76]*Arkansas Gazette*, December 20, 1849, p. 2, col. 2.
[77]Ibid., April 26, 1850, p. 2, col. 3.
[78]King journal original, October 3 to October 7; Owen Coy, *The Great Trek*, p. 257 also records names of camp.
[79]*Arkansas Gazette*, November 22, 1849, p. 3, col. 2.
[80]Ibid.
[81]Ibid., April 26, 1850, p. 3, col. 3.
[82]Ibid., December 14, 1849, p. 2, col. 3.
[83]Ibid., February 22, 1850, p. 2, col. 5.
[84]King journal original, October 18–November 10, 1849.
[85]King journal original, November 25–December 22.

Chapter V

Footnotes

[1]*Cherokee Advocate,* April 16, 1849.
[2]*Cherokee Advocate,* April 16, April 30, May 7, 1849; *Arkansas Gazette,* July 26, 1849, p. 2, col. 5; Foreman, *Marcy and the Gold Seekers,* pp. 67–68.
[3]Foreman, *Marcy and the Gold Seekers,* p. 68; *Arkansas State Democrat,* February 16, 1849, p. 3, col. 7.
[4]*Cherokee Advocate,* May 7, 1849, p. 2, col. 1.
[5]Foreman, *Marcy and the Gold Seekers,* p. 72.
[6]*St. Louis Republican,* July 4, 1849, p. 2, cols. 2 and 4; copied in *Arkansas Gazette,* July 26, 1849, p. 2, col. 5; and the *Cherokee Advocate,* July 30, 1849.
[7]*Cherokee Advocate,* July 30, 1849, p. 3, col. 2.
[8]Ibid.
[9]Ibid.
[10]Ibid.
[11]Ibid. Foreman, *Marcy and the Gold Seekers,* p. 69, p. 75, notes that Hicks was an important Cherokee and that his home was a well-known stopping place for the emigrants. *Cherokee Advocate,* June 25, 1849, p. 2, col. 1 recounts the sighting of the oxen.
[12]Ibid., August 6, 1849, p. 2, col. 2.
[13]Foreman, *Marcy and the Gold Seekers,* p. 76.
[14]*Cherokee Advocate,* November 12, 1849, p. 2, col. 2; *Arkansas Intelligencer,* December 8, 1849, p. 2, col. 5.
[15]Ibid., November 21, 1849, p. 2, col. 1.
[16]Ibid.
[17]*Arkansas Gazette,* September 20, 1849, p. 2, col. 2; another example November 15, 1849, p. 3, col. 5.
[18]*Arkansas Gazette,* September 20, 1849, p. 2, col. 2.
[19]*Cherokee Advocate,* November 12, 1849, p. 2, col. 1.
[20]Ibid., November 12, 1849, p. 2, col. 2; Foreman, *Marcy and the Gold Seekers,* pp. 76–78 elaborates on this celebration.
[21]Ibid., November 21, p. 2, col. 1.
[22]Ibid.
[23]George R. Stewart, *The California Trail* (New York: McGraw Hill, 1962), pp. 274–178.
[24]Foreman, *Marcy and the Gold Seekers,* p. 81.
[25]*Cherokee Advocate,* July 16, 1850, p. 2, col. 2.
[26]Foreman, *Marcy and the Gold Seekers,* p. 81.
[27]*Cherokee Advocate,* March 11, 1850, p. 2, col. 1.
[28]Georgia Willis Read, ed., *Gold Rush Journal, Drawings and Papers of J. Goldsborough Bruff* (New York: Columbia University Press, 1944), p. 569.
[29]*Cherokee Advocate,* January 7, 1850, p. 1, col. 1.
[30]Ibid.
[31]*Cherokee Advocate,* November 21, 1849, p. 2, col. 1.
[32]Letter from Thompson to *Cherokee Advocate,* February 9, 1850.
[33]Stewart, *The California Trail,* p. 230–32; 292.
[34]*Fort Smith Herald,* February 23, 1850, p. 2, col. 1.
[35]*Arkansas Gazette,* March 1, 1850, p. 2, col. 5.

Chapter VI

Footnotes

[1]*Arkansas Gazette,* November 15, 1849, p. 3, col. 3.
[2]Ibid., October 4, 1849, p. 2, col. 3.
[3]Ibid., September 6, 1849, p. 2, col. 3.
[4]Ibid., March 15, 1850, p. 2, col. 4.
[5]Ibid., March 29, 1850, p. 2, col. 7.
[6]Ibid., February 22, 1850, p. 2, col. 5.
[7]Ibid., March 22, 1850, p. 2, col. 4.
[8]Ibid., March 29, 1850, p. 2, col. 3.
[9]Ibid., p. 2, col. 3.
[10]Ibid., March 22, 1850, p. 2, col. 4.
[11]*Cherokee Advocate,* January 7, 1850, p. 2, col. 1; see p. 172 for letter.
[12]*Arkansas Gazette,* April 19, 1850, p. 2, col. 6.
[13]*Fort Smith Herald,* May 25, 1850, p. 2, col. 3.
[14]*Arkansas Gazette,* August 2, 1850, p. 3, col. 6.
[15]*Fort Smith Herald,* September 14, 1850, p. 2, col. 4.
[16]*Arkansas Gazette,* February 22, 1850, p. 2, col. 5.
[17]Ibid., March 22, 1850, p. 2, col. 4.
[18]Ibid., April 19, 1850, p. 2, col. 6.
[19]Ibid.
[20]Ibid., November 15, 1849, p. 3, col. 3.
[21]*Fort Smith Herald,* August 24, 1850, p. 3, col. 3.
[22]*Arkansas Gazette,* March 15, 1850, p. 2, col. 4, Ibid., March 22, 1850, p. 2, col. 4; Ibid, September 6, 1850, p. 2, col. 4; Fort Smith
[23]*Arkansas Gazette,* September 6, 1850, p. 2, col. 4.
[24]George W. B. Evans, *Mexican Gold Trail* (San Marino: Huntington Library, 1945), pp. 60–61.
[25]Ibid., p. 228.
[26]*Arkansas Gazette,* November 15, 1849, p. 3, col. 3.
[27]Ibid., April 19, 1850, p. 2, col. 6.
[28]Ibid., October 25, 1850, p. 2, col. 5.
[29]William W. Johnson, *The Forty-niners,* Time-Life Books, p. 176.
[30]Benjamin B. Richards, ed., *California Gold Rush Merchant: The Journal of Stephen Chapin Davis* (San Marino: Huntington Library, 1956), pp. 19–20.
[31]*Arkansas Gazette,* February 17, 1850, p. 2, col. 5.
[32]Ibid., March 22, 1850, p. 2, col. 4.
[33]Ibid., October 4, 1849, p. 2, col. 3.
[34]Johnson, *The Forty-niners,* p. 160.
[35]John H. Ward, letter to Dr. Lorenzo Gibson provided by George Toney of Little Rock.
[26]*Arkansas Gazette,* September 13, 1850, p. 3, col. 6.
[37]Ralph Beiber, *Southern Trails to California,* p. 254.
[38]*Arkansas Gazette,* October 25, 1850, p. 2, col. 5.
[39]John H. Ward, letter to Dr. Lorenzo Gibson provided by George Toney of Little Rock.
[40]*Arkansas Gazette,* September 13, 1850, p. 3, col. 6.
[41]Johnson, *The Forty-niners,* p. 131.
[42]Georgia W. Read, "Women and Children on the Oregon-California Trail in the Gold Rush Years," *Missouri Historical Review,* XXXIX, (1944), p. 6.
[43]Johnson, *The Forty-niners,* p. 131.
[44]Two sources especially helpful on California place names are Erwin G. Gudde,

California Gold Camps (Berkeley: University of California Press, 1975); Hoover and Rensch, *Historic Spots in California* (Stanford: Stanford University Press, 1933).

[45]Hoover and Rensch, *Historic Spots in California*, p. 168.

[46]George P. Hammond and Edward P. Howes, eds., *Robert Eccleston: Overland to California on the Southwestern Trail of 1849* (Los Angeles: University of California Press, 1950), p. 80.

[47]*Arkansas Gazette*, February 17, 1850, p. 2, col. 5.

[48]Howard C. Gardiner, *In Pursuit of the Golden Dream*, p. 82.

[49]David Potter, ed., *Trail to California: Overland Journal of Vincent Geiger and Wakeman Bryarly*, New Haven, 1945, p. 210.

[50]*Arkansas Gazette*, February 22, 1850, p. 2, col. 5.

[51]*Arkansas Gazette*, October 25, 1850, p. 2, col. 5.

[52]Ibid., April 19, 1850, p. 2, col. 6.

[53]Ibid., May 17, 1850, p. 2, col. 5.

[54]Ibid., October 11, 1850, p. 2. col. 4.

[55]Ibid., October 25, 1850, p. 2, col. 5.

[56]Ibid., November 22, 1850, p. 2, col. 4.

[57]Ibid., November 29, 1850, p. 2, col. 4.

[58]Ibid.

[59]Ibid., November 22, 1850, p. 2, col. 4.

[60]Ibid., December 27, 1850, p. 3, col. 4.

[61]Ibid., September 13, 1850, p. 3, col. 6.

[62]Ibid., October 4, 1850, p. 2, col. 6.

[63]Ibid., October 11, 1850, p. 2, col. 4.

[64]Ibid., September 6, 1850, p. 2, col. 4; October 25, 1850, p. 2, col. 5.

[65]Ibid., August 9, 1850, p. 3, col. 6.

[66]Ibid., November 8, 1850, p. 2, col. 3.

[67]Ibid., November 1, p. 3, col. 1.

[68]Ibid., August 2, 1850, p. 3. col. 6; also p. 2, col. 2; January 3, 1850, p. 2, col. 3.

[69]Margaret Ross, *The Arkansas Gazette: The Early Years*, p. 284.

[70]*Arkansas Gazette*, April 19, 1850, p. 2, col. 6.

[71]Ibid., October 10, 1851, p. 2. col. 2.

[72]Reminiscenses of son Thomas published *Arkansas Gazette*, July 5, 1914 and Ross "Chronicles of Arkansas."

[73]*Arkansas Gazette*, January 31, 1851, p. 2, col. 2; and p. 3, cols. 1 and 2.

[74]Ibid., November 22, 1850, p. 2, col. 1 and col. 4.

[75]Ibid., March 29, 1850, p. 2, col. 1.

[76]Reported in *Arkansas Gazette*, May 17, 1850, p. 2, col. 5.

[77]Ibid., August 23, 1850, p. 2, col. 4.

[78]Ibid., December 27, 1850, p. 2, col. 2.

[79]Ibid., September 23, 1851, p.

[80]*Fort Smith Herald*, July 20, 1850, p. 2, col. 1.

[81]Ibid., October 11, 1850, p. 2, col. 1.

[82]*Arkansas Gazette*, October 18, 1850, p. 2, col. 2.

[83]Margaret Ross, *Pulaski County Historical Review*, Vol. II, no. 1, March 1954, p. 5 ff.

[84]*Arkansas Gazette*, October 25, 1850, p. 2, col. 5.

[85]Ross, *Pulaski County Historical Review*, p. 6.

[86]Frank Weaver, "Hub from which the Western Gold Seekers went into the Wilderness," p. 59 in *Fort Smith Historical Journal*, Vol. 11, No. 2, September 1978.

[87]*Arkansas Gazette*, June 14, 1850, p. 2, col. 1.

[88]Foreman, *Marcy and the Gold Seekers*, p. 338.

[89]Patricia Etter, *American Odyssey: The Autobiography of Robert Brownlee.*

[90]*Arkansas Gazette*, February 2, 1856, p. 2, col. 3.

[91]Etter, *American Odyseey: The Autobiography of Robert Brownlee.*
[92]Ibid.
[93]*History of Napa and Lake Counties,* San Francisco: Slocum, Bowen & Co., 1881, p. 406.
[94]Johnson, *The Forty-niners,* p. 203.

Chapter VII

Footnotes

[1]*Fort Smith Herald,* February 15, 1850, p. 2, col. 2.
[2]*Arkansas Gazette,* February 15, 1850, p. 2, col. 1.
[3]Ibid., May 24, 1850, p. 4, col. 1.
[4]Ibid., April 12, 1850, p. 3, col. 4.
[5]*Fort Smith Herald,* November 14, 1849, p. 2, col. 3.
[6]*Arkansas Gazette,* November 12, 1849, p. 3, col. 2.
[7]Copied in the *Arkansas Gazette,* February 8, 1850, p. 2, col. 4.
[8]*Fort Smith Herald,* February 16, 1850, p. 2, col. 1.
[9]Copied from the *Arkansas Intelligencer* in *Arkansas Gazette,* March 1, 1850, p. 2, col. 5.
[10]Copied from *Arkansas Intelligencer* in *Arkansas Gazette,* March 1, 1850, p. 2, col. 5.
[11]*Arkansas Gazette,* March 1, 1850, p. 2, col. 1.
[12]*Fort Smith Herald,* April 6, 1850, p. 2, col. 1.
[13]Ibid.
[14]*Arkansas Gazette,* April 19, 1850, p. 2, col. 5.
[15]Ibid.
[16]Copied from the *Fort Smith Herald* in the *Arkansas Gazette,* April 26, 1850, p. 2, col. 4; May 3, 1850, p. 2, col. 6.
[17]Ibid.
[18]Ibid., February 2, 1850, p. 3, col. 6.
[19]Ibid., April 26, 1850, p. 2, col. 4; May 3, p. 2, col. 6; May 17, p. 2, col. 1.
[20]Ibid., May 3, 1850, p. 2, col. 6.
[21]*Fort Smith Herald,* April 13, 1850, p. 2, col. 1; *Arkansas Gazette* May 3, 1850, p. 2, col. 6.
[22]*Arkansas Gazette,* May 10, 1850, p. 2, col. 2.
[23]Ibid., May 3, 1850, p. 2, col. 6.
[24]Ibid., May 24, 1850, p. 3, col. 1.
[25]Ibid., December 12, 1850, p. 2, col. 6.
[26]Ibid., April 22, 1850, p. 2, col. 4, copied from the *Fort Smith Herald.*
[27]*Fort Smith Herald,* February 16, 1850, p. 2, cols. 5 and 7.
[28]Ibid., February 23, 1850, p. 2, col. 1.
[29]Ibid., May 4, 1850, p. 2, col. 3.
[30]Ibid., June 1, 1850, p. 2, col. 1.
[31]*Arkansas Gazette,* March 1, 1850, p. 2, col. 3.
[32]Ibid., September 20, 1849, p. 2, col. 1.
[33]Ibid., March 1, 1850, p. 2, col. 3.
[34]Ibid., October 4, 1849, p. 2, col. 3.
[35]Ibid., February 22, 1850, p. 2, col. 4.
[36]Ibid., August 2, 1850, p. 3, col. 6.
[37]Ibid., January 31, 1851, p. 2, col. 2.
[38]*Fort Smith Herald,* April 13, 1850, p. 2, col. 1; *Van Buren Intelligencer,* April 27, 1850, *Arkansas Gazette,* April 28, 1850, p. 2, col. 3, Ibid., May 3, 1850, p. 2, col. 6.
[39]*Arkansas Gazette,* May 17, 1850, p. 2, col. 2.
[40]Ibid., p. 2, col. 4.
[41]Ibid., p. 3, col. 7.
[42]Copied in *Arkansas Gazette,* May 24, 1850, p. 3, col. 1.
[43]Ibid., May 3, 1850, p. 2, col. 6.
[44]*Fort Smith Herald,* February 2, 1850, p. 2, col. 1.
[45]Ibid., August 24, 1850, p. 2, col. 2.

[46]Ibid., September 14, 1850, p. 3, col. 1.

[47]Weaver's article printed in *The Journal of the Fort Smith Historical Society*, Vol. II, No. 2, September 1978, p. 59.

[48]Copied from *Arkansas Intelligencer* by *Arkansas Gazette*, April 26, 1850, p. 3, col. 1.

[49]*Arkansas State Democrat*, July 27, 1849, p. 1, col. 7.

[50]*Fort Smith Herald*, July 4, 1849, p. 3, col. 4.

[51]Ibid., February 9, 1850, p. 3, col. 3.

[52]Ibid., p. 4, col. 6.

[53]Ibid., February 16, 1850, p. 3, col. 2.

[54]Ibid., February 23, 1850, p. 3, col. 4.

[55]Ibid., August 24, 1850, p. 2, col. 2.

[56]*Washington Telegraph*, July 31, 1850, p. 4, col. 1.

[57]*Fort Smith Herald*, February 2, 1850, p. 2, col. 2.

[58]*Arkansas Gazette*, March 29, 1850, p. 2, col. 7.

[59]Ibid., March 1, 1850, p. 2, col. 3.

[60]*Arkansas Gazette*, April 26, 1850, p. 3, col. 1.

[61]*Arkansas Gazette*, March 22, 1850, p. 2, col. 2.

[62]Ibid., p. 2, col. 1.

[63]Ibid., April 26, 1850, p. 2, col. 2.

[64]Ibid., p. 2, col. 2.

[65]Ibid., May 17, 1850, p. 2, col. 3.

[66]*Fort Smith Herald*, July 6, 1850, p. 2, col. 2.

[67]Ibid.

[68]Ibid.

[69]Foreman, *Marcy and the Gold Seekers*, p. 95 citing Department of Claims and Archives, Fort Myer, Book 32, No. 265.

[70]*Cherokee Advocate*, April 29, 1850, p. 2, col. 1.

[71]*Mitchell Diary*

[72]Ibid.

[73]Ibid.

[74]*Quesenbury Diary*, April 29 in *Flashback*, p. 18, Washington County Historical Society, February, 1979.

[75]*Cherokee Advocate*, May 27, 1850, p. 2, col. 1 from report written by secretary John H. Wolf on May 1; Foreman, *Marcy and the Gold Seekers*, pp. 100–101.

[76]*Mitchell Diary*

[77]Ibid.

[78]*Quesenbury Diary*, May 5.

[79]Foreman, *Marcy and the Gold Seekers*, p. 101.

[80]*Quesenbury Diary*, May 10.

[81]Ibid., May 14.

[82]*Cherokee Advocate*, June 24, 1850, p. 2, col. 1; Foreman, *Marcy and the Gold Seekers*, p. 102.

[83]*Quesenbury Diary*, May 17.

[84]Ibid., June 4.

[85]Ibid., June 15 and 16.

[86]*Mitchell Diary*, May 23.

[87]Ibid.

[88]Ibid., June 29.

[89]*Quesenbury Diary*, July 4.

[90]*Quesenbury Diary* and *Mitchell Diary*, July 5.

[91]Ibid., July 7.

[92]*Quesenbury Diary*, July 11.

[93]*Mitchell Diary* and *Quesenbury Diary*, July 12–14.

[94]*Mitchell Diary*, July 20.

[95]Joseph E. Ware, *The Emigrants' Guide to California,* Princeton, 1932, p. 34.
[96]*Quesenbury Diary,* August 1.
[97]David M. Potter, *Trail to California,* New Haven, 1945, p. 25.
[98]*Quesenbury Diary,* August 11.
[99]Ibid.
[100]Ibid., August 20.
[101]*Cherokee Advocate,* December 3, 1850, p. 2, cols. 1 and 2; Foreman, *Marcy and the Gold Seekers,* pp. 105–107.
[102]Ibid.
[103]Ibid.
[104]Ibid.
[105]*Cherokee Advocate,* February 4, 1851, p. 2, col. 1; Erwin G. Gudde, *California Gold Camps,* Berkley, p. 107.
[106]Diary Catherine Duval Rector, property Burley C. Johnston, Fort Smith, Arkansas.
[107]*Fort Smith Herald,* May 18, 1850, p. 2, col. 2.
[108]*Fort Smith Herald,* July 13, 1850, p. 2, col. 5.
[109]*Fort Smith Herald,* September 21, 1850, p. 3, col. 1.
[110]*Fort Smith Herald,* December 13, 1850, p. 2, col. 4.
[111]*Fort Smith Herald,* January 24, 31, 1851, and *Flashback,* Vol. 28, No. 1, February 1978, pp. 1–11.
[112]*Fort Smith Herald,* November 15, 1850, p. 3, col. 3.
[113]Ibid., p. 2, col. 3.
[114]*Arkansas Gazette,* November 29, 1850, p. 2, col. 2.
[115]Stewart, *The California Trail,* p. 296.
[116]*Fort Smith Herald,* November 1, 1850, p. 2, col. 1.
[117]Ibid., also *Arkansas Gazette,* November 1, 1850, p. 3, col. 5.
[118]*Arkansas Gazette,* February 2, 1852, p. 3, col. 6 from *Arkansas Intelligencer.*
[119]*Fort Smith Herald,* November 8, 1850, p. 2, col. 4.

Chapter VIII

Footnotes

[1]This diary is the property of Duval Johnston of Fort Smith and is quoted with his permission. Catherine's brother Ben Duval came to possess the diary and passed it on to his daughter later Mrs. Burley C. Johnston, the mother of the present owner.

[2]*The Goodspeed Biographical and Historical Memoirs of Northwestern Arkansas*, Chicago: Goodspeed, 1889.

[3]*Washington Telegraph*, November 28, 1849, p. 2, col. 2.

[4]*Fort Smith Herald*, November 15, 1850, p. 3, col. 3; see p. 287.

[5]Mrs. Dillard's son John was a member of Rector's company.

[6]John H. Ward, letter to Dr. Lorenzo Gibson provided by George Toney of Little Rock.

[7]Pyeatt letters. Original at University of Arkansas Special Collections Library; also published in the Washington County Historical Society's *Flashback*, Vol. 28, No. 3, August 1978.

[8]*Flashback*, Vol. 14, No. 1, January 1964.

[9]Hiram Davis letters published in Washington County Historical Society's *Flashback*, Vol. 9, No. 2, May 1959.

[10]Ibid.

Chapter IX

Footnotes

[1] *Fort Smith Herald*, April 4, 1851, p. 2, cols. 4–6.

[2] Margaret Ross, "The Chronicles of Arkansas," series published in *Arkansas Gazette*, November 28, 1960.

[3] *Fort Smith Herald*, April 4, 1851, p. 2, col. 3.

[4] *Arkansas Gazette*, April 4, 1851, p. 3, col. 2.

[5] This could be reference to Gold Bluffs on North Fork of Yuba River where new sources had been found.

[6] G. W. Patrick and David McLean from Clarksville.

[7] *Arkansas Gazette*, May 3, 1851, p. 2, col. 5.

[8] Ibid., June 13, p. 2, col. 4.

[9] Ibid., July 18, 1851, p. 2, col. 5.

[10] Ibid., January 24, 1851, p. 2, col. 3. Woodruff searched two columns to locate these Arkansas deaths.

[11] Ibid., June 6, 1851, p. 3, col. 4.

[12] Ibid., August 6, 1852, p. 3, col. 2.

[13] *Fort Smith Herald*, June 15, 1850, p. 2, col. 2.

[14] Reported by *Arkansas Gazette*, November 15, 1850, p. 3, col. 6.

[15] Ibid., December 3, 1852, p. 2, col. 2.

[16] Ruth B. Mapes, *Old Fort Smith* (Little Rock: Pioneer Press, 1965), p. 27.

[17] Donald Dale Jackson, *Gold Dust* (New York: Knopf, 1980), p. 315; Stewart, *The California Trail*, p. 301.

[18] *Fort Smith Herald*, February 21, 1851, p. 2, col. 1; March 14, 1851, p. 2, col. 3.

[19] *Arkansas Gazette*, January 24, 1851, p. 2, col. 1.

[20] *Fort Smith Herald*, April 4, 1851, p. 2, col. 6.

[21] Stewart, *The California Trail*, p. 303.

[22] Copied from *Arkansas Intelligencer* in *Arkansas Gazette*, February 20, 1852, p. 2, col. 4.

[23] Copies from *Fort Smith Herald* in *Arkansas Gazette*, March 12, 1852, p. 3, col. 5.

[24] *Arkansas Gazette*, August 20, 1852, p. 2, col. 2.

[25] Ibid., December 3, 1852, p. 2, col. 2.

[26] Ibid., December 24, 1852, p. 2, col. 3.

[27] Stewart, *The California Trail*, p. 303, p. 305.

[28] Ferguson & Atkinson, *Historic Arkansas*, p. 82. John D. Lee was finally executed after several years. A tall granite monument with the names of the Arkansas victims was erected at the courthouse in Harrison, Arkansas.

[29] New York, *The Spirit of the Times*, March 12, 1853, p. 38; May 7, 1853, p. 134.

[30] *Arkansas Gazette*, July 1, 1853, p. 2, col. 4; July 8, p. 2, col. 5.

[31] Ibid., p. 2, col. 5.

[32] King journal, April 1, 1849.

[33] *Arkansas Gazette*, May 14, 1852, p. 3, col. 6.

[34] Quoted by Kevin Starr, *Americans and the California Dream* (New York: Oxford University Press, 1926), pp. 123–124.

[35] See Bret Harte, "The Luck of the Roaring Camp," and Mark Twain, *Roughing It*, which was about the Colorado mines rather than the California mines.

[36] John L. Ferguson and J. H. Atkinson, *Historic Arkansas* (Little Rock: Arkansas History Commission, 1966), p. 80.

[37] William B. Worthen, "Elias Nelson Conway" in *The Governors of Arkansas*, edited by Timothy Donovan and Willard Gatewood (Fayetteville: University of Arkansas Press, 1981), p. 28.

[38] *Arkansas Gazette*, November 3, 1852, p. 1, col. 5.

BIBLIOGRAPHY

Newspapers

The Arkansas Democrat (Little Rock, Arkansas)
Arkansas Democratic Banner (Little Rock, Arkansas)
The Arkansas Gazette (Little Rock, Arkansas)
Arkansas Intelligencer (Van Buren, Arkansas)
Arkansas State Democrat (Little Rock, Arkansas)
Arkansas State Gazette and Democrat (Little Rock, Arkansas)
Cherokee Advocate (Tahlequah, Arkansas)
Clarksville Union (Clarksville, Arkansas)
Eagle (Batesville, Arkansas)
Fort Smith Elevator (Fort Smith, Arkansas)
Fort Smith Herald (Fort Smith, Arkansas)
The Southern Shield (Helena, Arkansas)
Southwest Independent (Fayetteville, Arkansas)
Southwest—Times Record (Fort Smith, Arkansas)
Washington Telegraph (Washington, Arkansas)

Diaries, Journals, Letters

Brownlee, Robert. *American Odyssey: The Autobiography of a 19th Century Scotsman, Robert Brownlee.* Patricia Etter, editor. Fayetteville: University of Arkansas Press, 1986. The original Brownlee manuscript (1892) is at the Arkansas Territorial Restoration and a typescript is at the Bancroft Library.

Durivage, John E. "Through Mexico to California: Letters and Journal of John E. Durivage." In Ralph Bieber's *Southern Trails to California in 1849.* Glendale, California: The Arthur H. Clark Co., 1937.

Davis Judge Hiram. Letters to wife. Published in Washington County Historical Society's *Flashback,* Vol. 9, No. 2, May 1959.

Freyschlag, Edward. Letters. Published in Washington County Historical Society's *Flashback,* Vol. 25, No. 1, February 1975.

Hodges, Howell. His 1915 recollections of the 1850 Cane Hill Company. Washington County Historical Society's *Flashback,* Vol. 18, No. 3, August 1968.

Johnston, Joseph C. Letters to his wife Malinda. Provided by Mrs. Charlie T. David (Sonny) of Little Rock.

King, A. D. Journal. Steve Logan published in the Sunday Magazine Section of *Arkansas Gazette* in 24 installments beginning January 19, 1941. The complete original has not been located, but the original portion of the second half is at the University of Arkansas Library Special Collections Department.

May, John, letters to wife Caroline, 1849–1851, University of Arkansas Library—Special Collections. Fayetteville, Ar.

Mitchell, James. Diary. Copy given to the Arkansas Restoration by Mrs. Frank Wait of Little Rock.

Pyeatt, John Rankin. Letters written to wife Elizabeth April 28, 1849–September 26, 1850. Originals at University of Arkansas Special Collections Department. Published in *Flashback,* Vol. 28, No. 3, August 1978.

Quesenbury, William. Diary, 1845–1861. Original at Duke University. Microfilm copy at the University of Arkansas Special Collections Department. Published in Washington County Historical Society's *Flashback,* 1979 issues.

Rector, Catherine Duval (Mrs. Elias). Diary. Property of Duval Johnston, Fort Smith, Arkansas. Published in *Southwest—Times Record,* July 19, 1936.

Ricks, Caspar S. "Diary of an Overland Journey from Albuquerque to Santa Cruz, New Mexico, 1849." In Owen C. Coy's *The Great Trek.* San Francisco: Powell Publishing Co., 1931.

Ridge, Rollin. Letters published in Washington County Historical Society's *Flashback*, Vol. 28. Nos. 1 and 3, February and August, 1978.
Sparks, J. H. Diary. Published in *Journal of Fort Smith Historical Society*, Vol. 11, No. 2, September 1978.
Thibault, F. T. "Excerpts from Journal." In *Arkansas State Gazette and Democrat*. January 31, May 9, July 11, 1851.
Ward, John H. Letter to Dr. Lorenzo Gibson provided by George Toney of Little Rock.

Other Sources

Audubon, John Woodhouse. *Western Journal: 1849–1950*, San Francisco: Book Club of California, 1957.
Bieber, Ralph P. *Southern Trails to California in 1849*. Glendale, California: Arthur H. Clark Co., 1937; also Vol. V in *The Southwest Historical Series*, Philadelphia, 1974.
Bruff, J. Goldsborough. *Gold Rush: The Journals, Drawings and Other Papers of J. Goldsborough Bruff*. Georgia Willis Read and Ruth Gaines, eds. 2 Vols. New York: Columbia University Press, 1944.
Butler, William J. *Fort Smith*. Little Rock: International Graphics, Inc., 1972.
Carr, John. *Pioneer Days in California*. Eureka, California, 1891.
Caughey, John Walton. *Gold is the Cornerstone*. Berkley: University of California Press, 1948.
Clark, Thomas D., Ed. *Gold Rush Diary: Being the Journal of Elisha Douglas Perkins on the Overland Trail in the Spring and Summer of 1849*. Lexington: University of Kentucky Press, 1967.
Couts, Cave J. *The Arthur M. Ellis Memorial Edition of the Journal of Cave J. Couts*. Los Angeles: The Zamoramo Club, 1933.
Cox, Cornelius C. "From Texas to California in 1849," *Southwestern Historical Quarterly*. Edited by M. E. Martin, Vol. XXIX, pp. 36–50, 128–146, 201–233.
Coy, Owen C. *The Great Trek*. San Francisco: Powell Publishing Co., 1931.
Eccleston, Robert. *Overland to California on the Southwestern Trail of 1849*. George P. Hammond and Edward P. Howes, eds. Los Angeles: University of California Press, 1950.
Eccleston, Robert. *The Mariposa Indian War, 1850–1851*. Edited by Gregory Crampton. Salt Lake City: University of Utah Press, 1975.
Etter, Patricia, *The Southern Route—1849 Journals: A Bibliography*. Unpublished manuscript.
Evans, George B. *Mexican Gold Trail: The Journal of a Forty-Niner*. Edited by Glenn Dumke. San Marino, California: Huntington Library, 1945.
Ferguson, John L. and J. H. Atkinson. *Historic Arkansas*. Little Rock: Arkansas History Commission, 1966.
Foreman, Grant. *Marcy and the Gold Seekers*. Norman: University of Oklahoma Press, 1939.
Gardiner, Howard C. *In Pursuit of the Golden Dream*. Edited by Dale Morgan. Stoughton, Massachusetts: Western Hemisphere, Inc., 1970.
Goodspeed Biographical and Historical Memoirs of Arkansas. Chicago: Southern Historical Press, 1889, 1891.
Gregg, Josiah. *Commerce of the Prairies*. Norman: University of Oklahoma Press, 1954.
Gudde, Edwin. *California Gold Camps*. Berkley: University of California Press, 1975.
Harris, B. B. *The Gila Trail*. Edited by Richard H. Dillon. Norman: University of Oklahoma Press, 1960.
Hastings, Lansford Warren. *The Emmigrants' Guide to Oregon & California*. Cincinnati, 1845, reprint Princeton, 1932.
Hoover, Mildred Brooke and Hero Eugene Rensch. *Historic Spots in California*. Stanford: Stanford University Press, 1933.

Jackson, Donald Dale. *Gold Dust.* New York: Alfred A. Knopf, 1980.

Johnson, William W. *The Forty-Niners.* New York: Time-Life Books, 1974.

Lavender, David. *The Overland Migrations.* U.S. Department of Interior: National Park Service, 1982.

Mapes, Ruth B. *Old Fort Smith.* Little Rock: Pioneer Press, 1965.

Medearis, Mary, Ed. *Sam Williams: Printers Devil.* Hope, Arkansas: Etter Publishing Co., 1979.

Oakley, Francile. "Arkansas' Golden Army." MA Thesis published in *Arkansas Historical Quarterly,* Vol. VI, No. 1, 1947.

Pope, William F. *Early Days in Arkansas.* Little Rock: Fred Allsop, 1895.

Potter, David Morris, Ed. *Trail to California: The Overland Journal of Vincent Geiger and Wakeman Bryarly.* New Haven: Yale University Press, 1945.

Richards, Benjamin B., Ed. *California Gold Rush Merchant: The Journal of Stephen Chapin Davis.* San Marino: The Huntington Library, 1956.

Ross, Margaret. "Chronicles of Arkansas Series." *Arkansas Gazette,* September 1957 to June 1968.

Ross, Margaret. "Chronicles of Arkansas Series." *Arkansas Gazette,* September 1957 to June 1958.

———. *The Arkansas Gazette, The Early Years.* Little Rock: Arkansas Gazette, 1969.

———. "The Watkins-Stevenson Family" *Pulaski County Historical Review.* Vol. II, No. 1, March 1954, p. 5. ff.

Sherwood, Diana. "Forty Niners in Arkansas." Sunday Magazine Section of *Arkansas Gazette,* April 23, 1939.

Starr, Kevin. *Americans and the California Dream, 1850–1915.* New York: Oxford University Press, 1973.

Stewart, George R. *The California Trail.* New York: McGraw-Hill Book Company, Inc. 1962.

Ware, Joseph E. *The Emigrants Guide to California.* Princeton: Princeton University Press, 1932.

Weaver, Frank. "Hub from which the Gold Seekers Went into the Wilderness," *Fort Smith Historical Journal,* Vol. II, No. 2, September 1978.

Index

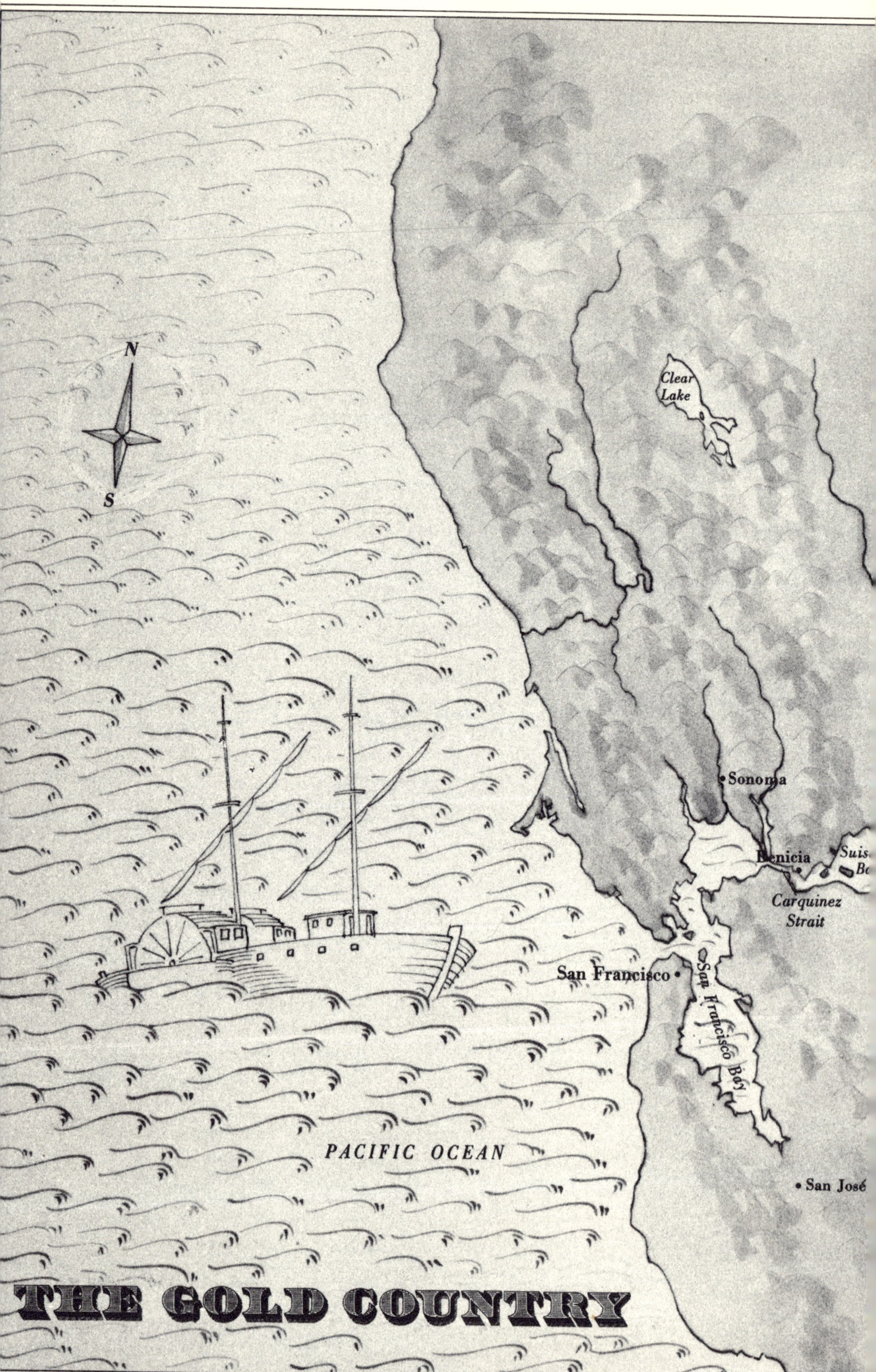
N
S
Clear Lake
Sonoma
Benicia
Carquinez Strait
San Francisco
San Francisco Bay
PACIFIC OCEAN
San José
THE GOLD COUNTRY